THEORY

AND RESEARCH

IN THE

COMMUNICATIVE

ARTS

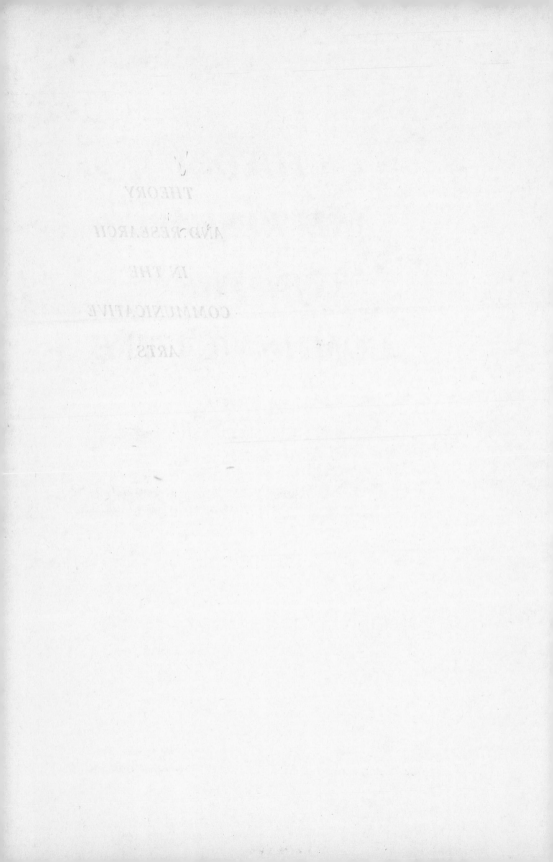

THEORY
AND RESEARCH
IN THE
COMMUNICATIVE
ARTS

ERNEST G. BORMANN, *University of Minnesota*

HOLT, RINEHART AND WINSTON, INC.
NEW YORK, CHICAGO, SAN FRANCISCO, TORONTO, LONDON

August, 1966

Copyright © 1965 by Holt, Rinehart and Winston, Inc.

All Rights Reserved

Library of Congress Catalog Card Number 65-12079

21026-0115

Printed in the United States of America

PREFACE

Theory and Research in the Communicative Arts grew out of two concerns. The first, a personal desire to explore and clarify the nature of theorizing in speech, led to a philosophical and linguistic analysis of the structure of speech theories and a comparison of these theories to the theoretical structures of other disciplines. The second concern was an outgrowth of teaching a course in research methods in the Department of Speech and Theatre Arts at the University of Minnesota. Having used an extensive bibliography for a number of years, it became apparent to me that there was a genuine need for a book that would bring the pertinent information on research methods together between two covers. To be sure a number of excellent books written for different purposes and different disciplines contain sections that deal with research methods similar to those used in graduate work in speech and theatre. However, these scattered references lacked focus and convenience for the student of research methods in my classes. In addition, the longer I studied the use of these methods in the actual conduct of research in speech and theatre, the more apparent was the fact that the content of the studies and the viewpoint and purposes of the researchers did change the methods in important ways. The research method used in a critical study of a speech or a play had to be bent to some extent by the nature of the materials. A rhetorical criticism was not the result of the same critical method used for literary criticism. An empirical study of small group discussion was not the same as an empirical study of a small group made by a social psychologist. In general the research methods borrowed from other disciplines such as social and experimental psychology were modified because of the techniques and materials employed.

These two concerns became fused into a unified work because of my experience in teaching the class in research methods. Inevitably I found myself drawing materials relating to speech theories into the discussion of method and vice versa. As these two came to be closely interrelated in my course, so they are related in this book.

The text is divided into three parts. The first deals with the functions of research, the justification of research, and the kinds of topics that are worth investigating. The second is devoted to the context of knowledge in which research in speech takes place. Here the nature of knowledge about speech is examined. Some of the issues are philosophical and some are several steps removed from the practical problems of method. Research, of course, both reflects and modifies theory so the analysis of the second portion of the book is frequently integrated with the analysis of research method in Part Three.

This latter portion of the book, Part Three, the largest of the sections, contains the detailed examination of research method. The chapters on scholarship, history, criticism, and empirical research contain many examples and illustrations for clarification and practical guidance. This is really the textbook part of the book and can serve to structure a course in research method. For the instructor whose course is already structured, the materials in Part Three can be integrated into the course by selecting and rearranging the chapters. For the course designed for graduate students in theatre that deals largely with creative projects and historical and critical theses, Chapters Seven to Eleven comprise a handbook of method. For the course dealing with empirical research, Chapters Twelve to Sixteen provide a similar handbook.

Part Two investigates some as yet relatively unexplored areas of speech theory. Part Three is a result of examining the best expositions of standardized research methods and collecting them together in terms of their use in speech research so they will be convenient to the student interested in conducting or reading and evaluating research. In this latter task, I am, of course, indebted to many excellent books on research method drawn from different disciplines. My debt to these works will be apparent from the bibliographies included.

In a more important way I am indebted to a number of teachers, my colleagues and my students. My teachers and colleagues furnished me not only with knowledge of method but also with inspiration and criticism to improve the analysis and clarify the writing, and in the case of A. Craig Baird, Gustav Bergmann, and Orville Hitchcock, they furnished me with the major portion of the impulse itself. In addition to these teachers, I should like to acknowledge the help of colleagues at the University of Minnesota, Robert Scott, George Shapiro, Gerald Siegel, Donald K. Smith, David Thompson, and Ronald Wendahl. These men read portions of the manuscript, criticized the presentation, and furnished me with information. Finally, I must acknowledge the dialectical skills of Samuel Becker and David K. Berlo who did a great deal to sharpen the analysis.

ERNEST G. BORMANN

February 1965

CONTENTS

PART ONE

BACKGROUND

CHAPTER ONE

THE FUNCTION OF RESEARCH

TO THE READER

The myriad diversities within the field of speech insure that those who read this book will have interests ranging from medieval mystery dramas to clinical problems related to aphasia. Any work on research method in speech must, consequently, cover a wide range of investigative techniques. The old bonds that held the Speech Association of America, The Speech and Hearing Association, and the American Educational Theatre Association together are no longer so strong as they once were; yesterday's students thought of themselves as "speech" people; you may identify yourself as a speech pathologist, a theatre student, a student of rhetoric and public address, a voice scientist, or a student of radio, television, and film.

You may be a graduate student in theatre primarily interested in acting and directing; you may feel that there is a tension between science and art, that science is antagonistic to art, and that in this conflict you will side with art. You may dislike mathematics in general and have a particular distaste for statistics. If this is the case, you may approach the sections that deal with these matters with some misgivings. Yet, theatre students have demonstrated that the sections in Part Three devoted to experimental design and statistics, while not simple, can be understood by a graduate student without previous background in higher mathematics and statistics. Research in the field of creativity indicates that a strong factor in creativity is the ability to break out of traditional ways of thinking. You should, therefore, be challenged to give the sections in Part Two dealing with science and scientific theories, and the sections in Part Three dealing with empirical research and statistics, a careful reading. Such a reading may convince you that there is much in the scientific method and in statistical mathematics that is helpful and even interesting.

If you are a graduate student in speech pathology or audiology you may consider the chapters on creativity, criticism, and historiography of little value to you personally. My hope is that you will read these chapters and find things relevant to your interests and your work in them. To know what writers of history and criticism in speech and theatre are doing and to know how they work is relevant to your general education if you never plan to write a history. If you are a dedicated specialist, however, I have arranged the chapters on research method in Part Three in such fashion that the section dealing with empirical research techniques is a self-contained handbook that can be read with or without reference to the handbook on critical and historical scholarship which precedes it.

If you are such a dedicated specialist in any of the areas that evolved from speech, you have been much on my mind while writing these pages. Parts One and Two are written for you no matter what your area of interest. These opening sections are, therefore, quite general. They trace the common heritage of all of us who specialize as rhetoricians, audiologists, theatre directors, television producers, or oral interpreters back to the emerging departments of speech in the early decades of this century. More importantly, Part Two analyzes the nature of knowledge about speech and examines the structure of theories in all areas of speech. If you are asking: how do I begin my research?, or, how do I draw up a prospectus?, you may feel that the opening chapters are too general, too far removed from practice. The handbooks on method in Part Three deal with the "nuts and bolts" aspects of research in detail. You may, therefore, wish to read these first. You should not put off reading the general chapters for too long, however, because an understanding of theory will help you in selecting a topic and in evaluating the worth of your project. Again, to know about the structure of knowledge in your discipline will be of value even if you never plan to do an extended piece of research.

Actual examples from research in voice science, speech pathology, audiology, radio, television, film, theatre, oral interpretation, rhetoric, and public address are used to clarify the exposition of theory and method. They have also been used to demonstrate how certain principles have worked in practice. However, hypothetical examples have been used frequently when a simplified problem will be easier for the beginner in research method to understand and when such examples will clarify the specific point under discussion. This book makes no attempt to survey the research literature in speech. In fact, the research studies that are cited are used primarily to clarify the exposition of theory and method.

Since the illustrative material is drawn from all interest areas, the speech pathologist may feel the hypothetical example of an acting test used to explain the various procedures for validating tests is not so helpful for him as a hypothetical test to determine articulatory problems. The student with an interest in experimental public address may feel the hypothetical example of an experimental design to test the effect of tranquilizers on stuttering therapy is less suitable than an example of the same design set up to test the effect of the prestige of a speaker on the attitude of his audience. In most instances, in the discussion of research method, the point remains the same whether the example is drawn from a history of the theatre or of public address, or from an experimental study in broadcasting or speech pathology.

Sharp as the divisions between some segments of the audience for a book in theory and method in speech have become, sharper still is the range of attitudes that graduate students bring to the notion of research itself. You, personally, may bring to this book an antipathy for research and all it stands for and may be turning these pages only because of the pressure of a graduate curriculum that requires you to know about and to do research in order to get an advanced degree. Or, you may be neutral and mildly curious about research because you have heard much about it and are, as yet, undecided as to whether it is an exciting enterprise that you will enjoy or whether it is a rather dull and routine business to be endured. Then, again, you may be thoroughly committed to research as one of the most important features of your graduate work and of your future career. No matter where you fall along this continuum, the thesis for an advanced degree will be one of your most important and difficult requirements. Only the language requirement and the comprehensive examinations will seem as difficult and, perhaps, as ominous as obstacles to your progress.

There are numerous old graduate-school tales about research. The resultant mystique is similar to the climate of truth, half-truth, superstition, and misinformation generated by all old wives tales. We need not be surprised that myths and legends should cluster around the birth of ideas as well as around the birth of babies. The graduate student is often frustrated by the emphasis on research and by the difficulty of the task. The person about to give an important speech may be treated by his friends as though he must of necessity be frightened and nervous until, under the prod of this suggestion, he begins to dread the event. In like fashion, the student starting his graduate career may absorb a sense of the importance, the difficulty, and, sometimes, a sense of futility about research requirements. He may soon get the notion that he will persevere or perish depending upon how well he does his thesis. He may well wonder why there are research requirements for graduate degrees and why research programs exist in colleges and universities.

THE FUNCTION OF RESEARCH IN A UNIVERSITY

The modern American university is a large and complicated institution engaged in many enterprises. Three basic purposes, however, run through all these enterprises. They are: teaching, research, and service to the community. Research is the most important work of many professors and graduate students. Only teaching challenges or surpasses it in importance. As might be expected, educators, administrators, and textbook writers tend to emphasize the ideal role of research in a university, while sociologists and journalists have, on occasion, tried to analyze the facts and point out the shortcomings in the practice of research. Here we shall adopt the textbook writer's viewpoint and outline this ideal role, and later (Chapter 17) we shall use a sociological approach and examine some of its faults.

THE IDEAL ROLE OF RESEARCH IN A UNIVERSITY

The major function of research is to discover new knowledge and test and modify old knowledge. The scholar's primary goal is to make a "contribution" to his field; but research can serve other ends of the university as well.

Research can vitalize teaching. The educational process is a joint dialogue participated in by the established faculty scholar and the student scholar. The teacher who is active in discovering new insights and principles should have the capacity to challenge students that increases the vitality of this dialogue.

Another way in which research can, under ideal circumstances, further the work of the university, is by serving the community. Through research the university can aid such diverse programs as slum clearance, labor relations, the formation of governmental policy and reform, agricultural efficiency, the conservation of natural resources, industrial efficiency, the improvement of underdeveloped countries, and international relations.

Finally, research can be an important part of individual education. The advanced student benefits from doing a hard and extended job of intellectual labor without typical undergraduate restriction and direction. The best research generates an atmosphere of excitement that is an important part of a graduate student's education. He learns about the limits of present knowledge in at least part of his field of interest and he learns to evaluate all the knowledge in his area more carefully because of his participation in the attempt to discover some part of it. In addition, he learns the skills that enable him to continue doing research after he graduates; even if he should decide not to continue doing research, he can read and evaluate research reports in his field in order to keep up with new developments.

THE FUNCTION OF RESEARCH IN SPEECH

Most of what has been said about research within the academic community applies to research in speech. The nature of gradute work and the backgrounds and interests of graduate students pose several problems that require some shift of emphasis in a discussion of the ideal role of speech research.

RESEARCH IN THE TRAINING OF SPEECH TEACHERS

The controversy over the relationship of research to teacher training is one that is felt most intensely in graduate training in speech. Many graduate students in theatre, rhetoric and public address, radio, television, and film are drawn to graduate work in speech because of their performance abilities. These skills-oriented undergraduates are the stars of the university theatre, the varsity debaters, the announcers and producers of the college radio and television stations. Their goals are to become teachers of speech or to find careers in theatre, radio, television, or film. Often those interested in teaching plan to continue directing plays, designing sets or costumes, directing and producing television shows, or directing forensics after they receive their degree.

Such students often think research is alien to their interests and nature. Why should the future director of a university theatre write a historical dissertation? Why should a future debate coach do a critical study of a speaker? Writing history, they say, seldom improves the student's talent for directing plays. Undergraduate interests and the career plans of graduate students in speech, thus, may combine to encourage a hurdle attitude toward research. A student with this attitude views the research requirement as another rather meaningless barrier that must be leaped in order to obtain the degree.

Sometimes research becomes an idol of academia but, when it does, it should not be sacrosanct. The student who raises questions about the research requirement deserves to have his questions discussed. Such questions are perennial and there is no easy answer to them, perhaps no answer at all. A strong case can be made for substituting a creative project for the research requirement of the graduate student who is preparing for a professional career or whose teaching will be largely in performance areas. Graduate faculties have debated and occasionally tried other plans such as waiving the requirement of a research project and replacing it with more hours of course work. All of these alternative proposals have met with little acceptance at the doctorate level because they have failed to match the prestige and status accorded the research degree.

Certainly a consideration of the role of research in the training of speech teachers raises questions that are difficult to answer in practical terms. A historical study in the theatre seldom has a direct and tangible bearing on a director's work; the values of such a research project are largely impractical but nonetheless worthwhile. Some of the subtle ways in which such studies are profitable will be examined in greater detail throughout this book.

THE RESEARCH BACKGROUND OF GRADUATE STUDENTS IN SPEECH

The production- and performance-trained undergraduate speech student may be unprepared for the problems posed by selecting a topic and planning and executing a research project. He may have little sense of the theoretical structures of his field and how they are developed. Part Two makes an analysis of some of the leading theoretical structures in voice science, speech pathology, rhetoric, and theatre. This analysis is important even though there is no immediate and apparent practical value in terms of selecting a research topic to be realized from it. A performance-oriented student may have little sense of the relationship between research and such theoretical structures, and he will search for a topic without relating it to these theoretical foundations. Many times he is drawn back to his interest in performance and production for a possible topic. He looks for a project which will produce something practical for a debate coach or a director in the television studio. He would like to improve the selection of high school plays or the quality of declamations in high school speech contests. He would like to see the requirements for teachers of speech in the high schools raised, or he would like to develop an argument in favor of more and better speech and theatre activities and courses in high schools and colleges. Such research projects, in the hands of a beginner in research, may result in trivia. The graduate student who begins his research in this manner must proceed with great care.

First, he may be tempted to design his study to prove what he wants to prove or to prove what he already knows. For example, he might set out to demonstrate the values of debate or to prove that higher standards for high school teachers are needed. Not that knowledge once discovered cannot be used for persuasion, but in the process of discovery the investigator must try to find out what is the case. He should not try to make a case. The researcher trying to draw up an argument for his position may consciously or unconsciously discover what he wants to discover. Every student conducting a research project is liable to have this sort of psychological bias but the investigator starting with a position he wishes to support is particularly vulnerable.

Second, among the most widespread techniques for investigating such questions are questionnaires and interviews. These research methods are deceptively simple. Almost anyone can draft a questionnaire or hold an interview; however, to use these techniques in such a way that the results are dependable and helpful requires skill and effort.

To avoid these pitfalls the graduate student in speech should begin early in his career to develop an appreciation for the worthwhile in speech research. One of the purposes of this book is to foster a taste for good research which is akin to the taste for good poetry, drama, or music. There are no set rules for discriminating between trivial and worthwhile music and drama. There are, likewise, no set rules to aid in discriminating the trivial from the worthwhile in research. Appreciation in these fields comes from the study of standards and methods and from the study of a number of works of some range of excellence. The graduate student needs to read research reports to supplement the information on method and theory presented here until he begins to have a feel for the good and bad research in speech.

RESEARCH AND KNOWLEDGE ABOUT SPEECH

The best justification of a research project is that the results will be a contribution to knowledge about speech. If the results of the study find their way into textbooks or if they are incorporated into theory they have made such a contribution. The first step in establishing a background to aid in evaluating the results of research in speech is to outline the sources of our current philosophies and theories of speech.

CLASSICAL RHETORIC AND POETIC

The first source in terms of influence and antiquity is the knowledge gained from the study of the classical sources of rhetoric, drama, and philosophy. The systematic and sophisticated analysis of the rhetoric of Greece and Rome is embodied in such works as those of Plato, Aristotle, Cicero, and Quintilian. Drama, too, had an impressive development in ancient Greece. One of the first influential statements of dramatic theory was embodied in Aristotle's *Poetics*. This work and the plays of such dramatists as Aeschylus, Sophocles, and Euripides have remained influential to the present day.

For many years a large number of scholars in Europe and the United States were classical in their outlook and were preoccupied with the study of Greek and Roman civilization. Until the last hundred years or so the amount of research into the classical sources of rhetoric and poetics has been one of the most voluminous and impressive areas related to speech. To be sure, much of this work was done before speech departments were established in this country and cannot, in this sense of the word, be called speech research. However, such scholarship remains the source of much rhetorical and dramatic theory. This research examined the classical sources to establish authorship and textual authenticity, to discover implications and meanings, and, most importantly, to find answers for the rhetorical and dramatic problems faced by the scholar and his contemporaries. An example of the latter type of research as conducted by scholars in speech is the study of Aristotle's *Rhetoric* to discover what is involved in the notion of the "enthymeme" and the implications of this concept for contemporary speakers or teachers of public address.[1]

HISTORY AND CRITICISM

Although the classical area is the oldest source of knowledge about speech, historical and critical scholarship in rhetoric and drama is also venerable and important. The practice of criticism followed the rise of rhetoric and drama in Greece. Greek and Roman historians furnish us with accounts of great speeches and speakers. Our record of Pericles' funeral oration, for example, is found in the account of Thucydides.

Criticism grows from the theory and philosophy of rhetoric and drama, but it also influences that history. In the fine arts and humanities, taste is one of the important intangibles, and criticism develops the powers of taste and discrimination. Both the writing and reading of criticism serve these functions.

History needs no further justification than that it keep a record of the past so that we may understand the present and have direction for the future, but as a byproduct of the study of the history of public address and theatre, models of speeches and the texts of plays have been preserved for study and analysis. We know of the speeches of Demosthenes, Cicero, Burke, and Lincoln because of the extant texts, to be sure, but because of the historical writings about these events, the texts take on added significance.

Since the development of graduate work in speech departments in this century, the study of the history and criticism of public address has flourished. The Speech Association of America has sponsored the publication of a number of volumes on the history and criticism of

---

[1] See, for example, James H. McBurney, "The Place of the Enthymeme in Rhetorical Theory," *SM*, III (1936), 49–74. Lloyd F. Bitzer, "Aristotle's Enthymeme Revisited," *QJS*, XLV (December 1959), 399–408. Charles S. Mudd, "The Enthymeme and Logical Validity," *QJS*, XLV (December 1959), 409–414.

public address.[2] In this same period, graduate dissertations in theatre have often been studies of a historical or critical nature.

EMPIRICAL RESEARCH

A third major source of knowledge about speech is of more recent origin and stems from empirical research in communications, speech and hearing disorders, voice science, experimental phonetics, radio, television and film, oral interpretation, public address, public discussion, speech education, and theatre. In a sense, the beginnings of the scientific method in the Renaissance can also be called the beginning of scientific research into speech. Early investigations in acoustics, the beginnings of the study of anatomy, early attempts at constructing a talking machine, were all forerunners of modern empirical investigations in speech. James Curtis suggests that Anton Ferrein did the earliest work in experimental phonetics and published the results in 1741. Ferrein's research dealt with the physiology of speech. He worked with the larynxes of human cadavers as well as those of dogs, pigs, and cows.[3] However, the organized use of empirical methods to investigate speech events is a relatively recent development. The Bell Telephone Laboratories, established shortly before World War I, was one of the first such organizations. Not until 1930 did graduate departments of speech develop voice-science laboratories. By that time, Russell's laboratory was established at Ohio State University, Robert West was at the University of Wisconsin, the laboratory at the University of Iowa was active, and J. Muyskens had a laboratory at the University of Michigan.[4]

Clinical investigations of speech and hearing disorders came still later. The work of Dr. Alexander Graham Bell in the nineteenth century was pioneering, but not until the turn of the century was there a noticeable growth of research in this area.[5]

Empirical research in rhetoric, public address, and theatre is the most recent development of all. In the 1920's such researchers as Charles Woolbert, Giles Gray, Sara Stinchfield, Robert West, Andrew Weaver, Alan Monroe, William Utterback, and Franklin Knower published findings of empirical research in general speech. As early as 1935, H. L. Hollingsworth's book *The Psychology of the Audience*

---

[2] See, for example, *A History and Criticism of American Public Address*, ed. William Norwood Brigance, Vols. I–II (New York, 1943); ed. Marie Kathryn Hochmuth, Vol. III (New York, 1955), and *Antislavery and Disunion, 1858–1861*, ed. J. Jeffery Auer (New York, 1963).

[3] "The Rise of Experimental Phonetics," in *History of Speech Education in America*, ed. Karl Wallace (New York, 1954), p. 359.

[4] Curtis, p. 365.

[5] Clarence Simon, "Development of Education in Speech and Hearing to 1920," in Wallace, p. 409.

drew on seventy-five research studies. By 1943 Howard Gilkinson could comment in his *Outlines of Research in General Speech,* "Over a period of years, and particularly during the last decade, an increasing number of statistical and experimental investigations of interest to teachers and students of speech have appeared in publication." [6] Gilkinson's bibliography contained 354 items. Of these, only two had a direct bearing upon the theatre.[7] But by 1943 E. C. Mabie and his students at the State University of Iowa were studying audience reaction in the theatre, using empirical research methods.[8]

A number of students and professors were conducting empirical studies in speech in the 1920's and 1930's, and World War II saw an increase in such work. The war focused attention on a number of communication problems in industry and the armed forces. Business firms and governmental agencies furnished funds for research in speech and speech-related areas. This additional financial support gave considerable impetus to the work. Today, research in experimental phonetics, voice science, speech pathology, and audiology is usually empirical in method. The empirical method is firmly established as a technique for investigating problems in radio, television, and film, rhetoric and public address, group discussion, and communications. It is gaining acceptance as a research method for the study of theatre and oral interpretation.[9]

OTHER DISCIPLINES

The fourth source of knowledge about speech and theatre comes from other disciplines. Because of their broad interests, scholars in speech have often incorporated the work of psychologists, sociologists, philosophers, literary critics, and logicians into rhetorical and dramatic theory. Some of the leading theoreticians in the field of speech in this century have applied the insights of psychologists to the problems of public speaking. James Winans, in his textbook *Public Speaking,* published in 1915, developed a set of speech principles based on the notions of such psychologists as E. B. Titchener and William James. Charles Woolbert made a similar synthesis of speech principles and behavioristic psychology particularly with the second edition of his *The Fundamentals of Speech* published in 1927. In the same way various schools of philosophy have been the basis for developments

---

6 (Minneapolis, 1943), p. 1.

7 Grant Fairbanks, "Toward an Experimental Aesthetics of the Theater," *QJS,* XXVIII (February 1942), 50–55; J. A. Tracy, "A Study of the Personality Traits of Mature Actors and Mature Public Speakers," *SM,* II (1935), 53–56.

8 E. C. Mabie, "The Responses of Theatre Audiences, Experimental Studies," *SM,* XIX (November 1952), 235–243.

9 The AETA Convention in Minneapolis in 1963 saw the establishment of a project devoted to empirical research in theatre.

of rhetorical and dramatic theory. Hegel and Sartre have influenced the theatre as Bertrand Russell and John Dewey have the philosophy of rhetoric. Recent developments in symbolic logic, and Toulmin's *The Uses of Argument,* have also made their imprint upon rhetorical theory.[10] General semantics, psychoanalysis, psychiatry, and experimental psychology have influenced speech pathology. Theoretical explanations of stuttering, for example, have often been drawn from these sources. The work of literary critics such as Kenneth Burke and T. S. Eliot has been interpreted and adapted to rhetoric and drama.

KNOWLEDGE FROM PRACTICE

The final source of notions about speech comes from the knowledge that grows with practice. In all areas of speech the development of techniques by people working in the clinic, or giving speeches, or directing in the theatre or studio has been an important source of information. Traditionally, the arts and crafts of speech are learned in an apprentice–master relationship. Speakers and dramatists have accumulated practical knowledge about writing, producing plays, and giving speeches in this fashion. Speech clinicians, too, have developed techniques of therapy that are effective, even though there are no adequate theoretical explanations for their success. Writers of handbooks and textbooks often incorporate these insights and the accumulated wisdom of much trial and error into their works. The last important source of knowledge about speech, therefore, is the knowledge accumulated by craftsmen and artists.

Research and practice furnish us with our knowledge about speech. Research into the classical sources of rhetoric and drama, into the history of speech and theatre, scholarly criticism, and empirical investigations furnish the bulk of what we know and teach in the classroom. Scholarly investigations of other disciplines with a view to applying the insights of these disciplines to the problems of speech have also been important. Only when clinicians, craftsmen, and artists have developed our knowledge about speech through actual practice has research been unimportant.

THE BASIC FUNCTION OF RESEARCH IN SPEECH

With this background as to the sources of knowledge about speech, we can place the function of research in speech into context. The ma-

---

10 See, for example, Donald L. Torrence, "A Philosophy for Rhetoric from Bertrand Russell," *QJS*, XLV (April 1959), 153–165; Wayne Brockriede and Douglas Ehninger, "Toulmin on Argument: An Interpretation and Application," *QJS*, XLVI (February 1960), 44–53.

jor function of research is to conserve the accumulated wisdom of the past, to amplify, clarify, and modify this wisdom, to make this knowledge more effective in improving the practice of the various arts of speech, and to create an appreciation of excellence in the various artistic areas of the discipline.

Each student embarking on a research project in speech should have some appreciation for the history of his discipline as well as a notion of how his project fits into the over-all network of theory and practice. The major emphasis of this book is upon research methods, but the importance of theory requires that some attention be paid to it as well. If this were a hunt for gold, our approach would be first to obtain a map of the treasure area and then the spade lest some might seize the spade and begin to dig in haphazard fashion. Thus, the next few chapters will outline in greater detail the recent developments in speech research and Part Two will consider speech theories.

Suggested Readings

Berelson, Bernard. *Graduate Education in the United States*. New York: McGraw-Hill Book Co., 1960.

Hunt, Everett Lee. "Research in the Training of Teachers of Speech," *QJS*, XXII (April 1936), 175–182.

Powers, Margaret Hall. "The Dichotomy in Our Profession," *JSHD*, XX (March 1955), 4–10.

Simon, Clarence T. "Graduate Study in Speech," *QJS*, XXXVI (December 1950), 462–470.

————. "Graduate Study and Research in Speech," ed. Clyde W. Dow. *An Introduction to Graduate Study in Speech and Theatre*. East Lansing: Michigan State University Press, 1960, pp. 352–383.

————. "The Teacher and His Graduate Work," *ST*, I (November 1952), 231–236.

Viner, Jacob. "A Modest Proposal for Some Stress on Scholarship in Graduate Training," *QJS*, XL (February 1954), 15–23.

Wallace, Karl, ed. *History of Speech Education in America*. New York: Appleton-Century-Crofts, Inc., 1954.

Projects

1) Read John Q. Academesis, "Too Many College Teachers Don't Teach," *The New York Times Magazine* (February 21, 1960), 14, and Charles A. Fenton, "The Sweet Sad Song of the Devoted College Teacher," *AAUP Bulletin*, XLVI (December 1960), 361–364. Write a short paper in which you state your opinions on the relationship between research and teaching ability.

2) Select a textbook in some area of speech and determine the major sources of information for the book. Does the text draw upon research in the classical sources? Upon historical and critical research? Empirical research? Upon the application of knowledge from other disciplines? Or does it reflect the experience and practice of the writer?

3) Examine the issues of the last few years of one of the major research journals in your area of interest. Select what seems to you to be the best study and the worst. Write a short paper in which you list the major differences between the two articles.

4) Each year the titles of masters theses accepted by departments of speech are listed in *Speech Monographs*. Examine the most recent such list and select three titles that indicate the student picked a topic growing out of an immediate personal and practical problem. What kinds of evidence could be used to investigate these topics? In what ways could the results of these studies be useful?

Questions for Discussion

1) Is science antagonistic to art? Would "scientific" studies in theatre be inimical to some features of the artistic enterprise?

2) If a student had the option to take the masters degree with a thesis or without a thesis, what arguments should he consider for and against the research thesis in making up his mind?

3) What dangers are there in borrowing ideas and research methods from other disciplines and applying them to speech problems and speech theories?

4) Should theatre be a separate discipline? Should voice science, speech pathology, and audiology be a separate discipline? Should radio-television-film be a separate discipline?

5) What are the advantages and disadvantages of retaining the traditional bonds that tied these diverse areas into the field of speech?

6) Should a graduate student expect his thesis to make a contribution to the knowledge in his field?

7) What forces might keep the research requirement from contributing as much as it should to the education of graduate students in speech?

CHAPTER TWO

RESEARCH AND THE FIELD
OF SPEECH SINCE 1900

THE EMERGENCE OF SPEECH DEPARTMENTS

The adoption of the department as the basic unit of administration was one of the major changes in institutions of higher learning in the nineteenth century. By 1900 most colleges and universities in this country were organized along departmental lines; although there were very few departments of speech at that time as English departments usually administered this work. Since 1900, however, there has been a rapid growth in the number of speech departments, and, to-day, departments of speech exist in a majority of colleges and universities.[1]

Several excellent historical monographs have been written on the reasons for the late organization of departments of speech.[2] A brief review of these factors will help us understand the background for the development of speech research in this century. In the eighteenth and early nineteenth centuries the emphasis in the teaching of rhetoric shifted from a balance of oral and written argument to a preoccupation with writing and the study of literature. During this same period the elocution movement grew and flourished. By the end of the nineteenth century elocutionists were teaching in professional schools, colleges, and universities. Teachers of elocution emphasized the study of voice, articulation, and gesture. The specialization on manner rather than content led some elocutionists into excessively minute attention to the details of delivery. These excesses were drawing criticism by the turn of the century. In 1892 when the National Association of Elocutionists was formed, strong opposition developed among the membership to the inclusion of the word "elocutionists" in the title of the organization. For some members of the new association the connotations of the term were already negative.[3]

---

[1] D. K. Smith, "Origin and Development of Departments of Speech," in *History of Speech Education in America*, ed. Karl Wallace (New York, 1954), p. 449.

[2] See, for example, Warren Guthrie, "The Development of Rhetorical Theory in America," *SM*, XIII (1946), 14–22; "The Development of Rhetorical Theory in America, 1635–1850," *SM*, XIV (1947), 38–54; XV (1948), 61–71.

[3] For a full discussion of these developments see Frank Rarig and Halbert S. Greaves, "National Speech Organizations and Speech Education," in Wallace, p. 491.

A group of teachers of elocution and oral English in the colleges and universities became dissatisfied with the emphasis on delivery in the elocution movement. They were also disturbed by the position of speech in English departments and with the philological research that was influential in these departments.

This small group of teachers banded together in the various national organizations of English teachers and elocutionists and eventually in their own national organization. They founded the Speech Association of America and many of the major speech departments in this country.

The research interests of the teachers of public speaking were a factor in this development. One of the leaders in the establishment of the Speech Association of America, James M. O'Neill, speaking at a banquet of the English Council in 1913 said, "The issue splits on the rock of standards of scholarship. The German Ph. D. ideal is not for public speaking, which must have its own standards of scholarship and teaching. . . ." [4] Another early leader in the speech profession, James A. Winans, writing in the first issue of *The Quarterly Journal of Public Speaking* reflected the same dissatisfaction. "We shall not," he wrote, "for some time be driven to the painful emendation of the text of Demosthenes or to studying the influence of Quintilian on Patrick Henry. We ought not to be led into dry-as-dust studies. . . ." [5]

RESEARCH AND NATIONAL ORGANIZATIONS

In the period from 1890 to 1920, the field of speech became a separate academic discipline. During these years speech teachers emphasized content as well as delivery. They began to use the term *public speaking* rather than *elocution* to indicate the changing emphasis. They formed new organizations dedicated to the study and teaching of public speaking. The Eastern Public Speaking Conference was formed in 1910 and the National Association of Academic Teachers of Public Speaking in 1914. In 1915 the latter organization began to publish *The Quarterly Journal of Public Speaking* which has since become the *Quarterly Journal of Speech*. These same three decades saw the formation of many new departments of speech.

All of these developments required a strong commitment to speech as a separate discipline on the part of the speech teachers. The national organization played an important role in establishing this *esprit de corps* because it furnished a rallying point and channels of communication for members of the new profession.

However, many of the teachers of speech were interested in writ-

---

[4] Rarig and Greaves, p. 498.
[5] James A. Winans, "The Need for Research," *QJS*, I (April 1915), 22.

ten discourse and *belles lettres;* they had roots in the English departments that were not easy to break. Once the struggle was over, the
new speech departments needed to find their role on the campus. The
soul-searching that accompanied the break with the English departments and the search for a suitable role was often reflected in articles
printed in the *Quarterly Journal of Public Speaking.*

James A. Winans wrote in the previously mentioned article in the
first issue, "I have no great humility before teachers in other lines.
Toward them we bristle with defiance." [6] In the July, 1915 issue,
Wilbur Jones Kay, President of the Eastern Public Speaking Conference, plead for more *esprit de corps* and applauded the new *Quarterly*
as a means for developing cohesiveness. He noted, "We are aware
that we are still somewhat on the defensive among our colleagues on
the faculty." [7] Everett Lee Hunt, in the same issue, stated the problem
directly, "Certain it is that teachers of public speaking have not the
academic standing accorded to the holders of long established chairs." [8]

Inevitably the place of research in the new departments and the
new discipline was an important issue. As we have seen, research methods used in departments of English had irritated some teachers of
speech. Research, too, could help establish speech as an academic discipline. "Research," Winans wrote in that early article, "will make us
orthodox. Research is the standard way into the sheepfold." [9] The first
report of the new association's committee on research was published
in the *Quarterly Journal of Public Speaking.* The committee noted
that public speaking "now aspires to become a scholarly subject," and
"Knowing that at present the countersign of the society of scholars is
'research,' it proposes to fit itself for, and engage in, research work." [10]
Although some, such as Everett Lee Hunt, argued against the emphasis
on research on the grounds that speech teachers should be more interested in teaching and performance than scholarship, the new association and the *Quarterly Journal* were strongly committed to the
importance of research.

EARLY RESEARCH INTERESTS

The issue of the importance of research to speech was settled early
but the question of what sort of research was appropriate for the new
discipline was not so easily determined. Some of the teachers of public
speaking had already rejected the philological scholarship that was

---

6 Winans, p. 17.
7 *QJS,* I (April 1915), 89.
8 "The Scientific Spirit in Public Speaking," *QJS,* I (July 1915), 185–193.
9 Winans, p. 17.
10 "Research in Public Speaking," *QJS,* I (April 1915), 24.

important in departments of English. But what would take its place? What is the nature of research appropriate to speech, and what sorts of questions are suitable for investigation? These issues are still important and will probably always need periodic re-examination. (In a sense, this book is an extended attempt to answer these questions.) One of the striking features of research in the field of speech is that from the very beginnings of the National Association of Academic Teachers of Public Speaking innovation was accepted. Members of the new departments tried many different research methods, investigated both practical and impractical questions, and often borrowed research techniques from other disciplines.

Some scholars continued to use the methods of literary and rhetorical scholarship that were traditional in the departments of English. Using these research techniques they studied drama, particularly Shakespearian drama, and oratory. Working in a similar vein were scholars in speech with close ties to the classical studies who worked on the classical sources of rhetoric and drama. The research in the Speech Department at Cornell University in this early period is indicative of these tendencies.[11]

Some members of the new association broke with these scholarly traditions and tried other methods. The second report of the Research Committee of the Association suggested that:

> Many teachers of public speaking could easily take courses in departments of physiology, psychology, sociology, or literature, which could give them a working knowledge of techniques of inquiry which they could adopt to their own field without great difficulty.[12]

Many investigators followed this advice. Psychology was one of the most popular fields of study for students of speech, and often they applied psychological research techniques to problems in speech. The first Ph.D. dissertation in speech at the University of Wisconsin in 1922 was an experimental study by Sara Stinchfield. This same tendency marked some of the early research at the State University of Iowa, where Dean Carl Seashore, a psychologist interested in the study of both the psychology of speech and of singing, established the voice science laboratory at Iowa.[13] As research in speech pathology and audi-

---

11 See, for example, the early reports of research work at Cornell in *QJS*, XI (June 1923), 237–238; (November 1923), 365–368.

12 *QJS*, I (July 1915), 195.

13 Paul Davee, "Definition of the Philosophy Underlying the Recognition and Teaching of Theatre as a Fine Art in the Liberal Arts and Graduate Curricula at the State University of Iowa," Ph.D. dissertation, State University of Iowa, 1950 pp. 65–68.

ology, in voice science, and experimental phonetics developed, the techniques of experimental psychology grew in importance for these fields.

A number of scholars used the methods of scholarship typical of English departments to do research in the history and criticism of public address, the history of the theatre, and dramatic criticism. As time went by, these scholars drew more heavily on research techniques borrowed from history, sociology, psychology, economics, and political science.

From the very beginning, a breadth of subjects and a diversity of method characterized the graduate research programs in the newly formed departments of speech. The directors of graduate study in speech made a strong effort to try different approaches and find research programs suitable to the field. The work ranged from creative projects such as writing plays to experimental work in voice science using complicated instruments and controlled laboratory conditions.

PROFESSIONAL ASSOCIATIONS AND PUBLICATIONS

The speech departments found a hospitable climate for growth after they established their departmental status. Graduate programs got under way at some of the larger institutions, and more students majored in speech both at the undergraduate and graduate level. New departments were formed; established departments and their graduate research programs grew. In 1935 approximately 200 master's degrees and 14 doctorates were awarded in speech. About 60 doctorates in all had been earned in speech up to 1935 and, according to Franklin Knower, "Ninety-three percent of the graduate degrees in speech" had been granted in the decade from 1925 to 1935.[14] By 1940 the number of degrees awarded in speech had increased to 375 master's degrees and 32 Ph.D. degrees. The twofold increase in the number of advanced degrees reported in speech reflects the steady and substantial growth in graduate enrollment during this five-year period. During the war years from 1942 to 1946 the number of advanced degrees earned in all areas declined, and speech was no exception, but this decline was followed after the war by an equally sharp increase. Over 800 master's degrees were awarded in speech in 1949—almost twice as many as had been awarded in 1948. Although the number of master's degrees earned

14 Franklin Knower, "An Index of Graduate Work in the Field of Speech, II," *SM*, III (1936), 2. The statistics on graduate degrees awarded in speech that are used in this section are all drawn from the reports published in the *Speech Monographs* by Franklin Knower. As Professor Knower has pointed out on occasion in these reports the statistics are not completely accurate. They are, however, among the best available on the subject.

in speech declined somewhat from 1953 to 1956, the number never fell below 700 master's degrees and the post-war plateau held at roughly double the pre-war figure. In 1959, for example, 818 master's degrees and 52 doctorates were awarded. In the twenty-four years from 1935 to 1959 the number of master's degrees awarded in speech each year increased about four times and the number of doctorates increased about twelve times. After 1960 the post-war plateau was broken. In 1961, for the first time, the number of master's degrees awarded in speech exceeded the post-war peak year of 1951 when 987 were reported. Over 1,000 master's degrees were awarded in 1961.

As the speech departments flourished and the graduate programs grew, so did the professional associations and research publications. As in other disciplines, these associations and publications have played an important part in encouraging and developing the graduate research programs in all areas of speech.

SPEECH ASSOCIATION OF AMERICA

The present Speech Association of America has evolved from the National Association of Academic Teachers of Public Speaking. The membership is predominately composed of college and university teachers, but it includes a large number of high school teachers, college and university students, and others. The plurality of members have interests in public address, but a large percentage have a primary interest in theatre, speech and hearing, general speech, interpretation, or radio-television-film.[15]

The Association has reorganized its structure periodically, with a major change taking place in 1956 when a system of interest groups was inaugurated. The primary purpose of the groups was to develop convention programs. In addition many of the interest groups have worked to promote research by such means as distributing bibliographies and circulating newsletters that report research in progress and research results.

Each year the Speech Association of America holds a convention at which time the interest groups present their sectional programs. The convention furnishes an opportunity for prospective graduate students to discuss graduate work with the faculties of the various graduate schools, and for members looking for teaching positions to interview and be interviewed by hiring officers. In this latter connection the Association maintains a Placement Bureau under the auspices of the Executive Secretary.

---

[15] See, for example, Franklin H. Knower and Thomas E. Richmond, "An Analysis of Some Characteristics of Members of the Speech Association of America," QJS, XXXIX (October 1953), 312–316.

One of the most important ways in which the Speech Association has promoted research has been through its publications. *The Quarterly Journal of Speech* is the oldest publication of the Association. Originally called *The Quarterly Journal of Public Speaking* (volumes 1–3, 1915–1917), the name was first changed to *The Quarterly Journal of Speech Education* (volumes 4–13, 1918–1927) and then to *The Quarterly Journal of Speech* (volumes 14 to date). In 1934 *Speech Monographs* was established to print research reports of monograph length. The *Quarterly Journal* continued to publish research reports as well as essays and articles. In 1952 a third journal, the *Speech Teacher,* appeared. It presents articles of interest to speech teachers in the elementary and secondary schools as well as those in colleges and universities. Although it prints a wide spectrum of articles dealing with educational philosophy, method, and practice in a range of curricular and extra-curricular speech teaching, research reports suitable to its audience and its purpose are also printed.

AMERICAN SPEECH AND HEARING ASSOCIATION

In 1925, Robert West and Sara Stinchfield (Hawk), led in the formation of a group interested in speech correction within the national Association of Teachers of Speech.[16] The following year the American Academy of Speech Correction was organized. The name was later changed (1927) to the American Society for the Study of Speech Disorders and renamed in 1936 as the Speech Correction Association. In 1948 the Association changed its name to the American Speech and Hearing Association. The membership is composed of public school correctionists, college and university teachers, and correctionists from special institutions, clinics, and hospitals.

The American Speech and Hearing Association functions as an accrediting agency for speech and hearing clinicians. In addition, it holds annual conventions, organized into sectional meetings, in which members discuss the theory and practice of speech and hearing therapy and receive research reports. The American Speech and Hearing Association has from its inception promoted research. One of the purposes of the original constitution of the American Academy of Speech Correction was to "make this leadership generally respected by our good work, i.e., by our scholarly research work, publicity work, and administrative skill." [17]

The publications of the American Speech and Hearing Association have played an important role in encouraging research in the field. The *Journal of Speech and Hearing Disorders* is the oldest publication of the Association. Inaugurated in 1936 under the title of the

---

16 See Robert West, "Ibi Fuistis," *JSHD,* XXIII (February 1958), 26–31.
17 Rarig and Greaves, p. 508.

Journal of Speech Disorders (volumes 1–12, 1936–1947), the name was changed in 1948 to its present title. In 1958 the Association began publication of the *Journal of Speech and Hearing Research,* a journal devoted to the publication of research articles. Another important research publication has been the *Monograph Supplements* consisting of longer reports of significant research. A more recent publication is *Deafness, Speech, Hearing Abstracts,* a compilation of abstracts of research work in the field. Another publication of the American Speech and Hearing Association is *ASHA,* a journal devoted to articles dealing with professional issues. It is less research oriented than the other publications of the Association.

AMERICAN EDUCATIONAL THEATRE ASSOCIATION

In 1931 the National Theatre Conference was organized to promote educational and community theatre. By 1936 the need for an organization devoted more directly to educational theatre became apparent. The result was the American Educational Theatre Association. In 1949 the AETA began publishing the *Educational Theatre Journal.*[18] The AETA has a strong interest in production and performance but also has worked to increase the amount and quality of scholarship in theatre. Yearly conventions furnish a forum for discussion of production and for reports on research. The *Educational Theatre Journal* publishes many research articles relating to theatre.

ASSOCIATION FOR PROFESSIONAL BROADCASTING EDUCATION

In 1925 the Association of College and University Broadcasters was formed to promote educational broadcasting. The name was changed to National Association of Educational Broadcasters in 1934. In 1957 a new group composed of teachers of broadcasting formed the Association for Professional Broadcasting Education. The same year the APBE began publication of the *Journal of Broadcasting.* The Association for Professional Broadcasting Education holds annual conventions and promotes research actively through its convention programs, a *Newsletter,* and committees charged specifically with this task. The *Journal of Broadcasting* is a publication outlet for research reports in broadcasting.

NATIONAL SOCIETY FOR THE STUDY OF COMMUNICATION

While separate organizations and publications were developing to meet the needs of various areas in the field of speech, the National Society for the Study of Communication was established in 1949 to cut

---

18 For a discussion of these developments see William P. Halstead and Clara Behringer, "National Theatre Organizations and Theatre Education," in Wallace. pp. 641–665.

across areas and disciplines. One of the purposes of the society was to disseminate research findings about communication, and in 1951 the *Journal of Communication* was founded to publish research articles dealing with communication problems. The NSSC meets in a summer conference and also with the SAA in its yearly convention.

OTHER ORGANIZATIONS AND PUBLICATIONS

A number of national organizations bear an important relationship to various specialities in speech, and their conventions and publications furnish an important outlet for research results. For the student of speech and hearing disorders, the following are of interest: the Acoustical Society of America and its publication *The Journal of the Acoustical Society of America,* the American Hearing Society and the *Hearing News,* the American Institute of Physics and *Noise Control,* the American Medical Association's publication *Archives of Otolaryngology,* the College of Speech Therapists and *Speech Pathology and Therapy,* the Conference of Executives of American Schools for the Deaf and its publication *The American Annals of the Deaf,* the National Hospital for Speech Disorders and *Logos,* and the Volta Bureau's publication, *The Volta Review.*

Organizations working in the area of theatre and interpretation include the American National Theatre and Academy, which publishes *Chapter One* and *World Theatre,* the Children's Theatre Conference, which is closely allied to the AETA, and the National Theatre Conference. In addition to the *Journal of Broadcasting* published by the APBE, the National Association of Educational Broadcasters sponsors the *Association for Education by Radio and Television Journal.* Of interest to students of general speech are the American Forensic Association and the various regional and state speech associations. The regional associations are assuming an important place in the development of research in speech. Typically they publish journals that emphasize research reports and have yearly conventions that furnish additional forums for scholarly papers. The five major regional groups are the Speech Association of the Eastern States, the Southern Speech Association, The Central States Speech Association, Western Speech Association, and the Pacific Speech Association. *Today's Speech* is a quarterly publication of the Speech Association of the Eastern States. While it accepts short research articles, it aims at a wider audience and is not as research oriented as the other regional journals. The *Southern Speech Journal* was started in 1936 and is issued quarterly. It publishes a wide range of research articles. *Western Speech* is quite similar in nature; it is also a quarterly and was founded in 1939. The *Central*

States Speech Journal is published quarterly and began in 1949. It, too, publishes research reports. The American Forensic Association publishes the *Journal of the American Forensic Association.*

RECENT RESEARCH DEVELOPMENTS

Commenting from the perspective of mid-twentieth century, one of the pioneers in the development of speech departments, Giles Wilkeson Gray, summed up the thirty years from 1890 to 1920 as "a period of transition and integration." He then asked, "Will it be said that by the end of the next thirty years a period of disintegration has set in?"[19] Certainly, the twentieth century has seen a remarkable growth in the size and diversity of the field of speech. Founded by a handful of men in the early years of the century, the organization grew rapidly in numbers and the interests of speech teachers proliferated into such specialities as audiology, experimental phonetics, broadcasting, scene design, oral interpretation, group discussion, industrial communication, rhetorical theory, persuasion, speech pathology, and play production. Whether this growth and specialization is called disintegration or healthy diversification, it has both affected and been influenced by research in the field.

The nature of their problems and the close ties that they had to experimental psychology drew the early researchers in speech and hearing disorders and voice science to the empirical method of research. Theatre research was largely creative or scholarly. Research in rhetoric and public address has tended to be more diversified in method, employing the whole spectrum of research techniques, from the experimental to those of the historian. Research in broadcasting has also ranged from creative projects to experimental studies. A good portion of research in radio and television has been empirical in nature, such as the investigating of audience reaction, the analysis of an audience's composition, and the determination of the effectiveness of educational television.

As these various interest areas grew larger, a market developed for specialized research journals. The same specialization developed in research reports given to national conventions. Before World War II the Speech Association of America, the American Speech and Hearing Association, and the American Educational Theatre Association held a common convention where papers were read dealing with theatre, voice science, speech and hearing, oral interpretation, rhetoric and public address, and radio. After the war, first the American

---

[19] Giles Wilkeson Gray, "Some Teachers and the Transition to Twentieth-Century Speech Education," in Wallace, p. 424.

Speech and Hearing Association and then the American Educational Theatre Association began to hold their national conventions separately.

In these developments research played an important part. Systematic research resulted in an accumulation of knowledge about speech that could only be dealt with through specialization. The increase in research encouraged the development of more and more sophisticated research techniques and this also increased the need for specialization.

Research, in turn, was influenced by the rapid growth of the field of speech. The large increase in graduate school enrollments stimulated research. The need for separate organizations and publications cut down the communication between areas of research interest and stimulated greater specialization of research techniques.

Certainly, in one sense the specialization of the areas of speech can be thought of as a disintegration of the field. In some institutions, the areas have split and separate departments have been established; in other institutions the department of speech still has jurisdiction over all areas, but the various divisions are largely autonomous. The graduate student in theatre reading a research report in the *Journal of Speech and Hearing Research* may find it as foreign as a study in a medical journal. The historical relationships to theatre, which was close to oral interpretation, which was close to voice production, which was close to voice science, or at least so it seemed in the early issues of the *Quarterly Journal of Public Speaking,* are slowly fading.

On the other hand, this same specialization has had a salutary effect upon the nature and quality of research. The early scholars in speech were unsure of the nature of the research methods most suitable to their discipline. They felt some sense of inferiority in regard to their research work as it related to the more established disciplines and, indeed, some of the early work was weak. Since World War II, however, research in speech has come of age; and the best of it can compete with comparable work in other fields. Specialization in research techniques was a prerequisite for these developments.

A POINT OF VIEW

In view of the well-established trend toward specialization in the various areas of speech, a book such as this which deals with research and theory in the field of speech might seem inappropriate. Would it not be wiser to write one handbook on research techniques for the theatre, another for research in speech and hearing disorders, another for research techniques in broadcasting, and another for research in rhetoric and public address? The graduate student in theatre and interpretation examining the table of contents of this book might well wonder about the relevance of the material on the scientific method to his research interests just as the empirically minded researcher in audiology or communications theory might wonder about the material dealing with rhetorical and dramatic criticism.

The first reason for examining research and theory for the entire field of speech is a practical one. Frequently, the introduction to research or the introduction to graduate-study course is the only place in the specialized curricula where students from all areas of speech are required to meet and learn about the other areas. Knowledge about speech pathology and public address is often of practical value to the student of theatre and vice versa. Many a new graduate has taken a job that requires him to teach speech courses tangential to his speciality. The new director of a college theatre may also teach courses in public speaking. The new forensic director may teach oral interpretation.

The major justification, however, is more philosophical. Surveying the entire field of speech gives researchers in all areas a broader perspective of their speciality and its relationship to theory and practice in all areas. It can serve as an antidote to some of the excesses of specialization. Specialization by emphasizing technique can give the beginner a mold or a pattern to follow in research. Such set patterns inhibit creativity in research and may develop technicians skilled in method but short on substance. To be broadly informed and knowledgeable is a virtue for the research specialist, for research takes place in a context of knowledge. There is also an interplay between theory and research in which historical traditions influence either by serving as models for current work or by forming a standard to react against.

Suggested Readings

Drummond, A. M. "Graduate Work in Public Speaking," *QJS,* IX (April 1923), 136–146.

Ewbank, H. L. "Trends in Research in Radio Speech," *QJS,* XXVI (April 1940), 282–287.

Gray, Giles Wilkeson. "Development of Graduate Work in Speech in the United States," *ST,* II (September 1953), 173–177.

Knower, Franklin H. "Some Present Problems and Next Steps in Graduate Work in Speech," *QJS,* XXIII (October 1937), 456–468.

McMillan, Carol. "The Growing Academic Recognition of Dramatic Production, *QJS,* X (February 1924), 23–29.

Merry, Glenn. "Research in Speech Education," *QJS,* VII (April 1921), 97–108.

O'Neill, J. M. "After Thirteen Years," *QJS,* XIV (April 1928), 242–253.

———. "A Bibliographical Introduction to Graduate Work in Speech," *QJS,* XIII (February 1927), 39–48.

"Research Papers in Process or Lately Finished—Compiled by the Committee on Research," *QJS,* IX (November 1923), 363–370.

Wallace, Karl, ed. *History of Speech Education in America.* New York: Apple-ton-Century-Crofts, Inc., 1954; Giles Wilkeson Gray, "Some Teachers and the Transition to Twentieth-Century Speech Education," pp. 422–446; Frederick W. Haberman, "English Sources of American Elocution," pp. 105–126; William P. Halstead and Clara Behringer, "National Theatre Organizations and Theatre Education," pp. 641–673; Clifford E. Hamar, "College and University Theatre Instruction in the Early Twentieth Century," pp. 572–594; Marie Hochmuth and Richard Murphy, "Rhetorical and Elocutionary Training in Nineteenth-Century Colleges," 153–177; Frank M. Rarig and Halbert S. Greaves, "National Speech Organizations and Speech Education," pp. 490–517; Mary Margaret Robb, "The Elocutionary Movement and Its Chief Figures," pp. 178–201; Donald K. Smith, "Origin and Development of Departments of Speech," pp. 447–470.

Weaver, Andrew Thomas. "Experimental Studies in Vocal Expression," *QJS,* X (June 1924), 199–204.

West, Robert, and Larsen, Helen. "Some Statistical Investigations in the Field of Speech," *QJS,* VII (November 1921), 375–382.

Whitehill, Buell, Jr. "Motion Picture Instruction, Production, and Research in Colleges and Universities," *QJS,* XXXVII (April 1951), 203–206.

Wichelns, Herbert A. "Research," *QJS,* IX (June 1923), 232–240.

Willis, Edgar E. "Research in Radio and Television by Graduate Students in Speech," *QJS,* XLI (October 1955), 261–270.

Woolbert, C. H. "The Organization of Departments of Speech Science in Universities," *QJS,* II (January 1916), 64–77.

———. "Report of Committee on Research," *QJS,* VI (June 1920), 62–72.

———. "Suggestions as to Methods in Research," *QJS,* III (January 1917), 12–26.

Projects

1) Trace the early history of your department. What were the research interests of the graduate students?

2) Select an area of interest to you and drawing from the articles on the suggested reading list, write a short paper outlining the history of research in this area.

3) Examine some of the reports dealing with research work in the early issues of the *Quarterly Journal of Public Speaking* and compare these with the reports of research in progress and completed in the latest volume of *Speech Monographs.*

4) How many of the publications of the national and regional organizations discussed in this chapter are available in your library? Find where they are kept and leaf through several issues of each. Prepare an annotated bibliography card for each publication.

5) Make a search for all the available indexes to the publications of national speech organizations. How many of these are in your library and where are they located?

Questions for Discussion

1) To what extent, do you feel, is the field of speech a result of the historic accidents associated with the development of separate departments of speech, and to what extent is it a function of common interests and common subject matter?

2) What, to your mind, were the major strengths and weaknesses of the early research in the field of speech?

3) How prophetic was James A. Winans when he wrote, "We shall not for some time be driven to the painful emendation of the text of Demosthenes. . . ."?

4) Have the various areas of speech been successful in achieving academic standing through their research?

5) Do you consider the development of separate areas of emphasis within the field of speech as disintegration or healthy diversification?

6) What, to your mind, are the major strengths and weaknesses of the current research published in one of the leading research journals in your area of interest?

7) What sorts of questions and what kinds of research methods are suitable for investigation at the graduate level in your area of interest within the field of speech?

PART TWO

THEORY

CHAPTER THREE

WAYS OF KNOWING

THE SCIENTIFIC METHOD CONTRASTED
WITH THE ARTISTIC METHOD

Three major ways are relevant to a search for knowledge about speech: the methods of science, of scholarship, and of art. Science, scholarship, and art, in our highly specialized society, often seem opposed in purpose, method, and style. The scientific culture seems unable, at times, to talk with the literary and humanistic culture and vice versa. Yet, there are similarities as well as differences; and all need to be understood by the student evaluating what we know about speech.

SCIENTIFIC DISCOVERY COMPARED TO TECHNOLOGY

Theoretical formulations in science are often associated with the names of a few men. Newton, Darwin, and Einstein come quickly to mind. The work of many other scientists prepared the way for these individual triumphs of theory construction. Some of these were ingenious and insightful men who opened up new areas of research. Others were dedicated but pedestrian workers doing the necessary replications of experiments and routine work that goes into accumulating data and testing hypothesis put forward by the more talented. The knowledge that accumulated as a result of the work of the pedestrian, the ingenious, and the genius was handed on from generation to generation. Newton could build on the work of Copernicus and Galileo. Einstein could build on the work of Maxwell, Hertz, Lorentz, Mickelson, Morley, and a host of others.

Once a scientific theory is discovered it can be taught to others, and practical applications of that knowledge usually follow. Learning and applying scientific theory are the work of the engineer. Using the laws of electricity, the engineer plans power plants and transmission systems. Using the laws of mechanics, he plans bridges. Using the laws of atomic physics, he plans atomic reactors. Applying scientific theories to invent machines and design buildings and bridges, technology results. In fact, the whole enterprise of finding practical applications for scientific knowledge can be termed *technology*. The number of technologists is always greater than the number of researchers looking for new knowledge. The number of basic researchers is always greater than the number of people who develop a theory.

ARTISTIC GENIUS COMPARED TO CRAFTSMANSHIP

In the arts great works are also associated with the names of a few men of genius in each generation. Frequently these men represent the culmination of an artistic movement in which they build, somewhat like the scientific genius, upon the work of previous artists, some of talent and some of dedicated competence, who have prepared the way for the great work of art.

In addition, each generation has many craftsmen who work with competence in painting, sculpture, writing, and music. Contemporary society supports and uses their work in much the same way that the results of technology are supported and used. These popular artists often draw sustenance from the works of genius, copying them or adapting their form and style to popular taste.

THE ENGINEER CONTRASTED WITH THE ARTIST

There is an analogy, therefore, in the way the engineer compares to the genius of scientific discovery and the way the craftsman compares to the artist. But the analogy is rough and should not be pushed too far. There are certain differences between the work of artists and the work of scientists. The genius who discovers a scientific theory begins with empirical information. He must use the evidence given by observations as a starting place. He cannot dream up a world to suit his fancy. He must suit his fancy to the world. If he fails to do so, the scientific method has a corrective feature that rejects his fancy. This mechanism is simple and consists of asking the theory for a prediction that can be checked out. The prediction must be unambiguous. The Delphic oracles also made predictions but usually in such fashion that any results could be explained by them. The scientific theory must predict in unambiguous fashion so observations of suitable events can result in a clear decision as to whether the prophecy has or has not been fulfilled. Failure of such prophecies causes the scientific community to correct or modify the theoretical formulations from which the prophecies were deduced. This corrective feature, too, is tied directly to the world of experience. Sometimes, to be sure, in the more advanced sciences the inferential steps from blips of light on an oscilloscope to theory may be long and complicated; but always, in the end, the scientist starts from and returns to stubborn features of his experience.

When the prophecies of the theory are fulfilled by the outcomes of experiments, the theory becomes part of the body of scientific knowledge. The theory is always held provisionally, subject to continual correction by the checking of the scientific method. Once the theory has been provisionally accepted the engineer can use it in his work. He can apply its prophecies to specific problems of a practical nature, and by exercising ingenuity and arranging materials properly he can prophesy *as well as the genius who discovered the theory.*

The body of knowledge accumulated by the scientific method continually grows by the addition of laws and theories. To be sure, some of this knowledge is modified or discarded because it fails to account for observed data; but in the long run scientific knowledge has proved to be cumulative. Thus the core of Newton's monumental achievement can be absorbed by a bright high school senior in a good physics course. By the time he is a senior in college this same student can be abreast of Einstein. At twenty-two or twenty-three he has as his heritage from these geniuses their accumulated power to look into the past or to prophesy. The engineer learns his job largely by studying the nature and application of these scientific laws and theories.

The artist, by contrast, is much freer to allow his fancy to dream as it will. The rigorous corrective mechanism of the scientific method has no claim on the artist. He may be "true to life" or not as he chooses. His sculpture may show a man with one head or two or a hand where the head is on most men. If he prophesies the end of the world in 1984 or Utopia by the twenty-fifth century and the prophecy is not fulfilled, it makes no difference to the artistic worth of his work. This does not mean that the artist ignores facts or the way things are; but when he moves from fact to fiction, he can stay with the historical record or leave it as he chooses.

Likewise, the artist develops his talent in a different way than the engineer learns his job. *Hamlet* is not analogous to Newton's *Principia.* The young playwright cannot gain Shakespeare's power as a high school senior in a creative-writing course. The artist does not have the accumulation of knowledge to help him in his work as does the engineer. In a sense, the young playwright is not much better off than was the young Aristophenes when he began to write plays several thousands of years ago. He must learn for himself the craft required for the practice of his art. He must appropriate these skills not only consciously but also in his foreconscious as he begins to feel the form of his work. Only then can he create art as well as explain how it is created. The number of young speakers who can describe how to organize a speech and yet are unable to organize their own speeches is always quite large. The same holds true for other artists. A playwright might talk knowingly of how to develop a character in a play without being able to write a play with well-developed characters in it. Each artist, therefore, must go through a period of apprenticeship in which he cuts his own way through to competence in his art. He can learn some things by watching an accomplished artist and by talking with him, but for the most part he must recapitulate in his own experience and training the way Aristophenes and Shakespeare developed their talent. Here is a crucial difference between the engineer and artist. This difference is explained by the difference between theories that deal with artistic creation and scientific theories. The burden of this section of the book is the explication of these theories and the differences between them.

THE ROLE OF CREATIVITY IN SCIENCE AND ART

The question of the role of creativity in science and in the arts raises further points of similarity and contrast between the two. The method of scientific discovery and the method of artistic creation contain large elements in common. The psychology of scientific discovery is quite similar to the psychology of artistic creation. Analogy is central to scientific theory as well as to artistic creation, and the esthetic quality of mathematical proofs and scientific theories is a prominent feature of successful scientific discovery. The beginning of the creative processes may differ. The artist often starts a creative project because he has a premonition focused on a stimulus that may be slight and capricious. The scientific discovery is usually the result of a contradiction or ambiguity in research results. The artist's creative machinery seems to have a radar focused inward for emotional clues, while the scientist's creativity is stimulated by cues from the outside that irritate his sense of logical consistency.

The final stage of the process is different as well. The artist will use his critical faculties in the revision of his work, in smoothing out rough places, catching the lack of proportion, and reworking to improve the form. The scientist checks his theory by making sure that his mathematical computations are right and by testing his work by observations.

SCHOLARSHIP, A WAY STATION

The third major way of knowing about man and his world is the method of scholarship. Scholarship is, in some respects, a way station between the method of the artist and the method of the scientist. The scholar is interested in what has happened in the past. Not that he is uninterested in the future, but his method restricts him to the past. He is more time bound than the artist or the scientist. The scientist is interested in finding a theory that transcends time, a theory that would describe the motion of the planets in Aristophenes time, in Shakespeare's time, and in the year A.D. 2500. The past is always part of the scientist's work. He builds upon it, but the present is even more important. The present experiment carries the day. Just as important is the future bridge or atomic reactor or space ship to the moon. The artist is still freer in his treatment of time. He may compress it or stretch it or ignore it or move into the future or the past. The scholar, however, is tied to the things that have been preserved from the past. These traces the scholar studies, carefully evaluating them, deriving meaning from them, and seeking to understand and explain them. From the records of the past he may seek to reconstruct an event or an incident. What took place when the Speech and Hearing Association was first formed? What did Patrick Henry actually say to the second Virginia convention on the occasion when William Wirt reported that he said, "Give me liberty or give me death?" He may study the literature and art of the past to give it new meaning. He may describe and evaluate the religious symbolism in Goethe's *Faust*. No matter what the particular focus of his study is, the scholar, like the scientist and unlike the artist, is tied to his observations. The scholar must find evidence from the past that he can observe and evaluate in order to assert that an event did or did not take place, and he must find evidence from the text of Goethe's *Faust* before he can describe and evaluate the religious symbolism in it. The scientist is tied to his laboratory; the scholar to his footnotes, both serving to restrict the researcher to the checking of the facts. Like the scientist, the scholar's work is cumulative. The scholarly work done on Aristotle can be used by the young scholar starting a study. He inherits, as does the scientist, the achievements of the past. The difference is that the scientist tends to inherit the theory and the scholar often discards the theory and keeps the specific facts established by studious examination of documents and sources.

The artist may or may not restrict himself even when writing historical plays or novels. Thus, Robert Sherwood, writing his play about *Abe Lincoln in Illinois,* supplied dialogue and an incident that might have happened; but there is no evidence that it ever did.[1] Such license is not allowed the scholar. If he reports dialogue or incidents, he must have evidence to support his descriptions.

When the scholar takes these historical traces and interprets them, fitting them into a plausible narrative, or setting up category systems to make sense out of the facts, he has room for creativity. Like the

[1] Robert Sherwood, *Abe Lincoln in Illinois* (New York, 1939), pp. 189–250.

scientist he is restricted in the range of creativity to the confinement of his sources; but as long as he accounts for the historical traces in plausible fashion, he may develop a structure to explain these in almost any way he wishes. This is the point where the very best works of scholarship outreach the merely competent ones. Careful, methodical, and thorough searching for traces and testing and evaluating their authenticity and meaning are important virtues in scholarship, and a work may be praised for these characteristics; but the great works of scholarship go further to discover structure in these materials that serve as explanations for historical facts. In this sense, scholarship is creative. A great deal of research work in the sciences consists of systematic observations—data gathering. The same is true of scholarship. The scholar must conduct a rigorous search for materials bearing on his study. This investigation requires more tenacity and hard work than creativity.

The artist may throw himself into an artistic project and dig out as much material as a doctoral candidate doing a scholarly thesis, but the use of the term *research* in this context is misleading. What the artist does is immerse himself in his material. If he is a playwright, he may read thoroughly background materials for his play, or he may take a job in the wheat fields, or go to jail, or work in a packing plant, or bum around the country. This kind of boning up until he is full of the topic and has the emotional feel as well as an intellectual grasp of the stuff of his play is not at all unusual. The scholar doing research, on the other hand, must keep careful records, making sure that names, events, times, and places are kept straight. When writing his scholarly paper, he ties his work back to the sources with footnotes.

THE CRITICAL ATTITUDE

Much scholarly activity is critical in nature. The focus may be on literary or dramatic or rhetorical criticism. Even when his book is not primarily criticism, it will entail evaluating sources and the work of other scholars. The playwright may well embellish the facts at a crucial point in his work because for what he wants to say the facts are not adequate, the form is wrong, the characters are not large enough. The scholar must rein in his fancy and pull it back to the record. The scientist is as severely restricted. He must strive for an objective critical attitude. His ideal is to be as free of psychological bias and emotions and prejudices as is humanly possible when checking the results of his observations. In short, at this stage of his work he tries to purge himself of the very elements that infuse life into the works of the artist. The dichotomy of art and science stems largely from these features of the two approaches. The scholar strives for a similar critical attitude in his analysis of the record of the past. This accounts for the scholar's claim of being scientific. He means by this not that he is searching for scientific theories nor that he is using the corrective feature of the scientific method but rather that he adopts a critical attitude similar to the scientist's when he does his research.

THE NATURE OF KNOWLEDGE

What is the nature of the knowledge generated by these three methods? The scientific method furnishes us with knowledge about the world that consists of generalizations and specific statements of fact. Astronomy tells us how many planets there are in the solar system and of the motion of the stars and planets through generalizations describing their motions. Physiology and anatomy tell us about the functioning of the circulatory system, the respiratory system, and the nervous system as well as the appearance and construction of the various organs. Experimental phonetics tells us about the process of phoneme production, and it describes the acoustic characteristics of the various phonemes. Because there is much generalization in scientific knowledge, it has a bearing on the future and the past. Experimental phonetics provides us with knowledge that will be useful in dealing with speech events in the future as well as the present.

Scholarship tells us about the events of the past. Because of scholarship, we know of Aristotle and Plato, of Demosthenes and Cicero, of Aristophenes and Sappho. Scholarship reveals the preoccupation of Greek thinkers with the nature of rhetoric and the ethics of teaching and practicing the arts of persuasion. Scholarship provides us with dissections and reconstructions of Shakespeare's plays, with descriptions of the theatre in St. Louis in the nineteenth century, and with the history of legal developments dealing with the broadcasting industry in the United States.

The knowledge generated by artists is much different. As a matter of fact, esthetic theory is composed largely of conjecture about the question, "What is art?" Such statements as "Art is play," "Art is an avenue to reality," "Art is a representation of the truth," reflect different answers to the relationship between art and knowledge.[2] Nonetheless, art does, in fact, tell us about the nature of human experience. Art can tell us much of how life was in Elizabethan England or in the

---

2 "This truth to life and truth to nature is the constant quest of the artist who is all the time looking more and more closely at life and nature, trying to penetrate more deeply into the way men's minds work, to understand man's place in nature and to see what are the permanent and deep principles that underlie all creation." H. Caudwell, *The Creative Impulse* (London, 1951), p. 7. For a basic survey of representative esthetic positions see James L. Jarrett, *The Quest for Beauty* (Englewood Cliffs, N. J., 1957).

ambulance corps in Italy in the First World War or at the *Oktoberfest* in Munich during the Hitler regime. Variously referred to as an intuitive or empathic approach to knowledge, art can be a stimulus to generate a kind of knowledge of the senses, an involvement in an experience that the knowledge of science or of scholarship cannot equal.

In a sense, these ways of knowing supplement each other. The knowledge of scholarship furnishes as accurate a mapping of the past as possible. The knowledge transmitted by art touching the map here and there adds sparks of experience so we know not only what happened from the knowledge of scholarship but also something of the experiences generated by these happenings. Art also illuminates such eternal questions as: What is the nature of God? Of man? What is the nature of the good life? Of evil?

BASIC AND APPLIED RESEARCH

Since the latter part of the nineteenth century there has been a strong pragmatic strain in much of the educational philosophy in the United States. The graduate student often reflects this pragmatism when he begins to think of a topic for research or when he prepares a research report. When he tries to justify a research project, he does so in terms of an immediate "cash value" for the results of his work. A history of the Alley Theatre in Houston, Texas, he suggests, may be helpful to other people interested in forming similar theatres. He may criticize a study he has read because there are no results that will help the speech teacher, or the speech clinician, or the theatre director, or the television producer.

The popular demand for practical results from research is so widespread that researchers in the natural sciences developed a frame of reference for discussing research in terms of *basic* and *applied* research. Basic research, sometimes called pure research, is work aimed at answering a question because the question arouses curiosity and is intriguing. The results may or may not have some apparent practical effects. The work is not undertaken to answer an immediate problem but rather to satisfy the researcher's curiosity about some feature of his environment. In the natural sciences there is a further connotation that basic research is aimed at the development of new information or new generalizations and that applied research is aimed at developing technology.

Such questions as: What is the action of the thyroid cartilage as a singer changes pitch? What is the energy distribution in the vowel sounds? What role does the most talkative member play in a group discussion? Do the means of persuasion vary from culture to culture? What

effect does television have on the family in the United States? are examples of questions in speech that would be analogous to basic research
questions in the natural sciences. This is not to say that practical implications cannot be found in these queries. A little ingenuity can
supply some practical justification for almost any research question or
any course of study. Study of the fine arts can be justified on the basis
that a coed will learn about home decorating in such a study and as a
result will provide her family with a pleasant and congenial home. The
essential feature of such questions, however, is that the researcher
seeks an answer for the sake of the knowledge that answer represents
and not because he hopes to make life easier or more comfortable or
longer.

Applied research is work aimed at solving a clear and immediate
practical problem. Much of the research and development work in the
space program is of this nature. Finding metals that can withstand the
heat of re-entry, developing guidance systems for rockets, discovering
solid fuels for rockets, these are problems for applied research. In
speech such questions as: Is group therapy as efficient in retraining
articulation problems as individual therapy sessions? Can educational
television teach the fundamentals of speech as effectively as the lecture
discussion method? How can the quality of high school dramatics be
improved? are questions of an applied nature. These two categories are
not mutually exclusive; and sometimes a research project may have
basic, that is theoretical, as well as applied or practical outcomes.

The basic–applied research dichotomy is useful in justifying research projects that seem wild-eyed and foolish. Supporters of research
and graduate students need to be reminded of the fact that many seemingly wild research projects eventually had important practical applications. In addition, the strange basic questions often result in knowledge that has a wide application, while the work on immediate practical problems often results in knowledge that is of limited use. The
general public has learned the value of basic as well as applied research
now; these days investment counselors study the amount of money a
given corporation spends on basic research as an index to the growth
potential of the company.

Certainly there are several grounds for justifying an empirical
research project in speech, and the fact that it is designed to meet some
practical problem is only one of these grounds. If the project is investigating a question of importance about speech events even though
there seems to be no direct application of the results, such research has
ample justification as basic research.

The words basic and applied have not been used much in discussing scholarship and art. To be sure there is a somewhat similar dichot-

omy in the notion of "commercial" art versus "fine" art; and it could be said that commercial art is more practical because it makes more money and is thus like applied research, but the analogy is quite strained. There would be little point in making a similar distinction in regard to scholarship, for if there is any direct cash value to such research, that feature is usually well hidden.

THE USES OF SCHOLARSHIP

The lessons of history are important, but they cannot be applied like the lessons of physics or chemistry to develop a new plastic material or to create an atomic reactor. The attempt to justify scholarship as though it were applied research is inevitably a bit difficult. Reading an essay criticizing the poetry of T. S. Eliot may improve the skill of a teacher of oral interpretation, but such results of scholarship are capricious byproducts that do not serve to justify the enterprise. Scholarship is somewhat like basic research in the natural sciences. The scholar is motivated by a desire to find out about things; and if the information and understanding that result from scholarship are some steps removed from the practical problems of the speech teacher, set designer, speech clinician, or television director, this is to be expected. However, while basic research in the sciences often turns out to have practical applications in the long run, as when Professor B. F. Skinner's research into learning resulted in the development of teaching machines, the results of scholarly work seldom have practical applications, even in the long run.

Of what use then is the knowledge gained by scholarship? Certainly it is of some use or the scholar would not have appeared so early in human history nor continued so stubbornly to go about his work. First and foremost, the scholar satisfies a curiosity about the past. He tries, in the tradition of scholarship, to keep the record straight. The function of this record of the past is subtle but important. Without such a record a family, a community, or a nation would suffer from a kind of collective amnesia. With the record a group has an identity, a heritage, a culture. Without the record the present has little meaning, the future has little purpose. With the accumulation of scholarship the present is enriched by the context of the past, and the future takes on purpose and direction.

There are records and group recollections other than the ones kept by scholars, and these recollections perform much the same function as the records kept by scholars. The components of these other records include myths, legends, and folklore. These make a record of the past composed partly of authentic record and partly of fanciful reconstruction. A recollection is essentially a synthesis of art, scholarship, and religion appropriated by society to give meaning and direction to its culture. If a nation such as the United States does not have a history, it must manufacture one; and in this process the story of Pocahontas and John Smith, of George Washington and the cherry tree, and of Patrick Henry saying, "Give me liberty or give me death" may be as important as the scholar's more authentic record.

George Orwell's book *1984* explains in fictional terms the subtle importance of this record. In his terrifying society one of the important ways of manipulating the present and future is to rewrite the record of the past. The controllers of society in *1984* continually rewrite the record. Names, places, dates appear and disappear depending on the needs of the manipulators. The practice of recent totalitarian societies indicates that Orwell's notion that whoever controls the present controls the past and whoever controls the past controls the future is essentially sound. The Nazis rewrote the German past. Hitler and Goebbels rewrote, for the German people, the history of World War I, the Versailles Treaty, and the Weimar Republic. More striking is the Soviet Union's erasing and modifying the record. Beria, Molotov, Stalin, even these recent names are erased from the record, stricken from avenue and street signs; removed from the maps as towns are renamed.

What distinguishes the record kept by scholars from these other records of the past is the ethical imperative that the scholar must, insofar as is humanly possible, generate an authentic record. The scholar tries to keep the record straight. This often makes him an unwelcome guest for those who wish to manipulate society. He will put in the record things that powerful people would rather suppress. Since he tries to keep the record accurate, he has a scholarly duty to enter all the relevant material as evidence. He will not record the fictions that people would like to have in their common recollections. For these reasons the scholar tenaciously clings to the principle of academic freedom. He knows that without such freedom to write of the past the record will be tampered with. He knows that if the keeping of the record ever falls into the hands of power elites, the temptation to manipulate it will be overpowering. This much he has learned from his study of historical traces.

AN ONGOING PROGRAM OF RESEARCH IN SPEECH

Graduate work in speech provides an opportunity for utilizing all avenues to knowledge. There are many basic questions dealing with the nature of speech production, propagation, and perception that need investigation. We need to know more about the basic process of speech, the process by which certain psychological states in individuals are connected to the production of speech sounds; and these speech sounds are then perceived by other individuals and these percepts connected to certain psychological states in the listener. Recently such disciplines as sociology, psychology, social psychology, and philosophy have found that speech, language behavior, group communication networks, and language itself are all of central concern for their work. This testifies to the importance of basic research in speech.

Many practical questions are worthy of investigation. Studies need to be done of speech education, clinical practices, radio and television audience analyses; ways of measuring, testing, or evaluating speech events need to be developed.

Much of the history of oratory, theatre, broadcasting, voice science and speech and hearing disorders remain to be written. Much dramatic literature and many speeches deserve careful criticism. Further research into the classical sources of speech is justified. And scholars should synthesize the results of previous studies. General works of history and criticism drawing together the findings of historical and critical dissertations and monographs are needed. Similar synthesis of empirical research is needed. Scholarship of an instrumental nature, such as compiling bibliographies, editing critical editions, and translating important works, also is most useful. In short, the justification of a research project can take many different forms and need not be confined to outlining the practical results that will result from the study.

Still, a graduate student needs to justify his study and he must try to do a worthwhile project. Maturity in speech research has come only with a mature attitude toward research. Ironically the more the researcher strives for prestige the less prestige his research tends to have. Merely turning out research articles is not the road to academic preferment. The research must be of value.

The graduate student's research should not be viewed as a hurdle. The candidate with this attitude often picks his thesis topic only after a careful analysis of the graduate adviser and graduate faculty. The student may be tempted to select a study that he feels his adviser is interested in and willing to accept. He may do some work for a research project that his graduate professor has under way. There are sensible reasons for so doing. If the student has come to study with a given professor because of similar interests, he might want to become competent in the very research techniques and areas that this person has developed. If the research program that is under way is of interest to the graduate student and he finds himself drawn into it, then such a procedure has much to commend it. If the graduate student finds himself at the limits of knowledge, utilizing research techniques that have been carefully developed to investigate a significant question, he is, indeed, fortunate. However, if the student searches for a topic and a method to please his adviser or if he accepts a suggestion from his adviser that he finds dull and uninteresting, he has made a serious mistake. If the research project seems dull, if the researcher must force himself to work on it, then the danger signals are up; and the graduate student should re-evaluate his motivation and his research project.

Every graduate student should ponder this pitfall as he draws up the prospectus for his research project. He may live with that project for several years. It will become as much a part of his life as his family, and he should look carefully at it to make sure that it has those qualities that will allow him to remain interested, better still, enthusiastic, two or three years later.

In addition, he will be bent by his graduate dissertation. His entire future is at stake. If he does a dissertation utilizing the historical method, he will be training himself as a historian; seldom will he change his research interests and competence later in his career. If he becomes an expert in stuttering or in British public address or in French drama as a result of his doctoral dissertation, his future as a teacher, scholar, and director of research will often be determined.

The student should also be aware that his attitude towards research will probably change during his graduate career. At the start of a graduate career the doctoral dissertation often seems a bit remote. Still, one should guard against developing attitudes toward research that may prove troublesome later. Frequently, graduate work stimulates the student's talent and curiosity and changes his orientation toward scholarship, the doctoral program, and his personal goals.

There is a need for the proper attitude on the part of students in speech and also a need for balance and proportion in ongoing research programs. The methods of science, scholarship, and art are all important and should be employed in graduate speech programs. Those who are drawn to the ways of the artist should not close their minds to the researcher who wishes to use the scientific method to investigate speech events. On the other hand, the researcher using the scientific method should not depreciate the work of the historian and critic because it cannot generate the same kind of knowledge as the scientific method. Scientific knowledge has virtue in dealing with facts. Its clarity of expression, power of explanation, and ability to lead to technology are evidence of this virtue. The knowledge of scholarship and art is basic to speech because it relates to the nonfactual but most important humanizing and intellectual activity of man—the development of tastes, values, purposes, and goals.

Suggested Readings

Art, Science, and Scholarship

Becker, Carl. *Everyman His Own Historian.* New York: Appleton-Century-Crofts, 1935.

Bergmann, Gustav. *Philosophy of Science.* Madison: University of Wisconsin Press, 1957.

Campbell, Norman. *What Is Science?* New York: Dover Publications, Inc., 1952.

Dewey, John. *Art as Experience.* New York: Minton Balch & Co., 1934.

Garrod, H. W. *Scholarship Its Meaning and Value.* Cambridge: Cambridge University Press, 1946.

Snow, C. P. *The Two Cultures and the Scientific Revolution.* Cambridge: Cambridge University Press, 1959.

Tolstoi, Lev Nicolaevich. *What is Art?* trans. Maude Aylmer, Oxford: Oxford University Press, 1950.

An Ongoing Program of Research

Aly, Bower. "The History of American Public Address as a Research Field," *QJS,* XXIX (October 1943), 308–314.

Bacon, Wallace. "Graduate Studies in Interpretation," *QJS,* XXXV (October 1949), 316–319.

———. "Scholarship and the Interpreter," *QJS,* XXXIX (April 1953), 187–192.

Baird, A. Craig. "Opportunities for Research in State and Sectional Public Speaking," *QJS,* XXIX (October 1943), 304–308.

Brigance, W. N. "Whither Research?" *QJS,* XIX (November 1933), 552–561.

Carson, William. "Some Thoughts on Graduate Theses," *ETJ,* VII (October 1955), 191–196.

Christopherson, Merrill G. "The Unfinished Work of the Research Scholar in the Carolinas," *SSJ,* XXIII (Fall 1957), 28–33.

Clark, Robert D. "Research Possibilities in Interpretive Speech," *WS,* XIII (October 1949), 16–19.

Dickey, Dallas. "Southern Oratory: A Field for Research," *QJS,* XXXIII (December 1947), 458–463.

———. "What Direction Should Future Research in American Public Address Take? *QJS,* XXIX (October 1943), 300–304.

Ehninger, Douglas. "Aspects of Current Research in the History of Speech Education," *SSJ,* XVIII (March 1953), 141–149.

Galloway, Marian. "Southern Materials for Graduate Research in Theatre," *SSJ,* XVII (December 1951), 125–129.

Gray, Giles. "Research on the History of Speech Education," *QJS*, XXXV (April 1949), 156–163.

Irvin, Charles F. "The Case for Creative Research," *CSSJ*, II (November 1950), 19–23.

Jeffrey, Robert C. "Men, Movements and Materials for Research in Public Address in Virginia," *SSJ*, XXIV (Spring 1959), 154–161.

McBath, James H. "Research Areas in Western Public Address," *WS*, XVI (May 1952), 169–173.

Minnick, Wayne C. "Graduate Study and Research in Propaganda," *SSJ*, XVIII (September 1952), 39–42.

Nichols, Ralph G. "Needed Research in Listening Comprehension," *JC*, I (1951), 48–50.

Nilsen, Thomas R. "Research Problems in Communication in Industry," *JC*, IV (1954), 98–103.

O'Brien, Joseph F. "A Re-Examination of State and Local Oratory as a Field for Study," *QJS*, XXXVII (February 1951), 71–76.

Oliver, Robert T. "The Speech of Diplomacy as a Field for Research," *CSSJ*, I (March 1950), 24–28.

Peterson, Gordon. "Speech and Hearing Research," *JSHR*, I (September 1959), 216–228.

"Research Needs in Speech Pathology and Audiology," Monograph Supplement #5, *JSHD* (September 1959).

Sandoe, James. "Riderless Horses and Empty Stables: Some Observation on Materials of Graduate Study," *ETJ*, II (October 1950), 230–245.

Templin, Mildred C. "Possibilities of Research for Public School Speech Therapists," *JSHD*, XVIII (December 1953), 335–355.

Thompson, Wayne. "Contemporary Public Address as a Research Area," *QJS*, XXXIII (October 1947), 274–283.

Timmons, William M. "Discussion, Debating and Research," *QJS*, XXVII (October 1941), 415–421.

Wiley, Earl W. "State History and Rhetorical Research," *QJS*, XXXVI (December 1950), 514–519.

Wolfson, Lester M. "On Selecting Subjects for Graduate Research," *SSJ*, XX (Fall 1954), 37–41.

PROJECTS

1) Prepare a list of twenty topics suitable for a masters thesis.

2) Select an article from the suggested reading list dealing with opportunities for research and write several pages re-examining the research opportunities in this field and bringing the article up to date.

3) Examine the abstracts of doctoral dissertations completed in speech as published in the latest volume of *Speech Monographs*. Compile a list of five studies that you judge to be *applied* research studies.

4) If your major interest in speech is theatre, radio, television, film, or rhetoric and public address, select five problems from these areas that would

be suitable for investigation by the scientific method. If your major interest is in voice science, speech pathology, and audiology, or communications select five problems from these areas that would be suitable for investigation by the historical or critical method.

QUESTIONS FOR DISCUSSION

1) How would you define knowledge?

2) How would you define art?

3) What are the basic purposes for using footnotes? How can these purposes be abused?

4) Is imagination an aid or a hindrance to the scholar?

5) Of what use are historical dramas? Historical monographs?

6) How does the creativeness of the scientist who elaborates a theory compare to the creativeness of a playwright?

CHAPTER FOUR

THE METHOD OF SCIENCE

THE PHILOSOPHY OF SCIENCE

An important group of twentieth-century philosophers have had a common interest in the systematic investigation of the language of science. This group incorporates scientists with a philosophical bent, and philosophers trained in mathematics, logic, and the theoretical aspects of science. P. W. Bridgman is an example of a scientist with an interest in examining the basic assumptions of the scientific method. His work in developing the notion of operational definitions was an important contribution to the philosophy of science. Bertrand Russell is representative of the philosophers who are also mathematicians and logicians. The philosophical analysis of the language of science draws from the work of such groups as the Cambridge analysts, the Vienna Circle of logical positivists, and some of the pragmatists in this country. In addition to Bridgman and Russell, some of the important figures in this movement are Rudolph Carnap, Ludwig Wittgenstein, A. J. Ayer, Gustav Bergmann, Herbert Feigl, Hans Reichenbach, Charles Morris, and Otto Neurath.[1] This list is by no means exhaustive, but it does contain the names of some of the representative individuals in this movement. The various "schools" that have participated in this strain of philosophizing differ as to style and method but their common emphasis on the study of the basic assumptions of science through the analysis of language justifies calling their work the philosophy of science.

The philosophers of science have used language analysis to clarify the nature of scientific knowledge and method. An interesting result of this analysis is that some statements that seemed to say something about the world turned out, upon careful investigation, to be empty of such content. These statements could not be verified scientifically, either because they were logical statements or because there was no way to gather empirical evidence for their verification.

---

[1] My own thinking has been influenced by the teaching and writing of Professor Gustav Bergmann of the State University of Iowa.

49

The members of this movement have concentrated on using the tools of the "science of science" or the "philosophy of science" to analyze the natural sciences. Recently, however, they have done considerable work in analyzing the language of the social sciences. Scholars at the Minnesota Center for the Philosophy of Science under the direction of Herbert Feigl, for example, have worked extensively on the philosophy of the social sciences. In addition to this work, the student of the psychology of speech will find the application of the techniques of the philosophy of science to experimental psychology by S. S. Stevens of particular interest.[2]

Although the philosophers of science have analyzed the language of the natural and social sciences, they have not studied so extensively the theories of the humanities and fine arts. The same tools can be applied to these theoretical structures but the philosophers have been preoccupied with the knowledge of the sciences. Certainly, a philosophy of speech can be developed by the systematic analysis of the language expressing theoretical notions about speech. Such analysis has proved helpful to research workers in the natural and social sciences and undoubtedly would be of help to researchers in all areas of speech. The next few chapters will consist of an outline of such a philosophy of speech developed by using the tools of the philosophy of science to examine the language of speech theories.

SPEECH RESEARCH AND THE PHILOSOPHY OF SCIENCE

What is the point of making such a philosophical analysis in a book on research? The bearing of a philosophy of speech on research practice and method may not be immediately apparent. Nevertheless, there are good reasons for doing so. A careful analysis of the nature of knowledge is a prerequisite to sensible research programs and projects. Applying the techniques of the philosophy of science to speech theories will yield clarifications of direct application to the research worker. Examples of such clarifications would include: this question is suitable for investigation by the "scientific" method; this question cannot be answered by the "scientific" method; this is a pseudo-question in the sense that it cannot be answered; this theory is not at all like a theory in physics, nor is it like a theory in experimental psychology, and therefore it cannot lead to questions for research in the same way; this theory is suitable as a guide to practice and an aid

---

2 See, for example, S. S. Stevens, "Psychology and the Science of Science," *Psychological Bulletin*, XXXVI (1939), 221–263, and "Mathematics, Measurement and Psychophysics," in *Handbook of Experimental Psychology*, ed. S. S. Stevens (New York, 1951), pp. 1–50.

in developing appreciation for the arts of drama and rhetoric but it cannot yield predictions as theories in the physical sciences often do. If the research worker understands these matters he will know how to take the advice that questions for research should grow out of and modify theory. In addition to such direct application to the research problems in speech, the analysis of speech theories will give the student some understanding of the nature of deduction and mathematics and the role of statistics in speech research. Statistical mathematics can, thus, be put into a perspective that will allow him to evaluate and understand statistical arguments as developed in research publications as well as to understand the use and misuse of statistics in speech research.

Of course, the task of developing a philosophy of speech along these lines is a large one and the next few chapters will make but a beginning. The discussion will start with the simplest issues and bypass a number of important and subtle problems in order to sketch the general structure of knowledge in the field of speech. A book would be required in each area to make a detailed analysis that discussed all the relevant issues. The effort will be to clarify without oversimplification, but complicated matters cannot always be made simple, nor should they be. You may find this way of looking at language a novel and diffi-cult exercise in concentration. Insofar as the philosopher of science purges his language of common sense ambiguities that make for easy comprehension, his arguments seldom make light reading. As Pro-fessor Bergmann used to remark in his lectures on the philosophy of language this is not "popcorn" reading, by which he meant that you cannot read this sort of material at a hundred pages an hour while eat-ing popcorn no matter what the speed-reading advocates may say. Hav-ing said this, let me assure you that the discussion assumes no prior knowledge in mathematics, the natural sciences, and philosophy, be-yond the background required of most high school and undergraduate students. It does assume above-average native intelligence and consid-erable motivation. The majority of graduate students in speech fulfill these requirements. So much for preliminaries.

THE ANALYSIS OF LANGUAGE

Before we can apply the tools of the philosophy of science to the analysis of speech theories, we must understand these tools and how they can be used. Let us begin with some techniques developed by one of the philosophy of science projects—the attempt to develop a unified basis for science. This project resulted in an important series of mono-graphs called the *International Encyclopedia of Unified Science* under the editorship of Otto Neurath. Charles W. Morris wrote the second number of the first volume of the *Encyclopedia* for the purpose of supplying "a language in which to talk about, and in so doing to improve, the language of science." [3] The monograph was called "Foundations of the Theory of Signs," and Morris succeeded in developing an approach to language analysis that has been used successfully in a number of disciplines. My terminology will be largely drawn from this monograph. The next few pages will be devoted to explicating these terms. They are gaining wider currency and, on occasion, appear in essays dealing with the field of speech. They may, however, seem new and you should become thoroughly familiar with them before proceeding to the next chapter.

Let us focus on the language of research workers studying such things as vocal fold movements, the action of vocal resonators, the composition of the sound wave, the gestures of a speaker, the nature of the audience that watched a television show, or the restlessness of a theatre audience. When an investigator talks of these events, he may use the words of a natural language such as English or German; or he may use the symbols of a logical language such as an analysis of variance or integral calculus. Such talk may be complicated enough, but there is good reason for beginning at this level for in this case the researcher's language will be concerned only with such objects or events as vocal resonators, theatre audiences, and sound waves. His language can be thought of as an object-language. Complicated as the object-language may be, the basic dimensions emerge most clearly at this level. As we shall see, more complete languages are required in speech research. The analysis of these languages can proceed along the same lines developed for the clarification of the object-language, however.

THE SYNTACTICAL DIMENSION

Whatever the symbol system (language) the researcher uses, one part of the process of using that system involves the relationship of symbols to symbols. This aspect Morris called the *syntactical* dimension of language. The disciplines of grammar, symbolic logic, and mathematics study this dimension of symbol systems, abstracted from the other elements of language usage.

THE SEMANTICAL DIMENSION

Another aspect of the symbol system used by a researcher involves the relation of the symbols to the objects of the world. This can be considered as an analysis of the rules that specify under what conditions a

---

[3] (Chicago, 1938), p. 3.

symbol can be used to denote an object. When this relation is abstracted from the process of communication, Morris labels it the *semantical* dimension.

This dimension of language may be studied scientifically or analytically. That is, semantics may be both a science and a tool of science. Scientifically, a sociologist or a psychologist might study how a given language is used by a community of people. The researcher in this instance *observes* the way the people talk and tries to determine the relationships that hold between the words of the language and the objects the people talk about. The scientific study of the semantical dimension of this language in use could result in a dictionary. Analytically, this dimension may be studied to keep the language of a discipline free of ambiguities and meaningless statements. My use of the tools of language analysis to examine the theoretical structures in speech will be of this latter sort.

The semantical dimension of language should not be confused with "General Semantics." General Semantics is the study of all dimensions of language. Thus, General Semantics is much broader in scope than the semantical dimension of language and corresponds roughly to Morris's term *semiotic*.

THE PRAGMATICAL DIMENSION

The third dimension of language is the relation of symbols to interpreters of symbols. In the United States the word *chicken* relates syntactically, to other symbols in English according to certain grammatical rules, and semantically it denotes a certain kind of fowl; but when interpreted, it may result in various physical and emotional responses on the part of the interpreter. If he thinks of chicken as food, he may respond with an increase in salivation. Or, if he interprets the word as an insult, he may respond with increased heartbeat, sweaty palms, and faster respiration. These additional features of language are included in the *pragmatical* dimensions of language.

A VIEW OF LANGUAGE

Language is the sum of the syntactical dimension, plus the semantical dimension, plus the pragmatical dimension. Each has certain special terms indicating the questions suitable for analysis in that dimension. For example, *implicates* is a term relating to the syntactical dimension. Thus, if you assert that one set of symbols implicates another set you are making a statement about the syntactical dimension. *Denotes* is a term in the semantical dimension, and if you say that a symbol denotes an object such as a chair, according to the conventions of a given language you are saying something about the semantical dimension. *Expresses* is a feature of the pragmatical dimension, and a symbol can be said to express its user.

THE LANGUAGE OF SCIENCE

When words are used according to the rules of a given language, they may be used for many purposes and arouse a number of responses; but one important usage is in talking about the world. This talk about the world is the distinguishing feature of the work of science. A certain subclass of statements used by any scholar in speech will have clear semantical relations to objects. Insofar as possible the scientist tries to emphasize the denotative (semantical) features of his language and keep the connotative (expressive) aspects of the pragmatical dimension to a minimum.

Robert Oppenheimer states this position from the viewpoint of an atomic physicist when he says:

> Common sense language is inherently ambiguous; when the poet uses it, or the rhetorician, he exploits the ambiguity, and even when we talk in ordinary life we almost need ambiguity in order to get by. But in science we try to get rid of that, we try to talk in such simple terms, and match our talk with deeds in such a way that we may differ as to facts but we can resolve the differences.[4]

STATEMENTS OF FACT

The way the scientist goes about talking in simple terms and matching his talk with deeds can be explained by examining a subclass of statements which I call statements of fact. Statements of fact can be distinguished from other well-formed sentences (syntactically sound) primarily because they stand in such a relation to objects (semantically) that *observations* can result in a decision as to the *truth* of the statement. Further, these well-formed sentences must be such that a decision about the truth or falsity of the statement *requires* observation. Statements of fact are *empirical* statements in that they say something about the world. They have content.

The statement, written in the research notebook of an experimental phonetician, that the "Vital capacity of subject *A* is 3,542 cc." is an example of a statement of fact. The sentence is syntactically sound. That is, it follows the formation rules of the English language and thus expresses a proposition. The jumble of words, "Over above vital capacity in between plus." does not conform to the syntactical rules of English and thus does not qualify as a statement of fact.

---

[4] "Analogy in Science," *American Psychologist*, XI (March 1956), 128.

"Vital capacity of subject *A* is 3,542 cc." is not empty. It is meaningful, in the sense that proper *semantical* rules can be specified to assure that the statement denotes something about the events that took place in the voice-science laboratory. This semantical dimension is important to the researcher. Oppenheimer suggested that the quest for objectivity, in a practical sense, eventually comes to the two requirements that researchers understand one another and that all qualified practitioners mean essentially the same thing.[5] The empirical researcher needs to communicate his research findings. The minimum requirement for scientific communication is a community of agreement about the rules governing the semantical relations of the discipline language. The fact that the scientist can tell his colleagues something about his findings implies the possibility that he can tell them something false about the events he is studying. Unless he is understood, in short, he cannot be objective, nor can he lie.

OPERATIONAL DEFINITIONS

The operationalism of P. W. Bridgman is helpful in dealing with the problem of specifying semantical rules. *Vital capacity* is a concept that can be defined operationally. That is, "vital capacity" can mean the set of operations the researcher went through to have subject *A* exhale three times into a wet-bath spirometer after maximum inhalation following maximum exhalation, with the selection of the largest displacement on the spirometer as the value used. The same sort of operational definition can be given to "3,542 cc." This concept can mean the operations the researcher went through to look at the gauge on the spirometer and read it. Bergmann and Spence in their article "Operationism and Theory" suggest that if we can trace the terms of the researcher's language back "to the immediately observable," then we "know what he means" and that is sufficient for *"operational definition of constructs* (italics in the original)."[6]

If the researcher's audience knows the *operations* the researcher went through in making his *observations,* they can understand what he means. The question "What do you mean by vital capacity?" becomes, therefore, an important one in the case of this statement of fact. We may well be confused because "vital capacity," like most concepts in speech, carries with it a large freight of the common-sense ambiguity so important in our daily traffic with language. "Vital capacity" can mean the room available in the lungs for the processing of air for the purposes of life (vital purposes). But when we define it oper-

---

[5] Oppenheimer, p. 127.

[6] Gustav Bergmann and Kenneth Spence, "Operationism and Theory Construction," in *Psychological Theory,* ed. Melvin H. Marx (New York, 1951), pp. 56–57.

ationally as we did above, *it means no such thing.* By operational definitions the scientist rids himself of the ambiguity of common-sense language. When operationally defined, vital capacity means simply the observations the researcher made and the conditions under which he made them.

TRUTH AND FALSITY

Finally, the operationally defined statement about vital capacity is such that observations can result in a judgment about the truth or falsity of the statement. The scientist tries, in principle, to find universal agreement as to truth or falsity of such judgment, or, in Oppenheimer's words, "we may differ as to facts but we can resolve the differences." That is, should any other competent observer make the same observations under the same conditions he would make the same judgment as to the truth or falsity of the statement, "The vital capacity of subject A is 3,542 cc." In practice, of course, this ideal is seldom reached. If observations are performed by several additional competent observers, the results might be that one observer says "The vital capacity of subject A is 3,542.1 cc," another "3,542.2," and a third, "3,542.15." Such fuzziness at the limits of a measuring technique is quite common but does not result in disagreement about the truth or falsity of the statement if the operational definition of "3,542 cc" is carefully determined. A definition such as "3,542 cc" is the equivalent of the set of observations of the marker on the spirometer in which the marker is judged to fall within the limits of 3,542 ± .5 on the scale" would take care of this sort of observational error. If a difference of .5 cc is important for the purposes of research, then a more finely calibrated measuring instrument would have to be used for the project.

The statement "Vital capacity of subject A is 3,542 cc," thus qualifies on all counts as a statement of fact. It is well-formed (syntactically), meaningful (semantically), and either true or false. The decision as to truth or falsity is made on the basis of observations; and the statement is, therefore, empirical and not a tautology or a formal statement empty of content.

DIRECTLY VERIFIABLE STATEMENTS OF FACT

If the researcher has observed carefully and reported his observations accurately, then the statement is true. It is true because of the semantical relationship between the statement and the observables. The objects (observables), in this case, include the person referred to as subject A, the wet-bath spirometer, the researcher, and certain events such as the subject's exhaling into the spirometer and the researcher's reading of the scale on each of three trials and selecting the maximum displacement for his reading. As in all scientific research, the final decision about truth or falsity of this statement was based upon direct observation of some selected elements of the researcher's environment. For this particular investigator the statement of fact concerning the vital capacity of subject *A* was *directly verifiable*. That is, he could personally check the relevant *facts* by observation and make his own judgment about the truth or falsity of the statement. In this case the statement of fact would be *true*.

Let us assume another instance in which an investigator has recorded on his work sheets that the "Personal Report on Confidence as a Speaker Score for Subject *A* is 25." [7] The researcher is careful, and he rechecks his scoring of the tests before making his final computations. He grades subject *A*'s test again and computes the PRCS score and finds that it is 23. He checks the test again and decides that his first notation was an error. The record on his work sheet was a *false* statement of fact. Again it was a *directly verifiable* statement of fact for the research worker because he based his decision as to its truth or falsity upon direct observation of facts, in this case the PRCS test taken by subject *A*. Thus a statement of fact may be *false* as well as true. The common-sense ambiguity which allows us to talk of "true friends" and "true facts" confuses the issue and must be avoided in a technical analysis. Facts (sets of operations in operational definitions) are never true or false; they simply are or are not the case. Only *statements* about these facts can be true or false. The notion that facts are true and truth is factual makes the age-old identification of the word with the thing. The notion of statements of fact, therefore, refers to *sentences* about facts that may be either *true* or *false*.

INDIRECTLY VERIFIABLE STATEMENTS OF FACT

Not all statements of fact are directly verifiable. An example of an indirectly verifiable statement of fact is "There are craters on the other side of the moon." This statement is well-formed, meaningful, and either true or false. However, no man has yet *directly* observed the other side of the moon since the moon always rotates in such a fashion that the same side is to the earth. Nonetheless, there is considerable *evidence* that there may be craters on the other side of the moon. There are craters on this side of the moon. The Russians maintain that they have photographs of the other side of the moon taken by

---

[7] The Personal Report on Confidence as a Speaker is a test of a speaker's perceived feelings of anxiety or confidence. It is a paper and pencil test consisting of one hundred items. The PRCS is explained more completely in Howard Gilkinson, "Social Fears as Reported by Students in College Speech Classes," *SM*, IX (1942), 141–160.

instruments in one of their space ships and that these photographs reveal craters. On the basis of such evidence, a judgment about the truth or falsity of indirectly verifiable statements of fact can sometimes be made. The statement "Subject A has less stage fright after taking a course in the fundamentals of speech than he had before taking such a course," is not directly verifiable. Of course, an operational definition can be given to the concept *stage fright,* and the statement then would be directly verifiable. Stage fright can be defined as the set of operations involved in giving and scoring the Personal Report on Confidence as a Speaker test, or the operations involved in giving a lie-detector test while the subject is speaking. But often this is not what the researcher is interested in studying. He may be interested in certain inner states and percepts of subject A. He calls these inner states "stage fright." Now subject A either has or does not have these inner states so a statement about them is a statement of fact, but the researcher cannot verify the statements directly because he cannot observe A's percepts. If the concept *stage fright* is defined in this way, then the statement: "Subject A has less stage fright after taking a course in the fundamentals of speech than he had before taking such a course," is an indirectly verifiable statement of fact. The researcher will have to make his decision about the truth or falsity of this statement on the basis of observations of the effects of the inner states. He may infer inner states from the observation of such behavior as subject A's shaking knees and quivering voice, or from reports gathered in interviews or by questionnaires, or from responses to tests.

The scholar deals with indirectly verifiable statements of fact quite frequently in his research. Such statements as "Francis Bacon wrote *Hamlet,*" or "Longinus wrote the essay *On the Sublime,*" are examples of indirectly verifiable statements of fact. The historian cannot, at least until a suitable time machine is invented, journey back to watch the writing of *Hamlet* to check if Shakespeare or Bacon is doing the writing. The same holds for the statement about Longinus. He can, however, examine directly certain historical traces such as manuscripts of the works, diaries, letters, and other documents that make statements about historical facts. On the basis of such *evidence* he may make a judgment that the statement "Francis Bacon wrote *Hamlet,*" is false.

When the scholar makes a decision as to the truth or falsity of a statement of fact that is indirectly verifiable, the statement is, for him, conclusively demonstrated as true or false. In the case of the statement about Francis Bacon, for many scholars, it has been conclusively demonstrated as false. The statement that "Abraham Lincoln debated Stephen Douglas at Ottawa, Illinois, in the Senatorial campaign of 1858," is also an indirectly verifiable statement of fact that has been conclusively demonstrated as true to the satisfaction of most scholars.

Some indirectly verifiable statements of fact have so little directly observable evidence bearing on their truth or falsity, or the evidence that is available is so ambiguous that a decision as to their truth or falsity is impossible. In such an instance the statement is said to be inconclusively verified. The remark about Longinus writing *On the Sublime* is such a statement for some scholars in rhetoric.

When a researcher feels that he has a good case for establishing the truth or falsity of an indirectly verifiable statement of fact, such as a statement about the measurement of meaning, or of stage fright, or of attitudes, or about the author of *Hamlet,* or about the shooting of Huey Long, he may publish his feelings. His readers will then examine his case. Typically such interpretations consist of the statements of fact that were directly verifiable for the investigator and which he asserts to have been true or false, plus his inferences from these directly verifiable statements to the truth or falsity of the indirectly verifiable statement of fact. The readers will examine the argument and will decide whether they are convinced or not. If they are not convinced and remain undecided, then, for them, the statement is an *indirectly verifiable inconclusive statement of fact.* For those who are convinced the statement becomes an *indirectly verifiable conclusively demonstrated true* statement of fact. For those who conclude from his evidence and his argument that the statement is false, it becomes an *indirectly verifiable conclusively demonstrated false* statement of fact.

Since much research in speech is concerned with indirectly verifiable statements of fact, there is a chance for bias, gullibility, personal dislike, and politics to intrude into the question of whether such statements have been conclusively demonstrated as true or false. The way is thus open for an occasional scholarly controversy and for contradictory findings in empirical research.

OBJECT-LANGUAGE AND META-LANGUAGE

The discussion of statements of fact has, so far, been confined to the simplest cases in which the researcher is discussing objects such as historical documents, gestures of a speaker, and wet-bath spirometers. At this level of direct description of observables the researchers is using an *object-language.* Since the object-language is used to discuss facts and only facts, it does not contain the words *true* and *false* because these words are not applicable to facts. They describe certain features of the semantical dimension of language. That is, because a given statement of fact bears a certain relationship to a set of facts (operations, observations), it can be characterized as true.

Of course, we must have a richer language which contains important terms like *truth*. Such a language can be called a *meta-language*. Figure 1 indicates the relationship of the meta-language to the object-language. The object-language is the more primitive in the sense that its vocabulary is confined to words describing objects.

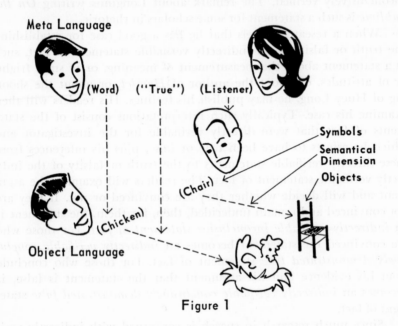

Figure 1

The processes of speech and communication could not be discussed in such a language since it contains no words that refer to language symbols, speakers, or listeners. Meta-language, however, is richer than object-language. It contains all the words of object-language. Thus, objects like chairs and chickens can be discussed in both object-language and meta-language. In addition, meta-language contains words that refer to symbols in object-language and words that refer to the syntactical, semantical, and pragmatical dimensions of language. There must be a symbol in meta-language to refer to such objects as chairs and chickens, but there must also be a symbol in meta-language that represents the word in the object-language that names the objects. In short meta-language must have a vocabulary large enough to talk about language, objects, and speakers. For example, a discussion of the syntactical dimension of the object-language would require the use of a meta-language full of words that referred not to objects but to symbols in the object-language. For example, a meta-language sentence such as "Chair is a five-letter word," or "Chair is a noun," is a sentence about the syntactical dimension of the object-language and a statement of fact. In this case, however, the truth or falsity of the statements depends upon linguistic occurrences for its verification.

The discussion of the semantical dimension of the object-language usually requires the use of meta-language statements containing words that refer both to things and to symbols in the object-language. If the meta-language is English and the object-language is German, the two levels of language can be distinguished without much trouble. However, when both the object-language and the meta-language are English, there is a possibility of confusion. Some convention is thus necessary to identify the meta-language words that refer to object-language symbols and keep them separate from the meta-language words that refer to objects. Typically, single or double quotation marks are used for this purpose. Single quotation marks will be used in this chapter to indicate meta-language words that name object-language symbols.

For example, if the semantical rules of English were being explained to someone who spoke only German, the *denotatum* (what is referred to) for the word *chair* would have to be specified. This could be done most easily, if the teacher also spoke German, by a statement such as *"Stuhl heisst* 'chair'." The explanation could also take the form of pointing to a movable four-legged piece of furniture used for sitting and vigorously asserting the word 'chair.' The statement in the meta-language that " 'Chair' denotes chair," is not nonsense as it may at first seem, nor is it a tautology of the order "A is A." Rather, this statement is an assertion in a meta-language about the semantical relation that holds in an object-language between the five-letter word 'chair' and the object that is a piece of furniture. " 'Chair' denotes chair," is similar to the assertion *" 'Stuhl'* denotes chair." The essential point of asserting that the word is not the thing is contained in this explication of " 'Chair' denotes chair." If the statement still seems trivial or confusing, you should read this section again. Understanding why the statement " 'Chair' denotes chair," says something about the world is the key to understanding the difference between object-language and meta-language.

Meta-language statements may be statements of fact in much the same fashion as object-language statements. Thus, a statement about the truth or falsity of a speaker's object-language phrased in the meta-language of a speech critic is also true or false. Should the critic say that "when the speaker said 'I did not accept the money,' he lied," he is asserting a statement of fact.

Statements of fact about speakers or scholars or experimental subjects and their object-language may be either directly or indirectly verifiable, and the same analysis that was made above of object-language statements can be made of meta-language statements.

LAWS OF NATURE

To this point, all the examples of statements of fact have been particular statements dealing with a single subject's vital capacity or PRCS score, or with one satellite, or one historical event. Not all statements that refer to observables deal with particulars. Of crucial importance to the scientist are general statements such as "Water when heated boils." Although it fulfills most of the requirements for a statement of fact in that it is well-formed and meaningful, the question of the truth or falsity of this generalization is a difficult one to answer. Certainly the statement refers to facts and is based upon observation. In addition, the observations of relevant facts have so far verified the statement. All the water that has been heated sufficiently has boiled. The reader with an empirical bent might feel some uneasiness at this point because of the vagueness of the concepts *heated* and *boil* in this formulation of the statement. His desire for precision may cause him to say that water has sometimes been heated and not boiled. The generalization can be made more precise by including all *relevant variables*. For example, the statement could be written as "H_2O, 99.9 percent pure, heated to 100° centigrade at a pressure of 15 pounds to the square inch, will boil."

When he cooks his eggs in the morning, all the research worker needs to know is that if he heats tap water sufficiently, it will boil. In the laboratory he will need the more precise formulation, particularly if he wants to *quantify* his measurements. Before he can assign numbers to the boiling point, that is, predict at what number on the scale of his thermometer the water will begin to bubble, he must isolate the invariable relationship between the heat and the boiling. This requires that all other factors important enough to influence this relationship must be taken into account. These are the relevant variables which in this case are the purity of the water and the air pressure.

The generalization about water boiling is based upon observation. It states an invariable relation between the heating of water and the boiling point of water and, to this point, universal agreement has been achieved that the relationship has never varied. The statement makes the claim that, without exception, every sample of water that has been heated, is now being heated, and shall be heated will boil. The claim is a bold one but by risking much the generalization gains much. If the statement were "Heating is correlated with boiling by a coefficient of .90," it would claim much less and gain much less. If the latter generalization were the best available, then the water would have to be watched each morning to see if it would boil for coffee.

PREDICTION, POSTDICTION, AND CONTROL

Because of the generality of the law of nature it covers *every instance* and so long as it works it enables prediction about every instance of water that is heated. Prediction allows control. In addition to prediction and control of future events, such a statement allows inference about past events. Given suitable heating in the past, the boiling water can be inferred. The determination of the historical age of a given object by determining the state of decay of carbon 14 in the object or the use of the laws of astronomy to determine the date of an historical eclipse are examples of the use of laws of nature to postdict.

When the cave man discovered the law of nature that "Water when heated boils," he no longer had to depend upon an anthropomorphic explanation for the phenomenon of water bubbling and vapor rising and the water biting his finger when he touched it. He could simply say that "Whenever water is heated, it boils." Before this discovery the bubbling water may have seemed capricious, the work of spirits and gods; afterwards it had a natural cause. The cave man equipped with a law of nature could arrange to bring water close to fire and make it boil. From that point on he could control his environment to some extent. He could eat soup instead of raw saber-tooth tiger, for example. The *technological* improvement in the life of the cave man is analogous to the more sophisticated technology of an engineer drawing up a blueprint for a machine and taking it to the shop and saying, "Build this machine, and I predict that putting tobacco in this hopper and cigarette paper here and cellophane here and turning on the motor will result in tailor-made cigarettes wrapped in cellophane coming out of this end of the machine." Such a machine may never have existed before but because of laws of nature such an innovation or invention is possible. Technology with its resultant modification and control of our environment rests upon laws of nature.

UNIVERSAL AGREEMENT ABOUT INVARIABLE RELATIONS

One of the important features of the scientific method is that it searches for universal agreement about invariable relations such as those expressed in laws of nature. Replication of experiments must result in agreement among the researchers as to the nature and extent of these relations. Since this is the case there is a universality to the statement of scientific laws. Specific statements of fact cannot, even in principle, be universally agreed upon. Only those having actually had an opportunity to observe the facts involved in a specific statement can agree about its truth or falsity. Scientific laws are stated in such a fashion that, in principle, everyone could replicate the conditions described by the law, observe the results, and agree that the promised invariable relations held. The beginning chemistry student goes through these steps when he replicates an experiment in the laboratory. He may produce oxygen by certain combinations of chemicals brought to reaction. The laws of chemistry are so firmly established that if his experiment fails to produce oxygen, the instructor does not question the laws but, rather, he examines the student's laboratory procedure. When the student does the experiment properly then he, like thousands of beginning chemistry students before him, agrees that oxygen is invariably produced under these conditions.

INDUCTION

With the rise of empirical observation as a way of knowing and with the development of modern science in the Renaissance, such philosophers as Francis Bacon (1561–1626), John Locke (1632–1704), and David Hume (1711–1776) examined the notion of *cause* as used in the sense that boiling water had a natural cause and with this analysis of the method of science came the analysis of *induction*.[8]

LAWS OF NATURE AND GENERALIZATION BY COMPLETE ENUMERATION

David Hume's analysis of causation is the culmination of this line of philosophy. It is one of the most important treatments of the problem of induction. Hume directed his attention to the relationship between the notions of cause and of induction. A law of nature, as opposed to generalization by complete enumeration of a class, requires an act of faith, according to Hume. The generalization that "All members of this seminar in dramatic theory are graduate students," could be based on an examination of the records of the five students enrolled. If such investigation revealed that students A, B, C, D, and E were all graduate students and all enrolled in the seminar, the generalization is true. This generalization is by complete enumeration of a class and is a shorthand way of expressing the same

---

[8] For a more comprehensive treatment of these developments see Hans Reichenbach, *The Rise of Scientific Philosophy* (Berkeley, 1951), pp. 78–94.

thing as the five particular statements of fact that assert of each student that the student is both a member of the seminar and a graduate student. Such a generalization, while often useful, is much different than a law of nature. Hume pointed out that arriving at a law of nature inductively required an act of faith because it covered many more instances than could be observed in making the generalization and, indeed, covered many more instances than ever *could* be observed. Thus, inductively arriving at a law of nature involved making the assumption that the regularities observed in the past would continue in the future. Hume maintained that there was no logical ground for such an assumption.

FALSIFYING A LAW OF NATURE

Hume's analysis points up one of the essential differences between a law of nature and a statement of a particular fact. "Water when heated boils," is a statement that has many features in common with the other statements of fact analyzed in this chapter and yet it is impossible to conceive of sufficient observations to judge its truth. Judgments about its falsity, however, can be made because only one negative instance is evidence enough to make the statement false. Even one thimblefull of H_2O of sufficient purity heated to 105° centigrade at 15 pounds per square inch of pressure that failed to boil would make the generalization false.

PROBABILITY STATEMENTS

Perhaps the most troublesome class of statements to analyze is the range that falls in the area between particular statements of fact and laws of nature. At least since Aristotle's time, logicians and rhetoricians have struggled with the knotty problems posed by an analysis of probability statements. Is the statement "If this water is heated sufficiently, it will probably boil," a statement of fact? On what grounds can you decide the truth or falsity of such a statement?

OPERATIONAL DEFINITIONS AND PROBABILITY STATEMENTS

Certainly, if a statement of this sort is to be a statement of fact, not only must operational definitions be given to 'heated' and 'boiled' but also to the term 'probably.' Mathematical statistics are useful to give this term an operational definition. For example, the statement "Heating is correlated with boiling by a correlation coefficient of .90," is a probability statement that includes an operational definition of the term *probably*. In this case, *probably* refers to the set of operations involved in computing a correlation between observations of water that was heated and water that boiled. Such a statistical probability statement can be evaluated by checking the observations and the statistical computations.

LAWS OF NATURE AND PROBABILITY STATEMENTS

When clarified in this way, the probability statement can be analyzed in the same fashion as a law of nature. If the investigator making such a statement says that for his two thousand samples of water the correlation coefficient was .50 and that this should not be generalized to another researcher's report that on one thousand samples of water he discovered a correlation coefficient of .90, he is generalizing by complete enumeration. Such a probability statement is essentially a statement of fact that can be judged true or false on the basis of the observations of the water and the mathematical computation of correlation coefficients. However, the probability generalization can also be treated like a law of nature. Observation, plus mathematical computation can lead to rejection of such a probability statement. For example, if for two thousand samples of water the result was a correlation coefficient of $+1.0$, the generalizations of correlation coefficients of $+.50$, $+.90$, and $+1.0$ would all be false if they were treated as laws of nature. Like a law of nature, however, correlation coefficients cannot be run on all samples of water so this probability generalization represents an inductive leap of the same sort a law of nature requires.

PROBABILITY STATEMENTS, PREDICTION AND CONTROL

Statistical generalizations that hold for all events enable some prediction and control. For example, assume that success in debating correlates .70 with scores on a verbal proficiency test, .68 with scores on an IQ test, and .82 with college grade point. When student A, who has a high score on the verbal proficiency test, the IQ test, and also a high grade point, wins the West Point Debate tournament, the explanation might be: debater A won for the probability is high that the winner of this tournament will be someone who scores high on the verbal proficiency test, the IQ test, and who has a good grade point. In addition, if the three measures were computed for all entrants to the West Point tournament and the prediction made that the winners would be in the top 10 percent rather than the bottom 10 percent on these scores, this would be a sound prediction. However, statistical generalizations could not have been used to invariably pick A as the winner prior to the tournament, as laws of nature would have.

PROBABILITY STATEMENTS AND GENERALIZATION BY COMPLETE ENUMERATION

There are occasions when the empirical researcher in speech wants to generalize about a class by complete enumeration. For example, he may wish to study the occupational patterns of radio, television, and theatre graduates of the University of Minnesota, and he would like to find out about the occupation of every such graduate. He may wish to study the television viewing habits of farmers in the United States, and he would like to find out about every farmer. The United States Census Bureau attempts to make some generalizations by class enumeration every ten years, and the task is staggering.

Probability statements are often used in such instances to estimate the results of complete enumeration of a class without actually observing every member of the class. Thus, instead of contacting every graduate student in radio, television, and theatre from the University of Minnesota, the researcher selects a random sample and uses statistical computations to estimate the results he would have gotten had he gone through the process of complete enumeration. If 20 percent of his sample indicate they are working full time in professional, educational, or community theatres and he knows the size of the total population of such graduates, he can make an estimate of the percentage of the total population that are working in theatre by use of inferential statistics. The statements about the selection of a random sample and the proportion of the sample that indicated they were working in theatre are directly verifiable statements of fact for the investigator. Random sampling procedure can be given an operational definition, indeed, it must be if statistical computations of a certain sort are to be used. Statements estimating the proportion of the total population working in theatre are also statements of fact, but in this instance the procedure used is like the procedure used to judge the truth or falsity of an indirectly verifiable statement of fact. That is, because of the difficulty of direct verification by complete enumeration, the researcher uses the directly verifiable statements of fact about his sample population to make a judgment about the truth or falsity of statements of fact about the total population.

THE USES OF PROBABILITY STATEMENTS

Because statements of this sort are estimates of the results of generalization by complete enumeration, they are much different from the probability statements that generalize about all similar events as do laws of nature, and the two must be clearly distinguished in any analysis of theory and research in speech. On occasion a student confuses the two sorts of probability statements by beginning in his opening chapter to justify the importance of his thesis on the grounds that discovering probability generalizations covering all similar speech events is a worthwhile research task and ending in the last chapter with the assertion that more research needs to be done in this area and that the statistical generalizations made in the study are by *complete enumeration* and refer only to the subjects of this study. This sort of confusion often leads to trivial results. A statistical estimate of the results of the complete enumeration of a large population is a useful research methodology as indicated above. To assert that the generalizations of a study set up to find probability statements analogous to laws of nature are generalizations by complete enumeration is seldom useful. The knowledge that I have found that, say, 200 students at Y University in 1950 reacted in a certain way to a speech is not very important information. No one can argue that a careful investigator is fully justified in saying that for the two hundred subjects in his experiment the difference between the experimental and control groups was significant at the one-percent level of confidence but about other speech events analogous to the ones he studied he can say nothing.

What does the fact that one researcher found a correlation of .90 and another replicating the experiment found a correlation of .50 mean? That more research is needed? Probably. But certainly if both experiments have been carefully done, it means that the general statistical statements asserting that whenever these two factors appear in a population they are associated by a correlation coefficient of .90 or .50 are both false. In practice, of course, researchers cannot be so harsh. Scaling techniques in speech are not always precise; variables are difficult to isolate and control, and results of .90 and .50 in two different experiments would be taken as evidence that there is a positive correlation between the variables in question, and until more precise research methods are worked out this is the practical thing to do.

STATEMENTS OF VALUE

Not all statements that are well-formed are statements of fact. Statements like, "Contestant *A* had a great oration," "His interpretation of the part was all wrong," "Tennessee Williams is a great poet," "It is unethical to make up evidence in the last rebuttal speech in a debate," "The ends do not justify the means," "It doesn't matter what you do so long as you feel good about it," are not statements of fact. There are no observations that will enable a researcher to make a judgment about the truth or falsity of such statements. Not that these statements are unimportant. Indeed, such statements are very important. Moral precepts are guide-lines for behavior. Value systems and taste prescriptions form the basis for criticism and appreciation of the arts. However, researchers in speech must be careful not to confuse such statements with statements of fact. Observation is the court of last resort for statements of fact. The scientist does not argue about how many teeth there are in the mouth of a horse. He goes and looks and counts. The clerics of the Middle Ages might well have argued about how many angels can dance on the head of a pin, for statements about angels dancing on pin heads are not statements of fact. Observations can not yield evidence for the truthfulness of such statements. Statements about the good life or the great play are open for argument, and they should be argued because they need to be accepted or rejected and there is no "true" or "false" answer. Each generation and each individual must decide which statements of this sort he will assert and believe and argument and disagreement are thus to be expected and welcomed about these matters. About statements of fact, men should not, in principle, disagree, or again in Oppenheimer's words, "we may differ as to facts but we can resolve the differences."

DEDUCTION

The final subclass of statements that are well-formed sentences but not statements of fact are logical statements that assert something about the syntactical dimension of the language being used and not anything about "facts." This brings us to the third part of the scientific method, deduction. Induction and observation are related to semantical dimensions and analysis of the relationships that hold between statements of facts and observables. Deduction relates only to the syntactical dimension, and for the scientist this often involves a good deal of mathematics.

EMPIRICAL AND LOGICAL STATEMENTS

The statement $2 + 2 = 4$ is a tautology, and a decision can be made about the correctness or incorrectness of arithmetic statements simply by examining and checking the form of the statement. That is, if you understand the rules and the assumptions of arithmetic, $2 + 2$ implies 4. Such statements are the province of the syntactical dimension of language. The study and development of such deductive systems is the province of the discipline of logic. Therefore, the tools of logic are important in analyzing the theoretical structure of speech because the distinction between empirical statements and formal statements must be made in order to clarify the philosophical bases of speech theory. Much of the confusion in the philosophy and theorizing of the past has stemmed from failing to distinguish empirical statements from tautologies. Plato's philosophy of absolutes has this confusion in it; Kant's search for what he called "a priori" synthetic statements was essentially a search for empirical statements that could be known or intuited without relying on observation, much as tautologies are intuited. Nevertheless, one of the major contributions of Kant's impressive critique of pure reason (deductive logic) and practical reason (empirical knowledge) was the distinction he made between synthetic statements and analytic statements. By synthetic statement Kant meant roughly what I call a statement of fact and by analytic statement he meant roughly what I have referred to as tautology or formal statement.

SYNTACTICAL ANALYSIS

The investigation of statements to discover if they are empirical or empty is the province of syntactical analysis. This branch of linguistic analysis is the most highly developed of the three dimensions of language, and it has proved more important than might at first appear. The study of the language of various disciplines in a purely formal way has resulted in distinguishing between empirical and formal statements, between empirically meaningful statements and non-sense statements, and between formally valid tautologies and formally invalid contradictions.

One interesting feature of the analysis of the logical syntax of the propositions of a discipline has been the discovery of a large number of statements that appear to be statements of fact but which, upon analysis, turn out to be empty or analytic statements. For example, the statement "Stuttering cannot be both a functional disorder and the result of a pathology of the central nervous system," appears to be a statement of fact that says something about the world. Syntactical analysis, however, indicates that the way these terms are used conventionally, the proposition that a behavior is the result of a functional disorder, is incompatible with the proposition that a behavior is a result of pathology. The statement then is a definition of "functional disorder" and records a decision as to how certain terms will be used. It is a statement about syntactical relations, not about stuttering. Researchers and theoreticians often use such statements in their work; and when the definitional statements are confused with empirical statements, pseudoproblems may result. Empirical statements or statements of fact must be distinguished from empty or analytic statements.

THE USES OF DEDUCTION

Deduction starts when induction leaves off. Beginning with statements of fact and generalizations that have been arrived at inductively, the investigator uses deduction to arrange the symbols of these statements of fact and generalizations into formal patterns permitted by the rules of logic or of mathematics to deduce or compute other statements of fact or generalizations that were implied but were not obvious in the original data. Mathematics adds nothing to the description of the world contained in the statements and generalizations provided by observation and induction. Mathematical statements are empty of content unless they are plugged into the world through observation and induction. When properly plugged in, they yield results that are just as reliable as the original inductions. What mathematical or logical deduction does in such a situation is make clear the additional implications of data. An infinite intelligence would not need mathematics because it would grasp all the implications of an induction or a theory immediately. Man, falling short of this infinite intelligence, must use mathematics as a tool to unravel the implications of his data which are not obvious upon inspection.

All that is required for a deductive system are a set of symbols and a set of rules governing the formation of the symbols into longer expressions. The rest is a purely formal matter of finding the allowable patterns. To discover that $2 + 3 = 6$ is not an allowable pattern in arithmetics does not require a pair of marbles and a trio of marbles. If the rules and axioms of arithmetic are known, the pattern $2 + 3 = 6$ can be checked as invalid simply by inspecting its form.

This emptiness should not be confused with triviality for mathematics is an indispensable aid to seeing the implications of a theory and the relationships among laws of nature. Neither Newton nor Einstein could have formulated theories without the aid of mathematics; indeed, Newton was forced to develop sections of calculus to work out his theory. Psychologically the relationship between the invention of theories and mathematics may be even closer than this. Perhaps Newton could not even think his theory until he had the mathematics for it.

On the other hand, the impressive role of mathematics in science should not blind the researcher in speech to the analytic nature of deduction. Statistics are helpful, often necessary; but they cannot tell the researcher anything that is not firmly bedded in his data.

If the observations are poorly done and the inductions unjustified, then the most elegant statistical analysis will not save the study.

SUMMARY

The necessary tools for a linguistic analysis of the theories and research work in speech are an understanding of the syntactical, semantical, and pragmatical dimensions of language and the distinction between object-language and meta-language.

The scientific method consists of three factors: observation, induction, and deduction. Observation is the basis for decisions as to truth or falsity of particular statements of fact. These statements may be either directly verifiable or indirectly verifiable. Generalization with empirical content may be laws of nature in which case they have so far expressed an invariable relationship. When such generalizations are formed on the basis of observation, the process is called induction. The observation of negative instances is evidence that a generalization is false but laws of nature can never be completely demonstrated as true. Probability statements may be statements of fact or generalizations analogous to laws of nature. In either case observation plays a similar role in truth decisions.

Not all statements are statements of fact. An important subclass of statements assert propositions in regard to matters of value, taste, morals, and esthetics. Such statements are not true or false, and observations cannot yield a decision about these matters. Another important subclass of statements that are not statements of fact are logical expressions that express linguistic relationships.

Logical statements are the province of deductive logic and for the scientists are most often expressed in terms of some mathematical model. They are without empirical content, and observations are useless for making decisions as to truth or falsity. Confusing linguistic statements with statements of fact has been the source of much trouble in various disciplines. Confusing statements of fact with statements of value and taste causes additional problems. Confusing meta-language with object-language statements is a third source of difficulty.

The business of the philosophy of science is to clarify the language of the various disciplines, to clear up confusions and ambiguities, and indicate where research is useful; decide what sorts of questions can be answered by observational methods, what questions are pseudo-questions, and what statements are essentially non-sense. The collection and philosophical analysis of knowledge thus become joint and complementary enterprises. The researcher collects knowledge and develops theories. The philosophic analysis of this material clarifies the structure and content of the theory and indicates where further investigation is needed.

SUGGESTED READINGS

Ayer, Alfred Jules. *Language, Truth and Logic*. London: Victor Gallanez, Ltd., 1948.

Bergmann, Gustav. *Philosophy of Science*. Madison: The University of Wisconsin Press, 1957.

Bormann, Ernest G. "An Empirical Approach to Certain Concepts of Logical Proof," *CSSJ*, XII (September 1961), 85–91.

Bridgman, P. W. *Logic of Modern Physics*. New York: The Macmillan Company, 1927.

Frank, Philipp. *Philosophy of Science*. Englewood Cliffs, N. J.: Prentice-Hall, Inc., 1957.

Oppenheimer, Robert. "Analogy in Science," *American Psychologist,* XI (March 1956), 127–136.

Reichenbach, Hans. *The Rise of Scientific Philosophy*. Berkeley: University of California Press, 1951.

Russell, Bertrand. *An Inquiry into Meaning and Truth*. New York: W. W. Norton & Company, Inc., 1940.

Stevens, S. S. "Mathematics, Measurement and Psychophysics," *Handbook of Experimental Psychology,* ed. S. S. Stevens. New York: John Wiley & Sons, Inc., 1951, pp. 1–50.

PROJECTS

1) Prepare a list of thirty statements containing five examples of each of the following six kinds of statements:

a) Directly verifiable true statements of fact
b) Directly verifiable false statements of fact
c) Indirectly verifiable statements conclusively demonstrated as true statements of fact
d) Indirectly verifiable inconclusively demonstrated statements of fact
e) Indirectly verifiable statements conclusively demonstrated as false statements of fact
f) Statements that are not statements of fact.

2) Select a recent research article from one of the speech journals and determine the proportion of statements of fact to the total number of statements. Estimate the proportion of indirectly verifiable statements of fact to directly verifiable statements of fact. Evaluate the truth or falsity of the statements of fact contained in the article on the basis of the evidence furnished by its author.

3) Prepare a list of twenty generalizations containing five examples of each of the following kinds of statement:

a) Generalization by complete enumeration of a class
b) Generalization that covers more instances than can be observed
c) Probability statements that estimate the results of complete enumeration of a class
d) Probability statements that cover all similar instances.

4) Select a recent research article from one of the speech journals and classify the language of the article as object-language or meta-language.

QUESTIONS FOR DISCUSSION

1) The paradox of the statement "This sentence is false," goes as follows: if the sentence is true then it is false, but if the sentence is false then it is true. How can the meta-language and object-language analysis of this sentence resolve the paradox?

2) Are higher levels of language such as meta-meta-languages implied by the analysis of object-language and meta-language?

3) In what ways are students of speech interested in studying the syntactical dimension of language? the semantical? the pragmatical?

4) Criticize the statement: induction is reasoning from the particular to the general and deduction is reasoning from the general to the particular.

5) Discuss the implications of the statement that deductive arguments are "empty" in the sense that they say nothing about the world.

CHAPTER FIVE

SCIENCE AND THE NATURE
OF KNOWLEDGE ABOUT SPEECH

THE KNOWLEDGE OF SCIENCE

UNIVERSALITY OF SCIENTIFIC LAWS

Science searches for universal agreement about invariable relations. Replication of experiments must result in agreement among the various researchers as to the nature and extent of these relations. The discussion of laws of nature in Chapter 4 outlined the basic features of scientific laws. The relations expressed, such as those between heating water and the boiling of water, must be invariable. In addition, all observers of all experiments must agree that water when heated boils. Bypassing all the philosophical niceties and problems raised by these broad requirements, the fact is that the natural sciences have achieved a community of agreement about a rather impressive number of such laws.

CONCEPT LAWS

Laws of two main types express the invariable relations in the natural sciences. The first is the concept law. Water is an example of a concept law. Iron, oxygen, and hydrogen are other examples of concept laws. The concept law *water* implies a host of invariable relationships. Once we determine that a given sample of fluid is water we know that it will boil at one certain temperature and freeze at another. We know that it will combine with other compounds and elements in a certain fashion. These relationships are invariable. If ever a sample of pure H_2O were discovered that did not combine with iron to form rust under suitable conditions, the whole structure of chemistry would be affected.

Iron, too, is a law of nature. If we test a given sample of metal and discover it has the density of iron, we can predict that the metal will deflect a magnetic needle, will rust, and will have a certain melting point. These invariable relations are called properties. Thus, iron has the properties of rusting and melting.

PROCESS LAWS

The second kind of law is known as the process law. It is expressed as a statement and is often represented in a mathematic formula. "Water, when heated, boils," is a process law. The law describing the invariable relations that hold between the distance traveled by a freely falling body on the surface of the earth and the time of the fall is also a process law. Expressed in a formula, the latter law is "$S = \frac{1}{2}gt^2$." This same law can be stated in words as, "the distance traveled is equal to half the acceleration of gravity multiplied by the time of the fall, squared." There is a close tie between process law and concept law. A concept law can be translated into process laws; and when all the process laws associated with the concept have been stated, the *meaning* of the concept law is exhausted. If a fluid is water, then a process law stating its specific gravity, another stating its boiling point, and another stating its freezing point can be specified. There is also reciprocal relation. Without the concept the process law could not be stated. The development of a concept such as "specific gravity" enables the statement of a process law involving both water and specific gravity.

SCIENTIFIC LAWS AND ANALOGY

Once laws of nature-stating concepts were discovered man began to look for other laws of the same type. The discovery of the earliest laws is lost in prehistory, but once discovered these laws led the way to other discoveries by analogy. The interesting fact is that analogies have often worked. Once a new concept law has been discovered, a new element for example, then by analogy a prediction can be made that the concept law will express a number of invariable relations of the order of a certain atomic weight, a certain melting point, and a certain specific gravity. Generally, these predictions have been accurate.

In like manner, when process laws were discovered, many similar laws of the same form were discovered by analogy. Both process and concept laws are suitable for physics and chemistry, and their discovery opened the way for the development of theoretical structures in these sciences. We have no guarantee that laws suitable for speech will have these forms and so far the attempts to find concept laws and process laws have been much less successful in the social sciences than in the natural sciences. If the behavioral sciences develop as the natural sciences did, however, once the appropriate forms for laws governing behavior are discovered, the way will be cleared for a rapid development of laws of a similar form.

THE KNOWLEDGE OF SPEECH

CONCEPT FORMATION IN SPEECH

Historically, concept laws have been one of the archtypes for laws of nature in the natural sciences. Concept formation plays an equally important role in knowledge about speech. Very few concepts in speech are laws of nature; and they, therefore, serve different functions and comprise a body of knowledge that is both like and unlike scientific knowledge. An explanation of the notion of definition will point up the ways in which concepts in speech are like and unlike laws of nature.

DEFINITION OF SPEECH CONCEPTS

Operational definitions are the basis for concepts in the natural sciences. The concept is a kind of a shorthand way of stating the operations that would be performed to determine specific gravity or temperature. Many definitions in speech are not operational in this sense. Sometimes the concepts should be given operational definitions because they are being used by an investigator trying to discover laws of nature. For example, a researcher dealing with stage fright may define the concept in common sense ways and then proceed in his experimental design to use the concept in operational terms. As Clevenger pointed out in his synthesis of a number of research projects in stage fright, the operational definitions of the concept used in these studies fell into three separate categories.[1] If the results were interpreted as bearing on the common-sense concept *stage fright*, confusion and contradiction resulted. Likewise, to define the concept *intelligence* as certain operations involving a paper-and-pencil test is much different from using the concept *intelligence* as we do in everyday conversation.

Quite often the definitions used in speech theory are not operational definitions. The nonoperational definitions are of three kinds: (1) conventional definitions, (2) descriptive definitions, and (3) prescriptive definitions.

Some definitions in speech are conventional. In a broad sense all language is specified by conventional rules for the syntactical, semantical, and pragmatical dimensions. Nothing about the world requires that a given object be called 'chair' rather than 'stuhl' or 'chaise.' If we speak English, we participate in the conventions that establish the rules of usage; and thus, we call the object a 'chair.'

---

[1] Theodore Clevenger, Jr., "A Synthesis of Experimental Research in Stage Fright," *QJS*, XLV (April 1959), 134–145.

The conventional nature of all language can be demonstrated by creating a language from the beginning. This requires an arbitrary set of symbols, some rules as to how these symbols can be related, and a set of semantical rules arbitrarily laid down. A nice example of this procedure is given by bidding conventions in contract bridge. No knowledge of the game is required to understand the nature of bridge conventions. The game is played with a deck of fifty-two cards divided into four suits. The suits are distinguishable because of different shapes, symbols, and colors. There are thirteen cards in each suit, ten with suit symbols varying from one to ten and three with pictures on them. These form the objects to which the language will refer. According to the rules of the game each player has a right to use a very limited vocabulary to discuss the holdings in his hand with his partner. The partners may bid or comment back and forth several times. The decision as to what this limited collection of statements may mean is conventional. Among the allowable statements are sentences such as "I bid one spade," "I bid one no-trump." Before such talk is meaningful a semantical dimension must be specified. For this purpose elaborate bidding conventions have been devised and published. "I bid one spade," can be agreed upon by the players to mean "I have five cards in the suit we agree to call spades, plus five additional picture cards spread throughout all suits." The statement can be made to mean something else but only if a convention has been established by those doing the bidding.

Natural languages such as English are not conventional in certain important respects. There are historical explanations of the way the symbols developed and are used. Psychological learning is a factor in language development. In this sense English is not a convention and phoneticians, anthropologists, and psycholinguists may study empirical data to find explanations of how the development of language is determined by the nature of man and his environment.

Nonetheless, within the restrictions imposed by history, there is room for some arbitrariness in the way a natural language such as English is used. One important kind of definition used in speech theory is the conventional definition. We may, within certain limits, make our terms mean what seems most suitable for our purposes so long as we agree about the meanings.[2] Thus, a speech textbook quite often begins in the early chapters to define certain terms that are important to the analysis of the rest of the book. *Persuasion* might

---

[2] This is the procedure used in debate when the teams agree upon definitions of key terms to facilitate clarity of argument. There may be compelling reasons for restricting these definitions because of the traditional usage of certain terms. Bizarre definitions often lead to confusion but the terms of a debate proposition may be defined in a number of different ways during the course of a debate season.

be defined carefully and arbitrarily. The definition found in a given book might be contrasted with those found in other books until the convention is clearly established. When definitions are made in this way, controversy over the definition is only profitable if it is carried on with a realization of what is at stake. The question that should be asked of a conventional definition is: "Does this definition serve the purposes of the discussion or analysis?" Thus, the argument over whether a definition of persuasion that includes all communication is more helpful to the study and analysis of public speaking than a definition that restricts its meaning to a certain subclass of communication is legitimate. In similar fashion such issues as the controversy over the persuasion–conviction dichotomy are worth pursuing.[3] For the most part, however, conventional definitions should not be the focus of argument. In debate such controversy is often called "quibbling over terms" and is usually not helpful.

When definitions are used in a descriptive way, however, controversy is useful. Many statements phrased as definitions in speech theory are not specifications of semantical rules for the use of a symbol but are statements of fact about objects and phenomenon. The conventional definition is a *meta-language* statement about how a term in the object-language is to be used in referring to objects. The single quotation marks (a convention we arbitrarily established in Chapter 4) around the term to be defined help keep this clear. For example, " 'persuasion' denotes the same phenomenon as 'communication' " would be a conventional definition of the terms 'persuasion' and 'communication.' The descriptive statement asserting in the object-language that there is a connection between all communication and persuasion is much different. It says nothing about the conventions of the object-language but does say something about the facts discussed in object-language. Thus, if the statement "All communication is persuasion," is an object-language statement, it says something about the world, namely that the events, communication, have the quality, persuasion. Although, on occasion, the two are confused, the second kind of definition is more widespread and important in speech theorizing than the first. For example, when Johnson defines stuttering as "an anticipatory, apprehensive, hypertonic avoidance reaction," [4] he is making an object-language statement, not a conventional definition. He is not saying that whenever we use the word 'stuttering' let us agree that we mean an anticipatory,

---

3 See, for example, Charles H. Woolbert, "Conviction and Persuasion: Some Considerations of Theory," *QJS*, III (July 1917), 249–264; Edward Z. Rowell, "The Conviction-Persuasion Duality," *QJS*, XX (November 1934), 469–482.

4 Wendell Johnson, *et al.*, *Speech Handicapped School Children* (New York, 1956), p. 217.

apprehensive, hypertonic avoidance reaction. Rather, he is saying that, in fact, the speech behavior, stuttering, has the qualities of being anticipatory, apprehensive, and hypertonic, and that it is an avoidance reaction. Such a statement is not so much a definition of a term as it is a description of the factors or phenomenon indicated by the term.

Finally, definitions may also be interpreted as prescriptive statements. Such definitions as "an orator is a good man speaking well," is a value judgment of the order, "good speakers ought to be good men." If tragedy is defined as a play dealing with highborn persons, the definition may be a value-judgment that tragedy *ought* to deal with highborn persons. If the purpose of speech-making is defined as communication, it is not a description of the purposes of actual speakers but rather an ethical imperative that other purposes should not motivate speakers. Many of the value judgments that comprise a large and important part of theorizing about the arts of rhetoric, drama, and oral interpretation are couched as definitions.

These three kinds of definition need to be distinguished in any scholarly discussion. If, for example, two scholars are discussing 'persuasion' and one of them is attempting a conventional definition for the purpose of conversation and the other interprets his definition as an attempt at describing the features of the world that the second scholar calls 'persuasion,' they may well get into a serious misunderstanding. Likewise, should one of them describe the world, as best he can, with a definition and the other scholar try to describe the world as he thinks it *ought to* be with his definition, they may again be involved in useless controversy.

The three ways of interpreting definitions can be illustrated by examining a famous definition in the field of rhetoric. When Aristotle's book on the subject is translated into English the term 'rhetoric' is sometimes defined as "finding all the available means of persuasion." This definition may be interpreted as a conventional, a descriptive, or a prescriptive definition. (At this point, the argument that Aristotle intended the definition to be of a certain kind, while an interesting scholarly question, is irrelevant to our analysis.)

If this definition is interpreted as a conventional one, then Aristotle would be suggesting that throughout the book whenever he uses the term 'rhetoric' he means in a given situation "finding all the available means of persuasion." Certainly, this is a legitimate way to begin a book and the only quibble a scholar might have with Aristotle in this regard would relate to whether or not some other definition might have been more helpful to the analysis in the rest of the book.

The definition might also be interpreted as an *object-language description* of the practice of rhetoric. In this interpretation Aristotle would be asserting that whenever the events called rhetoric are *observed* in the world they have the quality of "finding all the available means of persuasion." Some scholars have asserted that the Aristotelian approach to knowledge is based on descriptive definitions. G. Burniston Brown, for example, has interpreted Aristotle's definitional approach to knowledge as an attempt to apply the methods of geometry to *demonstrate* knowledge about the world. Geometry proceeds by starting with definitions and axioms and then deducing a number of unforeseen implications from the definitions. A triangle can be defined as a plane figure bounded by three straight lines and, given the axioms of geometry, a number of essential properties of triangles can be deduced. When all of these essential properties of triangles have been demonstrated we know all there is to know about a triangle. Aristotle, according to G. Burniston Brown, attempted to demonstrate knowledge about observables in a similar way. He began by defining concepts in terms of similarities (*genus*) and differences (*differentiam*).

Such definitions were designed to reveal the essence of a subject. Thus, the definition of man must reveal the essence of man just as the definition of triangle must reveal the essence of triangles. When the definition that contains the essence of man has been discovered Aristotle would use axioms suitable to the study of man to deduce, by means of syllogisms, the further essential properties of man. The definition of 'rhetoric' and 'tragedy' could proceed in the same way. 'Rhetoric' could be classified in the same genus as 'dialectic' and the definition could then proceed to establish the differences between rhetoric and dialectic. This process should lead to a definition that catches the essence of rhetoric and by using suitable axioms and syllogistic reasoning, we should then be able to deduce all the essential properties of rhetoric. When we have done this we know all about rhetoric and the task of science is finished.[5]

Stripped of all its elaborate Platonic and Aristotelian metaphysics, this sort of definition turns out to be a descriptive definition. That is, under this interpretation Aristotle's definition of 'rhetoric' is an attempt to describe the practice of rhetoric as he observed it in Greece. The scholar who interprets Aristotle's definition as a descriptive definition might well take issue with its adequacy and conduct his inquiry at some length. His argument should be based upon observation and judgment about the adequacy or inadequacy of the de-

---

[5] G. Burniston Brown, *Science, Its Method and Its Philosophy* (London, 1950).

scription as a reflection of the practice of speaking that the scholar observes. The scholar might assert that Aristotle's definition describing the facts of rhetorical practice is false because the scholar has observed speakers who did not find all the available means of persuasion.

Finally, Aristotle's definition could be interpreted as a prescriptive statement. That is, Aristotle is asserting a value statement that whenever a speaker practices the arts of rhetoric he ought to find all the available means of persuasion. The scholar who interprets Aristotle's definition as prescriptive may disagree with the definition but since it is a value statement and not a statement of fact about observables the scholar's argument will come down to some counter-statement such as rhetoric ought to have a broader (or narrower) function than finding all the available means of persuasion.

CONCEPTS OF LAWS OF NATURE

The concepts used in theorizing in speech that are established by conventional definitions, by observation of phenomenon, and as value-judgments, can be compared to the concepts in laws of nature. The definitions used for concept laws and process laws in the sciences are not conventional definitions in the narrower sense. The discovery of the concept of specific gravity was an important discovery based on empirical data. Scientists cannot say, "Let us agree that specific gravity means thus and so." Their experiments in the laboratory would force them to match their concepts with their observations. Yet, conventional definitions are helpful and important in theorizing in speech. The concept of ethical proof may be defined as the rhetorical devices used during the delivery of a speech or it may be broadened to include the reputation of the speaker and the actions that the speaker takes before he gives the speech. There is no laboratory to consult in a case like this and whatever definition is most helpful in the analysis at hand can be agreed upon by the people involved in using the concept. Indeed, this procedure is wiser than quibbling over whether 'ethical proof' *really* is one or the other, for 'ethical proof' is a label that can be assigned to any arbitrarily defined concept. If the statement is rephrased to say that traditionally *ethos* has meant what the speaker does before the speech and *ethical proof* has meant what the speaker does during the speech, then it becomes a statement of fact and is either true or false. Indeed, one of the important ways in which conventional definitions can be sanctioned is by tracing the way the term has been used in the past. Part of a scholar's task in a given research project might be to trace the way key terms have been used historically. These terms, however, may be defined conventionally despite their traditional usage. Words are essentially tools; and if we understand the difficulty in washing past connotations from a term, we can make the word denote whatever concept is most helpful to our analysis. If the traditional usage is likely to add confusion to the discussion, a new term may be coined for the concept. Introducing a new term insures that old language habits do not cause misunderstanding; however, inventing new terms exacts a price, too. The new terms must be learned and used, and too many novel terms can contribute to an abstruse style and make for heavy going until they become second nature. In addition, theoreticians can become addicted to making up new words. The result is often a pretentious jargon for the restatement of common sense. In any event, conventional definitions in speech have employed both strategies, sometimes redefining the traditional term in new ways,[6] and sometimes using a new term for the purposes of analysis. Terms such as 'feedback' and 'noise' are examples recently introduced in speech.

When the definition is an object-language statement describing the properties of the phenomena, the approach is similar to that of the scientist explaining a concept law. In this instance, observation is the court of last resort. The definitions of stuttering are attempts to outline the properties of stuttering. The contending positions on stuttering are based on such definitions. There is nothing conventional about their use. In making an analysis of stuttering, you do not say, "Let us agree for the purposes of our discussion that stuttering is a 'psychoneurosis caused by the persistence into later life of early pregenital oral nursing, oral sadistic, and anal sadistic components.' "[7] Such talk is not appropriate because those who feel that stuttering is a "disorder in which self-reflexive evaluative or semantic reactions play a determining role,"[8] could not agree to accept the other definition. They ought not to accept it because to differ about this matter is not a "quibble over terms" but a controversy over the nature of knowledge about stuttering. Descriptive definitions are attempts at finding concept laws in the field of speech. When successful, the definitions would express universally agreed upon invariable relations. For example, stuttering behavior would have to be invariably associated with anticipatory and hypertonic avoidance reactions or with a neurosis of a certain kind. The qualities associated with the

---

[6] For an example of redefinition of traditional terms see Ernest Bormann, "An Empirical Approach to Certain Concepts of Logical Proof," *CSSJ*, XII (Winter 1961), 85–91.

[7] Isador H. Coriat, in *Stuttering: Significant Theories and Therapies*, ed. Eugene F. Hahn (Stanford, 1943), p. 27.

[8] Wendell Johnson, in Hahn, p. 58.

concept such as hypertonic avoidance reaction or neuroses caused by early pregenital oral nursing needs must be defined in operational terms if a concept law analogous to those in physics and chemistry is to be worked out in stuttering theory. So far the investigations of stuttering have not resulted in concept laws. Yet, the descriptive definition is an important part of our knowledge about stuttering. Although we do not know as much as we would like to, we do know something and what we know is often expressed in the definition of concepts such as stuttering, stage fright, motives, group cohesiveness, and esthetic distance.

The differences among conventional definitions, descriptive definitions, and concept laws are reflected in one of the major theoretical frameworks for all disciplines. The setting up of classes in such a way that knowledge can be ordered, related, and explained is dependent upon concept formation. Systems of classification can be found in the natural sciences such as chemistry (table of elements), botany (classification of plants), zoology (classification of insects), and in speech, in such areas as drama (classification of plays), rhetoric (classification of rhetorical devices), speech pathology (classification of articulation disorders), radio and television (classification of program types), voice science (classification of phonemes), and oral interpretation (classification of literature as drama, poetry, and prose).

The classification of knowledge in the sciences is the result of concept laws or of descriptive definitions of considerable precision. The classification of knowledge in speech is often the result of conventional definitions. The difference is important in both the development and use of classifications as knowledge. For example, if the concept *swan* includes qualities *A, B, C, D,* let us say, swimming, long-necked, two-legged, white, we may build a classification system that has one category for swans. What happens to the classification system that has only one class for swans when an individual is discovered that is long-necked, swims, and is swanlike in all respects, except he is *black?* If the classification system is constructed on the basis of conventionally defined concepts, there is no problem. The system is expanded; and the definition of the concept 'swan' is cut so it includes only swimming, long-necked, and two-legged. There are now black and white swans. The class, swan, has been divided into two parts; and the classificatory system is a bit larger and, perhaps, more unwieldy but it still accounts for our experience. However, if the concept *swan* was a concept law like *iron,* then the discovery of a black swan would be a serious matter. One of the bases of classification would then be color, which is asserted by the concept law to be invariably associated with membership in a given class. When this is disproved by the discovery of a representative with an unpredicted color, doubt is thrown on all the rest of the invariably associated qualities upon which the system rests. The black swan is the equivalent of a piece of iron that has the wrong atomic weight. Such a piece of iron would cause a serious re-evaluation of the table of elements.

The classificatory systems in speech range from almost purely arbitrary ones to those based upon descriptive definitions as precise as those of the zoologist or botanist. If we classify plays according to a set of concepts such as tragedy, comedy, farce, and melodrama, the concepts are usually defined in arbitrary fashion.[9] Thus, when an individual play appears that has qualities *A, B, C,* which are the qualities included in the arbitrary definition of tragedy, but does not have quality *D,* and has several additional features, *E* and *F,* which were not included in the concept of tragedy, it is not at all unusual or disturbing. A new concept can be developed or the old concept can be divided into several subcategories. The classification system can be expanded to include classical and modern tragedies, or true tragedies and pseudotragedies. Speeches can be classified in the same way. They can be thought of as speeches to inspire, to inform, to persuade, and to praise or to blame. When a speech is discovered that does not fit into the category system, the system can be modified to accommodate the individual speech without doing violence to the entire structure.

The voice scientist's classification of phonemes in terms of the position of the articulatory mechanism during their production is an example of a classificatory system based upon precise descriptive definitions. To say that (b) is a bilabial plosive is to say something about its relationship to certain positions of the articulatory mechanism during its production. When a (b) is found that is not produced by making a small explosion by blowing apart the compressed lips, it is not as damaging as the discovery of an element that does not have the qualities predicted; but it is a surprise and may be considered as much of an anomaly as an albino pheasant. If too many such individuals are found, the whole classificatory system may need to be re-evaluated.

CONCEPTS AND PROCESS LAWS

Concepts play a crucial role in the development of process laws, as well as in classificatory frameworks of knowledge. Operationally

---

[9] See, for example, Edward A. Wright, *A Primer for Playgoers* (Englewood Cliffs, N. J., 1958).

defined concepts can be dreamed up by the gross, but they must not be random flights of fancy; they must be worth doing. Specific gravity is an example of a concept that was worth the trouble to develop. The reason it was worth developing is that it became part of a series of process laws. Specific levity could be an example of a concept that could not become useful in this way. Specific levity might be found by taking the weight of the speaker, times the number of hairs on his head, divided by the number of words spoken per each audience laugh. Specific levity could be determined operationally (although it is a bit tedious to do the necessary counting), but there would be little point in doing it unless we could find a process law or a probability generalization using the concept.

The importance of concepts like specific gravity in the physical sciences has led researchers in the behavioral sciences to try to develop similar concepts. Intelligence quotient is an example of an operationally defined concept in the behavioral sciences. The point of developing a concept such as intelligence quotient is to find a process law such as "If a student has an IQ of 140 or more, then he can successfully complete four years of college." This statement, however, does not hold true in every instance. Thus, the notion of IQ has not led to any process laws; but it is a more useful concept than would be the concept of specific levity because it has been the basis of a number of probability statements such as "IQ test scores correlate with the Brown Carlson Listening test with a correlation coefficient of .55." [10] Such probability generalizations are useful and comprise a part of our knowledge about psychological phenomena. They enable prediction, not about individuals, but about general trends when large numbers of individuals are involved; and they furnish a kind of explanation of events.

Some concepts in experimental phonetics are very close to concept laws. The concept of vowel *formants* is such a notion. Certain patterns of energy distribution in vowel sounds (formants) are closely related to the perception of the vowels. When this relation becomes invariable, the various discriminating formants will be laws of nature. The development of concepts such as *bel* in the area of psychophysical measurement is very close to a process law that states an invariable relationship between certain measureable qualities of the sound wave and certain other qualities related to sound percepts.

SPEECH CONCEPTS AND GENERALIZATIONS

A number of generalizations in speech take the form of process laws and incorporate concepts in the same fashion as a law of nature.

---

[10] Ralph G. Nichols and Thomas R. Lewis, *Listening and Speaking* (Dubuque, Iowa, 1954), p. 8.

In the field of public discussion such concepts as group productivity and group cohesiveness may be combined into a generalization that "Group productivity is proportional to group cohesiveness." Such knowledge is phrased in the same form and employs concepts in the same way as the natural sciences, at one level of perception, express laws of nature. The differences involve first the definition of the concepts. The concept of *group productivity* may be defined in somewhat arbitrary fashion as the ability of the group to do the job that it is set up to do. The notion of *cohesiveness* can be defined as the willingness of the individual group members to work for the group, the ability of the group to stick together, its *esprit de corps*. These concepts could also be defined in operational terms like the concepts in laws of nature. If the results of the group's work could be counted, this counting could be taken as the operational definition of group productivity; and some pencil-and-paper index of group members' attitudes toward the group could be taken as an operational definition of cohesiveness. With an operational definition for each concept the generalization could be tested empirically by gathering data on a number of groups and determining if the productivity, as operationally defined, varied proportionally to the cohesiveness, as operationally defined. When this is done, the results are seldom as neat and clearcut as the results of experiments in the first course in chemistry or physics. There is no invariable relationship between productivity and cohesiveness. For most groups it does seem that the more cohesiveness the more productivity, but not for all.

Teachers of discussion and group methods may also operate with knowledge in the form of this generalization and with concepts defined in a more general way. That is, the notion of cohesiveness, defined as sticking together and the generalization about the more cohesive a group the more productive it is likely to be, is asserted. What does such a generalization tell us, and is it worth asserting? In this age when science is so highly regarded, a statement of this order might not even be considered knowledge.

Certainly such generalizations tell us a great deal less than a law of nature. But they do tell us something, and they are worth asserting. They are like scientific laws in several important respects. First, they are based upon empirical data. People working with groups have observed how groups operate and have formed a concept that they labeled cohesiveness. Concepts are formed in such instances because certain features of the events under observation can be discriminated and seem analogous to other features of similar events. Watching $group_1$, $group_2$ . . . $group_N$ causes an observer to form the concept of cohesiveness. Working with this concept, he observes other groups and checks to see if he can use the notion to help him order his experience. When the concept seems linked to other important features of the discussion, he formulates generalizations like the one under consideration and keeps checking the generalization as he works with new groups. When the observations fail to verify the generalization, he often tries to *explain* its failure in terms of other factors that were unusual and thus submerged the operation of the relationship between productivity and cohesiveness. If the generalization fails repeatedly, it will be discarded. A group of such generalizations, imprecise as they are, used in concert by an experienced man can result in considerable explanation, prediction, and control of group phenomena.

A great deal of knowledge about theatre is of this sort. The concept of *protagonist* can be defined in general terms as was the concept of productivity. "Volition" or will can be defined in the same way. The result can be a generalization such as the following: "The most moving quality of a good protagonist is the quality of volition." [11] Such concepts in the theatre are formed by observations of plays; and when an example of a protagonist whose most moving quality seems to be something other than volition comes along, the exception may be explained in terms of other unusual features of the play or the hero. Nevertheless, if there are too many such protagonists, the generalization will be discarded. With such generalizations a playwright can explain, predict, and control, to some extent, the reactions of a theatre audience. The reason an Arthur Miller or a Tennessee Williams can write a more successful play than the graduate student doing a play for his master's thesis is that the successful playwright has developed such generalizations through practice and experience. The reason his plays are not always successful is that such generalizations are not laws of nature. They are imprecise, difficult to measure operationally, and sometimes wrong.

A few brief examples from other areas of speech will indicate how widespread and important this sort of concept formation and generalization is in our knowledge about speech. The generalization in public speaking that "Narrative material will hold the audience's attention better than expository material," is such a statement. The concept of *optimal pitch level* is such a concept in voice improvement. On occasion this latter has been given an operational definition such as being one-fourth of the way up from the lowest note in a male speaker's total range, including the falsetto. This same concept can be defined in more general terms as the ideal pitch level for a given individual's vocal equipment. The generalization that a

_____

[11] Marian Gallaway, *Constructing a Play* (New York, 1950), p. 67.

speaker's pitch flexibility will be increased as his habitual pitch level approximates his optimal pitch level is a typical generalization of this type. Another is that speaking with abdominal support of the breath and a relaxed throat will result in more vocal resonance.

PROBABILITY LAWS

Such generalizations are often the subject of more systematic empirical investigation. In these instances the concepts are given operational definitions and statistical interpretations are made of *correlation* between the concepts. When a generalization asserting a specific correlation exists between two operationally defined concepts in all similar contexts, the probability statement is a sort of half-way house between the generalizations that employ concepts defined in general terms and the laws of nature that characterize the natural sciences. The typical generalization formed by practitioners of the arts of rhetoric and the theatre or audiologists and speech clinicians are based upon direct observation and experience; the generalization asserting a statistical correlation between two operationally defined concepts is based upon more carefully specified observations and certain statistical inferences. There is inevitably more ambiguity in the former statement since it is closer to common-sense language. This ambiguity makes for more difference of opinion about the meaning of the nonoperationally defined concepts and about the reliability of the generalization. The probability statement's meaning is specified by operational definitions and statistical inferences. Are these probability statements then *statistical laws?* Can the statistical laws now developed plus those to be discovered furnish the basis for a *science* of speech or a science of communication? Like so many questions of this nature the answer depends on what one means by science. A more precise question can lead to greater understanding of the issue. Can statistical laws like those in physics become the basis of knowledge in speech? To answer this question a distinction must be drawn between the probability statements that express correlation between two operationally defined concepts and the statistical laws in the natural sciences. A good deal of mischief has been done because recent developments in the natural sciences at the *subatomic particle* level of analysis indicate that phenomena at this level of analysis seem to follow no regular laws of nature but operate lawlessly or follow statistical assumptions. For probability mathematics to be useful, several assumptions must be made. The first and most important of these is that the phenomenon under study is lawless, operating in random fashion, purely by chance. Having made this assumption, the researcher can apply probability mathematics to his problem; and if he is dealing with a large enough number of cases, he can predict fairly accurately what will happen at a *grosser* level of analysis.

The typical probability example of flipping an unbiased coin indicates how this is done. Assume an investigator wants to discover the laws governing the flipping of the coin. If he wants to know if a given instance of flipping the coin will turn up heads, he will try to find the laws of nature governing the movement of this particular flip. He must measure the force given the coin, the air resistance, the position of the coin before it was flipped, the distance of the fall, and other relevant information. By careful application of the laws of dynamics he could predict the toss. However, if the discovery of all relevant information proved too tedious and burdensome or proved to be impossible to determine, the researcher could begin to study the pattern of coin flips at a *grosser* level of analysis. He could ask himself if there are some laws governing the number of heads and the number of tails and the order in which they appear. He might, for example, compute the correlation between three heads in a row being followed by a tail. When this proves a dead end, he could decide to make the assumption that he should not look for laws at this level of analysis but rather that he should assume these events take place according to statistical assumptions or according to pure randomness and chance. Once he makes the assumption of chance governing the number of heads and tails he can apply the *laws* of statistics to his problem. Speaking of statistical laws in this way is much different from using the term to refer to probability statements indicating correlation between two variables. By statistical computation the researcher can now predict the number of runs of six heads in a row as larger and larger samples of coin tosses are collected. Such computation will also predict the equal distribution of heads and tails.

The important probability rule in such instances is the Law of Large Numbers. There is always a margin of error in making predictions on the basis of probability mathematics. The larger the number of events under consideration, the smaller the margin of error in probability predictions. If, for example, we want to be 99 percent sure of our predictions, the margin of error will depend on the number of tosses under consideration. For 100 tosses, if we wish to be 99 percent sure, we must say that there will be between 35 and 65 heads in 100 tosses. Obviously this is a crude sort of prediction when dealing with only a small number of events. Increasing the number of tosses and keeping our level of accuracy at 99 percent, probability laws predict between 450 and 550 heads in 1,000 tosses, and between

4,850 and 5,150 in 10,000 tosses. The margin of accuracy increases from 15 for 100 to 50 for 1,000 to 150 for 10,000, but the *percentage* of the margin in relation to the total number of tosses decreases from 15 percent to 1.5 percent.[12] With increasingly large numbers the percentage of error becomes so small that at a gross level of observation for extremely large numbers of events probability mathematics predicts with almost the accuracy of a law of nature.

Statistical laws of this sort are important where other methods of investigation seem inappropriate and where we can make the assumption of randomness and where large numbers of events are involved. In such cases, statistical computations can make predictions with considerable accuracy; and if *observations* verify these predictions, we can accept them as substantiated. The statistical rules governing the flip of a coin tell us nothing about the likelihood of the next flip turning up heads. Only when we observe a large number of events can predictions be made. Statistical laws can make no predictions about the next play of a slot machine, but over thousands of plays they enable more and more accurate predictions about how much money the machine will pay out. In terms of such statistical predictions the natural sciences have some advantages compared to the behavioral sciences. On occasion, the scientist investigates random activity in large numbers of atomic particles. This means that the statistical predictions can be made at the common-sense level of perception with such accuracy that the margin of error is not very noticeable. For example, radium, as found in nature, disintegrates slowly. If we have one gram of radium, we can compute the number of atoms it contains. Scientists have discovered that a portion of these atoms will split away each year. They have no notion as to which atom will split at any given moment. Any individual atom may split away in the next second or remain for a hundred years. If there are laws governing the splitting of an individual atom, the scientists do not know them. They take the alternate position of assuming that the process is a random one and use probability statistics to compute the rate of decay of radium with great accuracy. For a pound of uranium, for example, the rate of decay is about five million atoms a second which indicates the feasibility of applying the Law of Large Numbers to such phenomenon.

Statistical laws of this kind are not applicable to small numbers of events. Therefore, they have limited practicality for the researcher in speech unless he is dealing with mass media and can assume randomness in a million or so speech events.

---

12 This discussion of statistical laws is drawn from John G. Kemeny, *A Philosopher Looks at Science* (Princeton, 1959), pp. 65–81.

The analogy between such statistical laws in the natural sciences and statistical laws in speech does not hold. What about the probability statement that asserts that the null hypothesis was rejected at the 5 percent level of confidence or that there is a positive correlation of .87 between two test scores? Can such statements form the basis for a *science* of speech? Let us examine first the statement rejecting the null hypothesis with a certain amount of confidence. A researcher asserting such a statement is doing just the opposite of the researcher who first searched for lawfulness in the flipping of a coin and finding none decided to assume there was no lawfulness and used statistical laws to predict the distribution of heads and tails according to chance. Instead, this researcher *begins* by assuming that the events under study can be explained as happening by chance; this is the meaning of the notion of the *null hypothesis*. When the researcher tests the null hypothesis, he checks the notion that the results of his study can be explained by the operations of chance. When he finds that the odds are against such results as he found happening by chance, he can reject the null hypothesis. When he does this, he bets that there are laws operating in the data he is studying. If he asserts that he rejects the null hypothesis at the 5 percent level of confidence, he means that according to statistical assumptions of chance the odds are 95 out of 100 that he would *not* get such results. Thus, probability mathematics cannot be applied to these data as the scientist applies statistics to the decay of uranium. He has discovered that the variations in his data are not likely to be due to chance. What has he accomplished? He has established a strong case for assuming that there are laws operating in his data, and he must now try to find them.

Such probability statements can be thought of as the basis for a science of speech, but they remain different in important respects from laws of nature or from the use of statistical computations and the assumption of randomness to predict such things as the rate of decay of radium. They are a way station between the more crude formulations of common sense probabilities and the laws of the natural sciences.

SUMMARY

Science searches for universal agreement about invariable relations. These regularities are expressed in low-level laws of two general types. Concept laws which express a number of invariable relationships—*water* or *iron*. These invariable relationships are often called properties in concept laws. *Iron* includes the properties of rusting, deflecting a magnetic needle and so on. The second kind of law is the process law—water when heated boils.

Concept formation plays an equally important part in the knowledge about speech. Very few concepts in speech are laws of nature, but some of them are derived from experiences and observation and function in an analogous if less rigorous fashion.

In the sciences operational definitions are needed for concepts in process laws. Operational definitions are also used by empirical researchers in speech. Definitions of concepts that are useful in speech are not confined to operational definitions, however. Some definitions in speech are conventional, and are specified somewhat arbitrarily for a given scholarly or educational enterprise. The definitions that describe speech events are more like the operational definitions of science. A final important use of definitional techniques is prescriptive in nature. Definitions of an orator, or of the attitude of a member of a discussion group, are often ways of stating what sort of man the orator ought to be or what sort of an attitude a discussion member ought to have.

Conventional definitions are a legitimate part of the dialectic of speech study. Properly used they assist in clarity of expression and increase understanding. They should not be confused with definitions that outline the nature of phenomenon, as do descriptive definitions. Such definitions are an important part of what we know about speech events. They most closely approximate the concept laws of the natural sciences. Prescriptive definitions are unlike concept laws. They do not state anything about the nature of speech events. They are essentially a technique for asserting and clarifying value statements of the sort outlined in Chapter 4.

Concepts are the basis for one important type of theoretical structure in both speech and science. Systems of classification that order elements, species, phylum, plays, and phonemes are based on concept formation. If these concepts are conventional and arbitrary, the classificatory system resembles the theory erected on concept laws in the sciences but works in a different way. Classificatory systems in speech range from almost purely arbitrary ones to those based on concepts that are very close to laws of nature.

Concepts in the natural sciences are not only laws in themselves but frequently are required for the development of process laws. There are a number of generalizations in speech that take the form of process laws and use concepts in much the same way; however, such concepts are seldom operationally defined and the resulting generalization is usually a probability statement rather than a law of nature.

Probability statements can also be phrased in terms of operationally defined concepts and statistical inferences. These probability statements are sometimes called statistical laws. They must not be confused with the statistical laws said to operate in atomic physics. The statistical laws of physics are based on the assumption that random activity of large numbers of atomic particles will enable predictions based on probability mathematics. This use of statistical computation and the assumption of randomness and chance is quite different from probability statements that assert that the differences between two groups of subjects are significant (not likely to happen by chance) or that the correlation between two tests or measures is high.

SUGGESTED READINGS

Bergmann, Gustav. *Philosophy of Science*. Madison: The University of Wisconsin Press, 1957.

Braithwaite, Richard Bevan. *Scientific Explanation*. Cambridge: Cambridge University Press, 1953.

Campbell, Norman. *What is Science?* New York: Dover Publications, Inc., 1952.

Feigl, H., and May Brodbeck, eds. *Readings in the Philosophy of Science*. New York: Appleton-Century-Crofts, 1953.

Feigl, H., and Michael Scriven, eds. *The Foundations of Science and the Concepts of Psychology and Psychoanalysis*. Minneapolis: University of Minnesota Press, 1956.

Kemeny, John G. *A Philosopher Looks at Science*. Princeton: Princeton University Press, 1959.

Oppenheimer, Robert. "Analogy in Science," *American Psychologist*, XI (March 1956), 127–136.

Popper, Karl. *The Logic of Scientific Discovery*. New York: Basic Books, 1959.

PROJECTS

1) Give an operational definition to five speech-related concepts.

2) Give a conventional definition to five speech-related concepts.

3) Give a descriptive definition to five speech-related concepts.

4) Give a prescriptive definition to five speech-related concepts. Restate the prescriptive definitions as ought-to assertions.

5) Prepare a list of five generalizations (principles) dealing with speech events. Compare and contrast these generalizations with laws of nature in the natural sciences.

6) Suggest an area of speech research where statistical laws like those describing the rate of decay of radium might be appropriate. Write a short paper explaining how such an investigation might proceed.

QUESTIONS FOR DISCUSSION

1) Discuss the ways in which English can be characterized as a conventional symbol system and the ways in which it can be considered as historically determined.

2) When might it be helpful to give a conventional definition to such terms as *rhetoric, meaning, persuasion, tragedy, empathy, speech handicap,* and *articulation error?*

3) If an investigator wishes to study such phenomenon as stuttering, stage fright, critical thinking ability, creativity, ethical proof, or emotional proof what should be the relationship between the *operational* definition he gives the concept while gathering his data and the *descriptive* definition he would give it in everyday discourse?

4) In what way can we say that pure chance may lead to statistical laws in science?

5) In what way do statistical laws based upon chance and the Law of Large Numbers differ from statements asserting that two samples of subjects probably represent different parent populations or that two factors are positively correlated?

CHAPTER SIX

THEORY AND EXPLANATION
IN SPEECH

THE MEANING OF THEORY

Basic to the knowledge about speech is the elaboration of concepts of speech into structures that can be called theories. Because the boundaries of speech are nebulous and the field of speech encompasses such a variety of activity, the notion of theory in speech is equally nebulous. Learned men with much experience in the field have examined at length and with some perplexity the question "What is speech?"[1] They have attempted to categorize and label all the theories and diverse activities that are to be found in departments of speech.

Speech is, in some respects, a clinical practice like medicine or psychiatry, a humanity like history or the classics; or a fine art like music, literature, or painting.

In the sciences *theory* means one thing, and in the fine arts it means something quite different. A theory in history is not the same as Newton's theory. A theory about art is not the same as a theory about the learning of rats in a maze. The first step toward knowledge about speech is to understand the difference in these various ways of structuring information and concepts. These differences can then be used to analyze the theoretical structures of speech. An understanding of these theories is important to the development of research projects that will clarify and extend this knowledge.

A common use of the word *theory,* is to mean, in a general way, speculation some steps removed from practice. Using the notion of theory in this way we might say that the first course in speech contains very little theory and is more practical than some of the later courses. Graduate seminars might be described as primarily concerned with theory in this sense. Such statements as "That is fine in theory, but it will not work in practice," use the notion of theory in the same way. This usage is widespread and helpful for much of the day-to-day conduct of our business, but there are important distinctions. The

---

[1] "What Is Speech? A Symposium," *QJS,* XLI (April 1955), 145–153.

first kinds of theory to be described will be those of the natural sciences, and these will be contrasted with the theories of experimental psychology. With these two models as a basis of comparison and analysis, representative theories of speech will be described and evaluated.

THEORY IN THE NATURAL SCIENCES

NEWTON'S THEORY

Physics is a highly developed natural science and furnishes good examples of scientific theory. The first great theoretical model was Newton's theory of gravity. Other examples in physics include theories of electricity and magnetism, theories of optics, the dynamic theory of gases, Einstein's special and general theories of relativity, and quanta theories.

Newton's theory is a good starting place for an explanation of theory in the natural sciences because it is less complex than subsequent theories, requires less knowledge of a specialized nature about physics, and still has many of the essential characteristics of this type of theory. An understanding of his theory will also be helpful in preparing for a discussion of the dynamic theory of gases which will round out the analysis of this type of theory.

Newton's theory was not possible until a number of low-level laws of nature had been discovered. Galileo's work with pendulums, ballistics, and freely falling bodies had resulted in the formulation of a number of laws describing the motion (velocity and acceleration) of objects on earth. These laws were called *terrestrial mechanics*. The work of Kepler and Copernicus in mapping the paths of the planets around the sun in enough detail to allow for a description of their movement across the heavens furnished other low-level laws. Ptolemic astronomy had produced the same sort of laws many years before, starting with the assumption that the earth was the center of planetary movement. So long as the Ptolemaic system described the observable paths of the planets as accurately as the Copernican system, there were no logical grounds for choosing between them, except that Copernicus had a simpler, more elegant set of laws.

Newton's stroke was to see the analogy between the apple falling on the surface of the earth and the earth itself falling toward the sun. His unifying principle of gravity drew together terrestrial and celestial mechanics. His expression of that principle was much simpler than the conglomeration of low-level laws of Galileo and Kepler. It consisted of a formula of two parts. The first was a high-level generalization expressing an invariable relation concerning the speed of attraction between two bodies, their distance, and their mass. The law of gravity was expressed in such general terms that it covered the sun and the earth as well as the apple and the earth. The second part of the theory was a combination rule that explained how the generalization could be applied to specific problems. For example, the combination rule enables the computation of the effect of adding a third planet to a problem involving the sun and the earth. In this way the law of gravity can be applied to a complicated set of data such as that furnished by the sun and the planets of our solar system.

The laws of Galileo explaining the physical motion on the surface of the earth prove to be a special case of Newton's general law. The acceleration (pull) of gravity is a constant on the surface of the earth because the size of the earth is great in comparison to the apple, and the distance from the earth's center of gravity to the earth's surface is so much greater than the distance of the apple from the earth's surface, that the slight pull of the apple on the earth can be ignored. Indeed, any differences introduced are so small they cannot be measured. In this fashion, the laws of Galileo and the laws of Copernicus can be deduced mathematically from the law of gravity.

Newton's work resulted in the first elaboration of a theory in science. The essential features of the gravitational theory are that it expresses invariable relationships and that it has great scope. Mathematics plays an important role in the development and use of this theory. Typically there are more low-level generalizations implied in the theory than had been discovered at the time of its elaboration. New laws can be derived from the theory mathematically.

The deduction of such new laws makes possible the testing of the theory by means of a critical experiment, which tests a hypothesis derived from the theory, and if it is verified, the theory is strengthened. Newton's theory, once more accurate measuring techniques were developed for observing the paths of the heavenly bodies, failed to describe the path of the planets accurately. In such a situation, the tendency is to modify a useful theory and keep it as long as possible even though it fails at some points.

In this case the aberrations could be explained by the theory if the presence of another unknown planet of a given mass and orbit were postulated. This was the course taken by scientists; and when powerful enough telescopes were developed, Neptune was discovered in the orbit Newton's theory had predicted it would be. The theory was, thus, given additional verification. In subsequent years Newton's theory failed to account for some minor deviations of the planets and no amount of adjustment or accommodation would enable it to do so. The way was then open for the development of another theory that would account for these deviations. Einstein's work fulfilled these requirements.

Although such theories are abstract, they ultimately depend upon observations for their justification. Like laws of nature, theories are badly damaged by valid negative instances. Given the relevant data, Newton's theory can invariably predict the flight of an artillery shell. Since it does this in every instance, such a theory enables us to control the flight of a projectile by making the appropriate adjustments of the artillery piece. Thus, theories in the natural sciences enable prediction and control just as laws of nature do, but they enable such prediction and control for a much wider range of phenomena than do laws of nature.

Newton's theory, while it has most of the features of theory in natural sciences, is not as well suited to exemplifying the role of analogy and the use of an explanatory model in theory construction as is the dynamic theory of gases.

THE DYNAMIC THEORY OF GASES

A number of low-level generalizations expressing invariable relations about the property of gases preceded the formulation of this theory. Boyle's law, for example, states that the pressure of a gas varies with the volume and temperature of the gas so that the pressure is inversely proportional to the volume. Gay-Lussac's law states that there is a proportional relation between pressure and temperature. There are a number of such laws dealing with the relationship between pressure and the conduction of heat and so on.

Early in the nineteenth century the dynamic theory of gases was formulated to explain the laws governing properties. The theory includes a hypothetical model constructed out of rigid particles in random and rapid motion. The rigid particles are called molecules and, by analogy, are assumed to act according to Newton's mechanics. Gases, according to this model, consist of a large number of molecules moving randomly throughout the volume of the gas and colliding in haphazard fashion with each other and the walls of any containing vessel. The velocity of these molecules varies with the temperature of the gas, and the pressure on the walls of a container results from the impact of large numbers of molecules on the walls of the container. The effect of the motion of rigid particles such as those assumed in this model on the sides of a containing vessel can be computed mathematically. Further computation can then yield the number, mass, and velocity of particles required to yield the observable pressures. Particles such as those posited by the theory, when the general laws of mechanics are applied to them, will predict the invariable relationships between volume, pressure, and temperature of gases that Boyle's law and Gay-Lussac's law predict. The theory allows for the deduction of both these laws by mathematical computation. Notice that the notion of molecules and the model constructed from these molecules in random motion are not directly observable. Scientists did not directly observe little particles flying about in containers of gas. What they did observe was that gases acted *as if* they were composed of such molecules moving randomly and speeding up with increases of temperature.

The positing of a set of constructs that are not directly verifiable introduces a new dimension to theories. As the natural sciences grew more complex and as more and more was learned about atomic and subatomic physics, this sort of theory became quite common. In a sense, the molecule idea is a fiction in this theory, but it is a very important kind of fiction. Not just any hypothetical construct would do. The construct of a container filled with space and little particles in constant motion is called a model because it is not the same as gas, but it acts in the same way and *allows* for the prediction of results in the same way Newton's law did.

The basis of this theory is an analogy which brings the properties of gases within the theoretical framework of mechanics and thus simplifies, explains, and broadens the scope of the laws of mechanics. So now, the motion of the heavenly bodies, the falling apple, and the movement of molecules in gases are all special cases of the general theories of mechanics.

Like Newton's theory, the dynamic theory of gases yielded all the then known laws governing the properties of gases by deduction; but it, too, yielded some unknown laws. If the assumption was made that the molecules had some mass, the theory yielded laws that predicted the effect of great pressure on gases. With the molecules tightly restricted as they would be under great pressure, the theory predicted much different effects than when the gas was under little pressure and there were very few molecules distributed through the volume. Experiments designed to test these laws became critical experiments because so much was at stake. When these experiments were performed, they confirmed the new laws and thus substantiated the theory. The process of deriving new laws from theories and then subjecting them to experimental research is one of the impressive features of research in the natural sciences. The economy of such research and the importance of the results have caused researchers in other disciplines to try to do the same. The suggestion that experimental research in speech should be theoretically derived stems partly from this feature of theories in physics.

ANALOGIES AND THEORIES

In both of these theories the core is a particularly apt and fruitful analogy. Newton saw that the planets fell toward the sun much as
the apple fell toward the earth. The dynamic theory of gases is based
upon a model of greater complexity, but the parts of the model act
like the falling planets and the falling apple. The analogy must not be
thought of only as an aid to the discovery of the theory for in an important sense the analogy is the theory. The analogy does not become
unimportant after the theory is discovered; indeed, it continues to
be an important germinal influence on future theorizing, and it
helps explain the events covered by the theory. If all the theory
managed to explain were the laws it covered, a clever mathematician
could invent a dozen theories from which the process laws that deal
with gases could be deduced. As Norman Campbell points out in his
book *What is Science?*, analogies, far from being a help in the development of theories, are often a hindrance because finding the right
analogy is the key to developing a theory.[2] In the area of finding the
right analogy the innovating geniuses of science like Newton approach
a common ground with the geniuses of art.

DARWIN'S THEORY OF EVOLUTION

Charles Darwin's evolution theory is another important kind of
theory in the natural sciences. It is different in kind from Newton's
theory or the dynamic theory of gases. First, a distinction must be
drawn between (1) the conception of the origins and evolutionary
changes in species of plants and animals through time and (2) the
accounting for such changes. Darwin's work included both the conception of evolution and the explanation of it, but there is an advantage in thinking of only the explanatory part of his work as the *theory*
of evolution. Darwin fitted a host of specific facts dealing with such
things as vestigal structures, homologies, and embryology into a plausible pattern to demonstrate the *fact* of evolution. The evidence submitted for the truth of the conception of evolution has been conclusive. The theoretical part of his work involved the notions of
natural and sexual selection within a context of the struggle for
existence in which only those who are best adapted to their environment survive; the theory was designed to account for the facts of
evolution. Darwin suggested that many more of a species were born
than could survive. He further noted that there is always a variation
among the individuals of a species, sometimes slight and sometimes
great. There is constantly a struggle for existence in which some are

---

[2] New York, 1952.

better equipped because of individual variations and survive and reproduce, handing on the advantageous traits to their offspring. Darwin called this the process of natural selection. To account for variation between sexes in the same species, such as brighter plumage for male birds, Darwin offered sexual selection. That is, of those who survived some were sexually more attractive and thus more likely to have offspring.

In Darwin's theory there are no equivalents to laws of nature, and there is nothing like the logically consistent theoretical structure from which new laws can be deduced that characterized the theories in mechanics. Darwin's theory does not allow for prediction and control in the same way that Newton's theory does. Rather it gives a coherent and plausible accounting of the historical facts of evolution.

THEORY IN THE BEHAVIORAL SCIENCES

The learning theories of experimental psychology represent one of the well-developed areas in the behavioral sciences. Kenneth Spence points out that the term *theory* has a different connotation in psychology than it has in physics. According to Spence, theories in psychology are used to aid in the formulation of empirical laws. "They consist in guesses as to how the uncontrolled or unknown factors in a system are related to experimentally known variables." [3] Psychological theories are *aids in the development* of laws whereas Newton's theory is built upon a number of established laws. Psychological theories should aid in guiding research by suggesting possible areas of investigation, but they cannot yield by deduction the sorts of laws suitable for testing by a critical experiment.

The nature of psychological theory is clarified by distinguishing between *empirical* and *hypothetical constructs*. An empirical construct is the equivalent of the operationally defined concept that was explained in Chapter 5. Let us say that we establish an operational concept that is the number of times a rat correctly runs a maze. This is an empirical construct. On the other hand, let us assume that a number of animals are subjected to a stimulus, and the responses to the stimulus are carefully measured. If both stimulus and environment are carefully controlled and there is still a considerable range of response, we can suggest possible uncontrolled or unknown variables that we cannot observe and that intervene between the stimulus and the response and account for the observable variations in response. The psychologist Clark Hull developed a system of empirical and hypothetical constructs to account for the learning behavior of ani-

---

[3] "The Postulates and Methods of 'Behaviorism'" in *Readings in the Philosophy of Science*, eds. Herbert Feigl and May Brodbeck (New York, 1953), p. 557.

mals. The psychologist Charles Osgood used hypothetical constructs to account for meaning in the psychology of language. Between the perception of a word and overt response to the word Osgood suggested the hypothetical construct of representational mediation processes to account for the variations in response to word stimuli from individual to individual. Osgood suggests that there are unknown representational processes mediating between word and response. Osgood and his associates have worked on isolating and measuring these mediational responses, and the result has been the semantic differential.[4] Osgood's hypothetical construct has generated a great deal of research and has, thus, fulfilled the purpose of psychological theories.

The key to theories in this sense of the term is the hypothetical construct. There is a superficial similarity between the construct *molecule* used to develop the model for the dynamic theory of gases and a hypothetical construct in psychological theory. Both concepts refer to entities or variables that cannot be observed. The crucial difference, however, is that the constructs of the dynamic theory of gases formed a consistent deductive system from which laws of nature could be computed mathematically. The hypothetical constructs of Hull's learning theory or Osgood's theory of meaning do not yield such results. You cannot predict invariably the response of an organism in a learning situation on the basis of Hull's learning theory. Thus, theory in the behavioral sciences is quite different from the theories of physics. It consists primarily of guesses as to the unknown variables that relate to the empirical data, in such a way as to make the empirical results meaningful and point the way to new areas of research.

THEORY IN SPEECH

The organized knowledge included in dramatic theory, rhetorical theory, communications theory, and theories dealing with voice science and speech and hearing disorders can now be compared and contrasted to theories in the natural sciences and theories in experimental psychology.

THEORY AND HYPOTHESIS

The word *theory* is sometimes used as a synonym for *hypothesis*. In this way we also use it in everyday discourse as a synonym for *hunch*. We might say, "I have a theory that an affirmative team that

---

[4] For an analysis of Hull's learning theory see Spence, "The Postulates and Methods of 'Behaviorism' "; Gustav Bergmann and Kenneth Spence, "Operationism and Theory Construction," in *Psychological Theory*, ed. Melvin H. Marx, pp. 264–270. Osgood develops his theory in *Method and Theory in Experimental Psychology* (New York, 1953).

takes a large burden of proof and invites an argument will win more debates than one that tries to dodge arguments through the use of strategy." What we mean is that we have a hunch that this is the case. We do not have conclusive proof so it remains theoretical in this sense of the term. The "James-Lange Theory of Emotions" is a theory in the sense of a hunch or hypothesis. There has been a controversy over the nature of the sound wave produced by the larynx. One theory suggested that it was a simple sound wave that became complex during phonation because of the addition of overtones by the vocal resonators. An opposing theory was that the wave produced by the larynx is complex. Such theories are essentially statements of fact that have been inconclusively demonstrated. When more evidence was gathered, the *theory* that the sound wave produced in the larynx was a complex wave was accepted as a statement of fact conclusively demonstrated as true by many voice scientists.

The word *hypothesis* has also been used as synonymous with the way the word *theory* was used in our discussion of Newton. Theories like Newton's or the dynamic theory of gases are sometimes called *hypothetico-deductive systems*. Distinctions, however, need to be drawn between unproved hunches and Newtonian mechanics. Using the term *hypothesis* to refer to the former and *theory* to refer to the latter will keep the distinction clear.

SPEECH THEORIES AND SCIENTIFIC THEORIES

The framework for the analysis of theorizing in speech has now been established, and we can proceed to an explication of the structures of knowledge about speech. Clearly there are no equivalents in speech theory to Newton's theory or the dynamic theory of gases. The statement that there will be such theories is a statement of fact and until the evidence is in we cannot assert conclusively that it is true or false. To assert that such theories are better than the others analyzed is to assert a value judgment and not a statement of fact. Certainly we can all indulge in such voicing of value judgments, and we often do. We indicate our bias towards scientism by asserting that we must develop a science of communication. We indicate our bias against science by asserting that speech is an artistic enterprise and science would ruin the arts of rhetoric and drama. When such statements are recognized as value judgments and the inconclusiveness of the statement about the development of such theories in speech is understood, we can eliminate unnecessary conjecture about the possibility or impossibility of a science of the theatre or a science of mass persuasion.

Some theorizing in speech is similar to the use of intervening variables or hypothetical constructs in experimental psychology, and some is similar to the ordering of individuals into classifications and accounting for such classifications as in Darwin's theory of evolution. There are additional features of theorizing in speech that are not usually found in either the natural or behavioral sciences.

GENERAL CHARACTER OF SPEECH THEORIES

We shall begin with a general survey of sorts of statements and structures that characterize speech theories and then proceed to analyze some of these. Speech theories are typically structured and systematized collections of philosophical speculation, advice statements gathered from the practice of the arts of speech, value judgments and ethical rules, and statements of taste.

Theories of speech usually include some philosophical analysis of the sort exemplified in answering such questions as: What are the ends of rhetoric? What is the nature of rhetoric? What is the nature of tragedy? What are the purposes of drama? What is meaning? What is the nature of communication? What is a group? The definitions that are used to answer such questions may be arbitrary, in which case the philosophical analysis is devoted to clarifying the limits, boundaries, or scope of, say, rhetoric. They may be descriptive, in which case a certain set of plays might be selected as tragedies and then studied to see what qualities they possess. The definitions might be prescriptive, in which case they would be another way of asserting statements of values, ethics, or taste.

Direct assertions of value statements are often found in rhetorical and dramatic theory. Such statements might include the following: rhetoric should be used to defend the truth; the purpose of speechmaking is communication; the orator is a good man speaking well; high comedy and farce should not be mixed in the same production; television should be primarily an entertainment media; the basic purpose of theatre should be something more than entertainment.

Most speech theories also contain a large measure of statements giving how-to-do-it advice directly related to television or radio production, theatre production, treatment of stutterers, voice and articulation improvement, preparing and delivering a public speech, and orally interpreting literature. Some of these how-to-do-it statements are accompanied by an argument justifying their use. For example, the "method" approach to acting includes a number of statements justifying its validity. The advice to use a conversational style or a natural approach to the delivery of a speech is quite similar. Richard Whately in his *Elements of Rhetoric,* for example, advises that the speaker should pay no "studied" attention to his delivery but "dwell" on the meaning of what he is saying and trust to nature to suggest the proper emphasis and tone.[5] He then provides a justification for this advice. He does so by attacking the mechanical approach to delivery on three grounds: (1) using shorthand marks for stops, rising inflections, and other voice characteristics is imperfect because no system of marks is able to indicate the range of vocal inflections, (2) such mechanical planning is a circuitous route to first decide how a passage should be read naturally and then plan the way to simulate nature, and (3) the reader's attention being on his own voice he will project a studied and unnatural manner.

A number of advice-type statements derive directly from experience and often have little need for supporting arguments; they have worked for speakers and dramatists for many years. These how-to-do-it statements are often called *principles* or *fundamentals*. How-to-do-it advice that results in a definite style of speaking or production is likely to require a supporting argument (theory). The "method" approach resulted in a definite style of acting; critics who dislike this style of performance engage the proponents of the style in controversies over matters of taste and "theories" of acting result.

Advice-type statements (principles) drawn directly from practice include such things as the stock issues of debate, tips on how to select topics for speeches, outlining procedure for speakers, scenario writing for playwrights, advice on breathing for voice production, on gesturing, on improving articulation, on how to work up a part, on how to block a scene, on how to use color in a set and use lighting to get psychological effects, tests of evidence, and ways to use mirrors and group sessions in the treatment of stutterers.

CLASSIFICATION

The statements that comprise the raw material of speech theories are structured and systematized in several ways. Quite often the structure is one of sorting elements into classes and arranging these into a system. For example, the ends of eloquence can be classified: to enlighten, to please, to rouse, and to influence the will. The speech event may be classified into speaker, speech, audience, and occasion. Rhetorical proofs may be designated as emotional, ethical, and logical. The communication event may be classified into source, encode, message, decode, receiver. A play may be classified into plot, dialogue, theme, and situation. The elements of voice may be divided into pitch, loudness, rate, and quality. A group discussion can be classified into definition of terms, analysis of goals and problems, suggested solutions, evaluation and selection of the best solution.

---

[5] New York, 1834, pp. 264–270.

Classification is the process of selecting events and making decisions about equivalence. When two events are equivalent, they may be placed in the same class. The building blocks of a classificatory framework are, thus, concepts—concepts that are formed on the basis of finding analogies that hold among recurring events. The selection of the features of these events to use in making the decision as to equivalence is the next step in classification. In Chapter 5 the important difference between classificatory frameworks based on concept laws and those based upon concepts defined conventionally or descriptively was outlined. The major differences mirror the difference between concept laws and other concepts. No prediction can be deduced from classificatory systems based on conventionally or descriptively defined concepts. The concepts themselves are ambiguous enough to cause some difficulty in classifying certain speeches, communication events, or plays. This ambiguity is reflected in statements such as: "In some respects this production is a tragedy but in others it is a melodrama, and it also contains some elements of comedy." When a play or a passage from a speech is found that does not fit cleanly into a system as logical, emotional, and ethical proof, the classificatory system is not discarded. The overlapping of characteristics is merely noted in each case. In this respect they are more arbitrary than the classificatory frameworks of the natural sciences. If a given element were discovered that did not fit into the periodic table, chemists would seriously re-evaluate their theories.

As the process of sorting and classifying speech events goes on, a classificatory system is developed. In zoology and botany the classification system includes statements of fact about individual members of varieties of trees or species of animals. The classificatory systems in speech evolve from the study of speech events but information about individual speeches tends to drop away and the classificatory system that evolved during the study of individual speeches or plays remains abstracted from the speech events. These abstracted classificatory systems form a large share of what we call rhetorical and dramatic theory.

The fact that such classificatory systems are different from those of the natural sciences does not mean that they are without value; they serve a different function. Since they have evolved in this fashion, they work well when applied to a new selection of speech events. While not all such new events will fit neatly into the categories, many of them will; and when they do, we gain a good bit of information and understanding about the events. In addition, the classificatory system contains knowledge in its own right. Developing concepts that can lead to classifications and testing individual events for equivalence on common features results in the discovery of such features. The concept of logical proof names a feature of speaking that scholars have found both desirable and important. The classificatory system is thus more than an organizational scheme. It reflects the concepts that have been developed in the study of speeches and plays.

CLASSIFICATION AND THE PROCESS ANALOGY

A modification of the classificatory system that is sometimes used to structure knowledge in speech is to draw an analogy between speech events and laws of nature. Another way of referring to laws of nature is to call them *process laws*. "Water, when heated, boils," is a simple statement of process law. To formulate such a law we need to know the ingredients of the process—the water and the heat—plus the relevant variables such as pressure and purity of the water. We might go further and examine the relationship between the heat of the energy source and the time it takes to bring the water to boil. Process law states the invariable relations between ingredients and, if we include time dimension, the rate of interaction. Chemical process laws describe the same sorts of things only the process if often more complicated, more chemicals are involved, and the process may go on for some time before the reaction is completed.

An important type of theoretical structure in speech uses the notion of *process* as an explanatory analogy and discusses the processes of communication, persuasion, or public speaking. The ingredients of the process are listed as, for example, the speaker, the speech, the audience, and the occasion, or, the source, encoding, the message, decoding, and the receiver. These ingredients are then placed into the context of a process and various interactions described. Thus, the speaker can be said to react to audience response, and this in turn can stimulate the audience to greater response. The speech is influenced by the occasion, and by the variables in speaker and audience.

Using this framework of analysis is similar to the classification approach in listing ingredients for the process. The lists of ingredients are usually classifications of important parts of speech events. Knowledge about speech is also structured by the use of models in much the same way as the dynamic theory of gases was developed.

ANALOGY AND MODELS

Sigmund Freud's theories of psychology furnish a classical example of this way of structuring knowledge. Since Freud's ideas have been very influential in certain areas of speech and drama, perhaps they can be used here to illustrate this feature of speech theories.

Freud constructed a model of the psychological processes which included, first, the *id,* the unorganized bundle of psychological processes brought into the world with the child. The sole aim of the id is self-gratification. As the child comes in contact with environment, that part of the id which is closely connected with his senses is changed by the stubbornness of sense experience. This Freud called the *ego*. The ego is aware of the realities of the environment and tries to curb the undisciplined tendencies of the id. A neurosis might arise out of a conflict between the id and the ego. The superego is a portion of the ego modified through childhood experiences, particularly by parental influences.

This model can be used to account for human behavior. Certain manifestations of hysteria, for example, can be accounted for in terms of the repression of highly emotional experiences by the ego. In like fashion the repression of sexual energy, *libido,* might result in its expression through hysterical manifestations. Several analogies run through this model. The symbolism of dreams can be explained by use of the analogy of a censor standing between the id and the ego and protecting the ego from the dark forces of the id by changing shocking messages into symbolic ones that will be less disturbing to the ego. According to Freud, "the correspondence between the phenomena of censorship and the phenomena of dream-distortion justifies us in presupposing similar conditions for both." [6] A second analogy compares the model to the functioning of a hydraulic system. The libido is dammed up and flows into other channels.[7] Freud's model was unlike the model in the dynamic theory of gases, however, in that it was based upon clinical evidence and was not developed from low-level laws of nature such as Boyle's law; nor did it yield any new laws of nature by deduction.

THEORIES AS EXPLANATORY SYSTEMS

One of the most important functions of theories of all kinds is their power to explain events. Since this function is an important aspect, the nature of explanation requires further analysis.

EXPLAINING BY GIVING CAUSES

The notion of explanation is closely entangled with the concept of *causality*. Frequently when we talk in common-sense ways about "cause" and "effect," we refer to invariable relation in time. Thus, if an event B is always preceded by an event A and if the event A is always followed by the event B, we often say that B is caused by A or that

---

[6] *The Basic Writings of Sigmund Freud,* trans. and ed. A. A. Brill (New York, 1938), p. 223.

[7] For a detailed analysis of this feature of Freud's theory see Kenneth MacCorquodale and Paul E. Meehl, "Hypothetical Constructs and Intervening Variables," in Feigl and Brodbeck, pp. 608–609.

B is the effect of *A*. If someone is hit in the eye and the eye turns black, we say that the blow caused the black eye. If someone takes strychnine and dies, we say the poison caused the death, or that the death was the effect of the poison.

This viewpoint of cause and effect as an invariable relation in time is not enough to explain the logic behind these common-sense notions. For example, there are pairs of events that are invariably associated in time and yet we do not think of them as causally related. Birth invariably precedes death, but we do not think of birth as causing death. There are still other sequences in which event *A* invariably precedes *B* and then invariably follows *B*. Sunrise precedes sunset and then follows sunset, yet we do not talk of the sunrise causing the sunset. Actually the idea of causation as an invariable relation in time is rather sophisticated common sense. It transcends the cruder notion that the cause somehow is doing something to bring about the effect.

Both of these notions overlook the relationship between causality and laws of nature. Behind every statement of cause and effect a law of nature is implied. To say that heat causes water to boil does not necessarily mean that heat must precede boiling, for the heating and the boiling may take place simultaneously; nor does it mean that the heat is somehow in the water blowing bubbles. What it does mean is that *if* water is heated, *then* it will *always* boil. Assumed in every statement of cause is an if-then-always statement of this sort. The laws that state the relationship between pressure, volume, and temperature of gases do not imply a time dimension; but they can be used as the basis of cause and effect statements.

An important meaning of explanation, therefore, is to give the causes of an event. In the natural sciences this kind of explanation is furnished by laws of nature and theories such as Newton's. For example, if a curious child observes a book fall off the table and asks "Why?" an explanation can be given by furnishing a generalization that covers the specific event. Perhaps you answer "Because whenever an object is unsupported it falls." To the next "Why?" you may answer with a still broader generalization such as "Because the earth attracts all objects and causes them to fall." To the next "Why?" you may answer that in the universe all masses attract each other in a straight line with a force proportional to the product of the mass and inversely proportional to the square of the distance between their centers. To the next "Why?" you can give no further answer within the framework of Newton's theory because you have reached its broadest generalization.

For this meaning of explanation, therefore, the question "Why did that happen?" means, "According to what prior conditions and what laws of nature and theories did that occur?"[8] Scientific explanation of this sort has predictive power. You might say, "Be careful or you will knock the lamp on the floor." If someone asks "Why?" you may proceed as above to give an explanation of your prediction. Should the lamp be unsupported it will fall as you predicted.

Many explanations in speech theory take the same form as scientific explanation and use the terminology of *cause* and *effect* or *factors* to explain why something happened. The difference between speech theories based on probabilities and scientific explanation is that speech theories lack this predictive power. The work of a playwright might be explained as the outgrowth of a specific neurosis and certain biographical experiences after the plays were written, but given the antecedent conditions and the presence of the neurosis and the biographical experiences it would not have been possible to predict that he would write the plays he did before he wrote them. A student who has been a poised speaker may suddenly suffer a period of stage fright while giving a speech. The unexpected bout of stage fright may be explained after the event, but it could not have been predicted. A severe case of stuttering may be explained in terms of an overanxious mother, excessively high standards in the home, and harsh toilet training, but given these conditions it would have been impossible to predict accurately in every instance that the child would stutter.

EMPATHY AS EXPLANATION

When we use the form of prior conditions and general laws to explain an event, we understand the event in a theoretical or cognitive sense. We may also understand an event on empathetic grounds. The explanations furnished by works of art are largely of this kind. A play may make us feel an empathetic familiarity and we say, "I see. I understand the experience of the character." In this sense the characterizations of King Claudius and of Macbeth explain ambition and murder.

MOTIVES AND PURPOSES AS EXPLANATION

In addition to feeling an empathetic understanding, explanations in speech theory are sometimes developed in terms of motives or purposes. An individual's behavior may be explained in terms of a desire for money or out of jealousy; the behavior of men and animals by saying an organism hoped for or gained a reward. The

---

[8] This explanation follows the general analysis of Carl Hempel and Paul Oppenheim, "The Logic of Explanation," in Feigl and Brodbeck, pp. 319–352.

same teleological approach may be used to explain the behavior of plants. The shape of a tree may be explained by the tree's striving for sunlight or by the tree trying to be in the form of an ideal type.

PLAUSIBLE NARRATIVE AS EXPLANATION

Another kind of explanation is furnished by fitting specific facts into a plausible pattern or narrative. When the playwright draws his characters so their actions are plausible and when he develops an action line that is believable within the conventions established by his play he is making a similar kind of explanation. Another example is given by a lawyer's use of circumstantial evidence to develop a theory in a given case. The prosecuting attorney's theory may explain the facts in a case like this: the defendant was trying to obtain a divorce from his wife. She would not give it to him. The defendant and his mistress plotted to have the wife killed and hired a hoodlum to murder her. When the gunman failed to follow through as promised, the defendant and his mistress accosted the wife and asked again for a divorce. When the wife again refused, he shot and killed her. Therefore, the defendant is guilty of murder in the first degree. The defense lawyer may explain the same set of facts in some such fashion as this: his client did not try to hire the hoodlum to kill his wife. The hoodlum, who so testified, is a liar and a convict who stands to gain by helping the prosecuting attorney in this case. His client had a mistress and wanted a divorce; but he is intelligent enough to know he would destroy his life by committing murder, particularly such a crude and inept killing as this one. What happened was that his wife caught the defendant and his mistress in the garage of their home and threatened both their lives with her revolver. He grappled with her and in trying to take the gun away from her it accidently discharged and killed her. Therefore, his client is not guilty of first-degree murder.

The playwright Luigi Pirandello was skillful in developing explanations of this sort to account for information that the audience and characters shared. In such plays as *Right You Are If You Think You Are,* the dramatic device consists of furnishing several contradictory explanations for the facts.

SOME TYPICAL SPEECH THEORIES

Speech is a synthesizing discipline. It is often eclectic, drawing its method and its theory from diverse sources. Knowledge about speech reflects the general complexity of knowledge in many fields. Theory and explanation in speech is likewise complex. In the midst of this the scholar and researcher must clearly differentiate among the kinds of theorizing appropriate to the activities of speech and the kinds of explanations speech theories can furnish. A brief description of some representative theories in speech will show how linguistic analysis can clarify the nature of knowledge about speech.

ARISTOTLE'S RHETORICAL THEORY

No course in rhetorical theory would be complete without some consideration of Aristotle's writing on the subject. One of the salient features of Aristotle's theory of rhetoric is his classificatory arrangement.[9] In the *Rhetoric* he sets up four classes of the uses of rhetoric; he divides proof into "artistic" and "inartistic" means of persuasion and further divides artistic means into three main classes. Indeed, his work is a prototype for the classificatory structure in rhetorical and dramatic theory.

Aristotle also defined what the practice of rhetoric is or ought to be. He says that it is the counterpart of dialectic, that it is an art, that it is the faculty of discovering in the particular case all available means of persuasion. Such statements may be interpreted as descriptive or prescriptive definitions. In other instances his definitions are more clearly prescriptive. For example, when he defines the essence of persuasion as "argument" or "proof" and suggests that other writers have unduly emphasized emotional appeals, he is stating a value judgment.

When he lists twenty-eight topics for enthymemes, he is again classifying; but in this instance he is classifying how-to-do-it statements about how to find arguments and analyze a case.

A similar analysis could be made of Aristotle's *Poetics,* but it proceeds in the same fashion as the *Rhetoric.* Instead, let us take another example of dramatic theory.

HEGEL'S DRAMATIC THEORY

In *The Philosophy of Fine Art* Hegel suggested that the nature of the dramatic is man striving to assert and extend his finite ego through infinity. As he strives, he brings himself into collision with other egos in his environment. Two distinct and contradictory forces (call them protagonist and antagonist, hero and villain) take action to restore the kind of harmony they want. At the climactic moment the protagonist clearly succeeds or clearly fails.[10]

This theory is similar in form to Darwin's theory or Freud's

---

[9] These comments are based on *The Rhetoric of Aristotle,* trans. Lane Cooper (New York, 1932). The classificatory structure of Aristotle's rhetorical theory emerges in other translations as well.

[10] George Wilhelm Friedrich Hegel, *The Philosophy of Fine Art,* tran. F. P. B. Osmaston (London, 1920), I, pp. 209–288. For an analysis of Hegelian philosophy applied to dramatic art see Marian Gallaway, *Constructing a Play* (New York, 1950).

theory. Hegel takes the facts of dramatic construction and explains them by means of his dialectical model of harmony, collision, and a new harmony—his thesis, antithesis, and synthesis. He thus incorporates dramatic art into his philosophical system. Part of the charm of the Hegelian system is its ability to make this kind of plausible explanation for many different events. Marx was able to use this dialectical model to explain class struggle in terms of the ownership of the means of production, and John Dewey found the model applicable to the process of inquiry.

THE MATHEMATICAL THEORY OF COMMUNICATIONS

The mathematical theory of communications, sometimes called information theory, has a bearing on speech in two ways. In voice science and experimental phonetics, researchers in speech may use the theory for much the same purpose that engineers designing communications systems and computers do. Some scholars in public speaking have applied the concepts of information theory to serve as a model by analogy to the process of people talking to one another.[11]

The mathematical theory of communications was developed by communications engineers primarily to deal with technical problems involved in designing sending-and-receiving equipment and transmission lines of maximum efficiency. The semantic questions and psycholinguistic problems involved in human communication are not covered by this theory.

The theory is constructed in a manner somewhat analogous to the construction of a system of geometry. This is shown by the fact that Claude E. Shannon uses the term *theorem* in his paper on "The Mathematical Theory of Communication," when he develops the mathematical structure of his theory.[12]

The basic axiom of this geometry is that information be defined as uncertainty. In Warren Weaver's words, "information is a measure of one's freedom of choice when one selects a message." [13] Uncertainty is measured in terms of the logarithm of the number of available choices. The unit of measure is called a *bit,* an abbreviation of binary digit. The decision to make information mean uncertainty implies that noise in the transmission system that causes uncertainty must *also* be considered as information. Thus, static becomes information,

11 See, for example, Dale D. Drum, "Change, Meaning, and Information," *JC,* VII (Winter, 1957), 161–170, and R. Barry Fulton, "Information Theory and Linguistic Structuring," *CSSJ,* XIV (November 1963), 247–257.

12 Claude E. Shannon and Warren Weaver, *The Mathematical Theory of Communications* (Urbana, 1949).

13 "Recent Contributions to the Mathematical Theory of Communications," in Shannon and Weaver, p. 100.

and a distinction must be drawn between desirable and undesirable information.

When the axioms of the system are fulfilled by mechanical constructions of transmission systems or computing machines suitable for the use of binary arithmetic, the theory helps in assuring efficiency of transmission.

Wilbur Schramm's introductory essay in *The Process and Effects of Mass Communication* uses the concepts and the approach of information theory to form a theory of communication. He uses from the mathematical theory of communications the categories of source, encode, message, channels, decode, and receiver and such concepts as noise, feedback, and redundancy.[14] In a public-speaking situation the speaker would be the source, the speech would be the message, and the visual and auditory codes of the message would be sent through the channels of light and sound waves to the receivers, in this case the audience. Audience reaction cues noticed and interpreted by the speaker would be feedback.

STUTTERING THEORY

Another area in which speech theorists have worked out explanatory systems is in the area of stuttering. Although there is some disagreement about factual matters,[15] the greatest disagreement is found in terms of the explanations furnished about the agreed-upon facts.

Oliver Bloodstein has suggested that these explanations fall into three general patterns: (1) the "repressed need" explanation that accounts for stuttering by saying the stutterer blocks because he unconsciously wants to gratify infantile erotic or aggressive needs, (2) the "breakdown" explanation which accounts for stuttering by positing a breakdown of some sort in the complicated neuromuscular patterns required for more fluent speech, and (3) the "anticipatory struggle" explanation which suggests the stutterer blocks because he tries so hard not to block.[16]

The explanations are, of course, much more complicated than these sketches indicate; but their essential features emerge in this form. The repressed need accounts for stuttering in terms of inner motives. The breakdown approach is analogous to the hypothetical construct theories employed in experimental psychology. An unknown variable is posited to help explain the behavior of stuttering. The

---

[14] Urbana, 1960.

[15] See Wendell Johnson, "Introduction: the Six Men and the Stuttering," in *Stuttering: A Symposium,* ed. Jon Eisenson (New York, 1958), pp. xi–xxiv.

[16] Oliver Bloodstein, "Stuttering as an Anticipatory Struggle Reaction," in Eisenson, pp. 1–71.

breakdown explanation is based on statements of fact, however, and with advances in neurology and other sciences that deal with nerve and muscle functions it will be verified or disproved. The anticipatory struggle explanation contains elements of both of the other approaches. It accounts for stuttering by inner motives (trying not to block) and by a hypothetical construct (anticipatory struggle).

Bloodstein calls these explanations *hypotheses,* a term which draws a distinction between unverified hunches and established theories. These explanations of stuttering are certainly more like hunches than they are like the "dynamic theory of gases" and using the word 'hypothesis' will help keep this distinction from becoming blurred. They are in form, however, much like the combination of empirical and hypothetical constructs used to explain data in the behavioral sciences. Viewed in this latter way, they should be evaluated as to their ability to give a plausible accounting for empirical data and to generate helpful research questions.

SUMMARY

The first great theoretical model in physics was Newton's theory of gravity. His theory drew together the low-level laws of terrestrial and celestial mechanics. The dynamic theory of gases illustrates the use of models and the role of analogy in the formulation of theories in the natural sciences. The ability of theories of this kind to yield new laws by mathematical computations is an important feature for researchers. Experiments to test the new laws are important research projects. In this way the theory enables the researcher to concentrate his work in a significant area.

Darwin's theory of evolution differs in kind from either Newton's theory or the dynamic theory of gases. Darwin's work included the concept of the beginnings of a species, its gradual and continuous change to the present, and an explanation of why evolution took place. The proof of the concept of evolution was essentially a task of demonstrating the truth or falsity of a statement of fact. Species did originate and evolve in a continuous and direct line from less organized forms of life or they did not. To explain why evolution took place as it did Darwin suggested that the struggle for existence resulted in a selective process in which only those individuals with the ability to adapt to their environment survived.

In experimental psychology the structure of theories is again different. These theories consist of developing hypothetical constructs or intervening variables to account for data dealing with experimentally known variables. They are primarily guesses as to the unknown variables that relate to empirical data in such a way as to make the results meaningful and point to new areas of research.

There are no theories in speech that are equivalents of Newton's theory. Some of the knowledge in speech uses a structure similar to the intervening variable approach of experimental psychology and some is similar to Darwin's theory of evolution.

Speech theories are structured collections of philosophical analysis, advice statements derived from the practice of the arts of speech, value judgments, ethical rules, and statements of taste.

Quite often the structure of theories in speech involves classificatory systems. Another way of structuring knowledge about speech is to use the analogy of a physical process and apply it to speech phenomenon. The third way of structuring knowledge about speech is to construct models by analogy in the same fashion as the dynamic theory of gases was developed.

One important purpose of theories in speech is to explain speech events. The law of nature explains events in terms of an invariable relationship. Such explanation has predictive as well as postdictive power. It explains not only past events but also future events. Many explanations of speech theory take this same form of pointing to causes and effects or examining factors to explain a speech event. They do not have the predictive power of scientific theories, however. Explanations useful in speech can also be given by empathy, examination of motives and purposes, and plausible narratives.

Aristotle's theory of rhetoric is a good example of classificatory structure. Hegel's theory of drama illustrates the use of a model to structure knowledge. The use of the model of the mathematical theory of communications for a wide range of human communication by analogy is a good example of another way of structuring speech theories. Stuttering theory can, in some respects, be thought of as hypothesis rather than theory; but insofar as the various explanations of stuttering include hypothetical constructs or intervening variables to help explain the empirical data, they exemplify the structure of some of the theorizing in experimental psychology.

Questions for research projects should be related in some fashion to the theoretical structures in speech. Historical and critical research grows out of and modifies speech theories. The scholar may take as his frame of reference the speaker, speech, audience, and occasion as ingredients for a process analogy. He may, instead, use the classificatory system of Aristotle for his work. Empirical research problems may grow from advice-type statements dealing with the practice of rhetoric and drama. The advice that presenting both sides of a question is more effective than presenting only one and the advice that the climactic order of arguments is more effective than the anticlimactic order are two examples of advice-type statements that have been subjected to empirical investigation. Hypothetical constructs to explain empirical data may lead the researcher to ask questions designed to discover the nature of the unknown intervening variables.

The point about relating research directly to theory ought not be pressed too far. Good data has a life of its own even though it was developed in an investigation that had poor theoretical foundations. Good data may prove useful for subsequent researchers long after the theories that generated it have been discredited. Nonetheless, the difficulty of setting out simply to gather sound data is such that almost inevitably the researcher must start with some theoretical structure.

Suggested Readings

Bergmann, Gustav. *Philosophy of Science*. Madison: The University of Wisconsin Press, 1957.

Braithwaite, Richard Bevan. *Scientific Explanation*. Cambridge: Cambridge University Press, 1953.

Campbell, Norman. *What is Science?* New York: Dover Publications, Inc., 1952.

Eisenson, Jon, ed. *Stuttering: A Symposium*. New York: Harper & Row, Publishers, 1958.

Feigl, Herbert, and May Brodbeck, eds. *Readings in the Philosophy of Science*. New York: Appleton-Century-Crofts, 1953.

Marx, Melvin H., ed. *Psychological Theory*. New York: The Macmillan Company, 1951.

Shannon, Claude E. and Warren Weaver. *The Mathematical Theory of Communications*. Urbana: University of Illinois Press, 1949.

Projects

1) Examine a textbook in a speech area of interest to you and write a short paper analyzing the knowledge contained in it, using the tools developed in the preceding chapters.

2) Select a typical theory in speech and write a short paper comparing it with Newton's theory.

3) Select a typical speech theory and write a short paper comparing it to Freud's theory.

4) Select a typical speech theory and write a short paper comparing it to Darwin's theory.

5) Select a typical theory in speech and write a short paper describing

how the theory might "explain" an effective speech, or a successful play, or a successful treatment of a speech handicap.

6) Select an area of interest and construct a theory similar to one of the representative speech theories discussed in Chapter 6.

QUESTIONS FOR DISCUSSION

1) Why might Newton's work be called a hypothesis rather than a theory?

2) What is the role of analogy in the construction of theories in speech?

3) Assume that scientific theories such as Newton's that enabled prediction and control were discovered for speech events. What would be the implications for speakers, broadcasters, clinicians, and dramatists?

4) Discuss the implications of the assertion that to say a scientific theory is better than a speech theory is to assert a value judgment.

5) Discuss the ways in which scientific theories are superior to rhetorical and dramatic theories. What value statements are implied or expressed in your discussion?

6) Discuss the ways in which rhetorical and dramatic theories are superior to scientific theories. What value statements are implied or expressed in your discussion?

PART THREE

METHOD

CHAPTER SEVEN

CREATIVITY

▬▬▬▬▬▬▬▬▬▬▬▬▬▬▬▬▬▬▬▬▬▬▬▬▬

CREATIVITY AND RESEARCH IN SPEECH

THE CREATIVE THESIS

One of the solutions the new departments of speech tried when casting about for types of research appropriate to their needs was to substitute the creative project for the research thesis. For example, a pioneering institution in awarding the master's degree for creative projects, the State University of Iowa, gave three master's degrees in 1926 for planning and directing theatrical productions. In 1930 Iowa granted A. Dale Riley a master's degree for the writing and production of a play entitled *The Barong*. Six years later E. P. Conkle submitted a doctoral dissertation in playwriting.[1] Iowa has also awarded degrees for creative projects in stage design, acting, and costume design. Similar programs, particularly for the master's degree and the master of fine arts degree, are now widespread.

In general, graduate schools have resisted the use of the creative project in lieu of the doctoral dissertation. Some of this resistance stems from the traditional concept of a doctorate as a research degree and some from the difficult problems of establishing standards for creative work. Graduate facilities have set up rigorous standards for historical and critical scholarship and for experimental studies, but the evaluation of a new play or the design of a set is more difficult. How good must a new play be to be accepted? While a good play is an achievement comparable to a historical dissertation and a great play is an achievement only a few men of genius can attain, the bad play is within the competence of anyone who can write a hundred pages of dialogue.

The graduate faculties of the departments of speech and dramatic arts have debated these issues since the 1920's. Various schools

---

[1] Paul Davee, "Definition of the Philosophy Underlying the Recognition and Teaching of Theatre as a Fine Art in the Liberal Arts and Graduate Curricula at the State University of Iowa," Ph.D. dissertation, State University of Iowa, 1950, p. 315.

approach the problem differently and if you are interested in doing a creative project rather than a research project you should investigate the policy in regard to the creative thesis at your graduate school.[2]

If your department will accept the creative thesis you will quite likely be required to furnish rather substantial evidence that you are qualified to undertake such work. If you are planning to write a play, for example, you often will have to submit some plays for evaluation before your project will be approved. If you wish to do a directing project you may have to demonstrate your ability as a director with a one-act play or as an assistant to a staff director on a major production. The same requirements apply to students submitting design or acting projects.

We shall not include in this book a discussion of the arts and crafts of the theatre or radio, television, and film. In order to be accepted as a candidate for a creative thesis you will need to demonstrate competence in your field. Such artistic competence, as seen in Chapter 3, comes from a combination of talent and disciplined practice. If you are contemplating such a thesis you have probably read a number of how-to-do-it books as well as worked as an actor, director, technical director, or writer. This discussion, therefore, will be confined to the thesis paper and topics and to a general consideration of creativity.

Graduate schools differ rather widely in their requirements in regard to submitting plans for the work prior to approval of the project. Some schools require all candidates to submit a prospectus that describes the projected work. The requirements for writing up the thesis report differ as well. You should examine a number of studies that have been accepted at your school to discover a suitable form for writing up the creative thesis.

Some institutions accept the playscript, for example, in the case of a playwriting thesis, with a short preface discussing the play's source and the author's approach. Other institutions require that the script be supplemented with a more elaborate essay discussing the events surrounding the writing and production of the work. In the design, acting, and directing theses the general format often includes a section discussing the preplanning, a section reporting the production record, and a section of evaluation of the production.

Here are some representative titles of creative theses submitted for M.A. and M.F.A. degrees as reported in *Speech Monographs*.

---

[2] For a more full exploration of these questions see Richard Moody, "The Original Play," in *An Introduction to Graduate Study in Speech and Theatre,* ed. Clyde W. Dow (East Lansing, 1961), pp. 104–121.

An Analysis, Prompt Script, and Production Record of Shaw's *Candida*

The Problems Involved in the Directing of a Production of Carlo Goldoni's *The Mistress of the Inn*

A Study and Production of Sean O'Casey's *Juno and the Paycock*

A Project in Scenic Design for a Production of Jean Giraudoux's *Tiger at the Gates*

Costuming the *Comedy of Errors:* A Stylization Based on the Italian Renaissance

A Performance Thesis in Acting

P. O. A Play in Three Acts, with an Analysis of the Creative Process Which Utilized an Experimental Approach to Form

An Original Play, *Confirmation Rite*

A Tale from Sassyfras County, Film

Caesar and the Gaul, Screenplay

Three Television Plays

A Series of Original Dramatic Radio Scripts on United Nations Subjects for Presentation by Secondary School Students

The Pink Bathtub: A Musical Comedy

The Day It Was Night. A Ballet for Children

Although a handbook on playwriting or the arts and crafts of theatre, television, radio, and film would be inappropriate in a book such as this, the subject of creativity has a bearing on all graduate work in speech and deserves further exploration.

CREATIVITY AND THE PSYCHOLOGY OF DISCOVERY

The process of creativity relates in a practical way to the work of all scholars and researchers in speech. One of the persistent problems in graduate training is finding suitable topics for research. Even when a general area has been mapped out the student is still faced with the important matter of finding a significant question to investigate. He may solve this problem by imitating a previous study, by accepting the suggestions of his graduate advisor, or he may take the suggestions given him by previous studies and his advisor and move on to a different topic of his own. If he searches for his own topic, he will profit from an understanding of the creative process.

Finally, the actual work that goes on in laboratories and libraries as well as in studios and on stages raises important questions relating to creativity. At what juncture in the work of the historian, critic, or experimentalist does he utilize the creative process? What advice about work habits and mental sets do established artists and scholars give the beginner to increase his efficiency? Such questions can be illuminated by an investigation of the general features of creativity.

THE CREATIVE PROCESS

Man has long been beguiled by the process of introducing novelty, discovering new combinations, creating new patterns, and finding apt analogies. Oddly enough, only in recent years have empirical researchers begun an intensive and systematic research program to investigate the creative process. This research, however, is only now beginning to produce tangible results. As recently as 1963, a leading experimental psychologist, B. F. Skinner, could state in a speech at the University of Minnesota that we still know very little about the psychology of discovery.

One of the reasons that creativity has not been studied as much as perception and learning is that in this country much of the impetus for research in experimental psychology has been channeled into the various schools of behaviorism. Since the higher mental processes are difficult to observe, the behaviorists have tended to investigate other matters.

On the other hand, while Skinner is right in that we know very little about the psychology of discovery as a result of empirical investigation, we do know a good deal about creativity from other sources. Creative people have discussed problems pertaining to their craft in handbooks and magazines devoted to the practical problems of writing plays, painting pictures, and writing music. Professionals in the arts are often preoccupied with the creative process and they deal in informal essays and discussions with such topics as how to get ideas, how to break writer's block, how to shorten the daily warm-up period, and how to form material without losing the vitality of the original conception. Inadvertently, such shop talk reveals a great deal about the creative process.

The following description of creativity is drawn from the accounts of practicing artists, mathematicians, and scientists, from the scholarship that has ordered and structured such material, and from the findings of empirical researchers which are now reaching a point where they can be helpful.

Most accounts of creativity agree as to the general features of the process. Creativity is groping, random, and haphazard; and yet, it requires strict discipline. The process has both active and passive phases. It is subconscious and mystical and yet requires careful rational reflection and criticism. Since the creative process includes these contradictory tendencies, creative people may emphasize some features in their introspective description of their experience and neglect others. Literary men tend to use figures of speech and analogies to explain how they write. One familiar figure is that of the muse filling the artist and taking over the process of creation as the artist, dissociated, observes with some detachment. Another common analogy is that of conception and birth. Quite often when scholars assemble such accounts and search for a common structure they present the results of their study in an ordered pattern. John Dewey's explanation of "reflective" thinking was organized around the "steps" of the process.[3] Graham Wallas' description of the "art" of thought was organized around the "stages" of the process.[4] Creativity is seldom as neat and straightforward as the descriptions of it. These descriptions must, since they are presented orally or in writing, proceed chronologically. Both Dewey and Wallas warn that the process is one of doubling back from one step to another and, on occasion, skipping some of the steps. These warnings sometimes go unheeded because of the attractive simplicity of the step-by-step analysis.

GROPING AND SEARCHING

When describing the general features of the process of creativity we must be careful not to neglect the sometimes chaotic and often random nature of much of the preliminary searching. Although the results of the creative process are, typically, works of highly integrated form, such as a well-composed painting, a carefully-constructed play, or an elegant solution to a mathematical problem, the way to such disciplined form is often achieved by intensive groping first in one direction and then another. The path is strewn with unsuccessful attempts, false starts, and dead ends. The final product is tidied up in the revision and testing stages to cut away the evidence of strain and effort. In these periods of preparation the artist often is frustrated and unhappy. He says that "things are not going well." He does not seem to be able to "get it right." Here is the first paradox. Although he is doubling back and forth, trying first this way and then that, only vaguely aware of what he is doing and where he is going, it is at just this point that the creative worker must be disciplined. He must continue work, for until he is thoroughly immersed in his materials he cannot expect his subconscious to take over.

STARTING THE CREATIVE PROCESS

One of the mysteries of creativity is how the process begins.

John Dewey explained this getting under way with his notion

---

[3] John Dewey, *How We Think* (New York, 1910).
[4] *The Art of Thought* (London, 1926). A scholarly investigation into creativity, this book is one of the important works in the area.

of the "felt difficulty." According to Dewey, reflective thinking begins when the individual becomes aware that something is not as it should be. He feels a tension that seeks release. He wishes to bring his environment into more harmonious relationships with himself. Graham Wallas gives a somewhat different emphasis when he writes of "conception" as the moment when the creative process gets under way. In a sense, Dewey and Wallas may be referring to the same thing. Perhaps the psychologist, L. L. Thurstone, is right when he suggests "the working hypothesis that creative talent is qualitatively the same at all levels: in the trades and in the professions, as well as in the rare and extreme form that we call genius." [5]

We should note the difference, however, between the felt difficulty of a man in a prison camp and a playwright climbing a hill at night, seeing a child's swing caught in a tree against the moonlight, and suddenly conceiving of the central scene in a play involving a hanging. Prisoners of war are often surprisingly ingenious. They contrive musical instruments from bits of wood and string. They plan intricate and clever escape maneuvers. They have a clear and present "felt difficulty" which goads them to innovation. Shakespeare, when commissioned to do *Twelfth Night,* had little time to work on the play before it was produced, and he may have felt a similar clear and present difficulty. Many playwrights are under no such real and palpable pressures when they begin writing. Indeed, every creative person has at some time felt his first compulsion to paint a picture, compose a song, or write a play, and usually has had little or no external felt difficulty. He has had no commission and no deadline but for some reason has been motivated to do the creative project.

At this point, we must distinguish between the generalized desire to be a playwright and the specific stimulus that sets the creative machinery in motion and produces a particular play. One's life goal may be to become a playwright because of a desire to make money, or because of a longing for the prestige afforded a successful playwright in our society, or because of an urge to produce something worthwhile. Perhaps we need look for no deeper motivation than an instinct to symbolize. One may have to write plays whether he views this course as a sensible one to make money or gain status or not. We do not have much solid information relating to the question of motivation at this generalized level and writers on creativity have submitted a range of conjectures similar to the ones suggested above as possible explanations for creative activity in general.

---

[5] L. L. Thurstone, "Creative Talent," in *Applications of Psychology,* ed. L. L. Thurstone (New York, 1952), p. 19.

Given the generalized framework of an individual who wishes to write a play, the practical question of how to get started writing a play remains. The creative project is often set in motion by a minor and sometimes gratuitous stimulus. In his preface to *The Spoils of Poynton,* Henry James recalls the moment at which his imagination winced "as at the prick of some sharp point." He was having dinner with friends on a Christmas Eve when one of the ladies at the table made a remark about a lady with a good reputation who was "at daggers drawn" with her son over the ownership of furniture in a fine house inherited by the son from his father. The story of *The Spoils of Poynton* resulted from this small "germ." James was instantly aware of "the prick of inoculation; the whole of the virus . . . being infused by that single touch." [6]

Dorothy Canfield has described in detail how she came to write a short story. It started with a sentence spoken by an old and unhappy man, a moment so brief it "came and went between two heartbeats." She was going to a nearby farmhouse one pleasant spring evening, walking beside a brook full from the spring thaw. She found the old man sitting in front of his house watching the brook. They talked a bit and then the old man sighed and said, "Seems to me I never heard the brook sound so loud as it has this spring." There was something about the way he said this and the mood of the moment plus the recollection that his grandfather had drowned in the brook that made her feel "hot and cold with awe of that glimpse into a naked human heart." The story was under way. [7]

Getting under way is not quite as simple as these descriptions make it seem. Just as it is an oversimplification to maintain that the shooting of a Serbian prince started World War I, so it is an oversimplification to say that the creative process started with a chance remark. Dorothy Canfield comments that she knew for some time that a story was in the "offing" for all her stories began with a "generally intensified emotional sensibility." She could not explain where this "tide," comes from nor where it goes but when it began to rise she knew that a story was "hovering in the offing." The story started some days before the chance remark in a "shimmer" of "emotional tensity." [8]

Thomas Wolfe, in the *Story of a Novel,* reports much the same sort of intimation before he began to write. He felt that he had within him "swelling and gathering all the time, a huge black cloud . . .

---

[6] *The Novels and Tales of Henry James,* X (New York, 1908), pp. v–vii.

[7] "How Flint and Fire Started and Grew," in *The Creative Process,* ed. Brewster Ghiselin (New York, 1955), p. 170.

[8] Canfield, p. 169.

loaded with electricity, pregnant, crested . . . that could not be held in check much longer; that the moment was approaching fast when it must break." [9]

After the general vague feeling of excitement and intimation is focused on some concrete stimulus and the creative process gets under way, the individual begins to work to shape the product. As Dorothy Canfield walked away from the old farmer she was already thinking of suitable characters and situations to realize her purpose. In this period of preparation the artist's craftsmanship is important. He must know how to begin to build a story line or paint a picture. He must watch for such pitfalls as the character who begins to dominate his play and twist it out of shape, or the unnecessary complications that will make the play too long. Much of this preparatory work for a speaker or a playwright can be done in a purposive daydream. When difficulties arise concerning some technical feature of the work the creative process may be duplicated in a similar way within the general framework of the writing of, say, a play. Perhaps John Dewey's notion of a felt difficulty is more appropriate for these problems that arise within the context of a larger creative project. Such problems are often put aside and suddenly, when engaged in some other activity, their solution pops into mind. Faced with the problem of a character who had intruded into her story and did not seem to fit, Dorothy Canfield was working in the garden when she "laughed out suddenly, delighted with the whimsical idea of making him . . . the *deus ex machina* of my little drama." [10]

Many times the preparation goes on without pen touching paper or brush touching canvas. Creative people have often testified that in this phase of their work they are aided by regular monotonous physical exertion. They have reported such activities as walking, sawing wood, raking leaves, working in the garden, and, in the case of playwright John Van Druten, driving a car. Each individual has his own personal approach to the preparatory stage. One may work out most of the problems during long walks, another may need to write a scenario and character sketches. One may compose an entire speech orally, another may write it out and revise the drafts before discarding the manuscript to extemporize from an outline. Each individual must learn for himself the little personal tricks needed to aid him in preparation.

[9] New York, 1936, p. 37.
[10] Canfield, p. 172.

ILLUMINATION

Not always does the playwright respond to a stimulus by going to work on the play immediately. He may make a mental note that there is a play in this situation or experience and then put the idea out of his mind only to have it recur with additional impact. Sometimes, when the playwright goes to work on the play, immediately or later, the work flows to completion, but quite often it does not. After a period of casting about this way and that, trying a set of characters and incidents, the playwright may put his play aside and forget it for awhile. Graham Wallas called the period of putting the work aside the incubation phase.

After a passive, fallow phase, the solution to the problem or the play may come suddenly into consciousness. This moment, which the Gestalt psychologists call "insight" and which Graham Wallas calls "illumination," is one of the striking features of the creative process. Account after account of successful creative work tells of how, suddenly, at quite unexpected moments, the form of a play, or the solution of a mathematical problem came all of a piece, accompanied with a feeling of exhilaration. According to legend, such a moment caused Archimedes, who was in his bath when insight struck, to yell "Eureka!" and run through the streets naked. Creative individuals often interpret strokes of inspiration as mystical and beyond analysis and understanding because of their suddenness, stubbornness, and the feelings of excitement and delight that accompany them. Indeed, the lack of systematic investigation into creativity on the part of artists and writers is partly a function of their reluctance to tamper with illumination (or inspiration) for fear examination will destroy it.

Since insight or illumination seems to come all in a flash, a subject giving an introspective account of his experiences while doing a creative project has little to report about the moment. At one point in consciousness there is no solution to the problem, at the next moment there is. Between these two mental states there is little to describe introspectively. In the late nineteenth century Wilhelm Wundt and Oswald Kulpe and their followers in Germany discovered this feature of insight during early experiments in psychology using the introspective method.

ILLUMINATION EXPLAINED

Investigators of creativity have offered two general hypotheses to account for the suddenness and caprice of illumination. One explanation is that the central nervous system needs to be rested to effect the "stroke" of closure and that the entire process is a conscious one. The perception of the insight seems sudden because the brain, fresh from resting, gathers the necessary energy together to create the form or solution suddenly all of a piece.[11] A modification of this hypothesis adds that setting the work aside enables the individual to cast off the old mental sets that made the solution impossible and allows him to make a sudden fresh attack on the problem from a different angle.[12]

This hypothesis has the virtue of being the simplest explanation of the facts. One feature of illumination, however, cannot be accounted for by the notion that it is essentially a conscious process. If it is conscious, why does a strong emotional tonus often accompany the illumination? Since the second hypothesis gives an explanation for this feature as well as the other characteristics of illumination, it is more helpful than the first. Graham Wallas developed the second hypothesis using the Freudian model of consciousness, foreconscious, and the unconscious mind to explain creativity. Freud suggested that consciousness was the organ of perception. An individual is conscious of the mental percepts that he has at a given time. The individual cannot know the unconscious, however, unless he is made to dredge up experiences by hypnosis or free association under the guidance of a psychoanalyst. The foreconscious or preconscious is like peripheral vision. It contains percepts and memories that go unnoted unless the individual makes an effort to perceive or recall them.[13]

Wallas takes this model and elaborates on it by suggesting that there is a rising and falling of consciousness from full consciousness, through the foreconscious, to the unconscious. The continuum is recapitulated, according to Wallas, as an individual falls asleep. He begins with full and alert consciousness, moves through reverie to the dreams of sleep, then to complete unconsciousness. The model accounts for illumination in the following way: the idea comes suddenly into the consciousness; but if the individual could concentrate on his foreconsciousness during the period of incubation, he would find ideas being tested and tried as the foreconscious works on the creative project. Catherine Patrick in her study of poets supports the hypothesis regarding the role of the foreconscious. She found that final ideas and some lines of poems appeared early during the preparation and incubation phase in different forms and seemingly were forgotten by the poet until the moment of illumination.[14]

---

[11] This is the explanation of R. E. M. Harding, *An Anatomy of Inspiration: With an Appendix on the Birth of a Poem* (Cambridge, 1942) and Eugenio Rignano, *The Psychology of Reasoning* (New York, 1927).

[12] See, for example, L. F. Shaffer, B. von H. Gilmer, and M. Schoen, *Psychology* (New York, 1940).

[13] *The Basic Writings of Sigmund Freud,* trans. and ed. A. A. Brill (New York, 1938), p. 13.

[14] Catherine Patrick, *What Is Creative Thinking?* (New York, 1955), p. 60.

The model furnishes a plausible explanation for the emotional excitement of illumination. The foreconscious is the avenue for reaching the unconscious with its depths of emotional intensity. If the foreconscious works as a meeting ground for the form and order of consciousness on the one hand and the chaotic energy of the unconscious, on the other, the surfacing of an artistic form in the consciousness might well carry with it an emotional charge from the unconscious. Freud, in his examination of wit, suggested that the foreconscious works in this way. When a "cynical" witticism serves "unconscious tendencies," for example, "the unconscious tendency draws the foreconscious thought down into the unconscious in order to remodel it there." [15]

The second hypothesis also accounts for the frequent reports that invention seems spontaneous and involuntary. Writers often testify that the actual writing of a work of fiction was not a period of conscious calculation but rather that the characters of the play or novel seemed to take over the action. The writer reports the process as though his conscious mind watched with surprise as the work unfolded. Amy Lowell, in discussing the writing of poetry, says that the subject of one of her poems was dropped into her subconscious like one might drop a letter into a mail box. Some months later "the words of the poem began to come into my head." She notes that some poets talk of a voice speaking to them and of writing the poem as though by dictation. She does not hear a voice but does hear "words pronounced, only the pronouncing is toneless. The words seem to be pronounced in my head." [16]

Kipling spoke of his daemon as residing or not residing in his pen on a given day. Thomas Wolfe spoke of being "possessed" and "borne along as by a great river." Many other creative people, such as Shelley, Blake, Henry James, Spencer, Nietzsche, Gauss, Poincaré, Mozart, and Beethoven, reported that a large part of their invention was automatic in this sense.[17]

The hypothesis that there is a level of consciousness where the unconscious and the conscious meet, so that emotional energy and the desires of the unconscious are translated into symbols and analogies and formed and controlled by the conscious, explains both the automatic and emotional features in the production of creative works.

The practices of creative people furnish additional evidence for this hypothesis. They often use special tricks or techniques to concentrate their attention in order to better reach their muse or daemon. These tricks are usually similar to those used in the early stages of

---

[15] Brill, p. 759.
[16] Amy Lowell, *Poetry and Poets* (New York, 1930), p. 26.
[17] See Brewster Ghiselin, ed., *The Creative Process* (New York, 1955), p. 15.

hypnotism to reach the foreconscious. Kipling used only the blackest of ink because blue-black was an "abomination" to his "Daemon." He also used only large writing pads of off-white, blue sheets. Schiller liked to have a decaying apple in his desk. Other writers report they always smoke when writing or that they can only write at a stand-up desk.

Creative individuals often characterize the period of producing a long work as trancelike. An interesting feature of this trancelike state is that it can be regained after interruption. Since plays and novels take a year or more to write, their creators often develop special techniques to regain the proper trancelike mood. Ernest Hemingway was said to reread all that he had previously written each day to get back in the mood. Sometimes a writer will break off work when things are going well and he knows exactly what is going to happen next, because he feels that stopping after a scene or a chapter is completed will make it more difficult to regain the proper state.

All of these features of the creative process suggest that the Freudian explanation as expanded by Graham Wallas is both an aid to understanding and a help in the practice of creativity.

THE ROLE OF CRITICAL REASON

The role of the unconscious and the automatic nature of creative production should not be emphasized out of proportion. The writer may report that he watched with detachment as his daemon took over but he, nonetheless, watched. He watched with the cunning of his craft; and when the story began to go astray, he knew it and exercised conscious control. More importantly, not every solution considered in the foreconscious breaks through to the consciousness in moments of illumination. Poincaré, the famous French mathematician, suggested that the reason only a few combinations of ideas are allowed to come to consciousness is that there is a "delicate sieve" that lets only good solutions through. Poincaré argued that on those rare occasions when a solution to a mathematical discovery came in a flash of illumination and turned out to be wrong the pseudosolution was elegant and in the form of the right solution. He suggested that an element of creativity is an esthetic sensibility that allows only elegant solutions through to the consciousness.[18]

The notion of elegance is common in theoretical physics as well as mathematics. The Copernican solution to the structure of the solar system was more elegant than the Ptolemic, in the sense that it was simpler and its structure was more balanced and harmonious.

---

[18] Henri Poincaré, "Mathematical Creation," in Ghiselin, pp. 40–41.

Until the Copernican system was incorporated into Newton's theory, its elegance was the main advantage that it had over the Ptolemic system.

The same delicate sieve operates in the creation of works of art such as plays, symphonies, and paintings. In other words, the disassociation of consciousness from the production of a work is not complete. Part of the craftsmanship of any art is the sieve that allows only esthetically pleasing forms to surface from the unconscious. This sieve is sometimes called a "feeling" for form or structure and is developed both by working at the craft and by conscious critical study.

The fusing of the conscious and unconscious in the creative process is seen in many of the details of craftsmanship. If a student is learning to write plays, he may read a handbook that gives advice on how to handle exposition in the first act, and he may consciously understand all that is said about it. He may examine a number of plays and dissect the way successful playwrights have managed exposition in the early portions of their plays, and he usually understands this as well. Yet when he writes a play, despite all the conscious understanding of technique, his exposition rushes out awkwardly in a solid block of dialogue with characters telling each other things that they already know and that they are not particularly interested in discussing. If he keeps at his craft, however, there comes a time when he finds himself writing the opening scene of a play in which the exposition is woven skillfully into the opening action and suddenly, as it were, his fingers know how to write exposition. He now *feels* how it should be done as well as knowing how it should be done. He has appropriated the technique. It has become a part of his nervous system just as a hook shot becomes part of the nervous system of a basketball player after hours and hours of practice.

The craft can be studied and practiced intellectually under guidance; thus it is the element in creativity that is most teachable. Without the help of the conscious, the results of creative effort are chaotic and unformed. Without the foreconscious, with its forays into the subconscious, the results lack vitality. The characters of a play written intellectually are wooden and lifeless and seem manipulated by the conscious design of the writer.

The final phase is the most conscious and critical aspect of the entire creative process. In this phase the individual evaluates and revises his work. Poincaré had to work out the mathematics that verified or failed to verify his insight. The poet must check the word selection and order, the rhyme scheme and meter. The playwright must make sure his characters are consistent and the facts of the play are plausible. This is the stage of polishing, filling in blank spaces, pruning unnecessary exuberances, checking for proportion and balance.

Since the final phase of the creative process is rational and teachable it has been investigated more systematically and carefully than any other. The rules for verification in the various arts and sciences are well worked out. Rhetoric, logic, mathematics, the philosophy of science, historiography, all of these disciplines have developed rules to aid in the last phase of the creative process. Indeed, much of the practical advice on research techniques in this book falls into the same category.

THE CREATIVE PERSON

Since the general outlines of the creative process seem established, much of the current research into creativity deals with such questions as: what skills are involved in the process?, can individuals with these skills be identified? and, can these skills be improved through training?

The work of recent investigators has concentrated for the most part on these questions. Except for sporadic efforts during the early part of this century, the only sustained study of the creative process in recent years has been largely the result of work done by J. P. Guilford and his associates at the University of Southern California, C. W. Taylor at the University of Utah, and E. Paul Torrance and his associates at the University of Minnesota.

The traits most often suggested as being associated with creativity include fluency, flexibility, and originality. Fluency involves the ability to produce words, ideas, and sentences quickly and easily. The ability to change the approach to a situation is flexibility. It involves looking at the problem from another angle to break out of the mold of previous ways of doing things. Originality involves the ability to associate different ideas and to elaborate and redefine concepts in new ways.

E. Paul Torrance has compiled a list of characteristics that differentiate the highly creative person from less creative people. His checklist includes eighty-four items and was drawn from a number of studies that compared creative with less creative individuals. The creative person emerges from this checklist as adventuresome, sloppy, disorganized and accepting of disorder. He may feel the whole parade is out of step. He likes solitude. He questions rules and authority, holds conformists in some disdain, keeps unusual hours, has some oddities of habit, becomes preoccupied with a problem, and thinks of people as individuals. This is by no means an exhaustive portrait, but it indicates the nature of the results of such study.[19]

Some of the interesting research in creativity in recent years has dealt with developing tests as an index to creativity. Torrance and associates have developed such tests at the University of Minnesota and used them to study creativity in a wide variety of situations including foreign cultures, elementary schools, and department stores. Results of these researches indicate that, although there is correlation with some intelligence measures, for the most part, the relationship between creativity tests and intelligence tests is slight.[20]

One use of these tests is to evaluate techniques for identifying and improving creativity. The notion that creativity, though an art rather than a science, can be taught is an old one. In 1929 Hughes Mearns published *Creative Power* in which he outlined an approach to the "Education of Youth in the Creative Arts." The book is full of advice on how to encourage creativity in the classroom. In 1958 a revised edition of the book was printed largely because of the interest of the Children's Theatre Conference Division of the American Educational Theatre Association. The Children's Theatre Conference supported the book, because of its relevance to creative dramatics as well as creativity in other art forms.[21]

E. E. Thurstone, in a paper first delivered in 1950, suggested some of the characteristics of graduate students who were creative. According to Professor Thurstone, the students who were erratic and undependable often produced the most interesting and creative ideas; and those with the highest scholarship seemed to have a "certain degree of intellectual docility." He outlined the attitudes that seemed to favor the production of ideas and those that were hostile to new ideas. The graduate student, usually bright, who typically reacted in negative fashion to strange problems or new ideas and who seemed to be able to develop a clear and logical argument immediately as to why the proposal was wrong, demonstrated an attitude that was unlikely to result in the creative process. The better attitude is one of playing with the new notion and speculating about it. How would it change things? Professor Thurstone concludes that perhaps the creative graduate student should "have a certain amount of gullibility." [22] Graduate students should be encouraged to produce

19 E. Paul Torrance, *et al.*, *Assessing the Creative Thinking Abilities of Children, Bureau of Educational Research*, University of Minnesota (Minneapolis, 1960).
20 Torrance, *et al.*, pp. 13–15.
21 Hughes Mearns, *Creative Power*, 2nd ed. (New York, 1958).
22 Thurstone, p. 24.

ideas according to Professor Thurstone. Instead of asking a student to think of one dissertation topic, he should be asked to write twenty dissertation proposals in the course of a week.

Among negative attitudes that inhibit creativity in a graduate student is the attitude that the proper way to evaluate an article or book is to rip the work apart and point out its faults. Rather, he should suggest what he would have done with the same problem or how the materials of the article, faulty as they may be, can be used.

ENCOURAGING CREATIVITY

Drawing from empirical research and the advice of successful creative people the following general rules are suggested for the encouragement of creativity.

First, try difficult problems and projects. Intellectual laziness is an enemy of creativity. If you dodge difficult questions, ignore new attitudes and ideas, rely on answers furnished by other people, you inhibit the creative impulse. In short, the way to develop creativity is to take nothing for granted and tackle the difficult project that intrigues you.

Second, put aside some time for doing nothing. The contemplative life seems to have largely vanished from the academic scene. The picture of the college professor spending leisurely days strolling around a half-deserted ivy-walled campus, puffing on his pipe and thinking, seems like a daguerreotype from the past. Ironically, leisure to contemplate is now institutionalized in the form of "think tanks" like the Institute for Advanced Studies at Princeton. The popularity of "retreats" is another indication of the need to provide brains the leisure required for creative thinking. Constant activity can become a habit. Many professors find their days filled with conferences and committee meetings and consultative sessions and student counselling as well as with teaching and research. The graduate student often lives at an even more hectic pace. The leisure required for creativity is difficult to find in the graduate school where it should be most prized.

You may spend your leisure time in front of the fire with your feet up on a hassock, but this is not necessary nor always desirable. Repetitive physical activity, such as mowing a lawn or shoveling snow or painting a house or tending a garden or walking is often more productive than sitting comfortably inert. Reading is one of the insidious enemies of the kind of leisure required for creative thinking.

Reading allows the creative mechanism to dodge problems and projects. Reading is insidious because it is a praiseworthy intellectual activity. During the preparation phase of the creative process reading may be required to gather relevant information, but you must guard against the tendency of the reading to continue and inhibit the incubation and illumination phase of creativity. There is a time for reading and a time to stop reading.

Third, periods of prolonged and hard intellectual work improve creative thinking. One of the ways to get the habit of facing up to difficult questions and breaking out of unsatisfactory mental sets is to carry through an extended project of mental labor. The momentum of the project goads the worker to unusual effort and creativity. One of the important byproducts of graduate research requirements is that they force the student to carry through an extended intellectual project.

Fourth, training can prepare you to exploit the moment of illumination. The area of creative training has been thoroughly explored and needs only be mentioned here. The creative person must learn the craft of his discipline so that his creative muse is not hampered by an inability to express itself. The playwright must learn how to construct a scene, how to write dialogue, how to characterize, how to get people on and off the stage and so forth. The painter must know perspective and how to get visual effects. The speaker must know how to develop narrative material, how to adapt statistics to an audience, how to partition the subject of a speech and weave the parts together with transitions.

You need to know the fundamentals so well that they are almost automatic reactions. When they become automatic, you can concentrate on the flow and form of the content as you produce your work. The basketball player must be drilled in the fundamentals of dribbling, passing, and shooting so he can concentrate on the flow of the play and the momentary openings in the defense to drive for the basket and shoot without having to think if he should shoot with one hand or two. So, too, the creative person must know his craft well enough to keep his attention on his material.

The fact that the craft of an artistic discipline can be taught furnishes the rationale for courses in public speaking, playwriting, and scene design.

Fifth, develop creative mental sets. Do not repress wild ideas and daydreams. Occasionally, approach a problem with the notion of dreaming up as many solutions as possible no matter how strange they may be. On other occasions, determine to find the best ideas possible. When things are going nicely do not worry about grammar, punctuation, or awkward phrases. The rough spots can be tidied up in the revision and polishing phase of the work. You must test and reject ideas; but when the creative machinery is working smoothly you will be well advised to hold the critical set in abeyance.

You can develop a creative mental set by asking of a given problem or task: how many other ways might this be done? Instead of criticizing a speech for an inadequate introduction, try to think of twenty different ways this speech could be introduced to this audience. Student playwrights often do this unconsciously. No sooner do they hear one of the new plays read aloud for critical evaluation than they are off and rewriting it. Such mental sets increase an individual's ability to generate ideas fluently.

Flexibility is also increased by exercise. Successful ways of working tend to become habitual. After long training and specializing in a particular field an individual often develops a habitual way of approaching his materials and his problems. Specialization may cause inflexibility and encourage bias against other research techniques. Theatre students are among the most creative of graduate students. Yet, they often close their minds to the possibility of using empirical research techniques on theatre problems. Graduate students specializing in empirical research sometimes cannot see the point of dramatic or rhetorical criticism and do not see how these research techniques could be used to aid in solving their problems. When new problems arise that are not solved by the habitual methods of attack, the inflexible individual tries to solve the problem in the same or analogous ways. If he could return to his material with a different approach, he might have a better chance of success. Sometimes talking over a problem with a knowledgeable person who is naïve in the specialty can help break one out of his habitual set. Other ways of introducing flexibility include making the opposite assumptions, turning the problem upside down, or reversing time sequences.

The personal nature of each man's daemon limits the number of specific hints that can be given for improving creativity. What works for one man does not necessarily work for the next. Kipling's black ink and blue-white paper might not do for another writer. However, you should consider one technique that has been widely and successfully used. Since the moment of inspiration is capricious and may come at unusual times, many creative people keep a notebook or journal handy to jot down ideas as they occur. Typically, they carry their notebooks with them and keep them handy at a bed table at night. Ideas caught in a notebook can restimulate the creative machinery at a later time and be expanded. Unfortunately, the great idea unrecorded at midnight may be forgotten the next morning.

SUMMARY

The creative thesis is accepted in many graduate departments of speech as partial fulfillment of advanced degrees. Creativity also plays a role in other research projects. An understanding of the creative process is, therefore, helpful in most research areas in speech.

Often a feeling of heightened awareness is a prelude to the creative process. A slight stimulus then sets the machinery in motion. In the next period the individual actually works on the project even though much of this activity may be random and groping. If the work is not successfully completed during this stage, it is often set aside either by design or because the worker despairs of the project. After putting the work out of consciousness for a time he may experience a sudden stroke of closure where the main outlines of the work fall into place or where he gets the insight that will solve his problem. The final phase is also an active one as the worker checks the work and polishes it.

The Freudian model gives an explanation for many of the features of this process. The emotional penumbra surrounding creativity, particularly at the moment of conception and at the moment of illumination or insight, comes from the surfacing of ideas and materials from the unconscious into the conscious. The work of the unconscious and foreconscious during the period when consciousness has put the problem aside accounts for the sudden awareness of the answer that typifies moments of illumination. The role of the foreconscious also accounts for the sometimes automatic nature of the work of a creative person.

The traits commonly associated with creativity include fluency, flexibility, and originality. Studies comparing and contrasting people who have done highly creative work with those less creative indicate that creative individuals are often adventuresome, accept disorder, question authority, may feel the whole parade is out of step and prefer solitude, often become preoccupied with problems, and tend to think of people as individuals.

Suggestions for encouraging creativity include: (1) try difficult problems and projects, (2) set aside time for leisure and contemplation, (3) plan and carry through a program of prolonged and hard intellectual labor, (4) learn the craft involved in your project, and (5) develop mental sets that encourage fluency and flexibility.

Suggested Readings

Anderson, H. H., ed. *Creativity and Its Cultivation*. New York: Harper & Row, Publishers, 1959.

Dewey, John. *How We Think*. New York: D. C. Heath & Company, 1910.

Ghiselin, Brewster, ed. *The Creative Process*. New York: The New American Library, 1955.

Gibson, William. *The Seesaw Log*. Alfred A. Knopf, Inc., 1959.

Guilford, J. P. "Three Faces of Intellect," *American Psychologist,* XIV (August 1959), 469–479.

Johnson, Donald M. *The Psychology of Thought and Judgment*. Harper & Row, Publishers, 1955.

Jones, Robert Edmond. *The Dramatic Imagination*. New York: Duell, Sloan and Pearce, Inc., 1941.

Mearns, Hughes. *Creative Power*. New York: Dover Publications, Inc., 1958.

Patrick, Catherine. *What Is Creative Thinking?* New York: Philosophical Library, Inc., 1955.

Rowe, Kenneth Thorpe. *Theatre in Your Head*. New York: Funk & Wagnalls Co., Inc., 1960.

Simonson, Lee. *The Stage Is Set*. New York: Harcourt, Brace & World, Inc., 1932.

Stanislavskii, Konstantin. *My Life in Art*. Trans. J. J. Robbins, Boston: Little, Brown and Company, 1924.

Thurstone, L. L. "Creative Talent," in *Applications of Psychology,* ed. L. L. Thurstone. New York: Harper & Row, Publishers, 1952.

Torrance, E. Paul, *et al. Assessing the Creative Thinking Abilities of Children*. Minneapolis: Bureau of Educational Research, University of Minnesota, 1960.

Wallas, Graham. *The Art of Thought*. New York: Harcourt, Brace & World, Inc., 1926.

West, E. J., ed. *Shaw on Theatre*. New York: Hill & Wang, 1959.

Projects

1) Chapter 7 is a good example of the kind of knowledge we have about the arts. Apply the techniques of linguistic analysis discussed in Chapters 4–6 to the material in Chapter 7. Write a short paper outlining the nature and structure of the knowledge presented in Chapter 7.

2) Professor E. Paul Torrance and his associates at the University of Minnesota have experimented with having graduate students use creative sets in their outside-reading assignments. Here are the directions for the creative application set:

When you read, it is important that you think about the many uses of the information which you are reading. It is especially important that you think of the various ways the information could be used in your personal and professional life. In reading, do not just ask, "What is the author saying?" Also ask, "How can I use what the author is saying?" Do not stop with just one use. Think of as many uses as you can of the important ideas presented. E. Paul Torrance and Judson A. Harmon, *Effects of Memory, Evaluation, and Creative Sets on Test Performance* (Research Memorandum BER–60–17). Minneapolis: Bureau of Educational Research, University of Minnesota, 1960, pp. 2–3.

Select one of the following articles and read it with a creative application set. Make a list of all the possible uses of the material in the article that you can think of.

Bryant, Donald C. "Rhetoric: Its Functions and Its Scope," *QJS*, XXXIX (December 1953), 401–424.

Croft, Albert J. "The Functions of Rhetorical Criticism," *QJS*, XLII (October 1956), 283–291.

Geiger, Don. "Oral Interpretation and the 'New Criticism,'" *QJS*, XXXVI (December 1950), 508–513.

Hochmuth, Marie. "Kenneth Burke and the 'New Rhetoric,'" *QJS*, XXXVIII (April 1952), 133–144.

Murphy, Richard. "The Speech as Literary Genre," *QJS*, XLIV (April 1958), 117–127.

Powers, Margaret Hall. "The Dichotomy in Our Profession," *JSHD*, XX (March 1955), 4–10.

Berlo, David K. "Problems in Communication Research," *CSSJ*, VII (Fall 1955), 3–7.

Mabie, E. C. "The Responses of Theatre Audiences, Experimental Studies," *SM*, XIX (November 1952), 235–243.

Nebergall, Roger E. "An Experimental Investigation of Rhetorical Clarity," *SM*, XXV (November 1958), 243–254.

Hewitt, Barnard. "Gordon Craig and Post-Impressionism," *QJS*, XXX (February 1944), 75–80.

Deer, Irving. "Ibsen's Aim and Achievement in *Ghosts*," *SM*, XXIV (November 1957), 264–274.

3) Recall an incident when you solved a problem or created an interpretation of a reading, a theatrical part, a radio-tv-film role, or when you wrote or directed a play or television script, or when you solved a problem in clinical work or research design. Write a short paper describing your experience.

QUESTIONS FOR DISCUSSION

1) What is the difference between creative thinking and reflective thinking?

2) What is the difference between problem solving and artistic imagination?

3) Is it wise or possible to study creativity?

4) What do you think of the assertion that acting and playing a musical instrument are imitative rather than creative arts?

5) No mention was made in Chapter 7 of the role of accidents and of trial and error in solving problems. What is the relationship between accidental discovery and trial and error on one hand and creative thinking on the other?

CHAPTER EIGHT

SCHOLARSHIP IN SPEECH

THE ROUTINES OF SCHOLARSHIP

Just as a debater begins the analysis of his case by thinking of the stock issues of debate, so the scholar should begin his investigation once he has a subject with certain established routines. First, of course, he should prepare a bibliography, then he should read generally through the background materials, examine interesting books, and take notes on what seems pertinent. He will be as systematic, careful, and thorough with the machinery of scholarship as he can be. He will place bibliographical items and notes on cards and slips of paper of the same size. He will adopt and rigidly follow a uniform system of recording bibliographical and footnote information. He will write all notes with care to insure legibility and permanence. As notes accumulate, he will classify and arrange them around some general headings.

As the graduate student begins a scholarly investigation, he may react against what seems an irksome attention to picayune detail. Once he has found an important passage, must he stop and carefully record bibliographical information before transcribing a notation? Why not scribble a quick note to himself and get on with his research? He can come back to it later, he may reason, if it turns out to be useful. Such reasoning is wrong. The care practiced in detail work is one of the important symptoms of scholarship. It develops habits that carry over into all aspects of the investigation. Besides, the novice should learn to feel comfortable with the tools of scholarship. If he is to write a scholarly paper, he must learn to enjoy note cards and file boxes. The carefully transcribed notation that was irksome in the full flight of discovery becomes valuable as he begins to study and rework his materials. More than one beginner has been free associating at his typewriter in an attempt to write a scholarly paper when he remembers something that seems vital in the context of what he is writing. The quick note scribbled to himself on a ticket stub or on the back of an envelope or in a notebook is lost or inadequate; and his subconscious, having produced the detail, now nags at him to find the rest. So he must go to the library and search again for his materials.

To the person who has considerable experience in working up a part in the theatre and who has the technique to project that interpretation, the writing of note cards and bibliography cards may seem a dull pastime. Just so, the scholar dropping in at the rehearsal hall and watching an actor try several lines and bits of business over and over again to get them right may have much the same feeling about acting. The final written results of the work of the scholar and the finished portrayal by the actor both can be exciting and significant, and both usually were gained through hard work, concentration on detail, and thoroughness. The layman may find the length of a pause a trivial matter not worthy of attention; but the actor understands that such details, carefully attended to, are fitted into context with other details of technique, and the final performance depends upon such detail work just as it depends upon the creativity he has brought to the interpretation of his part. The careful collection of information is just as important to the final results of scholarship.

Once the researcher begins the routine of scholarship, he sets in motion his creative process. As he goes about making bibliography cards and reading documents and puzzling about the credibility of sources and trying to establish the truthfulness of particular statements of fact, he begins to get hunches about explanations for conflicting testimony or for certain sequences of events. Certainly his viewpoint will suggest the kinds of stock patterns to look for. As we have noted, the affirmative debater has a set of stock questions to aid him in getting started on his debate case. The good debater, however, reaches a point in his analysis of a case where he can discard the stock issues because he has suddenly gained insight into the specific issues of this *particular* question. They are still affirmative issues, but they are now issues that have grown out of his research and his skill at finding the fundamental questions upon which this particular resolution turns. In like fashion, the scholar will begin to find structure in his materials as the study continues.

Even when the sources have been tested, structure discovered, and adequate historical proof marshaled for the study, the actual writing of a scholarly work requires skill. Clarity of style is adequate for the presentation of results of empirical studies, but additional writing skills are necessary for historical and critical work. The scholar must be able to express subtle nuances of meaning. If he is a clumsy or inept writer, he may emphasize something he did not plan to emphasize or imply something he did not mean to imply. He may not do his findings justice. The scientist avoids expressing nuances of interpretation by the use of operational definitions and by reporting results quantitatively.

The scholar is assembling and testing evidence to be submitted in writing to the criticism of his peers and to the tests of time. His sources will be checked and his analysis criticized by the highest standards of scholarship.[1]

The routines of scholarship begin after a topic is selected and involve (1) the gathering of materials, (2) the critical evaluation of those materials, and (3) the writing of an account based upon the criticized materials that gives these structure and meaning. In this chapter we will discuss the techniques for gathering materials. In Chapter 9 we will deal with the critical evaluation of historical materials. We will examine the concepts of historical *viewpoint* and *structure* as they relate to the writing of history in Chapter 10 and apply these same concepts to critical studies in Chapter 11.

BEGINNING THE RESEARCH

An important consideration in a scholarly research project is the number and quality of sources available to the investigator. If the student is writing a master's thesis, he may reasonably expect to confine his research largely to his campus library. The student writing a doctoral dissertation, however, should expect to make a much more exhaustive search for materials. He may well need to travel to the primary sources during the course of his study. Before selecting a topic, the Ph.D. candidate should discover the location of important source materials. If the research will require a trip to the Vatican or London and he finds such a trip impractical, the topic will have to be abandoned. The primary sources may be widely scattered, even if they are in this country. Before the final selection of a topic, the researcher should make sure that he will be able to consult these basic materials.

Early in the investigation the student should find out what has already been written on the subject he is considering. Work with a direct or tangential bearing on his subject is helpful in gathering a bibliography and gives the student background information. Such

[1] See, for example, the critical evaluation of outstanding American historians in William T. Hutchinson, ed., *The Marcus W. Jernegan Essays in American Historiography* (New York, 1937).

a survey is necessary to indicate the current status of research in the area under study and should be included in his prospectus. Some graduate schools require the submission of a formal prospectus, which is essentially a blueprint or plan for the study, before final approval of a research topic is given. Such a formal prospectus is usually drawn up only after considerable preliminary research has been completed and the scope of the study determined. In Chapter 10 we shall discuss the way topics are selected and narrowed. The student might well draw up a less formal prospectus very early to aid him as his research gets under way. Such an informal written plan can also be a help to the graduate's advisor as he evaluates the project.

GATHERING THE BIBLIOGRAPHY

The scholar finds many of his sources in indexes. The indexed words that lead to relevant sources are key words. If the researcher does not exploit all key words bearing on his topic, he may overlook important sources and find that he must examine some of the same indexes again. He should try to discover all these pertinent key words early in his research. Generally, he will find a set referring to *persons*. Thus, if he is studying the oratory of agrarian unrest in the upper Midwest at the turn of the century, such names as Ignatious Donnelly, General Weaver, and William Jennings Bryan would be helpful. Another category of key words involves the *time period* covered by the study. The years from 1870–1910 would serve as a general key in this example. Another set might refer to events under study, thus such key words as agriculture, agrarian, Grange, Farmer's Alliance, oratory, and speeches would be useful. Another set of terms refers to *places*, and the scholar would look under Minnesota, Iowa, or Wisconsin, or St. Paul, Des Moines, and Madison. As the research gets well under way, the scholar finds more important key words that are unique to his particular project.

BIBLIOGRAPHIES AND REFERENCE WORKS

There are a number of bibliographies in history and speech.

A good place for a researcher to begin his bibliography is in the collections of bibliographies already compiled. Dictionaries, encyclopedias, indexes of doctoral dissertations in speech, bibliographies of material relevant to theatre, public address, experimental phonetics, and speech pathology are valuable reference sources. They should be used early in the research.

Specific bibliographies and reference works with which the scholar should become familiar include the *Guide to Reference Books,*[2] *Basic Reference Sources,*[3] the *Bibliographic Index: A Cumulated Bibliography of Bibliographies,*[4] and Franklin Knower's "A Selected Bibliography of Bibliographies for Students of Speech."[5] There are many historical bibliographies, a number of them international in scope, frequently arranged according to periods of history or around such topics as intellectual history, social history, political history and so forth. Some important ones are listed in E. M. Coulter and Melanie Gerstenfeld's *Historical Bibliographies: A Systematic and Annotated Guide.*[6] *The Harvard Guide to American History* is an excellent survey of bibliographical materials for American history.[7]

To discover what work has been done in the general area of a proposed research project, and also to discover what work is under way, useful indexes include: *Dissertation Abstracts: A Collection of Abstracts of Doctoral Dissertations in Complete Form on Microfilm,*[8] *Doctoral Dissertations Accepted by American Universities,* by Arnold Trotier and Marion Harman,[9] J. Jeffrey Auer's "Doctoral Dissertations in Speech: Work in Progress," an annual report since 1951 published in *Speech Monographs,* Franklin Knower's "Graduate Theses—An Index to Graduate Work in Speech," published annually since 1935 in *Speech Monographs,* Cheydleur and Golter, "Graduate Theses and Dissertations on Broadcasting,"[10] subsequently updated by Franklin Knower's supplements,[11] Clyde Dow's "Abstracts of Theses in the Field of Speech," published annually in the *Speech Monographs* since 1946. The most comprehensive bibliography of research in speech is *A Bibliographical Guide to Research in Speech and Dramatic Art* by Oscar G. Brockett, Samuel L. Becker, and Donald C. Bryant.[12]

In October, 1960 the American Speech and Hearing Association and Gallaudet College began publication of *DSH Abstracts,* a quar-

---

[2] Constance Winchell, *Guide to Reference Books,* 7th ed. (Chicago, 1951). Supplements by Constance Winchell covering 1950–1952, and 1955–1958. Continuation of work by Isadore G. Mudge (Chicago, 1936).

[3] Louis Shores, *Basic Reference Sources* (Chicago, 1954).

[4] New York, 1938–date.

[5] *SSJ,* XVII (December 1951), 141–153.

[6] Berkeley, 1935.

[7] Cambridge, Mass., 1954.

[8] Ann Arbor, 1938–date.

[9] New York, 1933–1934–1955.

[10] *Journal of Broadcasting,* I (Fall 1957), 377–383; also II (Winter 1957–1958), 55–90.

[11] See, for example, "Graduate Theses and Dissertations on Broadcasting: 1956–1958," *Journal of Broadcasting,* IV (Winter 1959–1960), 77–87; "Graduate Theses and Dissertations on Broadcasting: 1959–60," *Journal of Broadcasting,* V (Fall 1961), 355–370.

[12] Chicago, 1963.

terly compilation of research abstracts in the areas of deafness, speech disorders, and hearing.

After consulting bibliographies and reference works and noting the sources that look promising, the researcher should turn to the resources of the library in which he is working. He should first learn his privileges and responsibilities in regard to special collections, use of the stacks, and advice from reference librarians. Although the student may feel that he knows how to use the library, and he may know how to use it adequately for the purposes of writing term papers, he will probably discover that he has more to learn about the reference sources and other aids if he is going to do an extended research project. The student is well advised to become an expert in the use of the library for his particular topic, and he should not depend to a large extent upon reference librarians.

If the rules of the library allow, the researcher should get permission to use the stacks. Calling for books at the checkout desks is a time-consuming operation and does not allow opportunity for personal examination of the books on the shelves. Many libraries also have carrels or desk areas for scholars working on extended research projects where the researcher can keep books, his typewriter, file boxes, and other research materials.

Some of the nonuniversity affiliated research libraries will not allow researchers to go to the stacks—the Library of Congress, for example—but they all have procedures designed to aid the serious scholar. If the student is having difficulty finding materials in his library, he should consult a book on library use, such as *The Guide to the Use of Libraries*.[13]

THE CARD CATALOGUE

For many research projects the most useful tool in the library is the card index. This catalogue is cross indexed in several ways. There is a card indexed under the surname of the author, and one indexed under the first word that is not an article in the title. There may also be cards under subject entries of various kinds.

When the library catalogue yields the first useful item, it should be entered on a bibliography card. These may be note cards (3 by 5 or larger) or slips of paper cut from sheets of typing paper. The bibliographical information to be entered includes the name of the author, compiler, or editor, the exact title as it appears on the title page of the book, the place of publication of the book, the name of the publisher, the number of the edition, if it is a revised edition, the number of volumes, if there are more than one, and page num-

---

[13] Margaret Hutchins, Alice S. Johnson, and Margaret S. Williams, *The Guide to the Use of Libraries*, 5th ed. (New York, 1936).

bers for an edited volume where the reference is to a specific chapter or essay. This information should be entered on the bibliography card in the way it will appear in the thesis.

The student should decide, as he begins his research, on a form of note taking and bibliographical notation he will use. Although there are several acceptable styles for recording bibliographical information, the graduate student should learn and use the procedure recommended by his graduate school. He should check with a member of the graduate faculty about the preferred style for master's theses and doctoral dissertations at his institution. He should get the recommended style book and use this style for all term papers. Postdoctoral researchers should check the style preferences of the journals to which they plan to submit articles. When preparing book manuscripts, an author can get information about the preferred style from his publishing house. The *MLA Style Sheet* published by the Modern Languages Association of America is the accepted authority for the *Educational Theatre Journal,* the *Quarterly Journal of Speech, Speech Monographs,* and the *Speech Teacher.*[14] From time to time the editors of the *Journal of Speech and Hearing Disorders* and the *Journal of Speech and Hearing Research* publish information for contributors that outlines the proper style for articles submitted to these journals.[15]

The following examples illustrate the form recommended by the *MLA Style Sheet* for bibliographical items.

(1) For a book with one author

Davis, Forrest. *Huey Long.* New York: F. W. Dodge Corporation, 1935.

(2) For a book with two or more authors

Hutchins, Margaret, A. S. Johnson, and Margaret S. Williams. *Guide to the Use of Libraries.* 5th ed. New York: H. W. Wilson Co., 1936.

(3) For an edited book

Blain, Hugh, ed. *Favorite Huey Long Stories.* Baton Rouge: O. Claightor, 1937.

(4) For an article in an edited collection

Carter, Hodding. "Huey Long: American Dictator," *The Aspirin Age: 1919–1941,* ed. Isabel Leighton. New York: Simon and Schuster, Inc., 1949, pp. 339–363.

[14] Available for a nominal fee from the Modern Language Association of America, 6 Washington Square North, New York 3, N. Y.

[15] See, for example, "Information for Contributors to the Journal of Speech and Hearing Disorders," *JSHD* (February 1961), 99–103; "Examples of Manuscript Form," *JSHD,* XXVI (February 1961), 103–106; "Information for Contributors to the Journal of Speech and Hearing Research," *JSHR,* III (March 1960), 86–98.

(5) For a book of two or more volumes

Brigance, William Norwood, ed. *A History and Criticism of American Public Address.* New York: McGraw-Hill Book Company, 1943, II.

(6) For a translation

Tolstoi, Lev Nicolaevich. *What Is Art?*, trans. Maude Aylmer, Oxford: Oxford University Press, 1950.

(7) For an article in an encyclopedia

Cornyn, John Hubert. "Rhetoric," *Encyclopedia Americana.* New York: Americana Corp., 1949, XXIII, pp. 457–458.

(8) For a journal article, author given

Gassner, John. "The Meaning and Scope of the Playwriting Study," *ETJ*, IX (October 1957), 167–176.

(9) For a magazine article, author not given

"Louisiana After Long," *Commonweal*, XXII (September 27, 1935), 525–526.

(10) For a newspaper article

"The High School Rally—Numerous Students Competed in the Literary and Athletic Events," *The Reveille,* Louisiana State University, Baton Rouge, May 7, 1910, p. 1.

(11) For an unpublished thesis or dissertation

Davee, Paul. "Definition of the Philosophy Underlying the Recognition and Teaching of Theatre as a Fine Art in the Liberal Arts and Graduate Curricula at the State University of Iowa," Ph.D. dissertation, State University of Iowa, 1950.

The following examples illustrate a recommended style for bibliography in speech pathology, voice science, and audiology.

(1) For a book with one author

Lindquist, E. F. *Design and Analysis in Psychology and Education.* Boston: Houghton Mifflin, 1953.

(2) For a book with two or more authors

Berry, M. F. and Eisenson, J. *Speech Disorders: Principles and Practices of Therapy.* New York: Appleton-Century-Crofts, 1956.

(3) For an edited book

Travis, L. E. (Ed.), *Handbook of Speech Pathology.* New York: Appleton-Century-Crofts, 1957.

(4) For an article in an edited collection

Darley, F. L. The relationship of parental attitudes and adjustments

	to the development of stuttering. In W. Johnson (Ed.), *Stuttering in Children and Adults*. Minneapolis: University of Minnesota Press, 1955, pp. 74–153.
(5) For a journal article	Beck, J. and Shaw, W. A. Magnitude estimations of pitch. *J. Acoust. Soc. Amer.*, 1962, 34, 92–98.
(6) For an unpublished thesis or dissertation	Martin, Richard R. Direct magnitude-estimation scaling of stuttering severity utilizing auditory and auditory-visual stimuli. Unpublished Ph.D. dissertation, Univer. of Minnesota, 1963.

After noting all the bibliographical data in the recommended form on a bibliography card, the student should add every bit of information he can find bearing on the value of the book for his study. He should include information about the author's background, training, and position. Some of this information can be found by a brief examination of the book. Additional information about the author can sometimes be gained from *Who's Who in America* [16] and the *Dictionary of American Biography*.[17] Leafing through the book enables the scholar to make general comments on the bibliography card about its pertinence to his study. He will also note material that bears directly on the topic under investigation. These annotations should be kept separate from the bibliographical data proper but placed on the same note card. In addition to this information, the library call number should be added to the card. Here is a sample of an annotated bibliography card.

> Kendall, John S. *The Golden Age of the New Orleans Theatre*. Baton Rouge: Louisiana State University Press, 1952.
>
> John S. Kendall was a member of the editorial staff of the New Orleans *Picayune* and Professor Emeritus of Spanish at Tulane University.
>
> Eleane E. McDavitt reviewed Kendall's book in *QJS*, XXXVIII (April 1952), pp. 224–225. McDavitt judges the book "indicates painstaking research" but is not as helpful as it might be because of lack of documentation. Her over-all judgment is favorable.
>
> The descriptions of theatre houses will be useful in my study.

---

[16] *Who's Who in America: A Biographical Dictionary of Notable Living Men and Women of the United States* (Chicago, 1899–date).
[17] Allen Johnson and Dumas Malone, eds., *Dictionary of American Biography* (New York, 1928–1958).

Each work should be examined as soon as possible. If the works are not in the stacks, consult a librarian about tracing them. If the book has been checked out, the librarian will explain the procedure necessary to have it recalled.

While looking at particular books on the shelves, it is a good idea to examine the books in the immediate neighborhood. Since books are shelved by subject matter, frequently you will find in this way important sources that escaped your attention in the card catalogue. Often the researcher can walk through the stacks scanning titles in the areas of call numbers that are on his bibliography and find interesting and important materials. A quick glance down the index in the back of such a book, using his key words, will tell him whether or not there is much pertinent material in the book.

Really important books should be appraised, at least superficially, during this early stage of the research. The beginning scholar should not be overly impressed with a work until he gets some expert opinion about it. Although the *Book Review Digest* [18] is helpful in getting a general evaluation of an important book, a better approach is to check the reviews that the book received in the learned journals or in the leading general review magazines such as *The Saturday Review* and *The New York Times Book Review Section.*

The bibliographies in the books examined in this fashion should be carefully studied to see if they contain items not on the student's bibliography. He should check the footnotes also to find clues not only to other sources but also to the kinds of material found in these sources.

Bibliographical notes may be taken directly from footnotes found in books, although the source of the information should be noted and enclosed in brackets on the bibliographical card. Eventually, of course, the source itself will have to be consulted.

If a source is found in this manner that is not available in the library, this should be noted on the bibliography card. If subsequent investigation indicates that the source needs to be consulted, the library may purchase the book or a request through interlibrary loan may get the book. If this is not possible, the researcher may find the source in one of the other libraries he must visit.

PERIODICALS AND NEWSPAPERS

The general procedure used in consulting the card catalogue can be used in collecting a bibliography of articles in periodicals and newspapers. There are several major periodical indexes. The *Inter-*

---

[18] New York, 1905–date.

national Index to Periodicals covers the period from 1907 to the present and is a guide to periodical literature in the social sciences and humanities. General periodicals in this country are indexed in *Poole's Index to Periodical Literature,* which covers the years from 1802 to 1906, the *Nineteenth Century Reader's Guide to Periodical Literature,* which covers the years from 1890 to 1899, and the *Reader's Guide to Periodical Literature* which indexes about 115 periodicals for the years from 1900 to the present. *The Dramatic Index* contains a list of articles and illustrations relating to theatre in the periodicals of America and England from 1909 to 1949.

Newspapers pose a more difficult problem. The great majority of them are not indexed. Probably the most helpful indexes are those of *The New York Times* and the *London Times. The New York Times Index* is very detailed and since 1913 has indexed news stories, book reviews, editorials, and letters to the editor in that newspaper. The *New York Herald Tribune Index,* is helpful for a general indication of the important news stories from 1875 to 1906. The *London Times* has been indexed in *Palmer's Index to the Times* beginning 1790 and running to date, and in the *Times Official Index* which began in 1906 and continues to date.

These indexes can be helpful in searching other newspapers, by correlating the date the story was reported in *The New York Times* with the papers locally involved. For much research, however, the newspaper indexes will prove insufficient if papers other than those indexed are being examined. If the scholar is looking for letters to the editor or editorial comment, he will need to scan many issues of the newspaper rapidly and yet carefully enough to catch all relevant information. As he begins researching a newspaper file, he should read the first few issues rather slowly, examining every page. Typically, the newspaper will group certain materials in different sections of the paper. Thus, certain features are regularly carried in a women's section, certain others on an entertainment page, and still others on an editorial page. Theatrical reviews, for example, will tend to appear on the same page or the same section and to appear on the same days of the week. The student can scan the files more rapidly and efficiently as he becomes familiar with the format of the paper.

GOVERNMENT DOCUMENTS

The publications of the United States Government are especially valuable for the scholar. These documents are published in such volume and by so many diverse agencies that it is difficult to present helpful bibliographical information about them in a section as brief as this one. Most large libraries have a United States Government Document section, and librarians in such sections can help in finding a given document.

Of particular interest to the scholar in public address are the records of the debates in Congress. The debates which preceded the Constitution can be found in Worthington A. Ford and Gaillard Hunt's *Journals of the Continental Congresses*. The debates from 1789 to 1824 are reported in the *Annals of Congress* and the debates from 1824 to 1837 in the *Register of Debates in Congress*. The *Congressional Globe* duplicates the last few years of the *Register* and covers the debates from 1834 to 1873. Since 1873 the *Congressional Record* has kept an accounting (at times edited) of the debates in Congress. Not only does it furnish the texts for the criticism of oratory, but it also includes much additional information in the form of letters, articles, special petitions, briefs, and texts of speeches delivered off the floor of Congress which are "read" into the *Record*.

Early sessions of the Senate were held in secret, and the printed record is sketchy. *The Journal of William Maclay, United States Senator from Pennsylvania, 1789–1791*,[19] supplies some additional information on the first two years of the Senate and William Plumer's *Memorandum of Proceedings in the United States Senate, 1803–1807* [20] supplements the official record of the first decade of the nineteenth century.

Many state papers have been assembled and published as collections by the United States Government. For example, James D. Richardson collected *Messages and Papers of the Presidents* into a government document published by the second session of the fifty-third Congress.

There are several comprehensive indexes of government documents. Since 1893 a large catalogue to the government's documents has been prepared periodically by the Superintendent of Documents. This is called the *Catalogue of the Public Documents of Congress and of all Departments of the Government of the United States*. Documents before this period are indexed in Benjamin Poore's *Descriptive Catalogue of the Government Publications of the United States, September 5, 1774–March 4, 1881*, and the *Tables of and Annotated Index to the Congressional Series of United States Public Documents*, and the *Comprehensive Index to the Publications of the United States Government, 1881–1893*.

---

[19] Edward S. Maclay, ed., *The Journal of William Maclay, United States Senator from Pennsylvania, 1789–1791* (New York, 1890).

[20] Everett Somerville Brown, ed., *William Plumer's Memorandum of Proceedings in the United States Senate, 1803–1807* (New York, 1923).

SPECIAL COLLECTIONS

The Library of Congress prepares and publishes many bibliographies. On its shelves may also be found the personal papers of many prominent men. Special collections of regional and state materials can frequently be found through the help of the State Historical Societies. Many such societies have libraries and archives that contain the private papers of prominent citizens of the region. Special collections of documents may be found in unlikely places and need to be ferreted out by using all available clues. A good place to start this search is in *A Guide to Archives and Manuscripts in the United States.*[21] Two specialized guides to manuscript material of interest to scholars in drama are the *American Literary Manuscripts, A Checklist of Holdings in Academic, Historical, and Public Libraries in the United States,*[22] and *Performing Arts Collections.*[23]

A growing number of speech departments, working in conjunction with libraries, are establishing special collections of materials of interest to researchers in speech. The University of Wisconsin has a Center for Theatre Research that is collecting material in theatre and cinema. The University of Wisconsin also has in its Mass Communications History Center a collection of documents, including the archives of the National Broadcasting Company dealing with radio and television. The University of Pittsburgh Library has the Curtis Theatre Collection. The Ohio State University has a theatre collection and publishes *The OSU Theatre Collection Newsletter* to inform interested scholars about the materials available, and the research in progress. The Ohio University has a center for the collection of materials on contemporary public address, which stresses recording and filming contemporary speakers. Other important collections of material include the Theatre Collection of the Harvard College Library, the Theatre and Music Collection of the Museum of the City of New York, the Theatre Collection of the New York Public Library, and the Humanities Research Center of the University of Texas.

This list of special collections of research materials for speech and theatre is by no means exhaustive, but it does indicate the growing trend to establish such collections. The scholar working in these areas should explore these sources early in his work.

---

21 Philip M. Hamer, ed., *A Guide to Archives and Manuscripts in the United States* (New Haven, 1961).
22 Joseph Jones, *et al.*, ed., *American Literary Manuscripts, A Checklist of Holdings in Academic, Historical, and Public Libraries in the United States* (Austin, 1960).
23 Andre Veinstein, ed., *Performing Arts Collections* (Paris, 1960).

FILING BIBLIOGRAPHY CARDS

As the number of bibliography cards grows, some sort of filing system should be established. The most common is to file the cards alphabetically. Another good system is to divide the cards into two files, one for sources that have been consulted and one for sources that still need to be examined. As the bibliography grows even larger, it is frequently subdivided into types of documents, such as books, periodicals, government documents, newspapers and manuscripts. Within these subdivisions an alphabetical arrangement is usually followed.

NOTE TAKING

Research is seldom as neat and straightforward as it seems when described in textbooks. The bibliography is seldom completely and carefully compiled before note taking gets under way. In any extended research project there is much doubling back and forth between looking for sources and examining those sources for important material. With careful study and note taking come new clues that expand the bibliography; so scholarly research proceeds.

Recent technological improvements have lightened the burden of note taking considerably. Most research libraries now have fast and economical reproduction equipment. Microfilm and photostating procedures make it possible for the researcher to have complete copies of important documents available at all times. But even with the most modern of research aids the scholar must eventually come to the questions of relevance and expense, and he often decides that copying relevant material by hand is the most feasible method for his purposes. Note taking, thus, remains an important part of his research technique.

The same care must be taken with note cards as with bibliography cards. A uniform method for recording notes and filing them is essential. The smaller note cards (3 by 5) which may be adequate for bibliographical purposes will not be large enough for efficient note taking. For some projects, where the notes from a single source will be quite long, a complete sheet of 8½ by 11-inch typing paper filed in a large manila folder may be the best choice. For most projects, 6 by 8 note cards or 8½ by 11-inch sheets folded in half (5½ by 8½) make a good size for note taking.

Each note must contain an exact citation for the source of the information. If the bibliography has been carefully done, the student will have all the information he needs to make these citations in the same style that will be used for the footnotes in his writing of the study. This will save hours of work at a time when the hours will be most precious. In addition, the student should put some general heading on each note that will aid in filing the material. If this latter task is done with some care and creativity, it will be an aid in the outlining and writing of the first draft of the paper. When the note runs over onto two or more cards or sheets of paper, the heading should be repeated on each card or page.

There is considerable routine in the collection of bibliographical materials, but the process of note taking is less mechanical. If the student overlooks important information, he will have to retrace his steps. If he is not selective, he may flounder in irrelevant trivia. The decision about when to take or when not to take a note is a difficult one which calls for perception and judgment. Although there is no formula for this process, there are some guide-lines that can be kept in mind.

Secondary sources should be read to fill in background material on the specific topic under investigation. Here the note taking will be primarily for the student's general information. In such instances, abstracting or outlining pertinent sections will serve the purposes of the investigation. Such notes can be brief and of the kind that will best serve the researcher's needs with regard to the particular material. Here is a sample note card paraphrasing and summarizing material drawn from a secondary source.

> Thomas Harris, *The Kingfish—Huey P. Long Dictator* (New Orleans 1938), pp. 16–17.
>
> According to Harris, Samuel Blythe's articles in the *Saturday Evening Post* in the summer of 1914 had a profound influence on Huey Long. Blythe called his political sketches *The Fakers* and Harris maintains that while most readers took them as a humorous parody, Huey Long accepted them as a political "textbook for the masses." Harris quotes Long as telling a "close friend" that "The people want that kind of stuff. They eat it up. Why not give it to them?" Harris fails to identify the close friend. [Must keep in mind that Harris was an enemy of Long's and Long's bodyguards were alleged to have beaten him up in 1935.]

Secondary sources will contain statements of fact, arguments based upon these statements of fact, value judgments, and ethical judgments all woven together in an extended analysis that can be called an interpretation. In general, statements of fact from secondary sources should not be recorded. When documenting a statement of fact, the best source should be cited, that is, the first source of the information. For example: a scholar writing a history of intercollegiate debating for women, might find in LeRoy Cowperthwaite and A. Craig Baird's essay on "Intercollegiate Debating" a statement of fact to the effect that on May 12, 1921, a women's team from the University of Indiana visited the campus of the State University of Iowa to debate the issue of Philippine independence.[24] If this statement of fact is to be documented in the scholar's paper, it should not be documented by quoting the secondary source. One of the primary sources in this case would be the *Iowa Alumnus* for May, 1921. Not only that, but *the first source should be consulted* to check the accuracy of the secondary source and also to be honest with the reader about the extent and care of the scholar's research. To take a free ride on the secondary sources and then pretend that the work is based upon primary material is dishonest. Not only is this practice misleading and deceitful but it also works against one of the primary objectives of the scholar, which is to base his interpretations upon the soundest evidence available. Errors will certainly creep into scholarly work if the best sources are not continually re-examined by scholars when establishing factual statements. The following sample note card illustrates one good way of summarizing factual material drawn from a primary source. Notice, also, the use of a general topic heading to help organize notes.

LONG'S CAMPAIGNING IN LOUISIANA

The Times-Picayune, New Orleans, December 9, 1923, p. 6.

Speaking itinerary of Huey P. Long.
December 10—Jonesville, 11 A.M.
                   Jena, 7 P.M.
December 11—Alla, 10:30 A.M.
                   Columbia, 2 P.M.
                   Monroe, 7:30 P.M.
December 12—Tallulah, 11 A.M.
                   Lake Providence, 7 P.M.
December 13—Arcadia, 7 P.M.
December 14—Morringsport, 11 A.M.
                   Oil City, 2 P.M.
                   Vivian, 7 P.M.
December 15—Shreveport, 8 P.M.

Although taking direct quotations of statements of fact from secondary sources is generally unprofitable, it may be relevant to

[24] In *History of Speech Education in America,* ed. Karl Wallace (New York, 1954), p. 270.

copy argumentative statements, value judgments, ethical pronounce-
ments, and interpretations of events, if the scholar plans to support,
or modify, or refute these statements. Here is a sample note card
of a direct quotation from a secondary source. In Chapter 11 I use
this quotation because I hope to refute it.[25]

LONG AND SENATOR HARPER

Forrest Davis, *Huey Long* (New York, 1935, p. 73.

"A historian of the future I should judge, would be justified
in believing that Huey had entered into discipleship to Senator
Harper before the United States entered the world war and that
Harper shares with Moses and Winn's ancient radicalism the bulk
of the credit for inspiring Share-Our-Wealth."

The primary sources are the most likely places to find direct
quotations dealing with factual matters. The following sample note
card records factual material from a primary source by means of direct
quotation.

LONG AS A RADIO SPEAKER

The New York Times, August 2, 1934, p. 19.

"In a secret ballot officials of Washington broadcasting stations
have picked the five best political speakers in the nation." [Long
was not included in the five best but he was discussed as a leading
political speaker.] Senator Long has "microphone appeal" and
"the ability to hit the subject on the nose."

Finally, direct quotations will be useful to the scholar if the
material is unusually authoritative, expressed in an unusual or intriguing style, at variance with the accepted account, or if it is hard
to remember. This sample note card is a direct quotation from a
primary source that is unusually authoritative, and expressed in an
intriguing style.

LONG AND SENATOR HARPER

Huey P. Long, *Every Man a King* (New Orleans, 1933), pp. 35–36.

"The court again called to order after a recess, the Judge
began to read statements which I had made in the newspapers.
[Long was defending Senator Harper against a charge of obstruct-
ing the war effort during World War I.] It seemed apparent that
I was to be sent to jail. But to our great astonishment, after read-

---

[25] See below, pp. 239–242.

ing the entire list of statements I had made, the Judge concluded:
'The Court cannot let this and other matters pass without a
reprimand.' To the devil with the reprimand as far as we are concerned! All we wanted was a chance to clear our client."

When taking direct quotations, great care should be used to
quote the exact wording, spelling, and punctuation of the original.
The Latin word *sic,* should be inserted in brackets and underlined
immediately following any error in the original. The word means
thus and tells the researcher when he examines the note later that
the error was in the source and not in his copying of the source.
Ellipses (. . .) are used to indicate that words have been omitted
from the original. Underlined words indicate italics in the source.
If the note runs over two pages in the source (/) is used to indicate
the break over onto the next page so the page indicated in a footnote will be accurate. From time to time explanatory material will
have to be inserted in a direct quotation to supply a missing antecedent for a pronoun or to make clear a reference or to supply modifying context. Such insertions should be set off by square brackets.

Direct quotations should always be used in the spirit of the context and not used to misstate or oversimplify the statements of the
source. If there is any danger that the direct quotation may be subsequently misinterpreted by the student, he should make adequate
notations on the note card to keep the context of the quotation clearly
in focus.

When doing scholarly research that relies heavily on literary
works and speeches, the student should have these materials available, either in duplicated or printed form so that he can consult
them readily as he proceeds.

Sometimes the mass of data available to a student of public
address seems too large to be examined adequately. The Congressional
debates on the Foote Resolution in 1830, for example, or the Southern Senators' filibuster on civil rights in 1960, cover hundreds of
pages in the *Congressional Record.* In such instances, a quick reading of the material with the intention of discovering the representative arguments and materials, the ablest speeches, and the atypical
materials, will enable the scholar to select a sample of material for
more intensive investigation that represents the material fairly.

In the early stages of research, particularly, the investigator must
guard against being distracted by interesting but irrelevant materials;
and he should be quite careful not to make notes of such irrelevancies. For example, if the topic under investigation were the Congressional speaking of John Randolph of Roanoke, the scholar would

probably come across the vituperative exchange of letters between John Randolph and his cousin Nancy. These deal with an earlier scandal in which Nancy was accused of having an illegitimate child by her brother-in-law and of killing the baby shortly after its birth. Unless these letters have some bearing upon the study there is no point in taking notes on them, despite their sensational character.[26]

On the other hand, relevant materials should not be dodged because they are sensational. If a speaker was drunk when he delivered a speech, as President Andrew Johnson was sometimes accused of being, this fact would be relevant to a study of his speaking and should be included.

Perhaps at the beginning the student should err in the direction of taking too many notes, rather than too few, until his sense of what is relevant to his problem is sharpened by understanding. He should certainly err in the direction of taking too much care in transcribing his notes accurately and clearly. In conducting a scholarly research project, the student must cultivate a sense of history—that is, he must see time in perspective. He must not be impatient. He must be willing to take the time to do his research carefully. There is probably no other part of his research that will test his patience so much as will the gathering of a bibliography and the taking of notes. Some days the books that are needed cannot be found in the library. The exciting lead turns into a dead end. Not much progress is made. Other days, however, a chance remark and a hunch will turn up the previously undiscovered trunk filled with diaries and letters.[27] Searching for sources is by no means all dull laborious work, and those elements that are routine and laborious can be made bearable by establishing good research habits from the start.

SUMMARY

The scholar begins his work by discovering the sources of information available to him in doing his study. He compiles a bibliography of such sources and searches them carefully, keeping a record of relevant information so that it can be quickly found and used.

The first step in preparing a bibliography is to utilize the work of previous scholars and consult their bibliographies. The next step is to examine various general indexes to information such as the general card catalogue of the library, indexes to dissertations, indexes

---

[26] For a detailed treatment of the scandal see Francis Biddle, "Scandals at Bizarre," *American Heritage*, XII (August 1961), 10–13, 79–82.

[27] For an interesting account of some of the trials and triumphs of literary scholarship in tracing possible source materials see Richard D. Altick, *The Scholar Adventurers* (New York, 1960).

to periodicals and newspapers and government documents. The final and most important step is to consult reference libraries and indexes to collections of manuscript material to find original sources not available in printed form.

Note taking in secondary sources should be largely confined to information useful to the researcher in filling in background material. Direct quotations from secondary sources are generally confined to interpretations that will be further supported, modified, or refuted by investigation into primary sources. Direct quotations about factual matters are taken from primary sources. Direct quotations should always be made in the spirit of the contexts in which they appear and the scholar must transcribe his notes carefully, using explanatory symbols and statements whenever necessary to assure this accuracy.

SUGGESTED READINGS
Bibliographies

Baker, Blanch M. *Theatre and Allied Arts: A Guide to Books Dealing with the History, Criticism, and Technic of the Drama and Theatre and Related Arts and Crafts, 1885–1952.* New York: H. W. Wilson Co., 1952.

Billington, Ray A. "Guides to American History Manuscript Collections in Libraries of the United States," *Mississippi Valley Historical Review,* XXXVIII (1951), 467–496.

Broadus, Robert N. "The Research Literature of the Field of Speech," Association of College and Reference Libraries, *ACRL Monographs,* No. 7 (January 1953), pp. 22–31.

Broderick, Gertrude G. *Radio and Television Bibliography.* Washington: Government Printing Office, 1956.

Brown, Donald E. "Radio and Television: An Annotated Bibliography," *Journalism Quarterly,* XXXIV (1957), 378–386.

Caplan, Harry, and Henry H. King. "Dutch Treatises on Preaching: A List of Books and Articles," *SM,* XXI (November 1954), 235–247.

————. "Italian Treatises on Preaching: A Book-List, *SM,* XVI (September 1949), 243–252.

————. "Latin Tractates on Preaching: A Book-List," *Harvard Theological Review,* XLII (1949), 185–206.

————. "Pulpit Eloquence: A List of Doctrinal and Historical Studies in English," *SM,* XXII (Special Issue, 1955), 1–159.

————. "Pulpit Eloquence: A List of Doctrinal and Historical Studies in German," *SM,* XXIII (Special Issue, 1956), 1–106.

————. "Scandinavian Treatises on Preaching: A Book-List," *SM,* XXI (March 1954), 1–9.

————. "Spanish Treatises on Preaching: A Book-List," *SM,* XVII (June 1950), 161–171.

Dunham, Robert E., and L. S. Harms. *Index and Table of Contents of Southern Speech Journal, 1935–1960, Western Speech Journal, 1937–1960, Central States Speech Journal, 1949–1960, and Today's Speech, 1953–1960.* Central States Speech Association, Speech Association of the Eastern States, Southern Speech Association, 1960.

Eubanks, Ralph T., V. L. Baker [and James Golden]. "A Bibliography of Speech and Theatre in the South for the Year 1954," *SSJ*, XX (Summer 1955), 323–331; XXI (Summer 1956), 262–271; XXII (Summer 1957), 248–256; XXIII (Summer 1958), 211–219; XXIV (Summer 1959), 236–246.

Fairbanks, Grant, ed. "Cumulative Index, Volumes 1–15," *JSHD* (March 1951), Supplement.

Gray, Giles W. *Index to the Quarterly Journal of Speech. Volumes I to XL, 1915–1954.* Dubuque, Iowa: William C. Brown Company, 1956.

Grimes, Wilma H. "Oral Interpretation and Criticism: A Bibliography," *WS*, XXII (Spring 1958), 69–74.

Haberman, Frederick W. "A Bibliography of Rhetoric and Public Address." (Annually since 1948: in *QJS* from 1948–1950 and in *SM* from 1951 to date. Since 1957 edited by James W. Cleary.)

Hare, A. Paul. *Handbook of Small Group Research.* New York: Free Press of Glencoe, Inc., 1962.

Hiler, Hilaire, and Meyer Hiler. *Bibliography of Costume: A Dictionary Catalog of About Eight Thousand Books and Periodicals.* New York: H. W. Wilson Co., 1939.

Knower, Franklin H. *Table of Contents of the Quarterly Journal of Speech, 1915–1960, Speech Monographs, 1934–1960, and Speech Teacher, 1952–1960, With a Revised Index Compiled through 1960.* Bloomington, Ind.: Speech Association of America, 1961.

Kumata, Hideya. *An Inventory of Instructional Television Research.* Ann Arbor, Mich.: Educational Television and Radio Center, 1956.

McDowell, John H., ed. "A Bibliography on Theatre and Drama in American Colleges and Universities, 1937–1947," *SM*, XVI (1949), 1–124.

Strodtbeck, Fred L. and A. Paul Hare. "Bibliography of Small Group Research," *Sociometry*, XVII (1954), 107–178.

Thonssen, Lester, and Elizabeth Fatherson. *Bibliography of Speech Education.* New York: H. W. Wilson Co., 1939.

———, Mary Margaret Robb, and Dorothea Thonssen. *Bibliography of Speech Education, Supplement: 1939–1948.* New York: H. W. Wilson Co., 1950.

Welker, David, ed. *Ten Year Index of the Educational Theatre Journal: 1949–1958.* East Lansing: Michigan State University Press, 1959.

Method

Auer, J. Jeffrey. *An Introduction to Research in Speech.* New York: Harper & Row, Publishers, 1959, pp. 100–116.

Barzun, Jacques, and Henry F. Graff. *The Modern Researcher.* New York: Harcourt, Brace & World, Inc., 1957.

Hance, Kenneth G. "Bibliographical Source Materials," *An Introduction to*

Graduate Study in Speech and Theatre, ed. Clyde W. Dow. East Lansing: Michigan State University Press, 1961.

Hockett, Homer C. *The Critical Method in Historical Research and Writing.* New York: The Macmillan Company, 1955.

Turabian, Kate L. *A Manual for Writers of Term Papers, Theses, and Dissertations.* Chicago: The University of Chicago Press, 1955.

PROJECTS

1) Select a topic area that appeals to you as a possible source of a subject for a thesis or dissertation.

   a) What bibliographies of bibliographies will be helpful in gathering a bibliography for this topic area?

   b) Prepare an annotated bibliography of ten items pertinent to the topic, using an acceptable bibliographic form.

   c) Read five of the items on your bibliography, making notes of important materials. Write a comment on each note card explaining why you recorded the material and justifying the use of direct quotations, paraphrases, summaries, and abstracts.

2) Prepare a short bibliography of government documents bearing on one of the following topics:

   a) presidential inaugural addresses

   b) educational television

   c) blacklisting of film writers

   d) theatre

   e) speech pathology

   f) broadcasting

   g) experimental phonetics

3) Identify five of the following concepts by finding an authoritative article or book that explains the concept and relates it to the field of speech. Prepare suitable bibliography and note cards.

   a) the conviction-persuasion dichotomy

   b) optimal-pitch level

   c) James-Lange Theory

   d) speech synthesis

   e) the Second Great Awakening

   f) semantic differential

   g) tone

   h) delayed auditory feedback

   i) Marcus Cornelius Fronto

   j) Henrici harmonic analyzer

   k) Notker Labeo

   l) the Wisconsin sequential sampling audience analyzer

QUESTIONS FOR DISCUSSION

1) In what ways could the routine of scholarly investigation stimulate the creative processes?

2) What is the relation between the gathering of materials and the critical evaluation of the materials?

3) What technological aids to reproduce and retrieve materials are available in the libraries you use?

4) If a statement of fact is asserted to be true in a secondary source and documented to a primary source that is unavailable to the scholar can he use the statement of fact in his study?

CHAPTER NINE

THE HISTORICAL METHOD

HISTORICAL EVIDENCE

History is man's memory of the past. Since it is memory, it is often fragmentary. Some fragments of the past that are helpful for the historian include coins, monuments, potsherds, arrowheads, temples, inscriptions and any artifact that can give insight into what man has done and thought. Some of these historical traces have been preserved by design, because man has, from earliest times, developed his collective memory. Such records are preserved in sacred books and legends and myths that have been handed on from generation to generation. Some have been preserved by accident; some have been destroyed by accident.

Recent history is no exception. Valuable documents are lost or destroyed and others are altered or doctored. Some may be overlooked because the historian lacked diligence or was unlucky. Thus history must always be reconstructed from the inferences the scholar can make and insights that he can get from the traces left by preceding generations.

The winnowing of time has already sampled the evidence that was once available for the historian. He can never be sure that what remains is representative, for time can be capricious. Another process of selection takes place for the scholar often finds only part of the extant materials. Finally, the historian makes his own selections from the evidence that he has discovered.

Historians have carefully studied the method by which this selection is made and the rules that have been worked out have been standardized at least since the time of Ernst Bernheim's *Lehrbuch der historischen Methode,* first published in 1889.

HISTORICAL PROOF

The historian must observe facts and make statements about them. Thus, the student using the historical method must know on what grounds he may conclude that a statement of fact is true, probably true, doubtful, probably false or false. The grounds for such decisions can be thought of as historical proof.

Historical proof is but a special case of empirical proof. The framework of analysis established in Chapter 4 can be applied to the problems posed by historical demonstrations. The student using the historical method must discriminate between statements of fact and statements of opinion, value, and ethics. In regard to statements of fact, his primary interest is to conclusively demonstrate indirectly verifiable statements of fact. For example, let us take the case of a scholar studying a series of historical events alleged to have taken place in the Illinois Senatorial campaign of 1858 called "The Lincoln–Douglas Debates." The statements of fact about these debates are indirectly verifiable because the historian will be unable to observe the facts. The spoken words, the attitudes of the audience, their applause, their boredom, the tensions, thoughts, and feelings of Lincoln and Douglas are gone forever. Yet, Lincoln and Douglas were alive in 1858 and their actions that year left enough historical traces for a skillful scholar to conclude that the statement "Lincoln and Douglas participated in seven joint debates in the Senatorial campaign of 1858 in Illinois" is true. Such a statement is a statement of fact because it can be verified as true or false. Its truth or falsity depends upon what actually happened in the campaign of 1858 in Illinois. The historian will be interested in a number of other statements that will not be statements of fact because they cannot be verified as true or false. The claim that "The Lincoln-Douglas debates were the greatest debates in the history of the United States," is such a statement.

The verification of statements dealing in concrete terms with facts that were observed by many people is relatively simple. Such a statement as "The first debate was held at Ottawa," poses few problems. The historian, however, deals with more complex data. He may wish to examine Lincoln's mental states during the debates; to probe his emotional make up. In such a context the statement that "Lincoln believed that slavery was immoral," becomes a statement of fact. In this instance Lincoln's mental states become the facts that make such a statement true or false. Statements of fact about beliefs, ideas, attitudes, and emotions are frequently important to the literary historian and the writer of intellectual history. They become, therefore, of considerable importance to the scholar in speech using the historical method.

The first phase in a scholarly investigation is to discover the statements of fact relevant to the problem under investigation that seem to be conclusively demonstrated as true. (Sometimes, to be sure, it is valuable to discover those that are conclusively demonstrated as false.)

The grounds upon which the historian makes his judgments about truth and falsity in the end come down to facts that he can observe, such as newspapers, diaries, speeches, tape recordings, motion pictures, statues, inscriptions on cave walls, books, and other historical fragments.

Sometimes historians have observed the events that they wrote about. Thucydides took part in the Peloponnesian War; Leon Trotsky took part in the Russian Revolution; Winston Churchill took part in the Second World War. For the most part, however, the historian must use the facts that he can personally observe as mediating between the historical event and himself. He can report from direct observation that George Washington's bench mark is visible close to the natural bridge in Virginia. This is a statement of fact that the historian can verify for himself by going to the location and looking at the alleged bench mark. To move from this statement to the statement of fact that George Washington surveyed the territory around the natural bridge in Virginia is to use the observable fact as mediating between the historian and the historical event. To make such an inference is to make certain assumptions that the historian is reluctant to make without further mediating facts. It assumes, for example, that the bench mark is authentic and that the mark was actually made by Washington. The bench mark could be a forgery. It could have been forged by a businessman eager to exploit the tourist trade. The mark might be authentic and still not have been made by Washington. He could have contracted to survey the territory and then hired others to do the actual surveying using his mark.

The historian may make the statement that the *Illinois State Register* reported that at the Ottawa debate Lincoln "gazed over the audience as though at a loss for words." [1] The truth or falsity of such a statement is dependent upon what the paper printed in its report of the debate, and copies of that particular issue may well be available for the historian to examine for himself. It is quite another matter for the historian to take this fact (the newspaper which he can observe) and reason from there to the interesting statement of fact, that, "In the debate at Ottawa, Lincoln gazed over the audience as though at a loss for words." The latter statement is an indirectly verifiable statement of fact about Lincoln's speaking at Ottawa, Illinois, in 1858. Sometimes the historian must settle for the first sort of directly verifia-

---

[1] Mildred Freburg Berry, "Abraham Lincoln: His Development in the Skills of the Platform," *A History and Criticism of American Public Address*, ed. William Norwood Brigance, II (New York, 1943), p. 847.

ble statement because it is the only kind that he can assert with confidence. He must confine himself to telling what the sources assert without being able to make statements about the historical event itself. Of course, the historian prefers to be able to assert statements of fact about the historical events and not just about his sources; and he works to this end when he criticizes historical materials. Sometimes he does have enough mediating facts so that he feels justified in asserting the second kind of statement. To the questions of (1) what are mediating facts? and (2) what constitutes enough mediating facts in the above sense? the rest of this chapter will be devoted.

Is the report of the *Illinois State Register* sufficient evidence to prove that Lincoln gazed over the audience at Ottawa as though at a loss for words? Probably not. The *Register* was a Douglas paper strongly biased against Lincoln. Are there other traces left by the actual happenings that support or deny this report? Let us take a slightly different statement of fact about Lincoln, the speaker. Mildred Freburg Berry makes the statement that "Lincoln evidently suffered throughout his career from that bugbear of all students of public speech, stage fright." In addition to the above report in the *Illinois State Register,* she notes a similar report by Oliver Crissey of Avon, Illinois, who attended the debate in Galesburg. His statement was reported in the Galesburg *Evening Mail* of October 8, 1908. This date suggests that an observer was asked about his recollections of the event on the occasion of the fiftieth anniversary of the great debate. She quotes Lincoln's biographers, William H. Herndon and Jesse W. Weik, to the effect that "it seemed a real labor to adjust himself to his surroundings." Finally, she quotes from a letter of Lincoln's to Herndon in 1848 commenting on the same problem.

From the historical traces left by observers, (1) the reporter of the *Illinois State Register* who wrote up the debate at Ottawa, (2) the recollection of Oliver Crissey who attended the debate in Galesburg, (3) Herndon and Weik's assessment in their biography, and (4) Lincoln's statements in his letter to Herndon, this historian made a judgment about the truth of a statement asserting Lincoln suffered from stage fright. That this judgment was made with some reservations is indicated by the word "evidently" in the assessment.[2]

As this example indicates, the historian must, for the most part, depend upon the accounts of eyewitnesses to events that he is studying. These reports of observers may be direct or they may be secondhand. The historian does not rule out, as does the court, eyewitness testimony reported through another. For documents of the size of the crowd at

---

[2] Berry, p. 847.

the Charleston debate, the length of the Lincoln parade from Mattoon to Charleston and the kinds of carriages and wagons in the parade, the historian must depend upon the descriptions written by those who were there and saw it or by those who had it reported to them by someone who saw it.

For accounts of how people felt or thought or of what Lincoln believed and Douglas felt, the scholar relies upon introspective accounts of the people doing the feeling, thinking, and believing. The historical novelist may say that as Lincoln moved to the front of the platform at Freeport his thoughts turned back to Salem and Anne Rutledge. The historian cannot say such a thing unless he has a report in Lincoln's handwriting to this effect or unless he finds documents produced by others who heard Lincoln say that he had such a thought at this particular time.

Determining what took place in a recent traffic accident in a court of law with eyewitnesses available for extensive examination and cross-examination is not always an easy matter. The historian operates under more limiting conditions and often tries to find out what happened in a more complex situation and more remote time. His task is, thus, more difficult. The historian does have the advantage of being unhurried, if he wishes, and the passage of time may reveal some honest testimony that was not available at the time the incident occurred.

PRIMARY AND SECONDARY SOURCES

The historian wants the best testimony that he can get about the historical events of interest to him. Therefore he wants information from firsthand accounts of events. These are furnished by people or recording devices that directly perceived the phenomenon in question. Such sources are primary. In this sense the account of a newspaper reporter who observed the debate between Lincoln and Douglas at Jonesboro, is a primary source. In like manner the videotape recording of a John Kennedy and Richard Nixon debate of 1960 is a primary source.

The primary source need not be the original manuscript. The printed letters of Lincoln may be as good a primary source as the actual letters. On the other hand, original documents are not necessarily primary sources. A diary, for example, may give an account by someone else of the Jonesboro debate as described to the person writing the diary. The testimony of any person or device that was not present at the events reported is a secondary source. The motion picture film of a re-enactment of the Lincoln–Douglas debates would be a secondary source, just as a historical monograph on the Lincoln–Douglas debates by a scholar who had not observed them would be a secondary source.

Many times the same article, newspaper story, book, letter, or memoir will be a primary source for some statements of fact and a secondary source for others. When the reporter writes of what he has personally observed, he is a primary source. He is a secondary source when he reports information from "informed observers," or "sources close to the government," or "usually reliable sources." A biography may be a secondary source for the most part, but Forrest Davis's biography of Huey Long,[3] for example, contains Davis's personal impressions of Long speaking on the senate floor and reports of extensive interviews with Senator Long. Herndon's biography of Lincoln is also a primary source about some matters relating to Lincoln.

The same material may change from secondary to primary source material because of the focus of the study. If the scholar is studying Sartre, Eric Bentley's *The Playwright as Thinker*[4] would be a secondary source; however, if he were studying dramatic criticism in the twentieth century, he might be able to use the same book as a primary source.

TESTING THE AUTHENTICITY OF SOURCES

The first step in the critical evaluation of historical materials is to examine them to see if they are authentic. Historical documents may be forged for a number of reasons. Sometimes they are forged for money, to gain title to land or other property, to play a practical joke, or for political advantage.[5] The Kensington Runestone of Minnesota is an example of an alleged historical trace, with widespread implications bearing on the discovery of America, that has not been established as authentic. In 1928 the *Atlantic Monthly* published a series of letters reputedly written by Abraham Lincoln and Ann Rutledge.[6] In testing the authenticity of such doubtful materials the historian uses all the techniques available from other disciplines such as legal detection and archeology. The historian may examine the paper, handwriting, inks, seals, spelling, grammar, and style of writing to check authenticity of documents. The Lincoln letters in the *Atlantic Monthly* were revealed by scholars as frauds because of certain anach-

---

[3] Forrest Davis, *Huey Long* (New York, 1935).

[4] New York, 1946.

[5] For an account of some famous literary forgeries see Richard D. Altick, *The Scholar Adventurers* (New York, 1960), pp. 37–64, 142–176.

[6] Wilma Francis Minor, "Lincoln the Lover," *Atlantic Monthly*, CXLII (1928), 838–856; CXLIII (1929), 1–14, 215–225.

ronisms in the texts (i.e., the letters contained references that Lincoln would not have made). For example, the letters mention moving to Kansas which was not yet organized and opened for settlement at the time the letters were supposed to have been written. They also refer to a section 40 in reference to a piece of land and since sections are only numbered to 36 and Lincoln was a surveyor, he was unlikely to have made such an error.[7]

As troublesome as forgeries are the errors that creep into the documents by accidents. These errors include such things as a paragraph of material inserted as conjecture or explanation in a copy of the document for which the original is lost, or a subsequent cutting or addition printed as though it had occurred in the original. Many of Shakespeare's plays have been changed in this fashion.[8]

THE AUTHENTICITY OF SPEECH TEXTS

Of particular interest to scholars in speech is the problem of establishing the authenticity of speech texts. (The same problem faces the dramatic critic and the theatre historian in working with play scripts.) Students of public address have asked three questions in this regard: (1) who prepared the speech? (2) who gave the speech? (3) what did the speaker say?

GHOSTWRITERS AND COLLABORATORS

Scholars have always had difficulty answering the question of who wrote a given speech. Ironically enough, we remember the names of the ghostwriters of Ancient Greece while we forget the names of their clients. Most of the ten Attic orators, for example, were ghostwriters. Lysias's fame rests largely on the speeches he wrote for others. Yet, we attribute the speeches to him and not to his clients. Today the ghostwriter tends to be anonymous and the speeches he writes are usually attributed to his client. Ghostwriting has permeated history, and the ghostwriter is often extremely difficult to identify; and when he is discovered, his part in the writing of a historical document is often difficult to evaluate.[9] For the speech historian the process of discovering who contributed what ideas and what language to a speech is of great importance.

Another aspect of ghostwriting involves the multiple authorship

---

[7] "With Charity for All," *Atlantic Monthly*, CXLIII (1929), 288a–288b. For a skillful criticism of these materials see Paul Angle, "The Minor Collection," *Atlantic Monthly*, CXLIII (1929), 516–525.

[8] Pat M. Ryan, Jr., "Facsimiles, Fakes, Forgeries: Concerning Punctuation in Shakespeare's King Richard II," *SM*, XXVII (November 1960), 323–327.

[9] Claude M. Feuss, "Ghosts in the White House," *American Heritage*, X (December 1958), 45–47, 97–99.

of documents that are attributed to individuals. Speeches and letters and government documents may be worked up by administrative assistants and department heads and signed by the administrative chief. The student may assume that the document is a reflection of the thinking and the knowledge of the man who signed the document, if he is not aware of the process by which the material was composed.

Collaboration is most common in the preparation of speeches, but memoirs and letters are often ghostwritten also. In fact, almost all public documents must be checked for authorship.[10]

Even when the ghostwriter does little more than change the language of a document, he introduces difficulties for the historian. Stylistic features are important clues for the checking of the authenticity of historical materials. When the ghostwriter changes the style of a speaker or writer, he makes it much more difficult to discover the authentic statements and ideas of a historical figure. The ghostwriter often obscures the clues that a man's style can give to his character and intellectual abilities. In short, *who wrote the speech?* has been a perennial question for the historian but with the increase in ghostwriting in all areas of contemporary culture, it has become a much more important one.[11]

THE DELIVERY OF THE SPEECH

The second question, *who gave the speech?* is usually more easily answered. A speech is a public event, and often there are observers who make a record of their observations. Nonetheless, the historian must make sure he knows who, in fact, gave the speech.

THE CONTENT OF THE SPEECH

The question of *what did he say?* is again more difficult to answer. The record of what a speaker said may come down as the newspaper report of the speech. Newspaper stories about speeches can be misleading. Many a speaker has been dismayed to read an account of what he supposedly said in the next morning's paper. The speaker is certain that he either did not say what the paper quotes him as saying or if they have quoted him accurately, he is sure that he did not give the ideas the same emphasis, and, in general, he feels that the meaning has been distorted.

The record may come down as a written manuscript prepared before the speech was given. If the manuscript was prepared prior to

---

[10] Ernest R. May, "Ghostwriting and History," *The American Scholar*, XXII (1953), 459–465.

[11] Ernest G. Bormann, "Ghostwriting and the Rhetorical Critic," *QJS*, XLVI (October 1960), 284–288; Marie Hochmuth Nichols, *Rhetoric and Criticism* (Baton Rouge, 1963).

delivery the speaker may have done extensive platform editing.[12] The speech may come down through history as a manuscript written after the event, in which case there may have been extensive revision and editing by the speaker and his ghostwriters before publication. The speech may have been transcribed by court reporters or stenographers, in which case it may reflect what was said with considerable accuracy. On the other hand, early reporters of speeches, particularly legislative speeches, were frequently untrained and merely gave the main thread of legislative debate. Sometimes they omitted material because they thought it dull or unimportant and sometimes they admit to having been caught up in what the speaker was saying to the extent that they forgot to record all that was said.[13]

An electronic transcription on disc or tape is the most accurate text of the words of a speech available to the scholar. If the transcription is of high fidelity, it can be used for evaluating what the speaker meant as well as what he said. Voice inflections, phrasing, emphasis patterns will help in discovering satire, irony, strong emphasis, indecision and other shades of meaning that the written text will not communicate. To hear Huey Long in a recording of one of his national radio broadcasts say "Franklin Dee-Lan-Ooo Roosevelt" drawing out the vowels and making a mincing burlesque of the cultured pronunciation of "Delano," conveys a much different meaning than the written words "Franklin Delano Roosevelt" in the text of his speech.

Of course, such transcriptions must be authentic. If the tape has been edited in any fashion, it may be more misleading than a written text.

---

[12] For a study of such changes see Laura Crowell, "Word Changes Introduced *Ad Libitum* in Five Speeches by Franklin Delano Roosevelt," *SM*, XXV (November 1958), 229–242.

[13] See the analysis of the accuracy of the recording of speeches in Francis Childs ed., *The Debates and Proceedings of the Constitutional Convention of the State of New York* by Bower Aly in *The Rhetoric of Alexander Hamilton* (New York, 1941), p. 128. See also Elizabeth Gregory McPherson, "Reporting the Debates of Congress," *QJS*, XXVIII (April 1942), 141–148; McPherson, "Reports of the Debates of the House of Representatives During the First Congress, 1789–1791," *QJS*, XXX (February 1944), 64–71. Zon Robinson, "Are Speeches in Congress Reported Accurately?" *QJS*, XXVIII (February 1942), 8–12; Loren D. Reid, "Factors Contributing to Inaccuracy in the Texts of Speeches," in *Papers in Rhetoric*, ed. Donald C. Bryant (St. Louis, 1940), pp. 39–45. For studies in textual authenticity see Gregg Phifer, "Andrew Johnson at Cleveland and St. Louis, 1866: A Study in Textual Authenticity," *QJS*, XXXVII (December 1951), 455–462; Robert D. King, "Franklin D. Roosevelt's Second Inaugural Address: A Study in Text Authenticity," *QJS*, XXIII (October 1937), 439–444. David V. Erdman, "Coleridge in Lilliput: The Quality of Parliamentary Reporting in 1800," *SM*, XXVII (March 1960), 33–62. Ray H. Sandefur, "Logan's Oration—How Authentic?" *QJS*, XLVI (October 1960), 289–296. Theodore Clevenger, Jr., Donald W. Parson, and Jerome B. Polisky, "The Problem of Textual Accuracy," in *The Great Debates*, ed. Sidney Kraus, Bloomington, Indiana, 1962, pp. 341–347.

We are usually skeptical of the authenticity of speech texts from the colonial period in America or from the Middle Ages or from the classical period, but too often we take more recent speech texts at face value. Careful examination of the authenticity of recent speech texts reveals that this is not justified.

A CASE STUDY

An extended example of the problem posed by a relatively recent speech will illustrate most of the problems a historian meets when he asks of a given speech situation, "What did the speaker say?"

In March, 1935, Senator Huey Long, of Louisiana, delivered his most famous speech. This was broadcast over the National Broadcasting Company's network from coast to coast. Long was in the middle of a series of national radio broadcasts attacking the Roosevelt Administration when, several days before the March 7, 1935 broadcast, General Hugh Johnson, recently retired administrator of the National Recovery Administration, attacked Senator Long and Father Coughlin over the national hookup. General Johnson was a master of name calling and possessed considerable rhetorical flair in addition to a colorful barracks-room vocabulary. When he challenged Huey Long to a name-calling match he was up against a recognized champion in the art of billingsgate and the personal epithet. The duel caught the imagination of the news media and a large segment of the general public. When Long answered Johnson's attack his speech got unusual coverage. *The New York Times* printed a full text ". . . transcribed stenographically by representatives of the National Broadcasting Company." [14] As was his usual practice, Long had the speech read into the *Congressional Record*. *Vital Speeches* carried the text in the March 25, 1935 issue.[15] The speech also appeared in a collection of Long's speeches compiled by his administrative assistant, Earle Christenberry, and called *Speeches by the Late Huey P. Long*. There are, therefore, four texts of Huey Long's March 7, 1935, speech available for the historian to examine in an attempt to find out what the speaker actually said on that occasion. Close examination of these four texts reveals striking differences. In the absence of further evidence, the scholar faced with four texts of a document would resort to the technique of *variant* readings. That is, he would try to see if there is a pattern of relationships that holds among the copies. Was the Christenberry text a copy of the *Congressional Record* text? Was the speech as reported in *Vital Speeches* a copy of the *Congressional Record* text? Or was it a copy of *The New York Times* report? Or were all four independent copies of

14 *The New York Times*, March 8, 1935, p. 16.
15 I (March 25, 1935), 391–397.

yet another text? Or, perhaps, were all four independent copies of the speech itself? If the *Vital Speeches* copy could be revealed, by examining the texts themselves, to be a copy of the *Congressional Record* speech text, then, according to the procedure used in variant readings, it would be eliminated from further consideration and the testing of versions found in the *Times* and *Congressional Records* would continue. In fact, the speech text reported in the *Congressional Record* and the one compiled in the Christenberry publication are so nearly alike that the Christenberry version can be considered a copy of the *Congressional Record* speech and this text can be thought of as the official Long version. This reduces the number of texts to three. When all three versions agree on a passage in the text, there is a strong presumption that this is what the speaker actually said, particularly when the historian is dealing with at least *two* independent versions of a document.

The *Vital Speeches* text is almost identical, with one major exception, to the version printed in the *Congressional Record*. The *Vital Speeches* text has a conclusion that does not appear in either of the other two versions. However, it is so close to the Long version printed in the *Congressional Record* that it can be considered as a draft of the Long text. The differences can be viewed as the result of editing changes prior to publication. There remain, then, two independent versions agreeing substantially for the first two-thirds of the speech and reporting the final third of the speech in much different fashion. *The New York Times* speech text reported that the Senator ended his speech by reading portions of letters that had been written to him by his listeners and then delivering an emotional peroration. The *Congressional Record* version contained no mention of letters and the *Vital Speeches* text had the Senator concluding with a reference to attacks made upon him in front-page editorials in Philadelphia and New York newspapers.

In addition to the examination of the texts by the procedure of variant readings, the historian would take into account the reputable nature of *The New York Times,* and the fact that by 1935 the art of taking shorthand was well developed. He would also consider that Senator Long spoke very rapidly, that he preferred to speak extemporaneously, and that he generally did speak without manuscript over the radio. He would also consider the fact that this occasion was one of the few in which Senator Long did have a manuscript. On the basis of this evidence, what decision should be made about what Senator Long actually said in the final third of the broadcast? Before reading further, pause and make a decision between the report in *The New York Times* and in the *Congressional Record*.

We have additional evidence to help answer this question because the National Broadcasting Company had made electrical transcriptions of the speech; and it was possible to compare the written texts with the recording of the speech. The recording gave every evidence of being authentic. The speech was transcribed on both sides of four aluminum discs and requires a fiber stylus to be replayed. The recording was obviously a matter of indifference to the network. In 1951, they had difficulty finding it for me and apparently thought of it as too old to be significant as a contemporary record and too young to be important as a historical record. I could find no evidence that the discs had been tampered with.

All the printed texts of the speech follow the recorded text with considerable accuracy for the first two-thirds of the speech, as the variant reading technique would predict. Yet, even where they do follow rather closely the actual words of the speaker, they do not record exactly what the Senator said.

> For example, *The New York Times* text reads in part:
> Well, they are like old David Crockett, who went out to hunt a possum in the top of the tree, going from limb to limb, so he shot, but he missed.
> The *Congressional Record* reports the same section as:
> They are like old Davy Crockett, who went out to hunt a possum. He saw in the gleam of the moonlight that a possum in the top of a tree was going from limb to limb. He shot and missed.
> Long actually said:
> Why, they are like old Davy Crockett who went out to hunt a possum. He saw in the gleam of the moonlight that a possum in the top of the tree was going from limb to limb. So he shot but he missed.

The New York Times reports the final third of the speech as accurately as it does the first two-thirds. Apparently the editors of *Vital Speeches* were furnished with the manuscript that the Senator prepared before he gave the speech. This same manuscript with some editing was probably the one printed in the *Congressional Record*. On the air, the Senator did considerable editing and ad libbed a different conclusion for his speech. Instead of commenting on the newspaper editorials he read letters from his listeners.

I have dealt with this particular problem of determining the textual authenticity of a recent speech in such detail to indicate that even such sources as *The New York Times, Vital Speeches,* and the *Congressional Record* will not always, or perhaps, not even most of the time, yield authentic readings of a speech. The example also illustrates the changes that can be introduced by stenographic recording, by platform editing, and by the editing of a speech after delivery for publication. This example also illustrates the technique of variant readings to establish what was actually said. The scholar using this technique determines first which texts are copies of others and which are independent and then using the common elements of two or more independent texts he infers what was said or written.

AUTHENTICITY OF OTHER SOURCES

The authenticity of speech texts is a special problem for critics and historians of public address, but the scholar in speech must examine *all sources as carefully as he does the texts of speeches to establish their authenticity*. Who wrote the letter? Did the man whose signature is on the letter really sign it? Is this actually what was written in the letter? Who wrote *Hamlet?* Is this the text that Shakespeare wrote? Such questions must be asked of all sources.

EVALUATING ANONYMOUS AUTHORS

Even when all efforts to identify the author of a document fail, close examination of the contents can tell us something about him. If Daniel Webster's summation in the White murder case would fall into the hands of a scholar who was unable to identify the author, he could still discover a great deal about him from the speech itself. The speech reveals that the speaker is a lawyer, that he is making a plea for the prosecution in a murder trial, that he is a personage of more than average renown, and that he has been brought especially to aid the prosecution in this case. Most lengthy documents will reveal a great deal about the author's life and his biases and prejudices. That is, of course, if the document is the product of one man and not a committee of several ghostwriters.

EXTERNAL CRITICISM

Every important historical document should be criticized carefully and extensively to determine as accurately as possible the external circumstances that had a bearing upon its production.

In addition to discovering who produced the document and what sort of person he was, the historian should establish the time and place in which the document originated. Is this document dated? Will the style of the handwriting, or the language, or the words used indicate the approximate date? Will the paper and the ink serve to date the document? If dated, are the dates accurate? Sometimes documents are misdated purposely.

In what place did the document originate? If it is found in the expected place and originated at the appropriate time, there is a presumption in favor of its authenticity.

The student beginning his historical researches may view such thorough external criticism of sources as an impossible barrier. There must be, of course, some end to his questioning. But these methods have been developed over many years of scholarship and have withstood the tests of time. Fortunately, many documents have been studied by scholars previously. The authenticity or doubts about authenticity of such documents are well established. The historian can use such scholarship in his work. However, if he is dealing with new material that has not yet been evaluated, he must carefully criticize the documents along the lines discussed above.

INTERNAL CRITICISM

Having established the time, place, authorship, and authenticity of an historical document, the historian must now turn to internal criticism. From such reliable documents as he has found, he must sift out the statements of fact that he evaluates as true.

DECIPHERING THE DOCUMENT

The first step in this process is to decipher the document. What does it say? This is particularly important for any project that involves older materials that contain archaic expressions, words, and spellings. Before one studies Shakespeare, he must learn what the word and the idiom meant in Shakespeare's time. Some documents may be written in guarded language, in code, or in such poor style that the meaning is ambiguous.

DETERMINING THE MEANING

Having deciphered the meaning in a statement, the next question is: did the writer mean what he said? Is he writing ironically, figuratively, or literally? Speeches may contain large sections of figurative language and irony. Legal documents, on the other hand, are frequently to be taken quite literally.

TESTING THE SOURCE

Once the historian is certain that he understands the statements in the document and that he understands what the author meant to say by these statements, he must then test the competence of the witnesses whose testimony is recorded in the document. The first concern is to determine if the witness was an eyewitness, but even the testimony of an eyewitness must be critically examined. Was the witness a good observer? A professional soldier should be able to report a battle more accurately than a casual bystander. A lawyer should be able to report a legal summation more creditably than a butcher. A forensic director's account of a debate should be more reliable than a layman's account. Some men are trained for jobs that make a specialty of observation. Policemen, private detectives, and newspaper reporters are generally better trained in this than are laymen.

Was the witness in a good position to observe the facts under consideration? Was the reporter close to Lincoln at Ottawa? Or was he in a saloon, having filed his story, confident that his editor wanted the slant that he had given it? A common practice today is to prepare news releases for reporters and newspapers. Many news stories are based on these releases rather than observation. The scholar must take care not to evaluate such news stories as the reports of relatively unbiased newspaper reporters. Newspaper accounts of entertainment personalities often reflect the work of press agents. If the historian of the theatre is investigating the life and personality of a great actress, he must be careful not to be misled by this practice.

How long after the observation does the witness testify about the event? If he records his testimony immediately after the occurrence, it is more creditable than if he testifies fifty years later. The recollections of an observer recorded many years later are often unreliable. The unrevised daily journal or diary is generally more reliable than the memoirs of an individual.

How egocentric was the witness? A certain amount of ego involvement is inescapable in recounting personal observations; but if the scholar is not careful, he may gain the impression that the witness was more active and important in the affair than he actually was. The report of a ghostwriter about how many of his words and ideas found their way into the final speech of an important person must be examined critically to make sure that the witness is not overrepresenting his influence.

Assuming the examination of the source indicated that the witness was a competent one, that he was in a position to observe clearly and report accurately what took place, there is still the further question of whether he told the truth.

TESTING THE TRUTHFULNESS OF THE SOURCE

Was he willing to tell the truth? Did the witness have a reason for falsehood or distortion? The reporter of the *Illinois State Register* who covered the Lincoln–Douglas debates had reason to distort his description of Lincoln's delivery since he was writing for an anti-Lincoln paper. We suspect the claims of a salesman about his product; we expect a subordinate to say good things about the boss if the boss is likely to hear him, and we expect a political candidate to say bad things about his opponent. Likewise, if the witness has been injured or his ambitions frustrated or his friends harmed, we can expect willful distortion and falsehood. Thus, the historian must learn as much as possible about the relationships, friendships, and feuds of the people about whom he is writing and of the people whose observations form the basis of his history. The historian must also remember that people and their relationships do not remain the same. Lincoln in Salem is not the same Lincoln in Springfield. Lincoln's relationship to Douglas in 1848 is not the same as in 1858.

When testifying about highly emotional events such as labor strife, political campaigns, wars, economic dislocation, religious controversy, and intellectual battles, the bias of the witness may cause him to misstate or distort what happened.

The witness may misrepresent, overstate or understate the facts in a desire to please. Speakers in particular may adapt their material to what they think the audience wants to hear. Other source materials may be distorted for the same reasons. For example, may not the writer of a letter misrepresent the facts in order to please the recipient of the message?

Certain occasions have developed traditional forms of address and should not be taken at face value. Diplomatic communiqués often are of this nature. Reports coming from the headquarters of contending candidates for a presidential nomination after the convention has selected the candidate frequently follow a traditional form. Such statements seldom reflect the real attitudes and facts. Libel laws, or the fear of a duel in the past, politeness or tact may cause the witness to repress certain facts because they are considered libelous, impolite, unkind, or in poor taste. The historian, therefore, has a difficult task when he tries to establish the truth of statements of fact dealing with sexual abnormalities or promiscuousness, with drunkenness and alcoholism, and with dope addiction, even with manners and appearances.

If the writer is interested in creating an exciting account, he may distort the facts to heighten the dramatic impact of his report. He may exaggerate the stature of men and events for the same purposes. This exaggeration accounts, to some extent, for the evaluations of speakers and actors that seem unduly extravagant. The observer's desire to lend drama to his account may partly explain the reports of the wonderfully luminous eye of the speaker and his graceful and commanding gestures.

The style of writing in certain periods of the eighteenth and nineteenth centuries was florid by contemporary standards and given to elaborate descriptions. Some speeches were acclaimed the greatest since those delivered by Demosthenes and Cicero.

Writers of dramatic criticism for American newspapers in the nineteenth century frequently couched their reviews in such terms and overstated the quality of productions. When they described new theatre houses, they tended to grow poetic and reflect the general pride of the community in the progress that the new building represented for their city. Such accounts must be carefully evaluated with this in mind. Whether the result of conscious intent or stylistic conventions, such evaluations must be interpreted.

The witness may be misled by what he expects to see because of his preconceived notions. In observing a riot, he may see communists because he expects to see communists when there is mob violence. He may expect Englishmen to lack humor, Germans to be thorough, and actresses to be women of loose moral character; and his accounts are therefore warped because they reflect a witness who does not observe as fully and fairly as an observer with less strongly held expectations of what he will see in a given situation.

When a source is primary and the witness is competent to observe accurately and he is recorded authentically in the document under examination, the source can be considered sound for historical evidence.

EXAMINING SPECIFIC STATEMENTS

The student must remember, however, that even a tested historical source may contain statements that are not statements of fact and may contain some specific statements that are false. A statement of fact from a tested source should be corroborated by another equivalent statement of fact from another sound source, and the two reports should be *independent*. When this can be done, then the historian can judge that the statement of fact has been conclusively demonstrated as historically verified. In lieu of the second independent report, if other information corroborates the statement, it may be considered verified. For example, if the statement that George Washington surveyed the region of Virginia in the area of the natural bridge is found in a tested source and corroborated by the discovery of Washington's bench mark in the region, the historian will be justified in deciding the statement is true.

Sources that are suspect because of the bias or personality of the witness may contain true statements of fact. The historian should examine the details of each document as well as the document in its entirety. Perhaps not all of the statements of fact in such a document are perceived as important and interesting by the witness. Statements of this nature may well be truthful.

Statements of fact that are prejudicial to the witness' biases and interests may be considered as even more likely to be true than if the testimony came from a more objective witness.

Some statements of fact may be known to be true by so many people that it would be folly for the witness to maintain they were false, even if he wanted to. In this regard the scholar should ask if the statement under examination was made public so that its falsehoods could be refuted by others who were in a position to know what happened. If the statement was made and widely known by other observers who made no effort to set the record straight, this silence creates a presumption in favor of the truth of the statement. If the statement was not made until other eyewitnesses were dead and there was less likelihood of a falsehood being revealed, there is a presumption against its truth. Had John Smith published his account of the Pocahontas affair while she was still alive and able to testify about it, he would have had a better chance of being believed by subsequent historians.

Some factual information may be so incidental and probable that even highly unreliable sources will reveal it. One of the most abusive and scurrilous attacks ever made in print on Senator Huey Long was published under the title of *Kidnaped by the Kingfish* [16] and was attributed to a man named Sam Irby. Irby had disappeared under mysterious circumstances shortly before a crucial Louisiana election. Long's enemies charged that he had kidnaped Irby to keep him from revealing scandal about Long's personal and political life. On election eve, Long dramatically presented a man over a statewide radio hookup who said he was Sam Irby. The man then read a statement over the air exonerating Long. The newspapers charged that the man was not really Irby. In the book *Kidnaped by the Kingfish,* Irby recounts his side of the story, accusing Long of many unsavory crimes, including kidnaping; but he also tells how he was forced to read the statement over the air on election eve. Thus, although much of what Irby wrote can be discounted, his testimony does go to help establish the fact that he was the man who read the statement over the radio that night.

---

[16] New Orleans, 1932.

The statement that Lincoln's rally before the Charleston debate was small and unenthusiastic still helps establish the fact that Lincoln did have a rally. The statement that a given speaker's hands were shaking so badly that he could hardly hold his notes could still establish that the speaker used notes even though the witness might have reasons for reporting that the speaker was more nervous than he really was.

SPECIAL PROBLEMS

SECONDHAND ACCOUNTS

Sometimes there are no primary sources available, and the historian must then rely solely upon secondhand accounts. In such an instance the historian attempts to determine how accurately the secondary sources report what the eyewitnesses said and who the eyewitnesses were. He will then proceed to test the eyewitness as best he can, following the rules laid down above. Such accounts are particularly liable to the distortions common to rumors.[17]

Rumors tend to be simplified versions of the original event. Descriptions of events are seldom elaborated but rather details tend to be omitted or condensed as the rumor is repeated. This tendency is called leveling. With leveling comes a sharpening of certain details in the rumor which are selected for undue emphasis. Such things as movement, size, events contemporaneous to the recounting of the rumor, and familiar aspects of the original perception tend to be sharpened during the retelling of a report. The third tendency in hearsay reports is assimilation of details by condensing and twisting them to make the testimony more plausible and meaningful, or to make it conform to biases, prejudices, and stereotypes of the reporter.

Hearsay reports frequently have these characteristics because the individuals involved tend to confuse things in memory that happened at one time with those that happened at another time. Assimilation is largely a result of striving after meaning and the rationalization of emotional needs. Witnesses tend to reshape all experience into neat categories, thus doing particular violence to unusual features of the event which then become sharpened and exaggerated or reinterpreted. Rumors often contain distortions of fact regarding the time, place, and proper names of individuals involved in historical events.

---

[17] This description of rumor is drawn from Gordon W. Allport and Leo Postman, *The Psychology of Rumor* (New York, 1947). This book also contains a summary of psychological investigations into the psychology of recall and the studies of witness recall which is helpful in the internal criticism of primary sources.

Sometimes the historian is unable to get two independent documents bearing upon the same fact in order to corroborate the truthfulness of a given statement of fact. Diligent research may not turn up another statement bearing on this particular happening. Many questions of a psychological nature cannot be supported by more than one source because they deal with the inner states of individuals and only the individual who had the thought or feeling can really testify about these matters.

In such instances the rule of two independent sources breaks down. The source can be scrutinized, however, to determine whether it is a public or private document. Was it designed for publication or reserved for the eye of a confidant? Was it intended to be kept completely private? In general, a person is more likely to misrepresent his thoughts and feelings in a public document than he is in a private or confidential report. If his recorded introspections go counter to the mores of his time, there is a presumption in favor of their truthfulness. If his actions and his life support his introspective accounts, then there is a presumption that they are true.

NEWSPAPERS

Newspapers are an important source of historical information.[18] Most graduate students in speech, writing histories of the theatre or of public address, will rely heavily upon newspaper reports of theatrical events and speeches for their data.

The reporter's job is quite similar to the historian's. Like the historian, the reporter makes statements of fact about human events, but the reporter more frequently is an eyewitness to the event he is writing about. The best reporters are highly trained observers with experience in some particular field of reporting and therefore can be counted on to give reliable descriptions of what happened. On the other hand, the reporter works very rapidly and with very little perspective. The byline on a story becomes important for the scholar, for if a reporter is frequently identified, his ability can be evaluated. In the absence of a byline the student should discover the reputation of the paper for thorough or haphazard reporting or for bias to help him evaluate the statements found in its pages. He must disregard the newspaper's prior and subsequent reputation and

---

[18] Newspapers were not always considered suitable historical sources. James Ford Rhodes justifies and discusses the use of newspapers as primary material for a historian in "Newspapers as Historical Sources," *Historical Essays* (New York, 1909), pp. 81–97.

concentrate on the sort of paper it was during the period covered by his study. A paper with a reputation for accurate and objective reporting in 1950 or 1960 might have had a much different reputation in 1860.

Although reporters should make reliable reports, they often fail to do so. Not all reporters are good observers, nor are they all intelligent. Sometimes the reporter arrives on the scene of the event after it happened, and he must reconstruct what took place by interviewing what eyewitnesses he can. Sometimes he will suppress information that would be damaging to influential persons. Sometimes he is lazy and fails to do the necessary spadework to write a complete and accurate account.

Newspapers are useful for purposes other than establishing the nature of historical events. Newspapers frequently carry commentary about cultural events such as essays on the state of the theatre and reviews of specific productions. Such commentary or review is helpful to the scholar when he reconstructs the cultural climate of a given historical period. Frequently theatrical criticism is bylined which gives the historian of the theatre an opportunity to study the critic. He may evaluate a given critic by collating reviews of the same production by several critics, by studying the reviews and the other writings of the critic, and by reading comments made about the critic in letters to the editor and by actors, directors, and producers in interviews. Does he praise indiscriminately? Does he know theatre? Does he enjoy ripping apart a production with a clever phrase or figure of speech? The investigator needs to answer such questions when examining the work of a critic.

Newspapers contain much trustworthy material of an incidental nature. The advertisements will reveal quite accurately the price levels of the period. They will also reveal a great deal about the style and tastes of the time.

INTERVIEWS

Many graduate students in speech write dissertations that deal with contemporary theatre or public address and use the historical method. The study of contemporaneous events opens up some practical avenues for gathering and testing historical data and poses some special problems.

If the people involved in the study are still alive, the student may interview them for information. Such a source, if questioned about what he has personally observed, is undoubtedly primary. All the tests of primary sources mentioned above must be applied to data gathered in interviews. The historian, as interviewer, must be careful not to ask leading questions. A skillful lawyer knows how to structure leading questions so as to receive the desired answers. The historian must be careful not to do so for he is interested in the right answer, not the pleasing one. Asking loaded questions or questions that can be answered "yes" or "no" may further mislead the historian.

Unless the source's opinion is important to the study the interviewer is well advised to ask questions of fact and attempt to establish what the observer reports took place. He should try to avoid the interviewee's biases and emotions.

Two of the problems mentioned above in regard to testing written sources bear particularly on the interviewed source. The first deals with the time lapse between the event under observation and the report. Even an eyewitness recalling events of a year or more in the past can be expected to make mistakes about details. The superficial student will accept the interview as an accurate source of information if the interview is with a speaker or director or other great man who is the focus of the study. The more thorough student will check the facts in other sources and may find that the speaker actually did advocate a certain program, even though he denies it or that the play did not run two years as the star testified but actually closed in eleven months. In such a case he should not compensate by becoming so skeptical that he decides the interviews were worthless and not use any of the material. If two or more independent witnesses agree in interviews about a statement of fact, their testimony is evidence for the statement, even if each interviewee is mistaken about other details.

The second important problem in the interview for data is the egocentricity of the interviewee in a face-to-face situation. Frequently the source will present himself in a favorable light. Even when he was not an important participant, he may tend to select those events that indicate his importance to history. However, with special care, the problems posed by time-lapse and the egocentricity of interviewees, the interview can be an important tool of the student of contemporary history.

SUMMARY

Most statements of fact about historical events are indirectly verifiable and the scholar makes a judgment about their truth or falsity on the basis of the historical traces left by events. The historical method consists of the procedures utilized by the scholar to test and evaluate these sources.

The sources used in scholarship may be either primary or secondary. Firsthand accounts of the events under study are primary sources. All other accounts are secondary. The primary account may be found in an original manuscript of a speech, letter, or diary or it may be in a printed or recorded version of the same materials. An original document may or may not be a primary source, depending on its contents.

The first step in the critical evaluation of historical materials is to examine the circumstances surrounding their production. This step is called the external criticism of historical sources. The scholar must examine his materials to see if they are authentic. All historical documents must be tested in this fashion, but examining the authenticity of speech texts illustrates the basic problems. Three questions need to be asked in examining the authenticity of a speech text: (1) who prepared the speech?, (2) who gave the speech?, and, (3) what did the speaker say?

Additional considerations involved in external criticism include establishing both the time and the place in which the document was produced. In this regard the historian uses all available clues including the age of the paper, the kind of ink used, the style of the language, and the place where the document was discovered.

After the historian completes the external criticism of a document, he examines its contents more carefully. From the authentic documents he must sift out the statements of fact that he judges to be true. This step is called the internal criticism of historical sources.

Internal criticism involves deciphering documents, determining the meaning of statements, and testing eyewitness accounts in terms of witness ability and willingness to tell the truth. Even a source that seems sound after such evaluation may contain specific statements of fact that are false. Each statement of fact needs to be corroborated by another statement from an independent witness to the events under study. Such corroboration can also be furnished by facts as well as testimony. Even the testimony of a bad witness may contain true statements of fact. The student should examine all sources statement by statement to sift out the true statement of facts from the false.

If no primary sources are available, the historian may have to rely upon secondhand accounts. He tests secondary sources with the same rigorous methods that he uses in testing primary sources. He takes particular care because of the distortions that can be expected in hearsay accounts.

Scholars in speech find much useful information in newspapers, but students should examine these with special care. The scholar needs to study the competence of a given reporter or drama critic whenever possible. He finds bylines of considerable help. If there are no bylines, he may have to rely solely on the reputation of the paper at the time under scrutiny for bias or factual reporting.

The scholar who studies contemporary theatre or rhetoric may be able to interview eyewitnesses directly. These interviews need to be examined in much the same way as any other source of the historical period. Statements of fact asserted in interviews need corroboration as much as such statements found in letters or diaries.

Suggested Readings

Altick, Richard D. *The Scholar Adventurers.* New York: The Macmillan Company, 1960.

Bloch, Marc. *The Historian's Craft.* Trans. Peter Putnam, New York: Alfred A. Knopf, Inc., 1953.

Gottschalk, Louis. *Understanding History: A Primer of Historical Method.* New York: Alfred A. Knopf, Inc., 1950.

Handlin, Oscar, *et al. Harvard Guide to American History.* Cambridge: Harvard University Press, 1954.

Hockett, Homer C. *The Critical Method in Historical Research and Writing.* New York: The Macmillan Company, 1955.

Johnson, Allen. *The Historian and Historical Evidence.* New York: Charles Scribner's Sons, 1934.

Projects

1) Select a historical thesis or dissertation that has been accepted at your school and examine the use of historical proof in the study.

   a) Examine the sources and determine if they are primary or secondary.
   b) What evidence of external criticism do you find in the study?
   c) Evaluate the internal criticism of source materials.
   d) Select several controversial statements of fact that are asserted by the author and evaluate the historical evidence that supports the statements. Write a short statement evaluating this evidence similar to the statement concerning Lincoln's stage fright in Chapter 9.

2) Pick a statement of fact of limited scope from the history of your area and search your library for primary source material that bears on its truth or falsity.

3) Select a published copy of a speech or a play and determine the authenticity of the text.

4) Select a famous speech from history and search the newspaper files for reports on it. Compare these newspaper reports with the published speech text.

5) If you have recordings of famous speeches in your library or in your department, compare the transcribed version of the speech with the written texts.

6) Attend the performance of a play and then collect all the printed reviews of the production that you can. What sort of a reconstruction of the production might a historian in the year 2000 hope to make from these reviews?

Questions for Discussion

1) How might empirical researchers in speech use the historical method?

2) Why might a speech historian want to know who wrote the speech delivered by a famous personage?

3) To what extent is it justifiable to conjecture about the truth or falsity of statements of fact for which the historian cannot find much evidence?

4) On what grounds would you justify studying historical events such as ancient Egyptian drama or the oratory of the Dakota Sioux Indians for which there are few if any primary sources?

5) How would you answer the argument that the historical method is not appropriate to the study of acting, the dance, musical performances, or speaking because these events must be experienced in context, and the important features of the historical event leave no traces to aid in their reconstruction?

CHAPTER TEN

THE WRITING OF HISTORY

VIEWPOINT

According to Henry Adams, "Historians undertake to arrange sequences—called stories, or histories—assuming in silence a relation of cause and effect. These assumptions, hidden in the depth of dusty libraries, have been astounding, but commonly unconscious and child-like." [1]

The scholar in speech using the historical method for a research project will also subscribe to some notions about the method and its application, and he will acquire a viewpoint toward his material and the importance of various factors within it that will determine the kind of history he writes. The scholar should clearly avow the assumptions that form his viewpoint toward his material. Conscious avowal may reveal that the assumptions are, indeed, childlike and he may wish to change them; but when he is satisfied, a clear presentation of his viewpoint will strengthen the study for the reader as well as the investigator. [2]

A brief summary of the outstanding assumptions and notions that have been used by historians in the past will help to clarify the notion of viewpoint. In general, the viewpoints of practicing historians have reflected their conscious or subconscious view of man and his relation to the universe. They have viewed history as determined by the gods and god-inspired men, by fate, rational men, economic forces, military might, political and social forces, or by heroes.

The historian's point of view is usually restricted by his own history. Italian artists paint Madonnas that look Italian and Dutch

---

[1] Henry Adams, *The Education of Henry Adams: An Autobiography* (Boston, 1918), p. 382.

[2] This notion is developed in greater detail by W. Stull Holt in his article "Historical Scholarship," in *American Scholarship in the Twentieth Century,* ed. Merle Curti (Cambridge, 1953), pp. 95–96, and by John Herman Randall, Jr., and George Haines, IV, in "Controlling Assumptions in the Practice of American Historians," in *Theory and Practice in Historical Study: A Report of the Committee on Historiography,* Social Science Research Council Bulletin 54 (New York, 1946), pp. 19–24.

artists paint them to look Dutch. In much the same way German history reflects the German *zeitgeist* and a Russian and an English historian will each see the same events from a different angle. In this country such concepts as nationalism, liberalism, pragmatism, democracy, and capitalism are reflected in the writing of history. W. Stull Holt says of liberalism and democracy, "the influence of these concepts on historical scholarship has been vast. The result was that the worth and liberty of the individual person and of democracy as the proper way of organizing society were accepted as axiomatic." [3]

In addition, the historian's viewpoint is made up of what he condones and what he condemns. Does he view propaganda as a necessary adjunct to political activity or does he feel propaganda activity is essentially wrong? Does he view emotionalism as an important part of religious experience or does he feel emotional evangelism unethical?

Finally, the historian's viewpoint must include some notions about the nature of man. Is man essentially moved by subconscious conflicts and desires? What is the role of reason in his affairs? The historian will have to answer basic questions of human psychology of this kind whether he is aware of it or not. Such questions are particularly important for historical work dealing with individuals in a biographical way or as leaders of movements. Scholars in speech frequently write works of this type.

EXAMPLES OF VIEWPOINTS

Many of the historians of ancient Egypt, Babylonia, and Greece wrote with the viewpoint that heroes, priests, and gods caused historical events to happen.

THE THEOLOGICAL VIEWPOINT

Hebrew historians and early Christian scholars tended to emphasize the direct intervention of God in the affairs of men. Certain contemporary scholars accept the theological viewpoint and continue to reconstruct history through this focus. For example, in the foreword of Garraghan's *A Guide to Historical Method,* Jean Delanglez comments that Father Garraghan has based his book upon the *Lehrbuch der Geschichtlichen Methode* of Father Alfred Feder, a book which has a conception of history "which leaves room for the supernatural, for God, for revelation, for miracles." [4]

---

[3] Holt, p. 97.
[4] New York, 1946, p. v.

The theological viewpoint also was influential in early American historiography. Charles Beard suggested, in his book *An Economic Interpretation of the Constitution,* that there had been three schools that dominated American history up to the first decade of the twentieth century. The first he identified with Bancroft and characterized as explaining "the larger achievements in our national life by reference to the peculiar endowments of a people acting under divine guidance." [5] The following period, Beard called "Teutonic" and he described this viewpoint as one that "ascribes the wonderful achievements of the English-speaking peoples to the peculiar genius of the Germanic race." [6]

Historiographers have sometimes characterized this middle period as the era of the "germ" theory of history. This theory suggested that American institutions developed from European seeds or germs and could be explained by tracing them back to their sources in England and Germany.

The third period, according to Beard, was one that lacked a viewpoint and could not be characterized by a phrase. "It is marked rather by an absence of hypotheses." The historians of this school were aware of the errors of previous scholars and "turned aside from 'interpretation' in the larger sense." [7]

SCIENTIFIC HISTORY

Subsequently, scholars have come to regard this movement as the "scientific school" of history. German scholars, such as von Ranke, gave scientific history its original impetus. The movement spread to America because many of the first university faculty members to become historians were trained in German graduate schools. These German-trained historians often believed in "scientific" history or in the notion that American institutions grew from Teutonic germs.

For some scientific historians the application of the scientific method meant the discovery and establishment of laws of history similar to the laws of nature discussed in Chapter 5. This notion was difficult to apply and little history has been written along this line.[8] In the period discussed by Beard, scientific historians were placing emphasis on searching for facts that could be discovered and agreed upon and had, for the most part, renounced generalization, interpretation, and philosophy. The lodestone of scientific history was objec-

---

5 New York, 1913, p. 1.
6 Beard, p. 2.
7 Beard, p. 3.
8 Holt, p. 95.

tivity. To be objective meant to study critically the sources of history and without bias discover what actually happened. Reconstructing history *"wie es eigentlich gewesen"* (the way it actually happened) was the basic historical rule.

History written from this viewpoint had certain strengths and certain weaknesses. One major advantage was that scientific historians placed a high value on factual information, as we have indicated. They subjected sources to rigorous and thorough criticism and evaluation. The scientific historians are largely responsible for the procedure for testing historical sources outlined in Chapter 9. They introduced high standards of care and thoroughness into the historical method. Less commendable byproducts included an often heavy and dry style (as the historian tried for the accuracy of a physicist), a tendency to be timid about venturing any statement without a supporting document, and an unwillingness to make conscious interpretations of historical materials.

By 1913 such critics as Charles Beard and Carl Becker were seriously challenging the validity of the scientific approach to history. Their attack was concentrated on revealing the hidden assumptions of the scientific viewpoint. Critics pointed out that the scientific viewpoint towards history involved the following assumptions: (1) that the facts of history have an existence outside the mind of the historian, (2) that the historian can know these facts and describe them accurately, (3) that the historian can divest himself of all economic, political, philosophical, religious, social, and esthetic interests, (4) that there is a structure to the historical events that can be found by any suitably trained scientific historian, and (5) that other impartial historians will agree that the structure exists when they examine the same historical evidence.[9]

THE INFLUENCE OF SCIENTIFIC HISTORY

By 1920 the scientific approach to history was well on its way to being abandoned.[10] However, although most historians have modified, if not rejected, scientific assumptions, the tremendous influence of scientific history at the turn of the century has had a not always salutary effect on theorizing in the humanities and the social sciences. The student doing a historical study in speech may well have absorbed some of these assumptions almost below the level of consciousness and as a result may be working with a naïve and unexamined viewpoint towards his material. Probably the most commonly

---

[9] Holt, p. 96.
[10] Randall and Haines, p. 26.

held assumption is the common sense one that the student must reconstruct the events that he is studying as they really were. This is an impossibility. The best the scholar can hope for is to make a judicious selection of conclusively demonstrated statements of fact from carefully tested historical sources.

THE SIGNIFICANCE OF THE FRONTIER VIEWPOINT

The first modification of the germ theory of the development of American institutions came before the heavy attack on the scientific historians of the early twentieth century. Frederick Jackson Turner's famous paper "The Significance of the Frontier in American History," delivered in Chicago in 1893, was influential in developing the new point of view. Turner suggested that the influence of the settlement of new lands on American institutions was as important as the germs inherited from the forests of Germany. History, according to Turner, could be examined in terms of the unique characteristics imparted to American institutions by the frontier. The frontier furnished a continual rebirth and return to primitive conditions. This continual leveling process helped mold the American culture and character.[11] Turner's thesis influenced the viewpoint of many scholars. English historian H. Hale Bellot affirmed, "that the most distinctive feature of American historiography in the generation after 1890 was the work of the Middle Western school." [12] This work stemmed directly from Turner's thesis. For the Middle Western school the center of interest moved from federal and constitutional politics of the Eastern Seaboard to the history of states and minor localities in the middle regions.

THE SIGNIFICANCE OF THE CITY VIEWPOINT

In the introduction to his paper, Turner noted that the census report of 1890 showed no more clearly unsettled areas in the United States. The frontier line was gone. The waning of the frontier and the increasingly urban character of American society has furnished another viewpoint for the interpretation of history. In the last thirty years a growing number of scholars have used the urbanization of the United States as an explanation for many institutional and cultural changes. An article by Professor A. M. Schlesinger Sr. on "The City in American History," [13] suggests some of the elements of this viewpoint towards history.

---

[11] Reprinted in Frederick Jackson Turner, *The Frontier in American History* (New York, 1920), pp. 1–38.

[12] *American History and American Historians* (Norman, Oklahoma, 1952), p. 22.

[13] *Mississippi Valley Historical Review*, XXVII (June 1940), 43–66.

THE SIGNIFICANCE OF THE SCIENCE VIEWPOINT

For many historians, but for the writers of intellectual history in particular, the assumption that science has had an impact on society and thought has been an intriguing viewpoint to use in writing history. The effects of Newtonian mechanics and Darwinian evolution on intellectual history, the influence of science and the scientific method on the entire intellectual community, and the prestige of science with the general public, are elements within this approach. The viewpoint from which we examined the history of research in speech in Part one of this book and from which we will examine the current status of research in Chapter 17 includes, as an important assumption, the influence and prestige of science with both academic and general publics.

DETERMINISTIC VIEWPOINT

The scholar undertaking a study in speech and avowing his assumption must take a stand on another important issue. He must make an assumption about the freedom of the will. Sidney Hook, in his study of *The Hero in History*, states the question clearly: "to what extent is the character of a given leadership causally and, since men are involved, morally responsible for our historical position and future?" [14]

The determinists would answer that the influence of leadership and personality on historical events is negligible or nonexistent. One of the most important groups of historical determinists interprets history as being the result of economic forces. A major book of this type is Charles A. Beard's *An Economic Interpretation of the Constitution*. During the 1920's and 1930's the economic interpretation of history enjoyed a vogue in the United States. The viewpoints of these authors ranged from the consideration of economic factors along with other causes to the out-and-out economic determinism of Marxist historians who explained history in terms of the class conflicts resulting from ownership of the means of production.

Developments in psychology and psychiatry in this century furnished another deterministic answer. Scholars adopting this answer discarded the concept that man is a rational creature with a conscious will and replaced it with the viewpoint that man's behavior could be explained by a slightly more elaborate model of Pavlov's dog, if they followed the behaviorist psychologists, or by the viewpoint that man was pushed and pulled by powerful forces in his subconscious, if they followed the Freudian model. In either case, these approaches

---

[14] New York, 1943, p. 7.

led to the conclusion that since man was unable to control his thoughts and actions he could not be held responsible for them. This led to the further conclusion that man could not be looked upon as a motivating force in history, helpless as he was in the grip of conditioned responses or of subconscious desires and impulses. The hero forced along by a powerful neurosis developed because of the childhood treatment he received from his nurse is hardly a hero at all and certainly not responsible for his actions.

Still other deterministic forces were to be found in the work of sociologists and anthropologists who discovered that traditions and mores and group norms and pressures could result in the social control of individuals and ultimately determine the nature of society.

THE GREAT MAN VIEWPOINT

The opposing concept assumes that men can change the course of history and do so consciously, of their own free will, and they can be held responsible for their actions. This viewpoint towards life and towards history is an old one. It has often been called the "Great Man Theory" of history. Since at least the time of Carlyle's famous discussion of *Heroes and Hero-Worship* to Sidney Hook's *The Hero in History*, this question has remained an important one for scholars.

The question is pertinent for scholars in speech because so much of the history they write deals with flamboyant and dynamic orators, writers, actors, and directors. What influence did Eisenstein have on film? What effect did Stanislavsky have on acting? What did Eugene O'Neill do for the American theatre? Did Franklin Roosevelt's fireside chats have any effect on the course of events? Did the Lincoln–Douglas debates affect the course of history? What was the effect of Father Coughlin's radio speeches? Should Douglas have answered differently the second question raised by Lincoln at the Freeport debate?

To deal with such questions, the scholar must adopt the viewpoint that human personality does make a difference. The questions themselves assume the "Great Man Theory" of history, for there would be no point in asking them unless there was a possibility of discovering that Roosevelt's fireside chats did have an effect, or that Eisenstein did have an influence on world cinema. To view the world in this way is not in itself wrong, but it is wrong to view the world in this way *if you are unaware that you are doing so*.

Indeed, the student doing a historical research project in speech may find it helpful to look at history in this fashion. The question of whether or not it is possible to discover enough scientific laws to explain all human history is, as yet, a moot question. It is a question of fact because it either is or is not possible to do so, but the evidence is far from in. Should enough scientific laws be discovered to explain the action of every human being then the determinists would have considerable proof for their idea, and it would be wise to view history in this way. In the present situation, however, the scholar must operate on faith no matter what viewpoint he takes. The economic determinist as well as the believer in the freedom of the will, both take their position on trust until more evidence is accumulated. In such a situation, if the notion that human personality makes a difference in history helps the student illuminate his material and aids him in the interpretation of events, he might well take this viewpoint.

At any rate, scholars often find it difficult to write history from a consistently deterministic standpoint. Sidney Hook judges that social determinists of all kinds write history as though some individuals "at some critical moments play a decisive role in redirecting the historical wave." Even the communists fall into the assumption of human will. Engels refers to Marx as taking decisive action. Trotsky talks in the same fashion about Lenin. Theological determinists also slip into this view on occasion. Hook says of the Popes that they "speak of western culture since the reformation as if it had been created by Luther and Calvin behind God's back." [15]

The scholar using the historical method in speech often finds it difficult to refrain from writing as though individuals at critical moments in history make decisions that change the course of events. Certainly any scholar who attempts to evaluate the *effectiveness* of a speech, or a speaker, or the speechmaking of a rhetorical movement, assumes as part of his viewpoint the notion that these speakers affected history, and if they had not spoken things would have happened in a different way.

VIEWPOINTS APPROPRIATE TO SCHOLARSHIP IN SPEECH

The scholar in speech does not need to subscribe wholly or in part to the "Great Man Theory" of history. He may take the viewpoint of an economic determinist. He may explain the history of the commercial theatre in New York in terms of the effects of unionization of stage hands, musicians, actors, and carpenters. He may examine the effects of building codes on the income of theatre-building owners. He may study the rising costs of production in relation to the cost of theatre tickets and over-all box office income. He may explain the artistic qualities of the theatre in terms of these economic factors.[16]

---

[15] Hook, p. 12.

[16] For an article sketching such an interpretation see "World of Make-Believe: The Theatre Has Fallen Victim to Bad Economics," *Barron's* (June 6, 1960), 1.

He may examine the history of the theatre in St. Louis in terms of the effects of the frontier on the culture of the community. He may explain the developments of speech education from 1850 to 1920 from the same viewpoint, indicating how the pragmatic climate of the frontier demanded an elective system and the establishment of practical courses such as public speaking and debating.

He might, on the other hand, examine more recent historical developments in speech education in terms of the urbanization of our society. The rise of discussion courses could be explained in this fashion. The frontiersman hardly needed training in group discussion; the organization man certainly does.

In 1946 the Committee on Historiography of the Social Science Research Council published a bulletin on "Theory and Practice in Historical Study." In this publication the members of the committee laid down certain propositions relevant to the study of history. In Proposition VI they referred to the notion that all written history represents a selection of materials and an emphasis in the presentation of the data that, avowed or unavowed, affects the results of the research. They concluded that historiography should have as two of its purposes the clarification of this notion for all workers in history, and the setting forth of the "many schemes of reference, interest, or emphasis which have influenced written or spoken history." [17]

The members of the committee drafting this 1946 report thus advocated a pluralistic approach to the writing of history. The pluralistic viewpoint allows the historian to focus on any aspect of human endeavor for his research. He may write military, political, cultural, economic, social, intellectual, or literary histories. With such a viewpoint, a history of the theatre is as justifiable as a history of the War of 1812. With this pluralistic approach the historian may adopt a concept that emphasizes one aspect of historical explanation, such as the effects of heroes or literary giants, or the ownership of the means of production, or the urbanization of society upon the institutions and individuals with which he is dealing. The pluralistic viewpoint allows the scholar to take different approaches in different studies, depending upon circumstances and also to try to discover the multiple causation factors operating in any given situation.

He must, however, remember that he should develop his point of view consciously and with some care. More than likely, a student's viewpoint, while it can be consciously articulated and critically examined, cannot be easily changed.

---

[17] Social Science Research Council Bulletin 54 (New York, 1946), p. 134.

If a man is committed to a liberal or conservative position, or to a Marxist or Capitalist or Roman Catholic or Freudian position, he often will find it difficult to change his thinking at will. Nor, indeed, is his viewpoint likely to be arrived at through intellectual means alone.[18]

For the student in speech who brings not only a background in history to his task but also a background in public address, literature, and criticism, certain additional assumptions may well be implied in his viewpoint. If the student is making a historical investigation of the commercial theatre, he will have expressed or implied assumptions about the nature of the theatre, about its importance to the community, about the relationship between box office and the quality of the theatre, and about a host of other factors dealing specifically with theatrical matters and drama in relation to culture. In like fashion, the student investigating the history of speech education will be operating within a framework of assumptions about the importance of speech courses, about the desirability of the mechanical approach to delivery, about the importance of research to speech, about the elocution movement, and a host of other factors dealing with education in general and speech in particular.

The student making a historical investigation of public speaking will have a number of assumptions with which he examines the raw material of history to write his study. Perhaps he has a bias in favor of logical argument and debating. He may be preoccupied with persuasion. He may have a firm commitment to the notion of freedom of speech. He may believe that rhetoric is an art, style is the man, and eloquence is to be cherished and admired.

All of these assumptions can color the scholar's interpretation of historical speech events and some of them might seriously handicap his work with certain historical materials. For example, the scholar who believes that rhetoric and eloquence are to be cherished, might have difficulty doing a study of the speechmaking of the Nazi party in Germany from 1922 to 1932 and with a history of the speechmaking of the Communist party in the United States in the same period. He would find little eloquence to study in the monolithic style of Communist rhetoric in this country after 1929 and this would make it difficult for him to examine such material. The same investi-

---

[18] This sentence expresses my viewpoint towards human conditioning and motivation. While, in my opinion, it is possible to modify attitudes and biases developed over a lifetime, by the time a person begins embarking on a serious career as a scholar it will be difficult for him to change his viewpoint. Such assumptions as this color my presentation of the theory and method of speech research just as they affect the history and criticism that I write.

gator would find that a history of English parliamentary speaking from 1939 to 1945 was much more amenable to treatment from his particular viewpoint.

The historian of the theatre who believes that theatre is an avenue to knowledge and one of the major cultural expressions of a given society, might be comfortable studying the Provincetown Players and have considerable difficulty with a history of variety theatre in New York from 1900 to 1918. Many times such biases, hidden or articulated, will guide the graduate student to proper historical materials.

Sometimes, however, if the viewpoint is hidden from the beginning scholar in speech and from his faculty advisers, he may be counseled into a historical study that will be difficult for him to handle. He may find the material, if not dull, at least distasteful; and he may have considerable difficulty interpreting the meaning of its events.

SELECTING THE HISTORICAL METHOD

Since speech offers such a variety of topics for investigation and a considerable variety of methods of research for those conducting such investigations, the graduate student searching for a research topic should analyze carefully his background, interests, and talents before selecting a topic that requires the historical method of research.

An interest and background in general history is one indication that the student has a potential for such research. If the prospect of leafing through old newspapers and carefully compiling bibliography and note cards is repugnant to the student, he should seriously question the advisability of starting a historical study. If he has little talent for writing and little interest in developing his writing skill, he should consider some other form of research.

In any case, once the student has selected the historical method and a general area that he would like to study, he should develop a program of studies that will fill in his historical background. Adding a minor in history is an excellent idea. Developing proficiency in languages that will be helpful for his study is another good idea.

If the student can make some tentative decisions about his research project early in his graduate career, so that he can tailor his program to his research, he will be much better equipped to do his study when the time comes. If he cannot do so, he certainly should begin his study of history and historiography, formally in courses or on his own, as soon as he decides to do a historical study.

SELECTING A TOPIC

The student may look for a topic that grows out of his particular interests in speech. If he is interested in speech education, he may write a history of the elocution movement or the speech training in a specific institution. If he is interested in broadcasting, he may write a history of a network. If he is intrigued by speech pathology, he may write a history of speech correction in the public schools. If he is drawn to musical comedy, he may write a history of musical comedy on the Broadway stage.

The student may look for a topic that grows out of some cultural or economic interest that is not related to speech. He may study religious speaking, speaking in the labor movement, business, legal, or agrarian speaking. He may study the theatre of economic protest, vaudeville, melodrama, or the relationship of various religious movements to the theatre. He may have an interest in ethical questions that will lead him to study demagogues, evangelists, or saints, or public relations and advertising. He may be interested in the history of a particular region which will lead him to study Southern antisecession speaking or the history of abolition plays, or the speaking of the vigilantes in California. Or he may choose a topic that grows out of his desire to know more about the cultural climate and the activities of a great speaker, playwright, actor, director, designer, voice scientist, or teacher.

He should search for an area that excites his interest and curiosity, for if he really wants to know something about the events he is studying, the preliminary steps of historical research will be less painful. (Interest grows with information and understanding, however, and this problem is not troublesome once the study is well started, no matter what the topic.)

In one sense, everything that has happened to mankind is suitable for historical investigation. In another sense, however, every historical investigation needs to be evaluated for its worth. For the graduate student the justification of his study is a very tangible matter. He will be required to present a prospectus of his study to the graduate faculty for evaluation and approval. The postdoctoral researcher may not face such immediate and obvious problems of justification, but when he submits his work for publication, he can expect that his work will be evaluated by editors and readers.

In general, important events and individuals are more likely to result in worthwhile history than the study of unimportant events and people, although when searching for a topic for a historical monograph there are important reservations to keep in mind. If the question asked about important events is superficial, or of only momentary interest, the study may be more trivial than a study of less important affairs that probes more deeply and asks a more universal and persistent question.

Each year a number of graduate students in speech write historical studies as their master's thesis. You will find the titles of such studies listed in the summary of graduate theses published yearly in *Speech Monographs*. The following list of titles was selected from these summaries and illustrates the sorts of topic that have been investigated in master's theses using the historical method.

The Contributions of Alexander Graham Bell to the Fields of Speech Pathology and Audiology

A History of the Development of Speech Correction in the San Francisco Unified School District, 1915–1956

The Image of the Orator in the United States from 1890 to 1900

A Historical Analysis of Selected Sermons of Jeremy Taylor

A Historical Study of the Public Address of Margaret Chase Smith

A History of the School of Expression and Oratory at Nebraska Wesleyan University

The First Seventy-five Years of Forensic Activities at the University of Kansas (1867–1942)

A Historical Study of the American Forces Korea Network and Its Broadcast Programming

Order Out of Chaos: The Formative Years of American Broadcasting, 1920–1927

The History of TV College at the University of Detroit

A Study of the Development of Theatre in Greater Miami Until 1935

A Study of the American Repertory Theatre System from 1752 to 1852

The Development of Methods for Flying Scenery on the English Stage, 1800–1860

A History of Theatrical Unions in the United States

NARROWING THE TOPIC

Once the student has decided upon a general area of study he should systematically examine the history of the period. After he has a sound grasp of the historical background he should focus his study more sharply. As he becomes immersed in this more narrow topic, a structure should begin to take shape in his analysis of the material that will enable him to ask a specific question. That is, as the student studies the material some events will strike him as more important than others, some time periods will seem transitional, and the periods between these transition points may exhibit certain earmarks that will serve to characterize them. For example, in his study of the "low varieties" program in Memphis, Eugene K. Bristow discovered a transition point in the years 1861–1862 in the professional variety theatre in Memphis. By 1861–1862 variety programming had shifted from a dual purpose of instruction and entertainment to entertainment alone. At this time Federal troops entered Memphis and changed the character of both the city and the variety theatre. He found another transition point in the years from 1873 to 1878. The death of the leading entertainer, a can-can dancer whose stage name was Aline LeFravre, and the death of a leading manager, coupled with three yellow-fever epidemics, a national depression, and a rising city debt caused variety theatre to virtually disappear in Memphis. The period between these transition points contained a thriving public entertainment which he called the "low varieties" theatre. He judged this theatre's main characteristics to be "monotony, uniformity, similarity." A structure, thus, took shape in the material. After determining this structure, Bristow chose to examine the question of why manager after manager failed in the low variety business during this period. He ultimately found that success or failure could be ascribed to the way the managers planned and organized their shows.[19]

Such a specific question growing out of the structure discovered in the material can be answered with a thesis statement that will help limit and define the topic. The question is also helpful in determining the relevance of material to the study as the student begins to develop a prospectus. A sample prospectus can be found in the Appendix.

The student may well modify his plans in light of the results of his research. He does not know what he will find until he has been over the ground, and what he discovers should play a prominent role in his decision about the most fruitful question to ask and about the best answer that can be given to that question. He may, also, change the scope of his study because he discovers important transition points or boundaries within the material. Bristow found reason to narrow his topic to the low varieties program even though there was a family type variety theatre in Memphis at this time. He also found the years 1865–1873 as logical boundaries for his study because they

---

[19] "The Low Varieties Program in Memphis, 1865–1873," *QJS*, XLIV (December 1958), 423–427.

defined a characteristic period of variety theatre in Memphis. The student who proceeds in this way is on surer ground than the investigator who decides that he will study the history of the theatre or of public address for an arbitrary period of ten years, for example, from 1860 to 1870.

Graduate students have followed two general approaches to arrive at the scope or limits of historical theses. Some have started with a general area of interest and as their knowledge of the subject grew they have narrowed their topics. Others have started with a more limited study, for example, a term paper, and expanded the scope of the study for a master or doctoral thesis.

John K. Brilhart followed the first course. He began with an interest in forests, hunting, and fishing and first narrowed his topic to a study of speaking about conservation. Next, he focused on the speaking of Gifford Pinchot. After further study he decided to restrict his thesis to the most important year in Pinchot's speaking career. He picked 1909 as the most important and further narrowed the topic to seven speeches that he judged to be most representative. Finally, he focused upon one speech drawn from these seven.[20]

My own master's thesis evolved in much the same way. I began with an interest in studying the ethical responsibility of speakers. This led me to the decision to study a recognized demagogue. I selected Huey Long as fulfilling my requirements. As I studied his speaking career, I was drawn to his national radio broadcasts as some of the most spectacular and interesting speeches that he had given. In addition, they were delivered to a mass audience and the demagogue in Long should come out clearly in such a setting. Further study of the national radio broadcasts indicated that one speech was the most crucial and influential of the entire series. I selected it for the focus of my master's thesis.

Gregg Phifer followed the second path in establishing the limits of his topic. He reports that his doctoral thesis began with a term paper for a history class on Andrew Johnson's "swing around the circle." He enlarged this topic to include the relationship between Johnson's 1866 "swing around the circle" and the victory of the Radical Republicans in the congressional elections.[21]

Donald Parson used a combination of these approaches. He started his doctoral thesis with a term paper for a history course on the speechmaking of the isolationists. He decided to examine this area

---

[20] Reported in Elton S. Carter and Iline Fife, "The Critical Approach," *An Introduction to Graduate Study in Speech and Theatre,* ed. Clyde W. Dow (East Lansing, 1961), pp. 94–98.

[21] Gregg Phifer, "The Historical Approach," in Dow, pp. 72–85.

more intensively and soon found the topic too general for his purpose. He narrowed the topic to the speechmaking of the America First movement. Subsequently he found many state America First Committees as well as the national committee sponsored speakers. His final topic was limited to the speechmaking conducted under the auspices of the National Committee of the America First movement.[22]

BEGINNING THE RESEARCH

Historical studies often grow out of background courses and seminars. A seminar in the history and criticism of public address or the history of the theatre is an excellent place to begin the background study and early development of a topic for a thesis or dissertation. So also is a more specialized seminar in either the major or minor field. The advantage of this kind of birthplace for a research project is that the student is assured of guidance and criticism from the start. He is also forced into a pattern of deadlines which is of great help in getting the study under way.

In the absence of such seminars, graduate advisers usually furnish the deadlines and consultation required. In any event, the early selection of a general area for study is advisable if the student hopes to write a polished historical study.

In the early stages the student should attempt to clarify his viewpoint toward the historical materials with which he is dealing. What are his presuppositions about the theatre or about public address? How much influence on historical events does a great individual have? How important are economic factors? He should express for himself as clearly as he can, whatever presuppositions he has as he begins his study.

STRUCTURE

As he begins to examine the historical materials from this viewpoint, the historian should try to find *structure* in the materials. Structure in this sense is not the same as arranging the results of historical research on sheets of paper. The structure that the scholar finds may well serve the function of organizing his completed monograph, but that is a byproduct of the main function of structure which is to reveal a coherence and unity to the events under consideration

---

22 Mr. Parson and I discussed the way he narrowed the topic for his thesis while he was working on it at the University of Minnesota.

that help explain, in the sense of historical explanation discussed in Chapter 5.[23]

THE NATURE OF STRUCTURE

Contrary to the assumption of the scientific historians, the researcher does not "find" structure in his material as one might find a penny on the street because the penny happens to be there and any other passer-by might find it too. The structure he finds is a function of the historical events that he is studying, to be sure; but it is also a function of his viewpoint and his genius or talent. In a way, the scholar as much *invents* the structure as finds it. Two scholars studying the same events from different viewpoints will find or invent different structures to explain the materials and yet both studies may be excellent, indeed classical, works. Adam Smith and Karl Marx, studying economic events from different viewpoints, found very different structures in them and yet both wrote classical works in economics. This possibility of finding different structures in the same events partly accounts for the importance and necessity of reinterpreting history from time to time.

The classical works of scholarship have revealed this kind of structure in their materials. In addition, these classical structures are so apt, persuasive, and applicable to other materials, that the works expressing them remain relevant and interesting to succeeding generations of scholars. Applying classical structures to new materials is a risky business, however. When scholars apply in imitative fashion the framework developed in the study of a particular set of events to other events the results may do violence to the material under study. Quite often new material will have to be forced into inappropriate molds if the classical form is applied to them without adaptation. Marxist scholars who have used the structure of *Das Kapital* to explain diverse economic, historical, and cultural materials furnish an example of what can happen in this regard.

Not all scholars have the genius to write studies that will become classics; but unless the scholar has talent enough to find structure of some sort in his research, he can hardly be said to be writing a scholarly work at all.

STRUCTURE AND SPEECH SCHOLARSHIP

The discovery of structure in a historical work is pertinent to all historical investigation in speech but has particular pertinence to the writers of history of the theatre. A graduate student in writing a his-

---

[23] For the term "structure" and, to some extent, for the concept as I use it, I am indebted to C. Wright Mills, *The Sociological Imagination* (New York, 1959).

tory of the commercial theatre in Los Angeles, California, may be overwhelmed by the wealth of information he can collect about who appeared in Los Angeles when, where, and in what play. He may discover that there is much information about who owned what theatres at what time and where the theatres were located. Additional research may indicate the size, architecture, scene machinery, lighting facilities, fire escapes, and interior decorations of theatre houses in the period under investigation. He may find information about box-office prices, managers, producers, and theatre owners and financial failures and successes. Finally, he may be impressed by the work of several local critics who regularly reviewed the major theatrical events in the period he is studying.

Having gathered all this information, he is now faced with the problem of writing a history of the theatre in Los Angeles. Even if he has thought but little about his viewpoint towards history and towards theatre, if he has not searched for structure in this welter of information, he may, nonetheless, write a dissertation of some sort. What the student will do, then, in addition to collecting the information, is find some method of selecting and arranging the material. He can easily do this. He might, for example, do a chapter on famous actors and actresses who played in Los Angeles, another on theatre owners and managers, another on theatre finances, and yet another on critics of the theatre. But if he proceeds in this fashion, when he finishes, he will have a dissertation that looks like a telephone directory. A historian on the examining committee of a Ph.D. candidate who had just submitted such a history of the theatre to the graduate school was heard to mutter as he left the oral examination, "That just isn't history. Any competent secretary could have done it." Scholarship requires something more than this, namely, the bringing to bear of an articulate viewpoint on the materials, and the discovery of a structure that accounts for the events under study.

In selecting the following examples of structures from scholarly works in speech, I have drawn from readily accessible studies published in the *Quarterly Journal of Speech*. You may, therefore, examine in each case the entire descriptive article and see how the structure works in context. Of necessity, my treatment will be brief and will not do full justice to the explanatory power of the structure.

In examining how Eugene K. Bristow limited the scope of his history of the "low varieties" in Memphis, we saw how an explanatory form began to emerge. Bristow was not content to list the variety theatres, the managers, the performers, and the programs in chronological order. He found the terminus dates for what he judged to be a unique kind of variety theatre aimed at an all-male audience.

In summary, Bristow found the following structure in his materials. The advent of Federal troops encouraged the development of a unique kind of variety theatre in Memphis. This variety theatre flourished during the war and continued after the war but was no longer supported in the postwar period as it had been during the war. In the period of retrenchment, cut-throat competition developed among managers and expressed itself in attempts at novelty and frantic imitation of successful acts. A uniquely successful act, a can-can dancer, that could not be imitated climaxed this development and resulted in the death of this form of variety theatre in Memphis.

Another example of structure can be found in an article by Lenyth and O. G. Brockett called "J. M. Barrie and the Journalist at His Elbow." [24] This study was undertaken to answer the question concerning the influence of Barrie's apprenticeship in journalism on his career as a playwright. To do this the Brocketts examined the way Barrie wrote his plays. The structure they found in Barrie's creative process is similar to the structure of the creative process developed in Chapter 7. Barrie's creativity was stimulated by a number of personal observations, anecdotes, and stories told by others. He often moved from fact to fiction—picking a topic for a play that enabled him to use his personal experience. He characteristically would record an idea for a play in his journal and then turn it over in his mind for a considerable period of time before he actually was stimulated to start writing. During this period he did a great deal of preparatory work, making extensive and meticulous notes. These notes seemed to be used "as a device to stimulate his imagination" rather than as plans for the play itself. He often prepared scenarios but when he started to write he ignored these plans in order to let his story grow as it would. His muse frequently led him far afield. The period of lush inventiveness was followed by long periods of careful revision and pruning. He rewrote extensively and usually revised his plays during production. In summary, the structure consists of a moment of conception followed by extensive preparatory work, followed by a fallow period, followed by the actual writing when Barrie's inventiveness was given free rein, followed by extensive revision. The Brocketts judged that these features "all illustrate how far he had departed from what is generally thought of as the journalistic method." [25]

A final example of structure is the one found by Wilbur Samuel Howell in his study of "Ramus and English Rhetoric: 1574–1681." [26]

---

[24] *QJS*, XLIV (December 1958), 413–422.
[25] Lenyth and O. G. Brockett, p. 422.
[26] *QJS*, XXXVII (October 1951), 299–310.

Howell selected this time period because he judged the "period between 1574 and 1681 witnessed the death of the Medieval world and the birth of the modern world." [27] In this period, Howell found Ramus a transitional figure, not a rebel fighting medieval thought but rather a reformer who maintained the medieval outlook. Ramus insisted that the liberal disciplines should exist as separate and independent entities. He wished each subject to be rigidly defined. He found that rhetoric and dialectic overlapped in the invention and disposition of ideas. Ramus, whose primary interest was dialectic, tidied up this overlap by pruning from rhetoric the canons of invention and disposition. Rhetoric was then left with style and delivery as its province since the fifth canon, memory, was also detached from rhetoric and made part of disposition in dialectic. When Ramus' dialectic was translated into English in 1574 by Roland Mac-Illmaine there was an English system of dialectic and rhetoric. Thomas Wilson was representative of this rhetoric. The collision between the native English dialectic and rhetoric and the Ramist theory resulted in a complete victory for the French invader. Howell found, however, that almost as soon as the Ramist reforms won the field, they became obsolete. The separation of the investigative responsibilities of speakers and writers from their presentational responsibilities took place at a moment in history when other forces were working to bring these responsibilities together. The rhetoric that developed under the influence of Ramus' reforms had little to say to "the brave young science" of the time. The scientists, the representatives of the newly born modern world, wanted a theory of communication adequate to needs of scientist talking to scientist and of scientist talking to the public.

The basic figures underlying this structure are those of death and birth, conflict and collision. The broad general framework or outer structure involves the death of medieval thought and the birth of modern thought. Within this main structure is the collision of the ideas of the reformer Ramus with the rhetoric of Thomas Wilson. The Ramist reforms won the fight in England but the victory was hollow because developments within the broader structure were making the Ramist system obsolete.

To the extent that historians have developed a method for gathering evidence and testing documents so that general agreement can be reached by different investigators about the truth or falsity of specific statements of fact, history can be called "objective" or "scientific." To the extent that what actually happened controls and

---

[27] Howell, p. 300.

limits him, the historian functions as a scholar and differs from the playwright and the novelist.

Insofar as historians approach their task with different viewpoints and with varying talent for discovering structure in their material, it can be said that history is an art and requires the application of imagination. As the historian Frederick Marcham told the members of the Speech Association of America in 1948, "While we seek as much as we can of an authentic record our claim to respect as scholars, shall we say artists, lies in our ability to illuminate the fragments left us with the light of our imagination." [28] In short, as the scholar begins his careful investigation and testing of the sources, his imagination should begin to work on the material. The student should find useful hints for this phase of his research in the discussion of creativity in Chapter 7. If problems that cause frustration and seem dead ends can be put out of mind for a time, the subconscious will frequently go to work on them and find a solution. Regular work habits will set the creative machinery in motion more rapidly. If the student is lucky, he will begin to get hunches and ideas that solve some of his minor problems; and the excitement generated by this kind of creative thinking will add interest to his study. At some point, when he is deeply immersed in his subject, he should have a major insight and see the basic structure of his entire study. Such moments are not frequent; but when they come, they furnish the greatest intellectual excitement and deepest satisfaction for the scholar.

THE WRITING OF A SCHOLARLY STUDY

Creative insight is most likely to come to the student after he has started to write. The muse does not want to be commanded or forced. Each scholar must learn the nature of his talent and how best to use it.

STARTING TO WRITE

One of the most maddening features of creativity is that it fights work. There are pencils to be sharpened, typewriter ribbons to be changed, glasses of water to be drunk, and windows to be opened. When you are faced with a card file of notes and a clean sheet of typing paper, you may find that the first sentence is the most difficult of all. How you work in this stage of composition is a personal matter. An outline is not the logical starting place for everyone. Some people would be better advised to start writing to stimulate their

---

[28] Frederick G. Marcham, "History and Speech: Collaborative Studies, Present and Future," *QJS*, XXXV (October 1949), 288.

imagination. Major insight and the structure you are searching for may emerge as writing begins; however, in this approach there is considerable waste motion and effort. Unnecessary pages are written and must be discarded. A number of dead ends are run down before the right way is found. As in most artistic enterprises, the professional learns a better way, but he must always learn his own personal way. He must cut his own path through to artistic competence. As he writes more history, the student learns about writing, and he can do more of the preparatory analysis ahead of the actual writing. He conditions his muse to begin without the stimulation of pen and paper or typewriter.

Doctoral dissertations in speech that employ the historical method frequently suffer because this last, and very important, step in the writing of history is neglected or omitted. One of the reasons for this is the haste with which some graduate students attempt to synthesize their historical studies. They may spend several years gathering data, but they hope to write the dissertation in six months. If they can use outlining procedure before writing and if they can stimulate their imagination to find patterns and structure in their material before they begin to write, this is not an unreasonable schedule; but too many students have no notion about these matters when they begin to write. If they must follow the more circuitous route of most neophytes, then a more reasonable approach to a historical dissertation would be to divide the time available evenly between searching for material and writing the study.

USING AN OUTLINE

An outline is a practical time saver if the student has a personality that adjusts to such straightforward methods of planning. Every scholarly paper calls for some difficult intellectual decisions about selection, arrangement, and proportioning of materials. What quotations should be used and where? What arrangement will most clearly present the structure that emerges from the study? What matters are of greatest importance and need the most space? What matters deserve to be mentioned, but only briefly? If such questions as these can be answered by the use of the outlining technique, it should by all means be used; and it will simplify considerably the writing of the first draft.

The outline should be considered primarily as a tool to make the writer face up to specific questions of this type and not as a strait jacket for the writing of the first draft. Should the actual writing stimulate the creativity of the student into a more efficient arrangement of materials, or cause him to modify his original estimate of the importance of various materials, he should by all means adopt these amendments if they stand the tests of critical evaluation.

If the student discovers that the outline fails to get answers to the questions suggested above and fails to force him to specific organizational tasks, he may have to begin writing the first draft without benefit of an outline. He should, however, use an outline at any point along the way where it can help him check and strengthen the organization of his study.

THE IMPORTANCE OF DISCIPLINE

When the actual writing begins, the student should study his writing habits and set up deadlines and a writing schedule. The muse is stimulated by disciplined work habits; and if the writer waits for inspiration to come before he starts writing, he gets little inspiration. Most writers discover that their writing energies are highest at some particular time of day. Some prefer early morning, others like to write late at night; still others work at mid-day. Perhaps other duties make it impossible for the scholar to select the best time of day to schedule his writing; but if you can plan the writing and reschedule other responsibilities in advance, you should do so. If there are pressing demands for the morning hours, although that is the best time for you to write, you must work in a writing schedule at the next best time, or failing in that, at any time available. Some writers may be able to work all day and far into the night for short periods of time, but most of them prefer to write regular hours each day and usually from four to six hours every day. Certainly the beginning scholar who tries to write for extended periods, as he would cram for an examination, is going to encounter trouble. Physically he may persist, but his creative imagination will not survive such cramming.

The writing schedule should be rigidly adhered to. If the time set aside is 6 A.M. to 8 A.M., you should seat yourself at your work table and force yourself to write something during each two hour period. You may not feel like writing, and you may find dozens of excuses and distractions; but if you force yourself to write some each day, you will soon discover that you are disciplining your muse and it will take a shorter period to warm up before you get under way. Even if what you write seems very bad, you should push ahead, carving out the first draft.

THE WARM-UP PERIOD

In addition to sticking to a writing schedule, you can speed up the warm-up period each day by trying to write in the same environment each time. Using the same desk or table in the same corner of the room will help condition your creativity. Another secret is to stop in mid-flight rather than at the end of a chapter or section. If you stop when you know what the next sentence will be, you will be able to find that sentence more quickly when you start the next day. Reading the last few pages of the manuscript will often help create the proper mood to start writing again.

THE USE OF QUOTATIONS

As the first draft gets under way, the beginner meets one of the major differences between the creative writer and the scholarly writer. The scholar must curb his creativity when it begins to do violence to the evidence that he has collected about the historical events under study. He must tie his narrative back into the historical traces by means of quotations and footnotes. His account must remain firmly grounded in evidence.

This means that he must decide when to quote and how much to quote. A very common fault of first drafts by beginners is that they consist of little more than quotations with a few transition statements tying them together. The first draft should be written with an absolute minimum of quotation. Quotations can be kept to a minimum by condensing and paraphrasing the ideas and, when necessary, inserting direct quotations of short phrases from the original that contain the pith of the quotation. Of course credit must be given to the source even when the material is condensed and paraphrased. For an example of this technique examine the samples of structure used earlier in this chapter.

The scholar will benefit from using enough quotations from the original sources thereby providing the reader with a clear impression of the nature and quality of the evidence upon which the conclusions of the study are based.

If the words of the original are particularly apt or picturesque, direct quotations from them may have the added virtue of making the account more interesting. Sometimes the original puts the meaning so well that a paraphrase would be difficult and presumptuous if not impossible.

Short quotations (four or five lines or less) can be worked directly into the text if they are set off by quotation marks. Long quotations are set off from the regular text by indentation and are not enclosed in quotation marks.

Extreme care should be taken in selecting quotations and in paraphrasing sources to make sure that the context of the quotation is adequately accounted for in the way the material is used. The quotation and the comment made about the quotation should accurately reflect the meaning of the original document.

FOOTNOTES

All quotations should be footnoted to indicate clearly the source of the material. Footnotes should be indicated by Arabic numerals elevated slightly above the line indexed in both typewritten and printed texts. In printed texts the footnotes are commonly gathered at the bottom of the pertinent page, although they are sometimes collected at the end of chapters or even at the back of the volume. For theses and dissertations, a given graduate school or department will have a preferred method of collecting footnotes. The numbers in the footnotes should be elevated in the same fashion as the index numbers in the text with no space between the figures and the words of the footnote.

The footnote number should be placed at the end of the sentence containing the material referred to in the note. Sometimes it is necessary to refer to more than one source within a sentence. In this case the footnote should be placed at the end of the phrase containing the information drawn from that particular source.

Footnotes should be used to indicate not only the sources of direct quotations but also the sources of every statement of fact, opinion, and evaluation not the author's. The line between scholarship and plagiarism is not always clear but careful footnoting is the main technique that the scholar uses to maintain his integrity in this matter. This general rule needs to be amended in regard to information that is the common knowledge of the informed reader. The statement that Lincoln and Douglas held seven joint debates in Illinois in 1858 does not need to be footnoted in speech theses and articles. Such information may need to be included in order to place the study into historical context, but it is not necessary to footnote the secondary sources for such information, *unless*, of course, the interpretation of one or two works is followed closely in the development of the general history.

Footnotes are also used to refer to other portions of the work and to cite other discussions of the same material for the reader who may want to read more on the topic under discussion. In addition, footnotes are sometimes used to elaborate on textual material. This use of footnotes can easily become an abuse, and the impulse to use footnotes for irrelevancies and for important material that the author has not taken the time and trouble to work into the text should be carefully restrained. Footnotes can also be used to exhibit ability with foreign languages and in other ways put on a pedantic display.

Such abuses of the footnote will only serve to irritate and disturb the reader.[29]

When footnotes are used to document the source of information reported in the text, you should observe a consistent footnote form. The system of writing footnotes recommended by the *MLA Style Sheet* is often used for historical studies in speech and theatre arts. Footnotes documenting sources contain much the same information as bibliographical notations. For first references to books the following information, in this order, is recommended: the author's name, the title, the editor or translator, the edition, the series, the publication data, the volume number, and the page reference. First references to periodicals should include the following information in this order: the author's name, the title, the name of the publication, the volume number, the issue number, the page reference. The form of footnotes generally differs to some extent from the form suggested for bibliographical notations. In addition, when a footnote is used to refer to a source that has been cited previously it is abbreviated. The following list indicates the basic forms for first references to common sources.

(1) *One author*
      [1] C. Wright Mills, *The Sociological Imagination* (New York, 1959), p. 27.

(2) *Two authors*
      [2] Lester Thonssen and A. Craig Baird, *Speech Criticism* (New York, 1948), p. 9.

(3) *Three authors*
      [3] Herbert A. Smith, Kenneth E. Anderson, and Oscar M. Haugh, *Thesis Handbook* (Danville, Ill., 1957), pp. 100–101.

(4) *More than three authors*
      [4] Oscar Handlin, *et al., Harvard Guide to American History* (Cambridge, 1954), p. 32.

(5) *Editor of a collection*
      [5] Merle Curti ed., *American Scholarship in the Twentieth Century* (Cambridge, 1953), p. 31.

(6) *Translator of original work*
      [6] Marc Bloch, *The Historian's Craft,* trans. Peter Putnam (New York, 1953), pp. 138–189.

(7) *Article by one author in collection edited by another*
      [7] W. Stull Holt, "Historical Scholarship," *American Scholar-*

---

[29] For a spoof of some common abuses of footnotes see Richard Murphy, "On Footnotes and Citations. Shoptalk," *QJS*, XLV (October 1959), 345–349.

ship in the Twentieth Century, ed. Merle Curti (Cambridge, 1953), pp. 95–96.

(8) *Article in journal—author given*
    [8] Eugene K. Bristow, "The Low Varieties Program in Memphis, 1865–1873," *QJS,* XLIV (December 1958), 424.

(9) *Article in a periodical—no author given*
    [9] "Impeachment or Persecution in Louisiana?" *New Republic,* LVIII (April 24, 1929), 268–269.

(10) *For a book review*
    [10] Eleane E. McDavitt, Review of *The Golden Age of the New Orleans Theatre,* by John S. Kendall, *QJS,* XXXVIII (April 1952), 224

(11) *Newspapers*
    [11] *Chicago Tribune,* June 5, 1960, p. 1.

(12) *Theses and dissertations*
    [12] Paul Davee, "Philosophy Underlying the Recognition and Teaching of Theatre as a Fine Art in the Liberal Arts and Graduate Curricula at the State University of Iowa," Ph.D. dissertation, State University of Iowa, 1950, p. 42.

The first reference to a source may be modified if information such as the author's name or the title of the publication is included in the text. If such information appears in the text it is generally omitted from the footnote in the first reference to the publication.

When making a second or additional reference to the same source you may abbreviate the footnote substantially. Often you may use only the author's last name and the page reference. However, if you have previously cited another work by the same author you will have to add the title as well as the author's last name. Thus, the second or later reference to the work in sample footnote 1 above could be "Mills, pp. 100–101." If another work by C. Wright Mills has been footnoted previously a short title should be added as, for example, "Mills, *Sociological Imagination,* pp. 100–101." If you have cited works by two different men both named Smith you will have to include their first names in subsequent footnotes. The main thing to keep in mind in making second and later references is to be brief and clear.

If you are writing a scholarly paper or thesis you should become so familiar with these fundamentals of footnoting procedure that you need not pause in your work to consult a style manual for each footnote. However, you should have a good style manual at your elbow to help with the special problems of footnoting that are posed by government documents of various countries, privately printed and unprinted materials, reports, proceedings, legal citations, scriptural, literary, and classical references, letters, private files, and interviews. In general, the main requirements for footnoting the sources of information are clarity, completeness, and consistency.

In addition to documenting the source of information, you may wish to include explanatory material and other information in footnotes. Such content footnotes may consist entirely of explanatory material such as footnote 18 in this chapter or they may consist of comment supported by references to other works or annotations suggesting other references to be consulted on a particular point. For examples of this use of content footnotes see numbers 2, 16, 23 in this chapter.

On occasion, as we have noted, footnotes are used to refer to other parts of your paper. This can be done by using *"Supra,* p. 15" or "Above, p. 15" to refer to something mentioned previously and *"Infra,* p. 415" or "Below, p. 415" to refer to something that is dealt with later in the paper. Either the Latin or English terms should be used throughout; you should not alternate between the two.

THE SECOND DRAFT

Once the first draft is completed it should be carefully examined for major organizational flaws. Has one section grown all out of proportion in the writing? Is it now apparent that two sections would be better combined and condensed into one section of the study? Can certain parts be cut and do others need to be expanded and developed? Are there sufficient transitions and summaries? Are quotations woven skillfully into the narrative?

At this point some writers prefer to cut the paper apart literally, with a pair of scissors and paste it together again in more satisfactory order. Others prefer to run the whole thing through their typewriter once more. In addition to eliminating major organizational flaws the second draft should shape up weak points, revise faulty conclusions, and where necessary strengthen the development of ideas.

THE THIRD DRAFT

The third revision can then be used largely for stylistic polishing. Spelling, punctuation, awkward phrasing, trite language, and ambiguous statements, should be corrected at this stage. Because well-written history is generally dependent upon at least this much re-working, one should allot enough time for adequate revision.

THE SCHOLARLY STYLE

A perennial problem of the historian has been the question of the proper style for the writing of history. Should history be written in the precise, involved, and sometimes uninteresting style of the scientist, or should it be written in a literary style? In the period of the scientific historians, the more literary style of the older historians such as Bancroft was discounted, and the language of the natural sciences was preferred. As Carl Becker noted in discussing the difficulty that the scientific historians had in labeling Francis Parkman because he wrote well and was also meticulous about discovering and testing sources, "If Parkman had only written badly, no one could question his scientific standing." [30]

The controversy is probably not as real as it may seem on the surface. Insofar as the historian is using expository techniques to describe events, his language must be as accurate and precise as he can make it. On the other hand, the historian does not confine himself to the exposition of factual information. If literary style is interpreted to mean a misleading or inaccurate style, as it sometimes is, then of course that style is inappropriate to history. Hockett accuses Bancroft of using a "literary" style in describing the colonists at Lexington when he wrote:

> How women, with heaving breasts, bravely seconded their husbands! how the countrymen forced suddenly to arm without guides or counsellors, took instant counsel of their courage! The mighty chorus of voices rose from the scattered farmhouses, and as it were, from the very ashes of the dead. . . .[31]

Using language in this fashion undoubtedly does violence to the facts and is not defensible. If literary style is interpreted to mean the more florid and grand style of the nineteenth century which has since gone out of fashion, then its use would be inappropriate.

However, if "literary" is interpreted to mean using language in a graceful, accurate way, then the controversy tends to disappear. The historian must express many nuances of meaning to interpret accurately his analysis of the historical events under study. He must be careful to say what he means and connote the shades of meaning that are to be found in a study of history.[32]

---

[30] Carl Becker, *Everyman His Own Historian* (New York, 1935), p. 135.
[31] Homer Carey Hockett, *Introduction to Research in American History* (New York, 1950), p. 95.
[32] For an excellent statement on this problem see Marc Bloch, *The Historian's Craft,* trans. Peter Putnam (New York, 1953), pp. 138–189.

SUMMARY

The scholar in speech using the historical method should become aware of his view of man and the world as this will be reflected in his selection of data and his interpretation of historical events. These assumptions can be called his point of view. The major viewpoints used by historians in the past have included the theological concept, the "germ" theory, scientific history, the significance of the frontier, the importance of urbanization, the impact of science, the deterministic viewpoint, and the "Great Man" theory of history. The student in speech will have some assumptions that grow out of his study and practice in the field. He may employ one assumption primarily or he may take a pluralistic viewpoint. He should be aware of his assumptions and clearly avow them.

The graduate student is faced with a variety of topics and a number of suitable methods for research work. If history and the prospect of spending hours and days in the scholarly routine excite him, he might well pick the historical method.

Once he picks this research methodology he should develop a program of studies that will fill in his historical background and competence. The topic for his study may come before or after the selection of a research method. Sometimes the two come simultaneously.

When the general area of study has been selected, the student should become familiar with the background material. After getting a general picture he should focus his study more sharply. Background reading will usually point up some features of particular interest or pertinence for the student. Narrowing the topic in this way allows the researcher to concentrate his attention on the discovery and evaluation of primary source material. As his study of the primary material bearing on his narrowed topic continues, the investigator should find a structure in the material that will enable him to form a thesis statement. This statement of theme is useful as a working title for his study and helps to limit the topic.

In the early stages of a scholarly study, deadlines, guidance, and criticism are helpful to the graduate student. At this point, he should clarify for himself the viewpoint that he brings to the study. As this study proceeds, he should strive to find a structure in his materials. And the structure he finds will be a function of the historical events that he is studying and of his viewpoint. It will serve to reveal a coherence in the material and to give an explanation of the events.

There is often a temptation to prolong the gathering of data and cut short the period allotted for writing. The graduate student doing a scholarly study should leave enough time for his writing of the work. Outlining the first draft is helpful for some but others may have to start writing before they begin to digest and interpret the materials of their study. The first draft should be carved out in a disciplined fashion. A definite writing schedule should be established and followed. In this first draft quotations should be short and used sparingly. Footnotes should be employed primarily to indicate the source of statements of fact, opinion, and evaluation that are not the author's. The second draft should be used to remedy major organizational and developmental flaws. The third draft can then be used to polish the language and improve the mechanics of the work. Good scholarly monographs generally require three such drafts as a minimum for sound writing.

Scholarship can be considered a literary art and writing is an important part of the scholar's talents. The scholar does not have the license to create false impressions or to overdramatize by his use of language, but he does have a responsibility to communicate the nuances of meaning required for a scholarly work.

SUGGESTED READINGS

Becker, Carl. *Everyman His Own Historian.* New York: Appleton-Century-Crofts, Inc., 1935.

Bloch, Marc. *The Historian's Craft,* trans. Peter Putnam, New York: Alfred A. Knopf, Inc., 1953.

Gottschalk, Louis. *Understanding History: A Primer of Historical Method.* New York: Alfred A. Knopf, Inc., 1950.

Handlin, Oscar, *et al. Harvard Guide to American History.* Cambridge: Harvard University Press, 1954.

Hockett, Homer C. *The Critical Method in Historical Research and Writing.* New York: The Macmillan Company, 1955.

Hook, Sidney. *The Hero in History.* New York: The John Day Company, Inc., 1943.

Muller, Herbert J. *The Uses of the Past.* New York: Oxford University Press, 1953.

Nevins, Allan. *The Gateway to History.* Boston: D. C. Heath and Company, 1938.

The Social Sciences in Historical Study. A Report of the Committee on Historiography, Social Science Research Council. Bulletin 64, 1954.

Theory and Practice in Historical Study. A Report of the Committee on Historiography, Social Science Research Council. Bulletin 54, 1946.

Turabian, Kate L. *A Manual for Writers of Term Papers, Theses, and Dissertations.* Chicago: The University of Chicago Press, 1955.

Wecter, Dixon. "History and How to Write It," *American Heritage,* VIII (August 1957), 24–27, 87.

Projects

1) Assume you are thinking of writing a history dealing with some area of speech or theatre arts. Write a short paper in which you express the main assumptions regarding history, speech, or theatre that would be part of your viewpoint while writing such a history.

2) Select a topic for a historical thesis in speech or theatre and write a prospectus in which you:

a) describe the problem to be investigated
b) discuss the previous research in the area
c) justify the worth of the study
d) outline the sources available to you in doing the study
e) describe the way you would do the study.

3) Select a historical thesis written for an advanced degree at your school and write a short paper evaluating the structure used to explain the historical events.

4) Select a historical study published in a speech journal and write a short paper describing the viewpoint of the author as expressed or implied in the article.

5) Write a short paper in which you evaluate your personal qualifications as a historian.

Questions for Discussion

1) Compare and contrast scholarly history with historical fiction. What are the advantages and disadvantages of each approach?

2) How scientific is history?

3) To what extent can a historian reconstruct what actually happened in the past?

4) On what grounds would you justify studying the very same historical events that have been the subject of a previous scholarly work?

5) What are the advantages and the disadvantages of assuming that historical events are best explained by assuming that multiple causes of varying strengths account for historical change?

6) Would it be better for graduate students in history or graduate students in speech to write historical studies about speech events?

CHAPTER ELEVEN

RHETORICAL AND DRAMATIC CRITICISM

THE CRITICAL METHOD APPLIED TO SPEECH

THE NATURE OF RHETORICAL AND DRAMATIC CRITICISM

Even the most naïve member of an audience may be moved to discuss a play. He may talk of the things the playwright was trying to say. He may discuss the people in the play and why he has liked or disliked them. He may remember a particularly vivid or exciting bit of action. He may be impressed with the beauty of the language or how "true to life" it sounded. He may remember a clever or funny line. He may make some comment about the skill of the playwright as a craftsman. Such discussion can increase his enjoyment and understanding of the particular play and of drama in general.

Criticism is this sort of discussion refined by scholarship. The difference between naïve personal reaction to a play or speech and scholarly criticism of the same work is that scholarship furnishes the critic with a set of standards to guide his evaluation of the speech or play and a context of dramatic and rhetorical tradition to aid him in making judgments about the work.

Criticism may have practical byproducts such as the establishing of standards of taste and the developing of techniques of craftsmanship, but in the main it is an act of appreciation. An important aim of scholarly criticism in speech is increased appreciation and understanding of rhetoric and drama.

SCHOLARLY CRITICISM AND PLAY REVIEWING

Scholarly criticism should be distinguished from the journalistic practice of play reviewing. Dramatic critics write reviews of new productions to guide their readers in selecting plays or movies to attend. The television reviewer has a more ambiguous function. At first television critics presented reviews that were in the tradition of play reviewers. That is, comments on yesterday's television fare. However, since the television drama was seldom repeated the television critic, for the most part, was forced to become a popular columnist, who discussed television personalities and future programs, and who sometimes functioned as a critic of the entire industry.

Of course play reviewing and dramatic criticism are related, for some writers of play reviews also write scholarly criticism. George Jean Nathan and Eric Bentley have written theatrical criticism as well as journalistic reviews of theatrical productions. The two practices, while related, are not the same.

LITERARY, RHETORICAL, AND DRAMATIC CRITICISM

A close kinship exists between literary criticism on the one hand, and rhetorical and dramatic criticism on the other. Literary critics deal not only with novels and poems but also with speeches and plays. The literary critic functions in much the same way and for the same purposes as the rhetorical critic or the dramatic critic or the critic who views literature in terms of the oral interpreting of it for an audience. Literary criticism deals with the literary arts in order to explicate their nature and meaning as artistic expression. The literary critic sometimes changes the focus of his work and becomes a writer of literary or intellectual history, but for the most part, literary critics confine their attention to the description and evaluation of literature as art.

The literary critic generally uses the written text of the work as the basis of his criticism. He studies the text as an example of significant writing. The literary critic often views literature and writing as synonymous. In this respect, the literary critic differs from the rhetorical or dramatic critic and from the oral interpreter of literature. The scholar in speech who writes criticism views the speech, play, or story read aloud as an event involving an audience and an attempt to communicate with that audience by means of speech and gestures. In the case of the play the attempt at communicating with the audience requires, in addition, actors, sets, costumes, directors, and lighting effects. This difference goes far to answer the question of why a research project in speech involving the criticism of speeches, plays, or literature could not just as well have been written for a degree in the English department. The answer is that while a play of Shakespeare, Ibsen, or Shaw is a written manuscript, it is, when performed, also a theatrical event. In the same way, the manuscript of a speech is one thing; the same speech studied as an event involving the speech, the speaker, the audience, and the occasion, is quite different. A great poem is certainly literature; the same poem interpreted orally becomes, as with a speech, an event with additional factors requiring study. The change in viewpoint of the speech critic results, then, in significant changes in his criticism. A critical study of the theatricality of James M. Barrie results in a much different evaluation of Barrie's artistry than does a study of his plays as written literature.[1]

Much literary criticism of drama is based upon the idea that drama is drama whether it is read or viewed in production. George Jean Nathan suggests this position is the same as saying that music is music whether it is read from the score or performed by a symphony orchestra. However, he also remarks, "Why quibble? There is the printed drama—criticize it. There is the drama acted—criticize it." [2] The scholar in speech and theatre arts will criticize both printed and produced drama, but he will tend to do so with a full realization that plays are written to be produced and that there are important differences between a play in manuscript and the same play produced on the stage.

HISTORICAL VERSUS CRITICAL METHOD

The critic of drama or of rhetoric uses the same tools of scholarship as the historian. He exercises the same care when investigating documents and evaluating witnesses. He must footnote his factual statements and draw conclusions with the same logical rigor. Like the historian, the critic develops a viewpoint towards his critical project and attempts to interpret or find structure in the speech or play.

Since the two methods are similar in these elements, they can easily be confused. Unless this confusion is sorted out early in the research project, it will plague the researcher to the end of the study. Just as the speaker whose speech has two central ideas has difficulty organizing his speech clearly, so the scholar trying to write both history and criticism in the same study has difficulty focusing his work.

The differences between the two methods are to be found in the nature of the viewpoints and the kinds of structures for which the historian and the critic search. The historian, in looking at human activity, attempts to find a meaningful structure in the traces of the past that will allow him to write a narrative to explain the historical event. His viewpoint is important in that explanation, for it furnishes him with a framework of causes or factors to apply to a sequence of events. Speeches, plays, novels, and poems certainly qualify for historical study, but the historian approaches such materials as part of man's activity and he studies them with a view of explaining them as a part of man's history. The historian must of necessity be interested in the speaker or author as a person as well as an artist. The historian's

---

[1] William R. McGraw, "The Theatricality of James M. Barrie: An Analysis of His Plays to Determine the Source of Their Effectiveness in the Theatre," Ph.D. dissertation, University of Minnesota, 1958.

[2] George Jean Nathan, *The Critic and the Drama* (New York, 1922), p. 58.

viewpoint requires an examination of the historical setting in which the play was first written and produced, or in which the speech was given. The historian may well be interested in the ideas, the teachers, and books that influenced the playwrights and speakers he is studying. All of these materials are used by the historian to construct a plausible narrative explaining the theatrical activity of a given period in the past, or an orator's speechmaking, or certain plays written and produced in the past, or certain speakers and speeches. If he makes judgments and evaluations of plays and speeches along the way, they will tend to be tangential to his main concern. The historian writing about art is interested in telling the story of that art as it fits into man's cultural history.

The critic's viewpoint, on the other hand, is well expressed in Malcolm Cowley's definition of criticism as *"writing which deals with works of art."* [3] The critic searches for values and universals in art. In so doing, he necessarily works from a series of assumptions about the nature of drama, rhetoric, oral interpretation. These assumptions constitute the critic's viewpoint.

The critic will make assumptions about the importance of such matters as the life of the playwright or speaker in explaining the plays or speeches, the influence of the social background of the time, and the moral and political effects of the play or speech.

For example, a modern school of literary critics adopts the viewpoint that none of these matters is important in the criticism of literary works. Just as some historians believed in the nineteenth century that they should be scientific, this school of literary criticism suggests that the critic should be "scientific." [4] For both the historian and literary critic this use of the term *scientific* tends to refer to the careful collecting and testing of evidence and the use of rigorous logic in developing critical studies. However, this viewpoint often contains the notion that criticism should concentrate on the text and ignore the author's life, his other work, the social climate of the time, his purpose, and the effect of his work. [5] Critics working from these assumptions have made a contribution by focusing attention once again on a careful textual analysis of the work being criticized. [6] If criticism is to function as an aid to the appreciation of the work, the text should certainly figure in the criticism. [7] The critic may, of course, assume that

[3] Malcolm Cowley, "Criticism: A Many-Windowed House," *Saturday Review*, XLIV (August 12, 1961), 47.

[4] Northrop Frye, *Anatomy of Criticism* (Princeton, 1957), p. 8.

[5] For a discussion and criticism of this viewpoint see Cowley, p. 10.

[6] Rene Wellek, "Literary Scholarship," in *American Scholarship in the Twentieth Century*, ed. Merle Curti (Cambridge, 1935), pp. 120–121.

[7] Wellek suggests that this neglect can be traced to the Romantic revolt against neoclassicism which had "the inherited techniques of ancient rhetoric," that "only slowly has a new generation found its way back to these problems." Welleck, p. 136.

speech training, purpose, and skill, the influence of the occasion and the audience are all important in criticizing a speech.

Suffice it to say that the critic, like the historian, brings a critical viewpoint to bear on the works he is studying and like the historian he should become aware of his assumptions and avow them for his reader.

If he does study the life of the playwright and his other writings, he does so only to enable him to understand the play he is studying. If he examines the audience for a speech, he does so only to gain a greater understanding of the speech itself.

The critic's focus on artistry is the major difference between the critical and the historical method. The critic, to do his job fully, must make judgments about the excellence of the work he is criticizing. The historian may say in passing that Shakespeare was a great playwright or Webster a stirring orator, but the critic will explain in detail in what way Shakespeare was a great playwright and why he is judged to be great. To make such evaluations, the critic must establish standards of excellence. These standards should have a certain universality and permanence. The critic is aware of the historical context in which the play or speech was produced, but whether a play was written in three days or three years or whether it was the playwright's first successful play or the last, the critic's judgment may still be based on the merit of the work. He may say that considering the fact that this play was written quickly, it was quite polished, but that nonetheless haste is evident in the poorly constructed third act. In the end, although he may explain the weaknesses in historical terms, the critic must point out the weaknesses and judge the entire work against some artistic standard.

The historian might describe Roman roads as excellent and discuss their location, the reasons for their being built, and their function and effect during the time of the Roman empire. An engineer might discuss the same roads as would a critic of a play, first describing their construction and design, then applying certain standards to these features, and finally judging them to be good roads or bad.

The establishment of artistic standards for appreciating rhetoric or drama or interpretation and for judging the play, speech, novel or poem is the main difference between the function of the critic and the historian.

Can a scholar successfully shift back and forth from the historical method to the critical method in the same study? Such straddling of methods is difficult to manage. The difficulty is particularly pressing when the student does not realize he is using both methods. This question is an important one for students of rhetoric and public address and has some bearing for scholars in drama and interpretation.

Actually one of the most influential critical viewpoints in public address has been the "history and criticism of public address." Because of the importance of this particular field of research and because of its unique nature and problems, the combination approach needs to be examined in greater detail and the opposing schools (or viewpoints) contrasted and discussed.

HISTORY AND CRITICISM OF PUBLIC ADDRESS

THE EFFECT OF THE SPEECH

Herbert A. Wichelns of Cornell University wrote a germinal essay on speech criticism in 1925. He entitled his essay "The Literary Criticism of Oratory." After examining in considerable detail the literary criticism of a number of speakers, Wichelns decided that "the common ground of literary criticism is its preoccupation with the thought and the eloquence which is permanent." Literary criticism tends to view all literature as written literature and to ignore the difference between spoken and written works. Rhetorical criticism, however, "is not concerned with permanence, nor yet with beauty. It is concerned with effect. It regards a speech as a communication to a specific audience, and holds its business to be the analysis and appreciation of the orator's method of imparting his ideas to his hearers." [8]

In 1929, H. Clay Harshbarger completed his doctoral dissertation at Cornell on "Burke's Chief American Works." This study was one of the first to be developed along the lines suggested by Wichelns in his essay on "The Literary Criticism of Oratory." The "guiding principle" in Harshbarger's study was that Burke's "works are to be regarded as resulting from the interplay of three forces—speaker, occasion, and audience." [9] In addition, "The effect of the speeches on the debates in which they occurred is analyzed, and the effect of all the work on Burke's fortunes and those of his cause is recapitulated." [10]

Graduate students at other institutions were also beginning to write studies that examined speeches as resulting from the interaction of speaker, occasion, and audience and that evaluated the effect of those speeches. At the State University of Iowa, for example, A. Craig Baird was beginning a long and distinguished career of guiding graduate students in studies in public address. In 1930, one of the first of Baird's students to complete a doctoral study in public address, William Norwood Brigance, completed his study of Jeremiah S. Black. Baird

---

[8] Herbert A. Wichelns, "The Literary Criticism of Oratory," in *The Rhetorical Idiom*, ed. Donald Bryant (Ithaca, 1958), p. 35.

[9] From an abstract of the dissertation in *QJS*, XVI (June 1930), 384.

[10] Harshbarger, p. 386.

has directed more than one hundred master's theses and some fifty doctoral dissertations, largely in the history and criticism of public address. Basically Aristotelian in his approach to rhetoric, Baird uses classical canons in criticism, but follows Wichelns' doctrine of the importance of the audience and of effect.[11]

William Norwood Brigance edited two volumes of critical studies entitled *The History and Criticism of American Public Address* in 1943. In the preface to this collection, Professor Brigance stated of the studies that "final judgment is here based on effect instead of beauty, on influence instead of appeal to the imagination." [12] Indeed, the majority of the twenty-nine critical essays in these two volumes reflected the Wichelns-Baird approach to criticism. Wichelns contributed an essay on Emerson. A number of the contributors were trained at Iowa or Cornell and many of the essays were based on doctoral studies completed at those two institutions.

In 1947, Professor Baird coauthored, with his former student, Lester Thonssen, an article in the *QJS* entitled "Methodology in the Criticism of Public Address." In this article the emphasis is still clearly on criticism. "What is the goal of the rhetorical investigator?" the authors ask, and answer "It is chiefly criticism." While researchers may study many aspects of speechmaking as well as biographical material relating to the speeches under consideration, "The chief business of the rhetorical scholar, nevertheless, is the evaluation of a speech or speeches. His questions are, 'Is this a good speech? If so, why?' The answers are the essence of his primary research task." [13]

Further reflecting the distinction between history and criticism, the authors say of the process of criticizing speeches that the "judgment here is essentially like that of other art forms. The critic of speeches is confronted with an art, just as is the evaluator of a novel or play." [14]

The Wilchelns' notion that rhetoric "is concerned with effect" had become the central touchstone for evaluating a speech, according to Baird and Thonssen. They wrote, "The judgment concerns the effect of the discourse, or response. To what degree does the audience react favorably to the purpose of the speaker? Such a question, whatever may be the difficulty of interpreting the terms *audience* and *responses,* is the heart of the problem." [15]

In 1948, Professors Thonssen and Baird published a detailed

---

[11] See Orville Hitchcock, "Albert Craig Baird," in *American Public Address: Studies in Honor of A. Craig Baird,* ed. Loren Reid (Columbia, Mo., 1961), pp. xi–xix.

[12] New York, 1943, p. viii.

[13] XXXIII (April 1947), 134.

[14] Baird and Thonssen, 135.

[15] Baird and Thonssen, p. 136.

treatment of the methodology of rhetorical criticism entitled *Speech Criticism.* The book elaborates the basic position of the article on "Methodology in the Criticism of Public Address," and makes an important addition. It presents standards of criticism, developed from rhetorical theory. These standards are to be applied to a given speech and the speech will be found to measure up or to fall short. If it were not for the audience, that all-important feature that distinguishes rhetorical criticism from literary criticism, this would be sufficient for the critic to make a judgment. However, since the audience is involved, and the major canon is effect upon an audience, the rhetorical critic makes a further investigation into the historical context of the speech to discover if the speaker accomplished his purposes. If he did, then a judgment can be made not only about how well he followed the advice of rhetorical theory but also about the effectiveness of rhetorical rules themselves. If the speaker was ungrammatical and yet effective, and the rhetorical theory used as a criterion stated that ungrammatical language will hurt a speaker's ethos and thus his effectiveness, then the rhetorical theory itself must be modified.[16]

Thus, criticism can serve a practical function in that it can test and modify theory. Effectiveness becomes the crucial consideration in judging the worth of the rhetorical theory as well as the speaker's ability.

With *Speech Criticism,* the line of development begun by Wichelns' came to fruition. The viewpoint includes a classical, predominately Aristotelian, set of categories for the description and analysis of speeches. The emphasis in this criticism is upon the oral nature of speechmaking and the reciprocal interaction between speaker and audience. The nature of the audience and the occasion affects the quality of the discourse, according to this viewpoint, and the speech, in turn, influences the audience and, perhaps, the course of history. Finally, critics of this persuasion use rhetorical theory as an aid in evaluating speech practices but assume also, that the results of critical studies of effective speakers will serve to correct and modify rhetorical theory.

---

[16] That effective speakers do break the rules has often been noted. For example, William Trufont Foster, writing from a wide background as a speaker and teacher of public speaking, recalled that "In his talk to the brewers, H. G. Wells blithely violated some of the traditional rules of oratory. Again the truth was forced upon me that nobody can find out what moves audiences today merely by studying the classic utterances of other days. Some speakers who faithfully follow the models in the old textbooks leave the audiences cold—even when the audiences do not leave the speakers. The speeches are rhetorically correct but oratorically soporific. Teachers of speech may as well admit it. On the other hand, some of the best speakers of our time violate rules which were memorized by the old-time students of 'oratory.' These speakers do not respect even the right of a verb to agree with its subject, or the right of an antecedent to have something to antecede." "Random Notes on Public Speaking," *QJS,* XXXIII (April 1947), 139–140.

THE EFFECT VIEWPOINT EXAMINED

Rhetorical criticism written from this viewpoint has certain strengths and, on occasion, has revealed some weaknesses. The viewpoint that emphasizes the importance of studying the effect of speeches when making evaluations of their excellence has been the most influential in rhetorical criticism in this century and has resulted in some of the soundest critical scholarship in speech. Nevertheless, the position has come under attack from time to time. In 1956 Thomas R. Nilsen published an article in the *QJS* devoted to an analysis of the issue. Nilsen concluded his examination by supporting the importance and necessity of evaluating the social consequences of speeches, although he suggested that these consequences be viewed in the broader context of the ultimate effect for good or evil on society rather than in the narrower sense of the effectiveness of the speaker in realizing his purposes.[17]

Other writers on rhetorical criticism have stressed the need to consider effect. Leland Griffen, for example, discussing the rhetorical criticism of historical movements, took as "a first and obvious principle" that "the critic must judge the effectiveness of the discourse." [18] Albert Croft, writing of "The Functions of Rhetorical Criticism," in 1956, accepted the effect criterion as a starting place for his analysis.[19]

Despite the popularity and influence of the viewpoint that includes the study of effect of speeches, the criticism that has resulted from it has, on occasion, been weakened because the critic fell into a trap laid by the assumptions of the position. For example, the attempt by some graduate students to write rhetorical criticisms from this viewpoint has resulted in a confusion of the historical and critical method and a thesis that lacks structure or focus. The viewpoint developed in *Speech Criticism* is not confused. That work clearly focuses on criticism and the critical method. The book treats historiography and biography as it treats the techniques of other disciplines such as logic, sociology, and psychology, as supplementary to the main critical methodology. In practice, however, the emphasis on immediate effect of the speeches has sometimes caused a student to emphasize historical and biographical techniques.

In order for the critic to understand the speech, according to Thonssen and Baird, he has to view the speech as emerging from the interaction of speaker, audience, and occasion; and he has to study the subsequent effect of the speech upon the audience.[20] Therefore, the critic needs to study the speaker, particularly his speech training and

---

17 "Criticism and Social Consequences," *QJS*, XLII (April 1956), 173–178.
18 "The Rhetoric of Historical Movements," *QJS*, XXXVIII (April 1952), 184.
19 "The Functions of Rhetorical Criticism," *QJS*, XLII (October 1956), 283–291.
20 Lester Thonssen and A. Craig Baird, *Speech Criticism* (New York, 1948).

intellectual development; the critic needs to study the audience, and he needs to study the occasion. The critic needs to understand these elements before he examines the speech and tries to explain its nature. Then, the critic must study the events that followed the speech in order to discover its effect upon them.

The student has to exercise great care and considerable skill to keep all of this diverse material coherent and relevant to the speeches themselves and to make the speeches the center of his study. He can easily fall into writing biography and history unrelated to the speeches in the sections dealing with the speaker and the background of the speeches.[21] To be sure, historical and biographical material will have some relationship to the speeches but students sometimes fail to point out these relationships clearly and specifically. As a result the members of the student's graduate committee sometimes ask "Could this study not have been done better in the department of history?" The point of this question is not that historical studies are inappropriate to speech but rather, "How do these long passages of history and biography relate to the speeches and the speaking that you are investigating?"

But this question has not always been clearly answered in public-address dissertations. As more and more history and criticisms of public address was written, the historical elements tended to grow. Doctoral studies sometimes ballooned with historical narrative until they ran into hundreds of pages and were bound in several volumes. Long biographical sections were related in only a perfunctory way, if at all, with the sections criticizing the speech. The historical background grew in length and tended to be historical in viewpoint with little reference to the speeches under study. Such studies were, indeed, history and criticism mixed together.[22]

Using effect as the ultimate criterion for rhetorical criticism has also posed ethical problems. If we base our rhetorical theory on critical standards tested by their effect we run the danger of emphasizing the tricks that achieve the speaker's purposes. Thus, speech criticism based on effect may give sanction to any manipulative technique that works. Thonssen and Baird were troubled by this problem, and the last chapter of *Speech Criticism* discusses the importance of including ethical judgments in rhetorical criticism.

Awareness of a problem does not always suffice to solve it, however. Judging speeches by effect is essentially amoral and hence any attempt to bring questions of right and wrong to bear will result in

---

[21] See Loren Reid, "The Perils of Rhetorical Criticism," *QJS*, XXX (December 1944), 417.

[22] See Donald C. Bryant, "Rhetoric: Its Functions and Its Scope," *QJS*, XXXIX (December 1953), 423.

applying criteria external to the rhetorical standards. Baird's work is illustrative. He tended to use classical answers such as Aristotle's doctrine that rhetoric should be used to defend the truth and Quintilian's notion of the orator as a good man.[23] Another criticism of the effect approach to rhetorical criticism suggests that it has not in fact led to the modification of theory as it has promised. Despite the fact that hundreds of critical studies have been concerned with effective speakers who broke certain rhetorical rules, these rules continue to find their way into textbooks and lectures. Perhaps the fault is not so much with the critical method as it is with the failure of scholarship to survey the results of these critical studies and draw together the results for the purpose of modifying rhetorical theory. Whatever the reasons, the promise of this approach to yield practical results has not been fulfilled.

One of the virtues of *Speech Criticism* is that it sets forth a detailed and concrete set of categories for the analysis of speeches. However, although the authors recognize the arbitrary nature of these categories and warn against approaching every critical problem in the same way, on occasion students have applied these categories without modification in what is sometimes termed the "cookie-cutter" approach to criticism. These studies examine the speaker, speech, audience, and occasion. The speaker's use of supporting material is discussed; his organizational techniques, delivery, and style are studied, employing the categories of *Speech Criticism* in mechanical fashion. But in this process, sometimes the unique and salient features of the rhetoric under examination have slipped through the categories and been lost.

THE EFFECTIVENESS VIEWPOINT

Because of these problems, other approaches to rhetorical criticism have been advocated. One of these, also stemming from the Wichelns' approach, is represented by the writing of Wayland Maxfield Parrish. Parrish accepts the rhetorical viewpoint suggested by Wichelns, but modifies the notion of effect. In an introductory essay to a volume of *American Speeches,* of which he was coeditor with Marie Hochmuth, Parrish starts from an Aristotelian position and suggests that "the critic's concern is not with the literal results of the speech, but with the speaker's use of a correct method; not with the speech's effect, but with its effectiveness." For Parrish effectiveness means that not just any

---

[23] Thonssen and Baird, *Speech Criticism.* See also Croft, "The Functions of Rhetorical Criticism," and Earnest Brandenburg, "Quintilian and the Good Orator," *QJS,* XXXIV (February 1948), 23–29.

audience will do as a basis of judgment; certainly the immediate audience is not necessarily the guide to evaluating effectiveness. "We
admire Burke's great addresses, not because they were well adapted to
the boozy country squires who sometimes sat in Parliament, but because they were designed for better audiences." Thus, the critic will
"interpret and evaluate a speech in terms of its effect upon an audience of qualified listeners." [24]

THE ARTISTIC THEORY

Still a third viewpoint is offered by James H. McBurney and
Ernest J. Wrage in their book *The Art of Good Speech.* They reject
the effect criterion *completely,* and advocate in its place what they
call the "artistic theory" of criticism. Since speech is an art reducible
to principles, judgment of that art must be based upon those principles
and a speech in any situation for any purpose is good insofar as it
demonstrates adherence to the principles of the art of rhetoric and
bad insofar as it departs from them. On the basis of the "artistic theory," a critic should be able to judge the excellence of a speech in
manuscript before it is delivered to an audience or if, indeed, it is not
delivered to an audience at all.[25]

The *artistic theory* carries with it certain practical implications
that are different from those of the *effect* viewpoint. Certainly studies
developed from this viewpoint could do without much history, and
the confusions between history and criticism could be avoided. On the
other hand, this point of view allows little justification for the study of
effective but inartistic speakers. It also tends to blur the distinction
between the literary criticism of oratory and rhetorical criticism of
oratory as drawn by Wichelns.

PLURALISM OF VIEWPOINTS AND METHOD

While some critics have urged a monistic approach the tendency
has been to urge a pluralistic approach to criticism. Professor L. H.
Mouat is one of the few suggesting a unified approach to rhetorical
criticism. "It is not the purpose of this essay," he writes in *The Rhetorical Idiom,* "to make a brief for a particular set of principles that will
bind rhetorical concepts but rather to urge that there be a single set
of principles." Such unification of rhetorical principles would enable
rhetorical critics to "participate in a symposium or in a series of stud-

---

[24] Wayland Maxfield Parrish and Marie Hochmuth eds., *American Speeches*
(New York, 1954), p. 12. See also, Marie Hochmuth, "The Criticism of Rhetoric,"
A History and Criticism of American Public Address, III (New York, 1955), pp.
1–23; Marie Hochmuth Nichols, *Rhetoric and Criticism* (Baton Rouge, 1963).

[25] New York, 1953, pp. 28–31.

ies, so that unnecessary divergencies, confusions, and cross purposes can be minimized." [26]

Despite such calls for uniformity of approach, pluralism has been the dominant theme of the rhetorical critics in terms of viewpoint and method.[27] As William Norwood Brigance wrote in the preface of the first two volumes of *History and Criticism of American Public Address*, "the best scholars are not all adherents to the same philosophy of criticism. Some prefer a pure Aristotelian pattern. Some prefer their Aristotelianism diluted. Others abjure it altogether." [28]

A number of non-Aristotelian category sets have been recommended, and to a limited extent applied, to studies of rhetorical criticism. In addition to categories from General Semantics, readability categories such as Rudolph Flesch's formula,[29] the quantitative approach of content analysis, and the dramatistic approach of Kenneth Burke have been popular.[30]

The pluralistic approach to criticism has virtues of a theoretical and practical nature. Pluralism in critical viewpoint enables a critic to adopt a method for a given project in criticism that is most appropriate to the subject matter. Emerson could be profitably criticized from the effectiveness or artistic point of view.[31] A critical study of Huey Long's speaking from an artistic standpoint probably would give little insight into his rhetoric, whereas, a study that placed his speaking in its historical context and examined the effect of his speeches might well explain his speechmaking.

A pluralistic approach can also be adopted for the critical categories and method. The mechanical application of a set of critical categories for various rhetorical events so that critical studies are ground out like link sausage is to be avoided. Beginning with Aristotelian categories, straight or diluted, or with Kenneth Burke's categories, the critic should develop during the course of his study the most helpful categories for a given criticism. Not only do speeches contain enough unique elements to cause the critic with the "cookie-cutter" approach to lose important insights, but the mechanical applica-

---

[26] "An Approach to Rhetorical Criticism," in *The Rhetorical Idiom*, ed. Donold C. Bryant (Ithaca, 1958), p. 165.

[27] See Croft.

[28] William Norwood Brigance ed., *History and Criticism of American Public Address*, I (New York, 1943), p. x.

[29] Rudolph Flesch, *The Art of Plain Talk* (New York, 1946).

[30] Mouat's categories in "An Approach to Rhetorical Criticism," draw on Kenneth Burke. See also Virginia Holland, "Kenneth Burke's Dramatistic Approach to Speech Criticism," *QJS*, XLI (December 1955), 352–358; "Rhetorical Criticism: A Burkeian Method," *QJS*, XXXIX (December 1953), 444–450; Marie Hochmuth Nichols, *Rhetoric and Criticism* (Baton Rouge), 1963.

[31] See Herbert A. Wichelns, "Ralph Waldo Emerson," in Brigance, pp. 501–525.

tion of a set of critical machinery in this way is nonliterary. Criticism should be a literary art and that requires not only the ability to write in a literate fashion but also the freedom to structure the writing in an artistic way. The steady march of a critic from one Aristotelian category to another is, at best, a try for scientific agreement, or at worst, the substitution of method for insight.

Wayland Maxfield Parrish illustrates the virtues of adapting categories that are appropriate for a particular study in his essay on "The Style of Robert G. Ingersoll." He writes, in part, "Since no standard rubrics are generally accepted for the analysis of style, one may feel free to use whatever analysis seems most fitting for the study of a given writer or speaker. The qualities of Ingersoll's style most likely to strike the attention of a reader are, I believe, its vitality, its conversational directness, and its poetic quality." [32]

THE MEASURE OF INFLUENCE

The problems of measuring influence have to be met not only by the writer of history and criticism of public address but also, on occasion, by the literary critic and the writer of intellectual history.

FAME AND EFFECT

The problem that needs to be faced in determining influence is to discriminate between fame and effect. Fame or reputation is much easier to document and examine than is influence or effect. A man may be famous or infamous and still not have had appreciable influence on others or appreciable effect upon subsequent events. His fame may be largely posthumous and mythical, that is, wholly fictitious, like Oedipus Rex. Or his fame may be a legend that is based on a truthful fraction, like David Crockett's or Wyatt Earp's. As myth or legend a man's fame may be the basis of a cult or religion. Thus, the fame of such historical personages as Joan of Arc, Lenin, Abraham Lincoln, has had an appreciable effect on events. Whether the actual Joan of Arc had as much influence as has her legend is more difficult to discover. Fame, in and of itself, is not proof of influence. A critic, to establish influence must do more than demonstrate that a man or an idea, a speech or a play was often recalled and talked about after the event. Perhaps the frequently mentioned speech or person was less influential than a seldom mentioned speech or person.

---

[32] Wayland Maxfield Parrish, "The Style of Robert G. Ingersoll," in *Studies in Speech and Drama in Honor of Alexander N. Drummond,* ed. Herbert Wichelns (Ithaca, 1944), p. 395.

INTELLECTUAL INFLUENCE

When the problem of fame and effect refers to ideas or artistic phenomenon it becomes even more difficult to solve. Too often students will establish a similarity in two sets of ideas and argue that since the later set is similar to the earlier the first influenced the second. Such an argument is, of course, a version of the *post hoc ergo propter hoc* fallacy.

AN EXAMPLE OF THE PROBLEM

Certain biographers of Huey Long, including Forrest Davis and Carleton Beals, concluded that State Senator S. J. Harper of Winnfield, Louisiana, had profoundly influenced Huey Long's thinking. The evidence for such a conclusion was misleading. During World War I Senator Harper had published a book which he entitled *Issues of the Day—Free Speech—Financial Slavery*. Harper was indicted on a charge of violating the Espionage Act. Julius Long, Huey's oldest brother, was the chief attorney for State Senator Harper, but Huey helped defend the case.[33] During the course of the litigation Huey wrote a letter to the New Orleans *Item* in which he stated in part, "A conservative estimate is that about sixty-five or seventy percent of the entire wealth of the United States is owned by two percent of the people." [34] The letter continued in this vein reflecting some of the statistics in Senator Harper's pamphlet. Some fifteen years later, when Long actively began pushing the notion of "Share-Our-Wealth," he used some of these same statistics repeatedly in speeches and articles. Indeed, his ideas in 1933 were very similar to Harper's ideas in 1918. In addition to the evidence of the letter to the editor, Long had accompanied Harper to the state legislature to lobby for a bill to increase workmen's benefits. The conclusion was easy to draw, as Forrest Davis did, when he wrote:

> A historian of the future I should judge, would be justified in believing that Huey had entered into discipleship to Senator Harper before the United States entered the world war and that Harper shares with Moses and Winn's ancient radicalism the bulk of the credit for inspiring Share-Our-Wealth.[35]

Not everyone was convinced, however. Among the doubters were a number of citizens of Winnfield, Louisiana, who had known both Long and Harper. Included among these was Harley Bozeman who had

---

[33] *The Times-Picayune* (New Orleans), February 22, 1918, p. 15.
[34] *The Item* (New Orleans), March 1, 1918, ed. p.
[35] Forrest Davis, *Huey Long* (New York, 1935), p. 73.

gone through grade school and part of high school with Huey and who had worked with him in his early political career. Bozeman was sure that rather than being influenced by Harper, Long had used Harper for political purposes. The striking similarity between the ideas of Long and Harper as revealed by Huey's 1918 letter to the New Orleans *Item* and Harper's pamphlet of the same period can be explained without attributing influence to Harper. True, Long had not expressed any public interest in the unequal distribution of wealth until the time of Harper's trial, which suggests that Harper was influential on that issue, but from 1918 until the crash in 1929, Long was also strangely silent on the question of the distribution of wealth which suggests Harper was not very influential in this regard. Long wrote an article in his personal paper, *The Louisiana Progress,* in June of 1931 in which he claimed that he "began to broadcast speeches over the radio along this line about eighteen months ago." [36] In August 1931, he gave a speech to farmers and farm women attending a short course at Louisiana State University in which he discussed the unequal distribution of wealth; [37] from this time forward he came increasingly to stress these notions. Harper's influence upon Long, if he did indeed have much, apparently came equipped with a time fuse that was set to go off when the depression came on.

How can the letter to the editor of the *Item* be explained if not as the spontaneous effusions of a new disciple to equal distribution of wealth? One answer is that the letter was part of Long's strategy in defending Harper with every means at his disposal outside and within the courtroom, and only years later after the onset of the depression did he use the happy coincidence of the letter to pose as a long-time advocate of wealth sharing. Even at twenty-five, discipleship and spontaneous effusions were alien to Huey Long's character. Most of his actions were coolly calculated. He always chafed at working in harness with anyone; he wanted to be lead dog in any relationship. He also, characteristically, fought every lawsuit and every political campaign with a bewildering variety of methods, orthodox and unorthodox, ethical and unethical. For example, in his autobiography, he gleefully recalls how he caused the prosecution to waste their jury challenges by picking out prospective jurors that he felt would be biased against Senator Harper and then ostentatiously whispering to them. When questioned by the prosecution in regard to these whispered conferences with defense counsel they honestly answered that Long had not discussed the trial with them; but the suspicious prosecutor challenged them anyway.

---

[36] *The Louisiana Progress* (Hammond, La.), June 1931, p. 1.
[37] *The State Time* (Baton Rouge), August 13, 1931, p. 1.

More important to the issue at hand, Long began a campaign outside the courtroom to change public opinion. As part of that strategy he began to write letters to newspapers around the state reflecting Senator Harper's ideas. He also made strong statements in interviews with reporters and received statewide publicity for the first time. These letters and the statements that Long made to the newspapers about the maldistribution of wealth fit into his typical way of fighting through a lawsuit or court trial. Long's report in his autobiography indicates that the judge trying the case viewed the letters as part of the lawyer's strategy to win the case.

> The court again called to order after a recess, the Judge began to read statements which I had made in the newspapers. It seemed apparent that I was to be sent to jail. But to our great astonishment, after reading the entire list of statements I had made, the Judge concluded: "The Court cannot let this and other matters pass without a reprimand." To the devil with the reprimand as far as we are concerned! All we wanted was a chance to clear our client.[38]

After the Harper trial, Long seemingly forgot about the maldistribution of wealth until after 1929, when he suddenly began talking about the issue again. In 1931, when the first traces of Long's advocacy of Share-Our-Wealth began to appear in newspapers, Huey was about to launch his national political career; he needed a national issue and the maldistribution of wealth was the issue he chose. When this happened, he could point back to the happy accident that in defending Harper in 1918 he had written letters to newspapers around the state putting himself on public record as advocating the same ideas.

Was Harper influential in forming Long's ideas about the maldistribution of wealth? The two men used many of the same ideas and Long continued to use some of the same statistics in his national radio broadcasts until his death in 1935. But the actual influence, if any, is not so easy to discern. Long may well have shared Bozeman's opinion that Senator Harper was a kindly man but an intellectual lightweight and a crackpot, in which case the Senator's influence upon Long's thinking was probably negligible.

Perhaps the best way of puzzling out the nature and extent of influence is to ask: what if the alleged influence had not been present?[39] In answering such a question the student must be careful not

[38] Huey P. Long, *Every Man a King* (New Orleans, 1933), pp. 35–36.
[39] See Sidney Hook's analysis of "'If' in History," in *The Hero in History* (New York, 1943), pp. 119–137.

to indulge his imagination too much. Quite frequently, attempts to imagine what would have happened if at some key juncture in history a battle had gone the other way or a successful assassination had failed, turn into exercises in historical romance similar to the old folk tale about the loss of a battle because of the loss of a nail in a horse's shoe. But if, after carefully studying the evidence, the student cannot make some judgment about this question, he should not make a judgment about influences.

What would have happened if Huey Long, the young lawyer, had never met Senator Harper? Would he have advocated "Share-Our-Wealth" in 1934? He probably would have. Winn Parish was a Populist stronghold exploited by the lumber and oil interests. Natives of Winn Parish had a characteristic style of viewing exploitation and held a piney-woods rancor towards the planter aristocracy. Huey, needing a national issue in 1931, could turn only in one direction—to the problems of depression.

This extended example should indicate the danger of attributing influences, effects, or results on the basis of superficial analysis. The categorization of plays or playwrights into schools, movements, or periods, such as naturalism, expressionism, realism, romanticism, and impressionism may result in this fallacy. The tracing of the influence of impressionism on a given play, or the discovery of the influence of romanticism on a given playwright is a most painstaking task. Such stock ways of approaching intellectual and literary history can be extremely helpful if they are carefully done, but dividing events into periods or classifications if based upon superficial similarities may turn out to be misleading rather than helpful.

In examining influence, the scholar must be careful not to confine himself to studying the positive influence, that is, the bringing of sets of ideas into line with the ideas of the sources of influence. Sometimes an artist or a speaker exercises considerable influence because of the reaction against his art or his ideas. In his study of Jonathan Edwards, Orville Hitchcock concluded that Edward's greatest influence was not in bringing a resurgence of Calvinism but in hastening the reaction against Calvinism.[40]

THE WRITING OF CRITICISM

THE CRITIC'S BACKGROUND

The student considering a critical study as a research project should examine his interests, background, and abilities to see if he

---

[40] Orville A. Hitchcock, "Jonathan Edwards," in Brigance, I, pp. 213–238.

is suited to such an undertaking. As soon as the student decides that he would like to do a critical study he should build his understanding of rhetorical and dramatic theory and he should read and hear as many plays or speeches as he can. In this way he will develop the necessary background to establish canons of criticism and make evaluations as to the excellence of the works he is studying.

MATERIAL FOR CRITICISM

Unless the critic is attempting to test rhetorical theory by studying the practice of effective speakers, he should select speeches that in addition to being artistic have been neglected or misunderstood by previous scholarship. This does not mean that speeches already studied thoroughly from a historical point of view cannot be studied again from a critical standpoint. Nor does this mean that a play studied from a literary point of view cannot be viewed through the focus of the dramatic critic.

There can be little quibble about including plays in our definition of art. There is some possibility of quibbling about the inclusion of acting, scenic design, directing and producing in such a definition for purposes of scholarship. If acting is considered an art and not, as Nathan [41] argues, a craft then the critical study of such actors as Laurence Olivier, John Gielgud, and Maurice Evans would be justified. If other production activities are considered art, then critical studies of such designers as Gordon Craig, and directors such as Eisenstein in film, and Brecht in the theatre, would be justified.[42]

To be practical about such things requires some balancing of alternatives. Perhaps some studies should be developed from a historical frame of reference. Undoubtedly such pre-eminent men as Eisenstein, Gordon Craig, and Constantin Stanislavsky, deserve to have their work criticized as art.

Here are some representative titles of master's theses in speech and theatre arts that have utilized the critical method.

An Analysis of Invention in British Government Rhetoric in 1940

Senator Ervin's Speaking on Supreme Court Segregation Decisions. A Study in Evidence

Invention in Clarence Darrow's Defense of John T. Scopes

---

[41] See, for example, George Jean Nathan's Essay on "The Place of Acting," in *The Critic and the Drama,* pp. 83–110.

[42] See Barnard Hewitt, "Gordon Craig and Post-Impressionism," *QJS,* XXX (February 1944), 75–80; Barnard Hewitt and Aristide D'Angelo, "The Stanislavsky System for Actors," *QJS,* XVIII (June 1932), 440–446; Garff B. Wilson, "Versatile Tragedians: Edwin Booth and James E. Murdoch," *SM,* XIX (March 1952), 27–38.

An Analysis of Diestic Reference in Selected Speeches of Nine of the Attic Canon Orators

An Evaluation of the Speaking of Nikita S. Khrushchev in the United States During September, 1959

Schiller–Shaw–Anderson: Three Views of Saint Joan in the Drama

Meterlinck and the French Symbolist Theatre

Anthony and Cleopatra and *All for Love,* A Comparison of Two Dramatic Methods

Imagery in the Plays of Sean O'Casey

The State Politician: A Study of a Stock Character in Native American Comedy, 1870–1960

A Comparative Study of the Dramatic Techniques of Sarah Siddons, Ellen Terry, and Julia Marlowe

A Comparative Study of the Plays of John Webster and Tennessee Williams

Rhetorical Qualities in the Speeches of Winston Churchill

An Analysis of Some Persuasive Methods of Adolph Hitler's Rhetoric

A Comparison of the Use of Theological Terms in the Speaking of D. L. Moody and Billy Graham

This Is War: The Radio Documentary as a Medium of Persuasion

THE BEGINNINGS OF A CRITICAL STUDY

Although the critic may write of plays in manuscript or of plays in production, of speeches in text or as delivered, of films or viewed productions, his method will be similar. The critic should begin his study with the works of art under examination. He should begin with the electrical transcriptions, the tape recordings, the productions, the texts. Malcolm Cowley writes that "In practice . . . I always start and end with the text itself, and . . . I also try to start with a sort of innocence, that is, with a lack of preconceptions about what I might or might not discover. To preserve the innocence, I try not to read the so-called secondary or critical sources until my own discoveries, if any, have been made." [43]

If he has not already read most of the important speeches or works of the writer or speaker, the critic should next proceed to do so. The writings of other critics are usually troublesome for the beginning critic. Too often he is timid about making a critical evaluation without having several similar evaluations by other critics to support his judgment. Even worse, the student may simply collect the opinions of other critics and string the quotations that reflect

---

[43] Cowley, p. 47.

find its length and weight. If he has such standards and applies them to a given specimen, the critic of fish can describe the fish, if he has sufficient background, the critic can compare a given specimen to many other fish of the same species and decide that this particular fish is exceedingly long and thin, or short and heavy, or large and ill-proportioned, or well-proportioned, or well-formed and small. If he is a critic who feels that a well-proportioned fish is a better fish than a heavy one, he will pick a different specimen to stuff and hang over his mantel than if he is of the opinion that the important thing in a fish is its gross weight.

When the critic of rhetoric or drama begins to sort out the salient features of a given play or speech and tries to describe them in some fashion, he begins to develop a set of critical canons for measurement. This implies some categories of analysis and the critic generally develops a critical machinery to serve as the scale and yardstick for a given project in criticism. When the critic makes a decision to use Aristotelian categories, he should use these categories as an aid to select the relevant features of the drama or oratory that he is studying. That is, he should draw out of his careful study of the text those features that are relevant for his criticism and present a description of the work that includes these features organized and clarified. This is the main function of categories. As he does this, the critic should begin to discern a pattern or structure to his material that gives added insight, appreciation, and understanding of the work. When this happens, the original categories that were used to begin analysis of the work may be modified or discarded and a new critical strategy appropriate for the particular study may be adopted. Thus, the critical study becomes a function of the critic and the art that he is criticizing. Because of his viewpoint and the skills that he brings to his work he will view plays and speeches and describe them in a unique fashion. Yet, only in a limited sense is beauty in the eye of the beholder. The work itself will have a major effect upon the shape of the criticism and among capable critics of similar background and viewpoint a commonality of judgment about the worthwhile and the trivial in a given artistic field emerges.

If there is a case to be made for a literate, if not literary, style of writing for historical studies, the case can be made doubly for critical studies. Malcolm Cowley is of the opinion that criticism is one of the literary arts and that this implies "that it should be written in the same language of English literature and not, like a great deal of recent criticism, in some variety of philosophical or social-scientific jargon." [46]

---

[46] Cowley, p. 47.

Much of what has been said about the actual mechanics of writing a historical monograph in Chapter 10 applies to the writing of critical studies. The same techniques for stimulating the creative faculties, the same care in revision, and the same division of labor, apply.

SUMMARY

Scholarly criticism is essentially the description and evaluation of works of art. The difference between the naïve reaction to a play or speech and scholarly criticism of the same work is that the critic has a set of standards to guide his evaluation and a context of dramatic and rhetorical tradition to aid him in making judgments about the work. Criticism's main task is to increase the appreciation and understanding of rhetoric and drama.

Scholarly criticism differs from play reviewing in that it is interested in the long-range excellence of the work. The play review is designed as a guide for prospective playgoers. There are important differences between literary criticism and rhetorical and dramatic criticism. The major difference is the emphasis of speech researchers on the importance of the audience in evaluating speeches and plays. The literary critic tends to view these materials as literature and as writings rather than oral performances. The critic has a viewpoint toward his materials that is analogous to the historian's viewpoint. The unique features of a critic's viewpoint include such matters as the importance of the biographical and historical features in the evaluation and explanation of a speech or play.

The critic uses the same techniques of scholarship that the historian employs, but the critic focuses on the plays or speeches as works of art to be discussed by using the methods of scholarship. The critic usually makes judgments about the excellence of the work he is criticizing. The historian may or may not make such judgments; but if he does, they are tangential to his main concern for historical traces.

The major viewpoints used in the criticism of speeches have differed primarily about the need for and the importance of evaluating a speech in terms of its effect upon the immediate audience. One evaluates its immediate and long-range effects. This viewpoint also stresses the interaction of the speaker, the audience, and the occasion in forming the speech. The critic working from this position usually examines in detail the background for the speech, the speaker's life, the immediate occasion, and the nature of the audience. Another viewpoint stresses the effectiveness of the speech with a dis-

CHAPTER TWELVE

THE EMPIRICAL METHOD:
GENERAL CONSIDERATIONS

THE NATURE OF EMPIRICAL RESEARCH

EMPIRICAL RESEARCH AND SCHOLARSHIP

Among the statements that comprise the various theories in speech are a number of factually significant statements. Observation furnishes the most reliable basis for deciding whether such statements are true or false. When an investigator gathers data to support or refute such statements, he employs the empirical method. Of course, in one sense, today's observations are tomorrow's history. The rhetorical critic or historian of contemporary events may observe a speaker or a play directly and might be called an empirical researcher. Today's historian may find the results of empirical investigations of a decade ago useful for his study. For example, the future historian writing of television in the twentieth century might use the results of empirical investigations into the size and viewing habits of television audiences in the 1960's. Much of the empirical investigation in speech is as timebound as scholarship and deals with particular statements of fact. No sooner are normative descriptions of verbal behavior in preschool children completed than the norms change and the descriptions become dated. No sooner are television-audience attitudes toward Western dramas tabulated than the taste of the television audience changes and the results of the research become part of the historical record.

Despite these similarities, the empirical approach differs substantially from the methods of scholarship in technique and style. Because more data are available for the empirical researcher, he faces a problem in selecting the response to study. He must find the most relevant speech events or behavioral responses to observe or he must try to create these events and responses so he can observe them. He usually abstracts from these events and responses certain features which he describes numerically and interprets statistically. Empirical research can be divided, in terms of the purposes of the researcher, into descriptive and experimental types.[1] In terms of methodology, it can be divided into survey studies, field studies, and laboratory research. Whatever categorization system is used to make a systematic analysis of the empirical method, there are certain general characteristics that cut across purposes and methods. Empirical research relies upon observation for its data, typically quantifies this observation, and by mathematical deductions treats the data. Like the scholar, the empirical researcher has developed certain techniques and procedures to systematize his work, but before we discuss these practical matters we should deal with some general questions relating to characteristics of the scientific method.

EMPIRICAL RESEARCH AND SPEECH THEORIES

With the exception of the history and criticism of public address, which makes a definite attempt to modify rhetorical theory in terms of the effectiveness of public speakers, no other research technique in speech is as closely tied to theory as is the empirical method. The empirical researcher is trying to find out about speech events. He wants to observe them accurately and describe them objectively. He would like to discover evidence for probability statements, and, in some instances, for universally agreed upon invariable relations. His ultimate goal is usually the discovery of laws governing the operations and processes involved in speech and speech-related events.

Among other things he wants to find out what causes stuttering so that it can be averted or treatment improved. He wants to know the relationship between the acoustic stimulus (sound wave) and the perception of pitch, loudness, and voice quality. He wants to know how the vocal folds vibrate, what goes on in a group discussion, how words arouse emotional responses, if television violence causes juvenile delinquency, if clearness of language usage can be quantified, and if stage fright can be measured.

The empirically oriented investigator cannot do the job he is trying to do with qualitative insights as can the dramatic critic. Such descriptions as dynamic, forceful, lyrical, full, rich, resonant, are not very helpful for the empirical researcher. He prefers more operational descriptions and, in most instances, he prefers a quantified description.

OBSERVATION, INDUCTION, AND DEDUCTION

In his attack on his environment in order to discover knowledge, the scientist uses strategy and tactics in much the same way as the

---

[1] See, for example, J. Jeffery Auer, *An Introduction to Research in Speech* (New York, 1959).

military commander deploys his forces. The tactics of both reflect their over-all strategy. The investigator's tactics will be reflected in the research design for a given study. Governing the tactics (research design) of any given study will be some general strategic consideration. Such matters as the interrelationship between putting numbers to the observations he makes and selecting a statistical test belong to the strategy of empirical research. Strategic considerations cut across the diverse methods and varied purposes of the empirical researcher. They have a bearing on the worker describing normative data as well as on the researcher testing a hypothesis in a laboratory experiment.

Empirical research has three major components, (1) observation, (2) induction, and (3) deduction. No matter how far his speculative flights may lead him into statistics and system building, the empirical researcher begins and ends with observations. If he makes a survey of graduate education in the United States or an experimental study of the effect of structural changes in a speech on the retention scores of listeners, the researcher begins with observations, generalizes from his data, and tries to unravel all the implications of his generalizations by means of deduction.

The method of observation, the inductive framework, and the deductive analysis of empirical research data are all closely interrelated. Although observation, induction, and deduction need to be separated for the purpose of analysis, in actual practice the design of an empirical research project results from the interaction of these elements. Sampling procedures and the way numbers are assigned to properties restrict the kind of deductive treatment that the researcher can use in analyzing his data. The more carefully the observation and deduction are integrated, the sounder the evidence for an inductively arrived-at generalization. This chapter will be devoted to such basic strategic considerations as the nature of deduction, the process of quantifying observations, and the integration of these two features of empirical research in the design of a research project.

DEDUCTION

APPLYING DEDUCTIONS

Before a student can use mathematics to help him in a research project, he must set up the study in such a way that the assumptions of the deductive system are fulfilled by the way he goes about collecting his data. For example, before a surveyor can use Euclidean geometry to help him measure a distance across a river, he must set up an artificial condition that is the equivalent of the axioms of Euclidean geometry. Nature has few right angles and straight lines so the assumptions of Euclidean geometry are seldom met unless man manipulates his environment. The surveyor may set up the conditions that fulfill the requirements of the axioms of geometry, as in Figure 2. Once he does this, he can use geometry.

He begins by picking an object on which to sight across the river, such as the tree at point *B*. He then drives a stake at point *A* across the river from the tree at *B*. From the point at *A*, he sights a line towards *C* and selects the point *C* so that the line *AC* is at

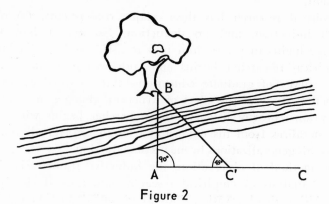

Figure 2

a 90-degree angle to the line *AB*. He then finds a point *C'* on the line *AC* so line *BC'* is at a 45-degree angle to *AC*. He now has fulfilled the axioms of geometry and he can compute that the line *AB* is equal in length to the line *AC'*, and measuring *AC'* will enable him to deduce the distance across the river from his stake to the tree, without crossing the river. In this way, deductions are a help in solving practical problems. Geometry was of no help to the surveyor until he created a situation that approximated the axioms of geometry.

STATISTICS

Deduction in empirical research is largely accomplished by the use of mathematics. Arithmetic is basic and the next most important branch of mathematics for the empirical researcher in speech is mathematical statistics. Graduate students in my research seminars have been both enchanted and dismayed by statistics. Some have embraced statistics and relied upon statistical deductions for most of their interpretations of research data. Others have rejected statistical interpretations and all mathematics as too difficult, too scientific to be suitable for the study of the arts of rhetoric and drama, or too dull. The extremists in both camps have tended to grow emotional about statistics. When faced with a study employing statistical treatment of data, the first group would sometimes examine the statistics for their elegance and novelty rather than for their suitability in the entire ensemble of observation, induction, and deduction. The latter group often pleaded ignorance. They preferred not to read the report at all. If they did read it, they often declared that they could not understand the statistics and so could not get much out of the study. For the consumer of research, this latter attitude, even for the accomplished and dedicated artist, is unfortunate. More and more empirical research is being done in the fields of rhetoric, oral interpretation, and theatre, and every scholar should be able to read and evaluate these research reports when they have a bearing on his field.

At least two levels of mathematical competence are required for graduate students of speech. The first is for the person who will develop his research along historical or critical lines and will not personally use empirical research techniques. Such an individual needs to develop an understanding of the nature of deduction and to adopt a positive attitude toward statistics so that he can read and evaluate empirical research reports intelligently. The second level of competence is required for the student who is doing or planning to do empirical research. Such a person needs to study the rapidly growing body of mathematical statistics in systematic fashion, so that he has a thorough grounding in the various statistical approaches available for the analysis of data.

Between the two levels of competence there necessarily is a considerable gap of expertise in relation to statistics. Yet, the two groups should remain close enough in attitude so they can discuss research matters with some understanding.

We shall not deal extensively with the principles of statistics in this book. The student who is preparing an empirical study for a doctoral dissertation or master's thesis will puzzle over a suitable research design for some time and take courses in statistics and consult with statisticians while planning the study.

At this point in our discussion a middle course somewhere between a primer in statistics and a detailed treatment of sophisticated statistical tests is indicated. We shall begin first with the nature of deduction, which is a necessary preliminary for both the relatively naïve and sophisticated statistician.

SYNTACTICAL NATURE OF DEDUCTION

In Chapter 5, the syntactical features of language were discussed. Deductive systems are syntactical systems. The major deductive systems are those of logic and mathematics. Mathematicians and logicians are interested in the *formal* relationships among symbols in carefully specified linguistic systems. (For this purpose mathematics can be considered a linguistic system.)

Deductive systems are composed of a set of symbols plus a set of syntactical or combination rules. The combination rules must be followed in discovering the allowable arguments, proofs, theorems, and formulas. For example, a deductive system can be developed which uses the symbols of English. Combination rules would have to be clearly defined and rigidly followed to make a deductive system out of the symbols of a natural language such as English. As used in day to day conversation, English seldom approximates a deductive system. Its grammar is much too loosely specified to allow for deductive combinations. The fact that arguments about the grammatical correctness of a certain sentence structure are possible in English points to this looseness. No such difference of opinion is possible about deductive structures. If the combination rules are understood, then a decision about correctness is always clear-cut.

We shall illustrate the sort of precision necessary in specifying combination rules by making a deductive system out of a few English symbols. First, we lay down the rule that all allowable sentences in our system are restricted to those that are either true or false. The allowable sentences are to be combined according to the following rules. Combination rules are generally expressed in logical words such as *or*. So let us turn to the specification of a rule for the use of *or*.

The syntactical rule for the use of *or* in conversational English is quite vague. It can stand for the combination rule that states, "Sentence *A* combined with sentence *B* by the word *or* means *A* is true and *B* is false, *B* is true and *A* is false, but not both *A* is true and *B* is true." Another way to specify such a combination rule is by means of a device called a *truth table*. This is a chart that indicates the allowable combinations for a given symbol. The combination rule specified above for *or* could alternatively be indicated by the following truth table:

A	*B*	*A or B*
T	F	T
F	T	T
F	F	F
T	T	F

There is nothing sacred about this combination rule, just as there is little sacred about the combination rules of mathematics.

The combination rule for *or* could just as well be specified as "Sentence *A* combined with sentence *B* by the word *or* means that *A* is true and *B* is false, *B* is true and *A* is false, both *A* and *B* are true." The truth table for such a combination rule is as follows:

A	B	A or B
T	F	T
F	T	T
F	F	F
T	T	T

Deductive systems of symbolic logic have been developed using either the *weak* or the *strong* form of this particular combination rule. We need not develop this deductive system in greater detail. Further logical words such as *and, not,* and *if . . . then* could be specified by truth tables and the allowable combinations could be deduced by computation from the forms of the argument.

The most important distinction between inductive logic and deductive logic for the empirical researcher is that deductive systems are pure syntax. They have no semantic features. Whatever meaning they have is in their form. They have no meaning in the denotative sense. They tell us nothing about "the world." The mathematician does not have to go into the field and examine a brace of pheasants and a trio of pheasants to check the deduction $2 + 3 = 5$, and decide that it is right. Should he be told "There are three pheasants in the ditch beside the car," he would have to glance at the ditch and look to see if the statement were true or false. The latter says something about the world and contains information. The former, $2 + 3 = 5$, says nothing about the world. The statement that some features of the world exhibit the property of number is an empirical statement that is either true or false. The discovery that this declaration is true is necessary for the use of arithmetic, as we shall see later in the chapter, but the correctness of $2 + 3 = 5$ as an arithmetic computation gives no guarantee that putting two pounds plus three pounds of potatoes into a container will result in the combined weight of five pounds. The fact of this connection had to be discovered by observation.

Only in two limiting cases are deductive arguments true or false and when they are true or false this is a feature of their *form* and not of anything external to the deductive system. The first limiting case is the one where an examination of the form of a deductive argument yields a decision that this argument must necessarily be true. The second limiting argument is when an examination of the form of a deduction yields a decision that this must necessarily be false. These two limiting cases enable the checking of an arithmetic paper or a solution of an analysis of variance without resort to any observation of the world. The correctness of the solution can be determined by checking the form of the solution.

TAUTOLOGY

In the first limiting case, when the form always yields a decision of truth, the argument can be considered a tautology. That is, the answer to the arithmetic problem and the conclusion of a syllogism are both simply restatements of what is given in the assumptions of the deductive system plus the premises for the specific problem or syllogism. For example, if the combination rule for *or* has been specified as *"or* can be used only if *A* is true and *B* is false or vice versa," then the argument "It is raining or it is not raining," is a tautology. Such a statement is necessarily true because of the combination rule for *or* and the form of the statement. The tautology can be demonstrated formally by means of truth tables. The truth table for *or* is as follows:

A	B	A or B
T	F	T
F	T	T
F	F	F
T	T	F

The truth table for *not* is as follows:

A	not-A
T	F
F	T

Substituting not-*A* for *B* in the truth table for *or* results inevitably in a statement that is true as the following truth table indicates.

A	not-A	A or not-A
T	F	T
F	T	T

If the combination rules for the logical words *or* and *not* have been specified, the statement "It is raining or it is not raining" is true no matter what the weather conditions happen to be. Such a statement is empty in that it gives us no information about the world. Until supplied with sentences that contain information resulting from observations, logic and mathematics contain no semantical features and can add nothing to what is already implied by the premises of the deductive system.

CONTRADICTIONS

The second limiting case, when an examination of the form of the deduction results in a decision that it must necessarily be false, can be called a contradiction. Assume that the combination rule for *and* is specified as "Sentence *A* combined with sentence *B* by the word *and* means that *A* is true, *B* is true." The truth table for this specification of *and* is then:

A	B	A and B
T	T	T
F	T	F
T	F	F
F	F	F

The statement "It is raining and it is not raining," is necessarily false with these combination rules. This can be formally demonstrated by use of truth tables. Again substituting not-*A* for *B* in the truth table.

A	not-A	A and not-A
T	F	F
F	T	F

In each case the necessary truth and falsity of the two statements was discovered by inspection of the form of the statements. If the proof of a mathematical solution is in the form of a tautology, it can be examined and called *true*. If such a proof is in the form of a contradiction, it can be called *false*. To assert that "*A* and not-*A*" is a contradiction may strike some readers as a restatement of Aristotelian two-valued logic. In one sense, of course, it is, because the combination rules specified above were an important part of Aristotelian logic; but the same combination rules play an important part in widely used contemporary deductive systems such as symbolic logic and much of mathematics. This does not mean that deductive systems could not be developed that would be three-valued or four-valued. Nor does it mean that a deductive system could not be specified in such a fashion that the statement "*A* and not-*A*" would be a tautology or an allowable theorem. However, if there is not a substitute rule for the contradiction rule, it would be possible to deduce any statement whatsoever from the axiom system. If the deductive system allows an assertion of both a statement and its contrary, it, in a sense, allows an assertion of every possible statement in the symbol system.

INDUCTION AND DEDUCTION

The objection that there is a meteorological state between rain and not rain, a time when one might say "It is not really raining but sort of raining," is a result of confusing induction and deduction. The deductive system is purely syntactical and the presence or absence of meteorological states that bear a semantic relationship to the statement, "It is raining," is irrelevant to the logic of a deductive system. Indeed, if there were no psychological experiences called *rain,* the tautologies and contradictions of the axiom system outlined above would still be true and false. This objection does point up the danger of using statements about which inductive truth decisions cannot be made as data for deductive computation.

In fact, deductive systems are much easier to work with when the distinction between syntactical rules and semantical rules of a symbol system is clear. To help keep this distinction clearly before the logician and mathematician, the general practice is to devise an arbitrary symbol system that is cryptic and strange enough so it is not easily confused with natural language symbols. In symbolic logic, where the danger is perhaps the greatest, a substitute symbol like V is used in place of the English word *or.* Arabic numerals, 1, 2, 3, . . . , N, or Latin letters, x, y, z, or A, B, C, or Greek letters may be used to symbolize sentences or variables.

If this is done, the tautological nature of statements is easier to determine. For instance, asserting that "If neither Lincoln nor Washington lived to be thirty-five, then Lincoln died before he was thirty-five," might lead to confusion because the truth or falsity of the statements of fact in the tautology distract our attention from its form. We may be misled by the obvious falsity, in the sense discussed in Chapter 5 of the sentence "Lincoln died before he was thirty-five." We may forget that the deduction asserts nothing about the age at which Lincoln died nor about the age at which Washington died. It simply asserts that *if* Lincoln died before he was thirty-five, *and* if Washington died before he was thirty-five, *then* Lincoln died before he was thirty-five. Putting the statement in the symbolic form, "If A and B, then A," helps clear up this ambiguity.

Statistical systems share these same characteristics with all deductive systems. Statistical theorems, computations, and formulas are simply long tautologies, expressed in symbols, that assert if the conditions assumed in the premises of this statistical treatment hold, then every conclusion derived according to the proper combination rules, holds as well.

Mankind took a long time to learn the lesson that mathematics was a formal syntactical system that contained no information about the world. Plato, for example, was impressed with the certainty of deductive inferences when compared with inductive inferences and assumed that mathematics yielded knowledge over and above the implications of its axioms. Immanuel Kant in his works on "pure" and "practical" reason tried to sort out the knowledge contributed by deductive systems. Kant's discussion of "synthetic" and "analytic" statements clearly made the distinction. Kant's synthetic statements are what were called statements of fact in Chapter 5, and his analytic statements are the equivalent of what is called a tautology above. The synthetic statement contains new information about the world. Adding such a statement to a book or an argument increases the knowledge contained in the book or argument. Analytic statements make no such contribution. They do serve to make clear some of the implications of the synthetic statements and assumptions in the argument. The function of making clear all the implications of a set of axioms such as those of Euclidean geometry is the primary contribution of a deductive system. If the statistician had a godlike intelligence, and could grasp at once all the implications of his data, he would not need to make statistical computations to interpret his results.

You should not infer from this clarification of the nature of statistics that they are not a significant aid to the empirical researcher. The point to be made here is that statistics, important as they are to the investigator in speech, cannot add any information to the raw data that have been gathered during the course of observation. The study can be no stronger than the data no matter how skillfully and elegantly the data are analyzed by statistical deductions.

DEDUCTION AND QUANTIFICATION

Since the data govern the amount of useful information in a study the use of statistics in their analysis requires a careful meshing of data and statistical tests. For the student in speech using the empirical method the problem of assigning numbers to the events he is studying in such a way that arithmetic can be used in computing the results is of great practical importance. If the student wishes to use arithmetic, one of the most important deductive systems, he should assign numbers only to those properties that can be *combined* in such a way that the combination results in a change in the property. The reason there must be a change of a certain kind in a property when it is combined with more of the same property is to be found in the foundations of arithmetic.

THE FOUNDATIONS OF ARITHMETIC

THE PROPERTY OF NUMBER

Collections of individuals have a property that can be called the property of number. This is as much a property of a class of speech students as their aggregate weight. Historically arithmetic evolved to describe the property of number. A flock of sheep, for example, is a collection of individuals. An important property of such a flock is the property of number. The property of number is as much a feature of the world as the property of heat or of redness. Interestingly enough, the world exhibits certain other properties that are so much like the property of number that the symbols (numerals) developed to describe number can be used to represent these other properties as well.

We will define the property of number operationally by describing the process of counting. In everyday affairs this process is so closely intertwined with arithmetic that counting without numbers is difficult to imagine. Nevertheless, numbers are not necessary for counting and the notion of counting is more primitive than the notion of numbers. In order to count two aggregations, one a collection of stones and another a flock of sheep, all we need is some way to separate individual stones and individual sheep from each aggregation and pair them up. If the last sheep is paired with the last stone, the collections are of the same size. If the stones are exhausted before the flock of sheep then the flock is larger than the collection of stones.

At this point several interesting features of this process of counting become apparent. These features are empirical and had to be discovered by observation. The first is that if a flock of sheep is counted against a collection of stones and found to be the same size, the collection of stones can be carried to another field and counted against a second flock of sheep. If the second flock can be paired with the stones, so both the flock and the stones are exhausted at the same time, then the first flock can be counted against the second flock with the same results. This discovery makes it feasible to have a portable collection to be used as a standard against which to count the individuals in various flocks of sheep. Carrying a bag of pebbles is much simpler than herding flocks of sheep around to count them.

The second important thing about counting is that the standard set of collections can be simplified. Even pebbles would become cumbersome for the counter if he had to carry a leather pouch with one pebble in it, another with two, a third with three, and so on up to a pouch that contained as many pebbles as the largest herd of sheep he might be likely to encounter. He does not need to do so because, at some point in history, someone discovered, once again an empirical discovery, that one large collection contained all smaller collections. He needed only a collection of pebbles as large as the biggest flock of sheep. By taking one pebble from this collection and adding another to it and taking another pebble and adding it to the first two, and by repeating this process over and over again, he could build up a series of collections so that one member of this series could be counted against any flock of sheep he wanted to count. To measure the number of a given flock with such a standard set of pebbles meant that he would count the pebbles against the sheep and when he ran out of sheep he would take that subset of pebbles from his bag of pebbles and call the number of the flock equal to that subset. He could simplify the process of calling the property of number of the flock equal to the property of number exhibited by the subset of pebbles by finding a name for the class of all classes exhibiting the same property of number. Numerals, either Arabic or Roman, fulfill this function. The numerals 2 and II, for example, are the name for the class of all classes of duets, twins, braces, and deuces.

A BASE TEN ARITHMETIC

These two discoveries made the use of a standard portable set of collections desirable and feasible. Primitive man carried two small sets of collections with him in the form of ten fingers and ten toes. After a time he must have discovered that when he had counted something against his ten fingers he could use one toe to stand for that collection of ten individuals that had been counted against his ten fingers and then proceed to use the ten fingers again. When he ran out of fingers again, he could set aside another toe to stand for that ten, thus, two toes, two fingers would represent 22. The fact that primitive man had these two handy collections to count against, perhaps, explains why our arithmetic is a base ten arithmetic. In principle, deductive systems can be manufactured in many different ways and arithmetics can be developed on any base, but historically deductive systems grew out of practical problems and usually reflect the necessities that caused their invention.

OTHER ARITHMETICS

Had primitive man been equipped with eight fingers and eight toes he probably would have developed an arithmetic to a base of eight. He would have counted a collection against his eight fingers and then set aside a toe for each octet in the collection and set aside an ear for each set of eight toes. 100 in base eight arithmetic represents the same size collection as 64 in the base ten arithmetic. An arithmetic can be developed on any base by proceeding in a way analogous to the development of the two arithmetics outlined above. Another important arithmetic has been worked out to the base two. This *binary* arithmetic has been important in the development of computers and one of the basic assumptions for the mathematical theory of communication is that information be measured in terms of a two-choice or binary arithmetic.

The binary arithmetic is appropriate to computers and the engineering of information because it is built up out of two digits, 0 and 1. Many engineering applications can be developed on the basis of an electrical or magnetic charge being present or absent, thus the binary arithmetic which is essentially a "yes" or "no" arithmetic is appropriate to machines that can be most easily built with this two-choice condition.

MINIMUM ASSUMPTIONS FOR ARITHMETIC

Although arithmetic grew out of experience, it is, nonetheless, a deductive system and like all deductive systems is based on certain combination rules or assumptions. When we analyze a deductive system, such as arithmetic, to discover the basic rules or assumptions required to reconstruct the system, a variety of assumptions can be used for expansion of the system. Two important sets of minimum assumptions have been developed for arithmetic. We outlined the first set of minimum ideas in the example of counting pebbles against sheep. The minimum assumptions included the notion of number, successor, and addition. Number is the property defined by the operation of counting. The notion of successor refers to the construction of collections of pebbles of various sizes by the procedure of adding a pebble at a time to the collection. In this fashion, so long as pebbles are available, any size collection whatsoever can be constructed. Addition is the rule that if the collection 1, 2, 3, 4, 5 is added to the collection 1, 2, 3, 4, the resultant collection 1, 2, 3, 4, 5, 1, 2, 3, 4 can be counted against the collection 1, 2, 3, 4, 5, 6, 7, 8, 9. To these primitive ideas Giuseppe Peano, an Italian mathematician, added the notion of 0 and was able to reconstruct arithmetic deductively from these postulates.

Bertrand Russell and Alfred North Whitehead, in the twentieth century, drove the analysis of the foundations of arithmetic to even simpler ideas. In addition, they demonstrated that the assumptions of arithmetic can be deduced from the basic assumptions of logic.

Thus, we see that arithmetic, and most of mathematics, is an extension of logic.

RELATIONS

Russell and Whitehead reconstructed Peano's postulates from the more general notion of relations. They asked what sorts of relations are sufficient and necessary to generate natural numbers. Since they approached the problem on this very general level, the natural numbers turn out to be but a small subset of all similar series produced by terms that can be ordered by these relations. This means that whenever observations reveal the same relations in data, as are required to generate the natural numbers numerals can be assigned to these properties and mathematical interpretations of such quantification will result in meaningful computations.

Russell and Whithead discovered that the simplest set of relations that would generate a serial order like the natural numbers includes asymmetrical, transitive, and connected relations.

ASYMMETRICAL RELATIONS

To generate an order, one term must precede another and the second term must always follow the first. If x precedes y, then y must not precede x. If 5 precedes 9, then 9 may not precede 5. If A is greater than B, then B is not greater than A. Such a relation can move in only one direction. Time is a good example of a feature of the world that exhibits this relation. If A precedes B in time, B cannot precede A. Such a relation is called *asymmetrical*. Not all terms are asymmetrical. Spouse is a symmetrical relation. If A is the spouse of B, then B is the spouse of A. If event A is simultaneous with event B, then event B is simultaneous with event A.

TRANSITIVE RELATIONS

To generate a serial order, the terms must be such that if x precedes y and y precedes z, then x precedes z. Such a relation is transitive. If A is greater than B and B is greater than C, then A is greater than C. Not all *asymmetrical* relations are transitive. Defeat in basketball, for example, is asymmetrical but not transitive for team A may defeat team B and team B defeat team C, but team C may defeat team A. One of the important differences found in empirical research data is that some relations are transitive and others are not. Judgments and evaluations of speaking excellence, for example, are rarely transitive.

CONNECTED RELATIONS

A relation is connected when it holds between any two terms in its field. The relation of *greater than* is connected when it can be said of any two terms N and M that either N is greater than M or M is greater than N. The relation *ancestor* is not connected, for you may find a Mr. Jones and a Mr. Smith, and you may not be able to say either that Mr. Jones is an ancestor of Mr. Smith or that Mr. Smith is an ancestor of Mr. Jones. In short, to have an ordered set of terms, it is necessary that for any given pair of terms from the domain, one must precede and the other follow. Ties, or the relation of equivalence, are not allowed. A relation, therefore, can be said to be a serial relation when it is asymmetrical, transitive, and connected.[2]

QUANTIFICATION AND MEASUREMENT DEFINED

When in the course of an investigation, the student observes some aspect of the events under study that exhibits a relation that is asymmetrical, transitive, and connected, he is fully justified in trying to assign numerals to that aspect. If he is successful, he can use arithmetic, statistics, calculus, or any mathematics that require arithmetical computation in interpreting his data. Since this sort of quantification is the most precise and helpful, it needs to be thoroughly understood. Only some properties of speech events are amenable to quantitative descriptions of this kind. Many other important and interesting properties of speech events do not exhibit relations that are asymmetrical, transitive, and connected. The researcher may assign numbers to these properties in some systematic fashion, but he should be extremely careful in using arithmetic in making computations when he quantifies in this way.

The term "measurement" can be used (and often is) in a way that fails to discriminate between assigning numbers to properties in such a way that they fulfill the assumptions of arithmetic and assigning numbers so that they do not. If measurement is defined as assigning numbers to properties the distinction between numbers that may justifiably be added and subtracted and those that may not be is lost. This distinction is so important to the rest of our discussion that we must take pains not to lose sight of it. To this end we shall make some arbitrary and conventional definitions of commonly used but ambiguous terms and keep strictly to these definitions for the remainder of the book. We shall use the term

---

[2] Bertrand Russell, *Introduction to Mathematical Philosophy* (London, 1950), pp. 29–41.

quantification as the generic term rather than *measurement*. Henceforth the term *quantification* will be used to refer to the operational procedures used by any investigator to assign numbers to the properties of the speech events that he is studying. The term *measurement* will be reserved for those quantifications in which numbers are assigned to properties in such a way that the resultant information (scale values) fulfills the assumptions of arithmetic.

EVALUATION AND ESTIMATION DEFINED

The term *evaluation* will be used for that subclass of quantification where numbers are assigned to features of the data in such a way that they do not fulfill the assumptions of arithmetic. The term *estimation* will be used for that subclass of quantification where numbers are assigned to properties that may fulfill the assumptions of arithmetic but for which the assignment procedures are so difficult or loosely specified that in practice the quantifications do not fulfill the assumptions of arithmetic.

A PROBLEM IN BASIC MEASUREMENT

Let us apply our terms to a simple case of an investigator who wishes to *measure* as many properties of a carload of potatoes as he can. Remember measurement requires that he be able to assign numbers to properties so the numbers fulfill the assumptions of arithmetic. He discovers that the potatoes are a variety called Idaho Red. He can *quantify* the property of Idaho Redness, but he cannot *measure* it. When he assigns a number to this property, he is essentially praising, complimenting, or evaluating it. Evaluations are made by judges of dogs, cats, beef cattle, diving and gymnastic competitions, and one-act play, oratory, and declamation contests. The judge quantifies his evaluation by giving points or assigning a number to some aspect of the event he is judging. Judging the excellence of an oration or a play or evaluating the severity of stuttering or voice and articulation problems is like the activity of a scholarly critic described in Chapter 11. Quantifying such evaluations can make them appear like measurements, and they may be confused with measurements in such a way that the necessarily arbitrary nature of an evaluation is forgotten. If the judge of a speech contest rates contestant *A*'s performance at 75, contestant *B*'s at 80, and contestant *C*'s at 85, such a judgment means that the judge asserts, "I liked *B*'s oration better than *A*'s and *C*'s better than *B*'s and, of course, *C*'s better than *A*'s." It should not be interpreted to mean that if *B*'s oration were combined with *A*'s oration the result would be an oration with a rating of 155. Yet, if the evaluation of the judge were to fulfill the assumptions of arithmetic, this is exactly what it would have to mean. Nor should the judge's evaluation be interpreted to mean that there is a property named *oration excellence* and *B*'s oration had five more points of this property than *A*'s.

The researcher trying to measure the degree of Idaho Redness in his carload of potatoes is bound to fail. He can assign numbers to this property (quantification), but when he does so, combining a bushel of his potatoes with another bushel of his potatoes does not change the amount of Idaho Redness in the combined batch of potatoes.

Next, the investigator decides to measure the quality of two batches of potatoes drawn from his carload. He gets three experts to examine each batch and carefully grade them. Two experts evaluate the potatoes as grade 2 Idaho Red potatoes since they are a bit small. The other expert evaluates them as grade 1 despite their size because their other excellent qualities make up for their small size. The experimenter places both batches together and again asks the experts to evaluate the quality. The experts can see no additive change in the quality as a result of combining the two batches of potatoes. Therefore, this property is not measurable, either.

The investigator decides to measure the property of number in his carload of potatoes. He assigns a numeral to each potato in the carload, and these numbers can be used in arithmetic computations. When he takes an aggregation of fifty potatoes and combines them with another of twenty-five potatoes, the resulting pack contains seventy-five potatoes, as arithmetical deductions predict it will. He discovers that expert judges are not required to assign numbers to this property. Counting potatoes is a routine matter and disagreements such as those he encountered with expert judges ascertaining the excellence of the potatoes are rare and easily settled.

Encouraged by his success with counting the potatoes, the researcher decides to quantify the space filled by the carload of potatoes. Taking a yardstick he lays off lengths of the yardstick against the length of the car. His yardstick is divided into thirty-six equal parts. He has available, also, a meter stick divided into one-hundred equal parts. He finds that he is assigning numbers to a continuous surface or a continuum rather than counting individuals but each dividing point on his yardstick can be treated as an individual and he can count each alignment of the yardstick as thirty-six until he reaches the end of the car, when he discovers that his yardstick projects beyond the end. He solves this problem by deciding to count the units up to the closest line on the yardstick. He tries the operation several times and discovers that he assigns the same number to the length of the car each time. He then tests to see if this method of quantification is a measurement by taking two lengths of board and assigning numbers to each. He finds that the first board is 24 units long and the second is 10. When he places the two boards end to end and aligns his yardstick, he assigns a number of 34. This quantification procedure yields a measurement because the property of length when treated in this fashion fulfills the assumptions of arithmetic.

He is puzzled, however, by one feature of his measurement procedure. When he uses the meter stick, he assigns larger numbers to the two boards. The measurements still fulfill the assumptions of arithmetic, but the results are expressed in different numbers. When he counted the potatoes he did not have this problem. Careful examination of the two sets of measurements indicates that both sets contain the same information for there is a constant relationship between the two measurements. Once he discovers this constant he can translate his measurements from one set of calibrations (inches) to the other set (centimeters) without difficulty.

He still wishes to test whether he can measure the space filled by his carload of potatoes. He tries to derive the volume deductively from his measurements of the length, width, and depth of the car containing the potatoes. Checking the corners of the car with a T-square he determines that they are right angles and using the axioms of geometry he computes the volume. In this instance he has used two deductive systems, arithmetic and geometry, successfully because he has been careful to fulfill the basic assumptions of both systems.

Finally, the researcher decides to quantify the property of his potatoes that causes them to exert pressure on his hands when he holds a batch of them above the surface of the earth. He begins by taking a batch of potatoes in his right hand and estimating the pressure they exert in terms of the kinesthetic cues he gets from muscle strain. He discovers that this procedure results in an assignment of numbers that is unreliable. That is, he does not assign the same numbers to the batches of potatoes when he repeats the operation. However, in a general way these numbers seem to indicate that the more potatoes he lifts the greater the muscles strain. He decides to make his assignment more precise by taking a batch of potatoes in his right hand and then adjusting the number of potatoes he holds in his left hand until he feels they are equal. He feels this procedure is more precise but such quantification is not additive as were his measurements. Although combining batches results in assigning a larger number, the resultant numbers do not fulfill the laws of arithmetic. He now must confront the basic problem of whether the property he is quantifying is the result of an evaluation or of a measurement. In many respects it seems to be like a measurement. Perhaps his method of assigning numbers is not as refined as it should be for a measurement. In this case he is assigning numbers by *estimation*. When there are large differences, he always judges that one batch exerts more pressure than another; but when the differences are small, he has difficulty. He next tests the notion that the problem is a psychological one and that he cannot discriminate pressures with much accuracy when he depends on muscle-tension-cues. To aid him in testing this notion he constructs an instrument to help his powers of discrimination. Instead of balancing the potatoes on his hands he uses one of his boards and places it on a rock until the board is balanced on the rock. He puts a batch of potatoes on one end of the board and uses it as his standard batch of potatoes. He balances this standard batch with another batch adding and subtracting potatoes from the other side until the board once again balances. In this way he creates ten standard batches of potatoes. He calls each batch by the numeral 1. Putting five such standard batches on one side of the board he balances it with potatoes. This batch he quantifies as 5. He then places three standard batches on the board and balances it with another batch of potatoes which he quantifies as 3. When he adds the batch of 5 to the batch of 3, he discovers that it takes 8 standard batches of potatoes to balance the board. He now knows that he has measured another property of his carload of potatoes.

DERIVED MEASUREMENTS

The investigator examining the measurable properties in a carload of potatoes did not go beyond the processes of *basic* measurement. Scientists, however, invent concepts that describe properties that can be measured in the sense that numerals can be assigned to them. Such concepts require the scientist to move beyond the common-sense level of the basic measurements that were illustrated in the example of the carload of potatoes.

The assignment of numbers to such invented properties is always dependent upon measurements of the basic kind outlined above. For this reason these measurements can be called *derived measurements*.[3]

Density is such a derived measurement. If two liquids are mixed together, an investigator might notice that one of the liquids floats on the other. If he decides to investigate the relation *float*, he could

---

[3] This is the terminology of Norman Campbell, *What Is Science?* (New York, 1952), pp. 124–129.

proceed in this fashion. He discovers that if A floats on B and B floats on C, then A floats on C. He discovers that if A floats on B on one occasion, A always floats on B subsequently. He also finds that this relation holds for any two substances, so that either A floats on B or B floats on A. The relation is asymmetrical, transitive, and connected. However, this relation differs from the basic measurements in that adding more of a substance to itself does not change the property described by the relation *float;* adding more oil to the oil on top of the water does not cause the oil to sink. The property remains uniform; indeed, that is the unique characteristic of the concept of density. The concept describes a uniform feature of substances.

Let us say that he orders his substances in serial order, A, B, C, D, E, F, and G. He still needs to assign numerals to the *density* of each substance. He might do so by assigning numerals in this way, 1, 2, 3, 4, 5, 6, and 7; or he could use 2, 5, 9, 10, 13, 14, and 21. He could not use numerals such as 5, 2, 8, 10, 6, 9, and 8; but as long as each subsequent numeral was larger than the preceding one, he could assign almost any series of numbers to his rank-order of substances in regard to this relation. In making the basic measurements of weight and volume, the researcher examining the carload of potatoes had no such freedom. In an important sense this freedom to assign numerals is a drawback because the empirical researcher examining this property feels that his ability to rank the substances in this way represents an important regularity in the events under question. He sees a relation of lawfulness here that is not fully exploited by simply discovering the rank-order relationships. His solution to the problem is the invention of a concept to describe this regularity. The concept invented is density, and it is defined in terms of the basic measurements. One gallon of water weighs 10 pounds and one gallon of mercury weighs 135 pounds, thus mercury should sink in water; and if the investigator divides 135 by 10, he can assign a density of 13.5 mercury and if he divides the weights of the water by 10, he can assign a density of 1 to the water. Proceeding in this way, he can assign a number to each substance derived from the fundamental measurements of weight and volume by dividing the weight by the volume. This number agrees with the rank order relationships he discovered when he investigated the relationship of floating. To make his measurements more meaningful he translates them to a base or standard reference point; in this instance, the density of water is assigned the numeral 1 and all other measurements are then derived relative to the standard of water as 1.

Further investigation indicates that new substances can be measured by the fundamental measures of weight and volume, and that they fit into the rank order *as predicted*. Further, the formulation of the concept itself states a law of nature; weight is proportional to volume; if the density of a substance is to remain constant then the weight must vary at the same rate as the volume.

MEASURING THE SOUND WAVE

While the man with the carload of potatoes may seem to be dealing with relatively simple measurement problems and using obvious measurement techniques, his problem, in principle, is little different from the experimental phonetician trying to measure all aspects of sound production, distribution, and perception. The phonetician studying the sound wave produced by a singer sustaining a vowel may play the recording of the sound wave and decide that it is a soprano, alto, or tenor sound, just as the man with the potatoes judged them to be Idaho Red potatoes. Should the phonetician decide to measure the "altoness" of the voice, he will be as unsuccessful as the man trying to measure the Idaho Redness of the potatoes.

The phonetician studying the sound wave will discover that there is a characteristic of the wave that has the property of number. This is the recurring feature of certain parts of the wave. He refers to an individual recurrence as a cycle, and he can count these cycles as the investigator counted his potatoes. Further, he discovers that there are changes in air pressure associated with the sound wave as it moves through the air and that these changes can be increased or decreased by adding another sound wave. So this property is suitable for basic measurement. The ruler required for such measurement is likely to be an electronic instrument that takes minute deflections of a diaphragm and translates them into an electrical analogue of the sound wave, in much the same way as the crude balance scale measured weight. Our phonetician is not content to make what basic measurements he can. He wishes to discover additional laws governing the sound wave, so he develops several derived measures that prove important. One of these is what he calls *cycles per second*. This is the number of individual waves counted during a second or the number of cycles in the sound wave divided by the number of seconds of wave duration.

So long as he confines himself to measuring the sound wave, the voice scientist can assign numbers to properties of the wave with good results. However, he is not content to simply measure the sound wave. He wants to make some connection between physical events such as sound waves and psychological events such as *pitch, quality,* and *loudness.* He starts by asking about the relationship between the sound wave and the percepts of that sound wave such as pitch and loudness. Since he can measure the sound wave with accuracy, he must attempt to measure the psychological percepts with similar accuracy if he is to establish any sort of invariable relationship. He begins by trying to measure *pitch*. Is pitch a psychological percept with properties that fulfill the requirements for measurement? Is it like "altoness" or like cycles per second?

The researcher lets some subjects hear two different tones in a series of experiments. He discovers that he gets more uniform reports of change in tone from his subjects when he varies the number of cycles per second than when he increases the intensity of the sound wave. Not only that but the results are such that if the relation "higher in pitch" is used the various sound waves of different cycles per second can be ordered so that pitch X is higher than pitch Z.

He is still far from his goal but he has made progress and discovered that pitch has some of the requisite qualities needed to make it a measurable phenomenon. One of the stumbling blocks is the range of ability in his subjects to discriminate pitches. They are somewhat like the man assessing weight from muscle tension. But this is only a momentary difficulty because in the beginnings of physics and chemistry the researchers often posited an idealized situation to assure that they could find the invariable relationships. Galileo had to posit that his freely falling body on the surface of the earth was falling in a vacuum. The phonetician feels justified in positing an idealized ear. He could posit an idealized ear that he calls *normal* and define it in terms of the statistical concept of normal curve. Thus, in measuring hearing discrimination he may establish a base-line for his measurement of hearing on the threshold of the *normal* ear as discovered through testing many ears. He could, in this instance, posit an idealized ear that had *perfect pitch* and use only subjects that fulfilled some operational definition of "perfect pitch" in his experiments.

Using these subjects with better powers of discrimination, he finds that they arrange their reported pitch-percepts in a rank order that is a direct function of the number of cycles per second in the sound wave. He is now in the position of the researcher working with the concept of density. He can assign numerals to these rank orders, but he can pick almost any serial order of numerals he wishes. He next tries to assign numbers in such a way that they reflect what seems to be invariable relationships. He first looks for the simplest connection between the number of cycles per second in the sound wave and the reported pitch percepts. If raising the number of cycles per second from 100 to 150 were to increase the pitch percepts by 50 units and if an increase from 150 to 200 were to increase the pitch percepts by an equal interval of 50 units, he would have a measure of both the property of number of the periodicity of the wave form and the property of pitch reports.

When he performs an experiment to check this hypothesis, he discovers that his subjects report their pitch percepts do not follow this sort of equal-interval increase in pitch with an increase in cycles per second. Indeed, when a 50-cycle-per-second sound wave is increased to 100 cycles per second, the subjects report much greater pitch change than when a 10,000 cycle sound wave is increased to 10,050.

The investigator discovers that one of his problems is that while he has a basic measurement of the sound wave in terms of the number of cycles he counts he has no such measure for pitch percepts. He attempts to develop a unit for measuring pitch in which subjects serve as yardsticks. He stimulates the ears of his subjects with a sound generator equipped with a modification so that the number of cycles per second of the wave can be adjusted slowly. He then changes the sound wave a few cycles at a time and asks the subjects to indicate the point where a noticeable difference in pitch occurs. He calls this unit the "just noticeable difference" and hopes to find a consistent relationship between this measure and the changes in cycles per second of the stimulating sound wave. The relationship is not clear-cut but it is quite good. If he wishes to measure pitch in terms of the frequency of the sound wave, he must do so on the basis of ratios instead of direct intervals. To achieve an interval of pitch increment, he must provide a ratio of increase in cycles per second. Doubling a 220 cps sound wave causes the subjects to report an increase in pitch roughly equivalent to the interval of increase when the sound wave is again doubled from 440 cps to 880 cps. A ratio scale would be appropriate for this sort of measure. The phonetician has now achieved a measurement of pitch percepts, in that he no longer assigns numbers to his rank-order of pitches in arbitrary fashion.

He needs, still, to find some name for his unit of measurement; and he must have some standards for that unit and a base point. The researcher in this instance uses the octave of the even-tempered musical scale as his unit of measurement; and he uses as his base point the pitch percepts associated with *A* above middle *C*, a tone of 440 cps. He further subdivides the octave into tones and labels the tones with letters of the alphabet. Whenever the phonetician wishes to make precise measurements, he must be sure that his 440 cps tone is close enough to 440 cps for his purpose. It is only through

the use of standard weights and measures, for example, that researchers can compare very precise measurements.

The phonetician does not know how accurately he is measuring
variations in pitch percepts. He is dependent upon observation of
the responses of his subjects, when he stimulates them with various
sounds, for his measurements. He has to verify indirectly their pitch
percepts because he cannot observe them directly. Still, the behavior
of his subjects exhibits a kind of uniformity that fulfills the criterion
for a measurement. The experimental phonetician measures pitch
percepts quite well, as well as most other empirically oriented investigators in speech and theatre arts, and better than many.

RELIABLE AND VALID QUANTIFICATION

Why does he do better than many other investigators? Because
his subjects tend to make reliable reports about their pitch percepts.
Subject A reports a pitch percept he calls "A above middle C" almost every time he hears a tone of 440 cps, and subjects C, D, E, F,
and G all report a pitch percept that they call "A above middle C"
when they hear a tone of 440 cps. To return to the man with the
potatoes, if he re-counts a basket of potatoes in two weeks' time and
discovers the same number of potatoes as his last count or if a number of different people count the potatoes and they all agree as to
the number of potatoes in the basket, the measurement would be
reliable. However, if the man measured the volume of the potatoes
in the boxcar and came up with a different answer two weeks later,
his measurements would not be reliable; and he would be hard put
to decide which measurement to use. The same would be the case if
another person measured the volume of the potatoes and came up
with a different answer.

The experimental phonetician does well, also, because his measurements have considerable *validity*. Validity means that he is assigning numbers to the property he wishes to study. As we shall see in
greater detail in Chapter 13, validity is one of the most troublesome
problems facing a researcher when he attempts to quantify the properties of speech events.

SUMMARY

Empirical research relies upon observation for its data, typically
quantifies these observations, and makes mathematical computations
to interpret the results. No matter how far his speculative flights
may lead him into statistics and system building, the empirical investigator begins and ends with observations. There is a close tie

between the method of observation and the deductive analysis of empirical research data. If observation and deduction are carefully integrated, the conclusions of the study are more likely to be sound.

The basic requirement for using mathematics in a practical situation is to set up observations in such a way that the assumptions of the mathematical system are fulfilled by the data.

To use arithmetic, one of the most important deductive systems, numbers can only be assigned to properties that can be combined in such a way that the combination results in an additive change in the property. In addition the property must demonstrate the relations of being asymmetrical, transitive, and connected.

Since assigning numerals to properties in such a way that arithmetic computations can be made with the results is an important feature of empirical observations, it should be distinguished from other ways of quantifying properties. This subclass of quantification will be termed *measurement*. The term *evaluation* will be used for assigning numbers to features of the data that do not fulfill the assumptions of arithmetic. The term *estimation* will be used for assigning numbers to properties that may fulfill the assumptions of arithmetic but for which the assignment procedures are so difficult or loosely specified that the quantifications do not fulfill the assumptions of arithmetic.

Basic measurements can be made of such properties as weight, length, and time. Derived measurements are more complicated than basic measurements and are dependent on basic measurements. Derived measurements result from the invention of operational concepts such as specific gravity and cycles per second.

Two important features of quantification of observations in empirical research in speech are the reliability and validity of the process of assigning numbers. If the process of quantification is repeated at different times by different observers and they always assign the same number to the property, the process is called *reliable*. If the number is assigned to the property under investigation rather than to some other features of the observations, the process of quantification is termed *valid*.

Suggested Readings

Bergmann, Gustav. *Philosophy of Science*. Madison: The University of Wisconsin Press, 1957.

Campbell, Norman. *What Is Science?* New York: Dover Publications, Inc., 1952.

Feigl, H., and May Brodbeck, eds. *Readings in the Philosophy of Science*. New York: Appleton-Century-Crofts, 1953.

Russell, Bertrand. *Introduction to Mathematical Philosophy*. London: George Allen and Unwin, Ltd., 1919.

Stevens, S. S. "Mathematics, Measurement and Psychophysics," in *Handbook of Experimental Psychology*, ed. S. S. Stevens. New York: John Wiley & Sons, Inc., 1951, pp. 1–50.

PROJECTS

1) Work out the symbols of a base-eight arithmetic that would describe the property of number equivalent to the property of number described by the first twenty-five symbols of our conventional base-ten arithmetic. Here, as a hint, are the equivalent numerals for the next five collections.

Base ten	Base eight
26	32
27	33
28	34
29	35
30	36

2) Find three examples of each of the following kinds of relations:

a) asymmetrical relations
b) transitive relations
c) connected relations

3) Using the tools of linguistic analysis developed in Chapters 4 and 5 analyze the definitions of *quantification, measurement, estimation,* and *evaluation,* furnished in this chapter. Write a short paper discussing the advantages and disadvantages of these arbitrary definitions.

4) Construct a syntactical system along the lines suggested in this chapter. Let capital letters A, B, C . . . Z stand for statements that are either true or false. Let "#" stand for the combination rule that A#B means A is false and B is false. Let "__" stand for the combination rule that A means A is true. Let "*" stand for the combination rule that A*B means A is false and B is true or A is true and B is false but not that A and B are both either true or false. You may add more arbitrarily defined combination rules if you wish. The final assumption is that all allowable combinations must result in false statements as conclusions. For example, these theorems result in false conclusions and are allowable:

premise	A#B	premise	A#B
conclusion	A	conclusion	B
premise	A*B	premise	A*B
premise	A	premise	B
conclusion	B	conclusion	A

See how many other theorems you can develop from these few symbols and a limited number of combination rules.

Questions for Discussion

1) Why must the conclusion of a deductive system necessarily be true if the premises are true?

2) If the premises of a deductive argument such as a problem in addition are false what can be said about the conclusion? (Sample problem: The two false premises are that John has five apples and Bill has five apples. The problem is how many apples does Bill have if John gives him all of John's apples? In point of fact John has eight apples and Bill has two apples.)

3) When a speech teacher assigns a number to a student's speech, oral reading, or acting performance would this be quantification as defined in this chapter? Would it be a measurement? An evaluation? An estimation?

4) Are there any measurable properties in plays or speeches?

CHAPTER THIRTEEN

QUANTIFICATION AND STATISTICS

QUANTIFICATION IN SPEECH RESEARCH

Chapter 12 contained an extensive explication of the nature of measurement. During the course of that discussion the concepts of evaluation and estimation were briefly defined and discussed but they were not explained in detail nor applied to the problems of quantification in speech. Another method of quantification that is often employed in speech research—the use of tests—has not yet been examined. We shall begin our consideration of quantification and statistics by a more detailed examination of evaluations, estimations, and tests.

EVALUATION

The empirical researcher in speech sometimes studies aspects of speech events that cannot, even theoretically, be measured. For example, he often quantifies evaluations. If we recall the discussion of statements of fact and of taste developed in Chapter 4, we can see that evaluations based upon statements of value or of taste will result in conflicting judgments. In Chapter 11 we examined the process of evaluation as it unfolds in a critical work of scholarship. The empirical investigator uses much the same procedure when making evaluations except that he usually assigns numbers to the judgments that are made. The process of quantifying judgments can result in confusion, however. The addition of numbers to the process may deceive a student and he may feel that he is dealing with statements of fact when he is, indeed, dealing with statements of taste. Let us see how this might happen. The student using evaluations will often have trained judges, such as a certified speech correctionist or a debate coach or an experienced drama director, respond with evaluations to standardized stimuli. That is, the investigator will, let us say, ask a panel of experts to "judge" some aspect of the vocal production of a series of subjects—perhaps the "pleasantness" of voice quality. In such cases, the investigator may quantify the judgments of the experts by assigning numbers to the evaluations. This is done to facilitate interpretation. What the investigator says, in effect, is that "Judge *A* rates subject *z* at the *5* level and subject *y* at the *4* level with regard to this quality." If he is not careful he may infer from this statement another statement such as "Subject *z* has more of a property called 'pleasant voice quality' than subject *y*, because *z* has *5* units of that property and *y* has *4* units of that property." The second statement is phrased like a statement of fact and may be misinterpreted as a statement of fact. Actually both of these statements reflect additional statements of taste or opinion that express the judges *criteria of evaluation*. The check marks on the rating scale should be interpreted as sentences of the order, "I *like z's* voice quality better than *y's*."

In making judgments of this kind, even highly trained observers disagree. One judge may prefer a voice quality that is the result of systematic study under the guidance of a teacher of voice improvement. Another judge may dislike this voice quality and consider it affected and unnatural. He may prefer the kind of voice quality that has developed without systematic study. Two drama directors may disagree about the quality of acting because they disagree about "method" acting. Two certified speech correctionists may disagree about stuttering because one may prefer a certain kind of block and rate a stutterer who blocks in this way as less severe than another stutterer who blocks in a different way.

To add to the possibility of confusion, investigators, on occasion, may give an operational definition to such concepts as "good voice quality" or "stuttering severity." If the concept of "stuttering" is given an operational definition such as counting the number of blocks per unit of time, then the number assigned to a given sample of stuttering would be a derived measure. That is, it would be like cycles per second or specific gravity in that it would be based upon the basic measurement of the number of time units and the counting of the individual blocks. The fact that a stuttering block may be difficult to isolate and count and therefore the reliability of the counters would be lower than the reliability of counters examining sound waves does not change the fact that such operational definitions translate evaluations into measurements. However, the concepts usually lose something in the translation. Stuttering severity as *measured* by the counting of the number of blocks per minute is not always the same experience as stuttering severity evaluated by trained judges.

ESTIMATION

If the investigator is interested not only in a property of the stimulus (speech event) but also in the response to that stimulus (attitude, meaning, pitch percept), he may be dealing with measurements or, if not a measurement, an estimation as well as an evaluation. For example, let us take the student who wishes to study the change of attitude of an audience that results from manipulating the structure of a speech from weakest argument to strongest and vice versa. He begins first with an evaluation in which he develops a number of arguments and asks a panel of judges to rate them as to *strength*. Next he arranges his stimulus events into the order he feels will best manipulate the variable he wishes to study and he plays these speeches to new audiences. Now, he asks not for an evaluation of the strength of the argument but for an estimation of the change of attitude *within the subjects* as a response to the speech. The subjects might mark an attitude scale with a check at number 5 (strongly agree). The investigator observes the number on the attitude scale and infers that the indirectly verifiable statement of fact that "Subject z has a positive attitude of weight 5 with the speaker's position," is true. Since *agreement* and *positive attitude* can be names for psychological states just as *pitch* can be a name for a psychological state, these are statements of fact and might be measured rather than evaluated. If psychological states are to be measured, however, they must have the properties required for measurement. Let us assume that the subjects understood directions, interpreted their psychological states accurately and described these states on the attitude scales as honestly as they could. They must still assign numbers to the intensity of the attitude. Certainly when they try to place the scale on their perceptions and assign numbers to them they are likely to make errors. The problem is analogous to the problem of measuring pitch percepts considered in Chapter 12. Since the techniques for assigning numbers to meanings, attitudes, and opinions are as yet loosely specified they can, at best, be termed *estimation* procedures.

TESTS

Another way in which empirical researchers quantify their observations is by the use of tests. Tests differ from evaluations, estimations and measurements. Testing procedures are usually based upon a correlation between two sets of responses. For example, the test a teacher uses in the classroom is often based upon the assumption that the student's answers (the first set of responses) are correlated with what the student has learned in the class (the second set of responses). In general, the testing procedure establishes a set of responses to the test and correlates these responses with the behavior under study. The correlation is often computed statistically by means of a correlation coefficient.

The differences among measurements, estimations, evaluations and tests can be illustrated by examining how these various quantification procedures have been used in the considerable body of research into stage fright. Stage fright has been intensively studied. Investigators have used all of the techniques of quantification described above. They have used instruments to count heartbeat and rate of breathing and to assign numbers to the amount of perspiration in the palms of subjects giving speeches. The results of such quantification procedures are measurements.

Investigators have also used estimation procedures to quantify such things as a speaker's voice tremor or the shaking of his knees. An observer could also be asked to estimate rather than measure such things as rate of breathing if he were presented with a scale and asked to check somewhere between the polar extremes of *very slow* and *very rapid* or, in the case of amount of perspiration the equal appearing interval scale could be labeled *very little* and *very much*. The estimation differs from the measurement because the counting of heartbeat, for example, results in numbers that can be added and subtracted and further counting will verify the conclusions of such addition and subtraction. The scaling of knee shaking is an *estimation* because the investigator could *measure* knee shakes if he thought the increased precision would be helpful. He could, for example, photograph the speaker's knees with a high-speed motion picture camera, slow down the playback, carefully define the amount of movement required for one tremor, and count the number of shakes in much the same way that the number of cycles in a sound wave are counted. Such counting would result in a measure of knee shakes.

When the investigator asks a judge to observe the speaker and assign a number to an equal-appearing interval scale ranging from *poised* to *anxious* the result is an evaluation. The judge rating the amount of stage fright is like the judge rating an oration's merit by assigning a number between 70 and 100. The two situations are similar because in each instance the judge must decide what to look for in making his rating and he must decide on the relative importance of each factor in his final score. Thus, if he is looking for the amount of stage fright he must decide what to look for. He may decide on tremor in voice, shaking of knees, changes of color in face, amount of perspiration, and difficulty in swallowing. He must then make some decision as to the relative importance of these factors in his evaluation. The judge evaluating an oration does the same. He may decide to look for the appropriateness of the topic, the use of language, the development of ideas, the use of gesture, and the use of voice. He also makes some decision as to the importance of these various factors in the over-all evaluation of the oration.

If the investigator gives the subjects of his study the test called "Personal Report on Confidence as a Speaker," his procedure is still different. In this case he asks the subjects to respond to a hundred statements such as "Audiences seem bored when I speak," or "I look forward to an opportunity to speak in public." The subject marks "yes," "no," or "?" in response to each statement. The investigator then assumes or demonstrates that this set of marking responses is correlated to another set of responses to a speaking situation.

In practice the confusion of various quantification procedures in stage-fright research has lead to difficulty. Clevenger made a synthesis of the research into stage fright and discovered what appeared to be conflicting results. Upon closer analysis he concluded that much of this disparity stemmed from assuming that these various techniques for quantification all *measured* stage fright.[1] If they had all been measures of stage fright, the low correlations between such things as judge's evaluations and "Personal Report on Confidence as a Speaker" test scores would indicate poor research technique or low reliability of measurement. Some of these factors may have been present but Clevenger suggests instead that each quantification procedure is related to a different factor in the situation. Various investigators often worked with different *operational* definitions of the concept of stage fright. None of these quantification procedures by themselves resulted in an index of the property of stage fright; rather each procedure resulted in a measure, an evaluation, an estimation, or a test of a factor related to stage fright. How important any one of these factors is to the whole complex of behaviors called *stage fright* is an interesting but unanswered question at this point in the research into stage fright.

Many important concepts in speech and drama theory that are useful to teachers in the classroom are like the concept of stage fright. When these concepts are taken into the laboratory for study, they may be given different operational definitions by separate investigators. Becker has examined the research bearing on the concepts of *emo-*

---

[1] Theodore Clevenger, Jr., "A Synthesis of Experimental Research in Stage Fright," *QJS*, XLV (April 1959), 134–145.

tional and *logical* proofs and discovered a similar problem. He noted that "A weakness in the research on emotional appeals is the multitude of operational definitions used for the term. This would not be so bad except that the researchers and the consumers of research then treat the studies as though all of them are concerned with the same phenomenon." [2]

When an investigator examines the relationship between the operational definition of a concept, which is often the quantification procedure used in the study, and the phenomenon he wants to study he is concerned with the validity of his numbers as an index to what he wants to know. What is the relationship between pulse rate and stage fright? Between palmar sweat and stage fright? Between the evaluations of observers and stage fright? Between PRCS test scores and stage fright? Finding the answers to these questions *validates* the quantification procedures.

VALIDITY

Validity refers to the usefulness of the numbers that result from a given quantification procedure. The validity of a measure, for example, is its ability to measure what it is supposed to measure. If you count the number of sheep in a flock, the resulting number is a valid index to the size of the flock. Counting the number of heartbeats per minute to assign a number to anxiety states is less satisfactory. A high pulse rate may accompany a perception of anticipation and exhilaration rather than a perception of anxiety.

When we probe the relationship between operational definitions and the common sense concepts that pointed the way to our research, we should clarify our language, refine our theories, and add to our knowledge. Operational definitions of common sense concepts often vary from study to study. When this is the case, the complexity and ambiguity of the common sense concept is revealed. Becker's survey of attempts to give operational definitions to the concepts of emotional and logical proofs demonstrates the complexity and ambiguity inherent in the rhetorical concept of logical proof. If certain operational procedures enable us to quantify an important factor in the phenomenon in question, then we have moved from the ambiguity of common sense to a helpful precision and we have, also, learned something about stage fright or emotional proofs. Thus, some of the empirical studies that we may characterize, with the wisdom of hindsight,

---

[2] Samuel L. Becker, "Research on Emotional and Logical Proofs," *SSJ*, XXVIII (Spring 1963), 198–207.

as badly done, may still have made their contribution to knowledge by aiding our understanding of speech concepts.

Nevertheless, if you wish to study the anxiety reactions accompanying speaking to, or acting before, an audience you should try to establish the relationship between the numbers you get from your observations and quantifications and the anxiety states you want to study. In short you must establish the validity of your quantifications.

The problem of validity, which is troublesome enough in regard to measurements, is even more difficult to solve when we deal with estimations, evaluations, and tests. For example, let us take the attempts to test aptitudes, traits, achievement, and personality factors of individuals. Often traits or aptitudes are a function of a complex network of variables. Pause to consider what you think "critical thinking" involves. Or what, to your mind, is "stage fright"? In the case of ambiguous concepts, the validity of test scores that purport to be an index to the phenomenon described by the concept, must be clarified and established. Psychologists, attempting to deal with these complex problems of testing and evaluation, have worked out systematic procedures for establishing the validity of their tests. Four important procedures for this purpose are (1) content validity, (2) predictive validity, (3) concurrent validity, and (4) construct validity.

CONTENT VALIDITY

At some institutions the speech departments make an attempt to evaluate the aptitudes and achievements of entering students in regard to such things as acting, public speaking, and voice and articulation skills. One way in which theatre staffs make such evaluations is by having general tryouts for new actors. Each individual taking part in the tryouts prepares a cutting from some play and presents it to a panel of evaluators who make a judgment about the student's acting ability. The same can be done for a student's speaking ability. The school may require each student to prepare and present a five-minute speech which is evaluated by a speech teacher. Also a speech pathologist may evaluate each student's voice and articulation by listening to the student read selected passages of test material. Such tests have *content validity*. That is, the subject is required to do the thing that is being tested. A test of acting ability that requires the actor to present a sample of his work for evaluation assumes that this sample will be representative of the actor's ability. Although content validity procedures have merit, there are some problems in establishing the validity of such tests. First, the test situation, in acting, must furnish a response for evaluation that is a sample of the total acting responses of the individual. The test situation may bias the results so the acting that is sampled is different from the acting that the individual would do in a production. Such factors as the lack of a regular audience, sickness, nervousness, having a poor day, or picking a poor selection to work with, might bias the individual sample—even granting that the acting sample is similar to the acting performances of the actor. Finally, the observers must take valid judgments. They must base their evaluation on acting and not on sympathy for the actress, her physical attractiveness, or other traits that are not pertinent to the study.

PREDICTIVE VALIDITY

If an empirical researcher wanted to examine the tryouts of a university theatre to determine their validity, he might examine their *predictive validity*. He could check on the individuals tested during the tryouts to see how well they did in the university theatre during their collegiate career. If the students who received high ratings in the tryouts subsequently were active and successful in the university theatre productions and the students who received low ratings turned out to be unsuccessful, the tryouts would have predictive validity.

Tryouts are time-consuming and require skilled evaluators to be successful. Many times we would find some index of ability useful but we cannot employ elaborate procedures such as voice and articulation screening of freshmen or tryouts for actors. If an empirical researcher tries to develop a paper and pencil test of acting ability to save manpower and time, he obviously will no longer have a test with content validity but he could still check the validity of his test by using the predictive validity check.

CONCURRENT VALIDITY

An extensive predictive procedure is, of necessity, time consuming and the researcher may want some evidence of validity in the interim as he waits for the results of predictive validity. He could use a *concurrent validity* check to furnish such evidence. To do so he would select several groups of actors of different levels of demonstrated ability. He might have a group of professional actors of recognized skill as representative of high ability in acting. He might have a group of actors who are members of the National Collegiate Players as representative of moderate acting ability. He might set up another group of freshmen students interested in acting as a group of still lesser ability and a final group of freshmen engineering students as representative of the least amount of acting ability. He would then give his test to all four groups and check to see if his test discriminated among the four groups.

CONSTRUCT VALIDITY

If his test fails to have high predictive or concurrent validity he could still justify its use on the basis of construct validity. He may feel that his test does correlate with acting ability although there are so many other factors involved in success as an actor such as luck, politics, and drive that acting ability is not a large enough factor to show up in his predictive and concurrent validity checks. In this situation the investigator might turn to construct validity. That is, he would attempt to justify the test by utilizing the theoretical constructs that served as the basis for the test's development as an argument in favor of its usefulness. Let us say that among the theoretical constructs that led to the development of the test were the following: that actors tend to be more senstive, to have more feminine characteristics, and to have more exhibitionary tendencies, than nonactors. The researcher could then justify the inclusion of test items to measure these traits by saying the test measures the traits which are an important part of acting ability. He might go further and empirically test some of the constructs; for example, he might put untrained subjects who had high scores on the exhibitionary items into a tryout situation with a control group that scored low on these items. He might try to correlate scores on the acting test with scales of other psychological tests. Thus, his construct system might predict a high correlation with certain scales of the Minnesota Multiphasic Personality Inventory and a low correlation with a mechanical aptitude test. He could then run such correlations; and, if the results agreed with his predictions, he could use them as part of his construct validity procedures.

Ordinarily he would use every available means of determining the relevance of the test for the behavior under study when he examines the construct validity. If predictive and concurrent validity can be used in construct validity, they will be. In addition, evidence from many different sources will be integrated to make a final evaluation of construct validity.

STATISTICAL INFERENCES OF VALIDITY

Statistical procedures such as the correlation coefficient are useful in interpreting the predictive and concurrent validity of tests. Let us say that the investigator administering the paper and pencil test of acting ability wishes to use the results to aid him in selecting students for enrollment in an acting class. Assume that he must restrict enrollments. (At some graduate schools a similar decision must be made in regard to the Miller Analogy test and its relation to admission to graduate school.) As the test in acting is used for selection purposes, the effectiveness of the test should be evaluated. A statistical solution to the problem of evaluating the effectiveness of a test is to determine the *validity coefficient*. The first step in determining the validity coefficient of the acting test is to determine, by means external to the test, the acting achievement of each individual taking the test. This index of achievement in acting is called the *criterion* because it is the yardstick against which the test is validated. Let us assume that the researcher selects as his criterion the performance of students in the acting class. He does this by dividing the class into thirds. He then computes the correlation coefficient between scores on the acting test and rankings in the upper third, middle third, and lower third of the acting class. As he continues to use the test on other classes the size of the criterion group increases. Usually the validity coefficient will tend to stabilize when the group reaches a certain size. When this happens the test can be used as a predictor of success in the course. Table 1 indicates the effectiveness of the test in predicting success if three different validity coefficients are assumed. If the validity coefficient is .00 and if candidates who scored in the upper half of the test are selected to take the acting course, Table 1 indicates that seventeen of this group would be in the top third of the class, sixteen in the middle third, and seventeen in the lowest third. Selecting the students who scored in the lower half of the test would

Table 1

EFFECTIVENESS OF A HYPOTHETICAL ACTING TEST ASSUMING THREE
DIFFERENT VALIDITY COEFFICIENTS

| Validity Coefficient | Criterion Score | Number of Candidates With Test Scores in | |
		Lower Half	Upper Half
$r = .00$	Top third	17	17
	Middle third	16	16
	Lowest third	17	17
$r = .50$	Top third	9	25
	Middle third	16	16
	Lowest third	25	9
$r = .80$	Top third	4	30
	Middle third	16	16
	Lowest third	30	4

result in a similar class record. The test with the validity coefficient of .00 is of no help as a predictor of performance in the class.

If the validity coefficient is .50 and the same selection procedure is used the test will pick students half of whom will rank in the top third of the acting class and only about 20 percent of whom will be in the lowest third. With a validity coefficient of .80 the test would discriminate more sharply. Selecting the students who score in the upper half of the test under these conditions would result in over half of those selected ranking in the top third of the acting class. If the students in the lower half of the test scores took the class over half would rank in the lowest third of the class.

EXPECTANCY TABLES

Another way of interpreting the validity of a test is by means of expectancy tables. Let us assume that 100 students have taken the acting test and then completed a course in acting. Table 2 is an example

Grades in Acting

Scores on Acting Tests						Totals
80-89					I ¹	1
70-79				I ¹	IIII ⁴	5
60-69			III ³	LHT LHT IIII ¹⁴	LHT ⁵	22
50-59			LHT IIII ⁹	LHT III ⁸	LHT I ⁶	23
40-49		III ³	LHT LHT III ¹³	LHT I ⁶		22
30-39	I ¹	III ³	LHT IIII ⁹	III ³		16
20-29	I ¹	IIII ⁴	III ³			8
10-19		II ²				2
0-9		I ¹				1
	2	13	37	32	16	100

Table 2

of an expectancy grid showing how the grades in acting might be distributed with respect to the scores on the acting test.[3] The expectancy grid in Figure 2 is developed with an N of 100, mean test score of 48.58, a standard deviation of 15.2, and an γ of .71. Examine, for example,

[3] My discussion and my example of expectancy tables follows, with some adaptation, A. G. Wesman, "Expectancy Tables—A Way of Interpreting Test Validity," *Test Service Bulletin 38* (New York, 1949), 11–15.

the group that scored between 60 and 69 on the test. Twenty-two individuals fell in this category and nineteen of them made a grade of B or better. They all made a grade of C or better. Thus, a score of 60 or better on the mythical test of acting ability would be a good predictor of success in the acting course. What does a test score of 65 mean in terms of this distribution? It means that on the basis of past distributions with a given sample of students the individual making a 65 is likely to do well in the acting course. Past experience indicates that betting on a B or higher grade is fairly safe. The bettor will win about 86 percent of the time. Betting on an A is not so safe since A's tend to turn up only about 23 percent of the time for individuals making similar scores.

The empirical researcher in speech who uses a test as part of his procedure needs to know the basis for the validity of the test; and if the test has been validated against some criterion statistically, he needs to know the meaning of the statistical report and the group that was used to validate the test. In the example above the norms were developed from students taking a course in acting. Some tests give data on the general population, some on high school seniors, others on entering college freshmen. The selection of a test requires not only a check of the validity of the test but also the norms upon which the test is based. If there are several tests available, the one with norm tables that are most relevant to the purposes of the study should be selected.

RELIABILITY

Validity, in a sense, is the primary problem in assigning numbers to properties by measurement, estimations, evaluations, or tests; but reliability is almost as important because of its effect upon validity. Validity is influenced by the reliability of observations and a test or measure with low reliability "will necessarily have a low validity in all predictions." [4]

Even in such an elementary measurement task as counting potatoes there is a possibility of error and thus the reliability of such a measure is not perfect. In measuring the side of the boxcar there is some lack of reliability of measurement because of error and sometimes because of a systematic bias such as always looking at the yardstick from an acute angle. Should the carload of vegetables discussed in Chapter 12 contain not only potatoes but carrots, onions, sweet potatoes, and parsnips, the investigator might have decided to separate the contents according to these categories and count the number of individuals in

---

[4] Helen M. Walker and Joseph Lev, *Elementary Statistical Methods,* 2nd ed. (New York, 1958), p. 156.

each category. After this task was completed he could make a quantitative description of the content of his boxcar. Such a description might be that the contents of the boxcar consisted of 40 percent potatoes, 15 percent carrots, 12 percent onions, 13 percent sweet potatoes, and 20 percent parsnips. On occasion he may find a vegetable that is difficult to classify. He may not know for sure if it is a potato or a sweet potato. One day he may count it as one, at a later time as another. Other counters may have a similar difficulty. With these additional possibilities for error the reliability of these measurements will drop.

COMPUTATION OF RELIABILITY

The statistical test for reliability between counters or observers is the coefficient of correlation. The same statistical tests that were used to determine the validity coefficient can be used with suitable data to determine the coefficient of reliability. Sometimes the data is such that the agreement among coders or observers is computed on the basis of percentages of agreement. If two counters divided 100 vegetables into suitable categories and agreed on 92 of them, the reliability could be expressed in terms of 92 percent agreement.

RELIABILITY OF EVALUATIONS

Although the graduate student in speech doing an empirical study may find the problem of making reliable measurements a difficult one, it is not nearly as troublesome as are the problems posed by evaluations. Since subjective elements are a larger part of judgments than of measurements, completely reliable decisions are not possible even in theory. In principle, every measure should be reliable. In matters of evaluation, however, disagreement is to be expected.

The graduate student in speech often needs to use evaluations in his work. A student who asks why one speech has greater merit than another or why one artist is better than another or if one method of therapy or teaching is better than another must rely on evaluations for his study. Although judges do not always agree, we continue to ask them to judge competition in debate, drama, declamation, and public speaking. We try to get the best judges we can and abide by their decisions. The empirical researcher often does the same.

Generally, judges, whether they are highly trained or not, can agree about the very good and the very bad. Evaluations tend to be less reliable in the middle ground where events are of almost equal quality. Judges will differ, but the contestants who are finally selected for the state high school final competition in, say, oral interpretation, will be good, just as the teams in the semi-finals at the West Point Debate tournament will be of high calibre. If the student is interested in investigating the difference between excellent and poor speakers, he can pick the top ten and the bottom ten from a group of one hundred speakers evaluated by five judges with some confidence.

You may treat the problem of the reliability of evaluations in a fashion analogous to the problem of the reliability of measurement. You may use the coefficient of correlation or you may use percentages of agreement. You must answer the question of how high a coefficient of correlation is required or how great a percentage of agreement is necessary on the basis of the purposes and procedures of your study. Generally a higher correlation is to be expected from measurements and estimations than from evaluations and should probably be required. If the correlation falls too low, there is little meaning in the evaluation. For example, if three judges rated an extemporaneous speaking contest as indicated in Table 3, there would be little point in announcing a winner.

Table 3

HYPOTHETICAL EVALUATION OF AN EXTEMPORANEOUS SPEAKING
CONTEST

| | Speakers | | | | |
	First	Second	Third	Fourth	Fifth
Judge *A*	3	5	4	1	2
Judge *B*	1	3	2	4	5
Judge *C*	5	1	3	4	2
Totals	9	9	9	9	9

Table 4 indicates a situation in which six speakers are ranked by two judges. The Spearman's rank order coefficient formula is given at the bottom of the table. The computation of the correlation coefficient indicates it is .83. The evaluations are in agreement except in the cases of speakers *A*, *C*, and *E*. Only in the case of speaker *C* is there a substantial difference of opinion. The coefficient of correlation gives a numerical index of this high reliability.

Agreement can be increased by selecting a wide range of data. Judges usually have an easier time agreeing in a speech contest at the local level where there is a considerable range of talent on display than they do at the state contest where the range of abilities is more restricted. If the researcher confines his study to stutterers at the University speech clinic and then has observers evaluate the severity of their stuttering, they may have trouble agreeing because the range of stuttering responses has been restricted to those severe enough to be

Table 4

HYPOTHETICAL EVALUATION OF SIX SPEAKERS BY TWO JUDGES
WITH A CORRELATION COEFFICIENT OF .83

Speaker	Rank Assigned by		Difference	Square of Difference
	Judge 1	Judge 2		
A	2	1	1	1
B	4	4	0	0
C	1	3	−2	4
D	6	6	0	0
E	3	2	1	1
F	5	5	0	0
Sum				6

$$R = 1 - \frac{6(\text{sum of square of differences})}{N(N^2 - 1)}$$

$$R = 1 - \frac{6(6)}{6(36 - 1)}$$

$$R = 1 - \frac{6}{35} = \frac{29}{35} = .83$$

R is the rank order correlation of **Spearman**.

N is the number of speakers.

referred to the University clinic for treatment. The same problem must sometimes be faced when college students are used as subjects and their responses evaluated by observers. The college selection procedures may have restricted the range of responses. The researcher should be on the alert for this problem if he selects his subjects from speech courses and asks his judges to evaluate some feature of their speech.

RELIABILITY OF TESTS

There is a close relationship between the validity and the reliability of a test. Lack of reliability is sufficient to demonstrate lack of validity. Techniques for checking the reliability of a test include using the same items in a test and then in a retest, using two sets of test items drawn from a pool of similar items in a test and then in a retest, and using the same items from the same testing situation by dividing them into halves and comparing the reliability of the two halves.

Each procedure has advantages and disadvantages. The test and retest with the same set of items assures that there is no variation introduced by a change in questions. However, the researcher must try to sort out the amount of the change in the two test scores that is due to lack of reliability of the test and the amount that is due to changes in the person taking the test. The subject may remember the test to some extent or he may have practiced the skill or learned some of the information since he first took the test, and thus the change in score may reflect a change in the subject rather than a lack of reliability in the test. The researcher must balance the advantage of keeping his test items constant with the possible changes in the subject because of having taken the test before and because of other influences upon him.

If two forms of the same test can be developed, some additional reliability checks are possible. In addition to testing first with one form and then retesting at a later time with the other form, the two forms of the test could be administered at the same time. Testing with two forms of the test at the same time cuts down on the changes in the subjects that might affect test scores.

The procedure for developing two forms of a test is similar to the procedure for developing any test. A large pool of test items is developed. A random sample of the test items is drawn for each of the two test forms. In the test and then retest check of reliability the two forms should be administered so any changes due to fatigue or environment are not reflected in the scores. The time interval should not be so long, however, that the factor being tested can have changed appreciably. If the two forms of the tests are administered at the same testing session, the difference in scores will indicate variability of sampling from the pool of questions as well as a check on reliability of the test. Assume that the original pool of questions contained 1,000 items. If 50 tests, each containing 100 questions, were drawn at random from this pool of questions and given to a subject, he would not make the same score on each test. Thus, even assuming all other variables remain constant, the sampling procedure itself will introduce some variability into the scores.

When only one form of a test is available and the researcher wishes not to retest, he often divides the test into halves and compares the score on these two halves. This procedure is really very much like administering two forms of the test at the same testing session. The number of ways in which a test can be halved is very large. If the test items are of similar difficulty and comparable in other respects, the test can simply be split in half and each half used as a subtest. Another way of dividing the test under these conditions is to put the odd-numbered questions into one subtest and the even-numbered into another. If the test items are not comparable, then the split half and odd-even ways of dividing the test may be unsuitable. For example, if success on prior questions governs to some extent success in answering a given item, these ways of splitting the test would not be appropriate.

SCALES AND STATISTICS

Observation is the ultimate base for empirical research. The empirical researcher's first important task is to specify his operational definitions in such a fashion that they yield the most reliable and valid numerical descriptions of his data that are possible under the limitations imposed by his study. His second task is to analyze the nature of the properties described by his data to decide what deductive systems can be used to analyze this information. Of course, if he has discovered a property that exhibits the relations of being asymmetrical, transitive and connected, and if he has been able to assign numbers to this property in such a way that they fulfill the assumptions of arithmetic, he may use arithmetic and most branches of statistical analysis in his computations. Quite often, however, the investigator in speech cannot make these assumptions. In any case, he should examine his data carefully to discover the relational characteristics of the property he is investigating and the assumptions that can be made about the information contained in the numbers he assigns to the properties under study. Empirical researchers in the social sciences have developed the concept of a *scale* to aid in discovering what assumptions can be made about a given set of numbers and what computations are justified. A scale is an orderly arrangement of data that allows for the assignment of numbers in a systematic fashion. There are two sides to the scaling procedure—objective and subjective. The objective side reflects the characteristics of the relations that order the data and the subjective side refers to the procedure of selecting numbers to describe the data. The actual length of an object being measured (objective side) plays a determining role in the decision that the object is 39.37 inches long. The length of the object can be described as 39.37 inches long or 100 centimeters long, however, and the decision as to which unit of length to use is a subjective decision. Data may be ordered in nominal, ordinal, direct interval, and ratio scales.

THE NOMINAL SCALE

The simplest sort of scale is the *nominal* scale. A researcher assigning numbers to events according to a nominal scale, uses them as names. A speech teacher might use a nominal scale in assigning numbers to the teams at the start of a debate tournament. He might call school *A*'s representatives affirmative 5 and negative 5. The basic observational process for developing a nominal scale is the determination of equality. If the affirmative team is from the same school as the negative team it would be assigned the same number. The relations that must hold between two events in order to generate a nominal scale are those of being symmetrical, transitive, and reflexive. In the case of our hypothetical example of debate teams, a symmetrical relation is one in which if the affirmative team is from the same school as the negative team, then the negative team must likewise be from the same school as the affirmative team. If team A is from the same school as team B and team B is from the same school as team C, then team A is from the same school as team C, so the relation is transitive. Team A must always represent the same school. Such a relation is reflexive. The assignment of numbers to various events on this basis is arbitrary, and the numbers may be drawn from a hat. The tournament director makes no assumption of difference between the events named by the numbers nor does he make any assumption of *distance* on any dimension of difference. The numbers do not describe any amount of difference along a scale analogous to the distance of length along a yardstick. The nominal scale fulfills few assumptions of statistics and the statistical treatments suitable for such a scale are limited. The statistical computations that are justified include the determination of the number of cases within each category (number of debaters from school 5), the determination of the mode (which school had the most debaters), and some contingency statistics, including the contingency correlation.

THE ORDINAL SCALE

The next scale in simplicity is an *ordinal* scale which is defined by connected, asymmetrical, and transitive relations. A rank order evaluation or estimation would exemplify this scale. The ranking of pitch percepts into an order discussed in Chapter 12 illustrates this scale. The basic observational process for an ordinal scale is the determination of difference along some dimension. Along the dimension of pitch the difference was "higher than" or "lower than." Of any two pitches it could be said that one was higher than another; that if A was higher than B, then B was not higher than A; that if A was higher than B, and B higher than C, then A was higher than C. Although an ordinal scale assumes distance along some relevant dimension, the observational technique is not refined to the point where numbers can be reliably assigned to describe the distance. The statistical treatments that can be used with an ordinal scale include the median, percentiles, and rank-order correlation formulas such as the Spearman *rho* or the Kendall *tau*.

DIRECT INTERVAL SCALE

If the investigator has refined his observational process to the point that a serial order can be determined and the order is discovered to be additive, then he can use a *direct interval* scale to describe his data. To use the direct interval scale he assumes a difference along some dimension and a unit of measurement, expressed in equal intervals, that can be used to describe the amount of distance. The basic observational technique is the determination of equality of intervals. The hypothetical example in Chapter 12 where the investigator established a standard interval for measurement of the weight of potatoes is an example of the determination of equality of intervals. The direct interval scale illustrates the subjective and objective features of scaling in that the objective relations that order the property are asymmetrical, transitive, and connected, and the subjective procedure for assigning numbers to the property requires the determination of equality of intervals. If we measure the vital capacities of a group of subjects and make a series of measurements, which show that A has a vital capacity of 3,500 cc, B has a vital capacity of 3,550 cc, and C, 3,600 cc, the result is a direct interval scale. Not only can we say that C has a greater vital capacity than B but the magnitude of the difference can be assigned a number that describes the amount of difference in equal interval units. The objective side of the scale is the magnitude of the difference; the subjective side is our choice of the unit to use in describing the size of that difference. The use of cubic centimeters or cubic inches will make a difference in the numbers we use on the scale. The information about the data contained in the scale remains the same in either instance, however.

The direct interval scale marks a crucial dividing line between measurements and other quantification procedures. It has wide ramifications in terms of the statistical treatments that can be used to interpret the data. Many of the quantification procedures used in speech research result in nominal or ordinal scales and the statistical treatments that are justified are therefore restricted.

Most of the common statistical tests are applicable to data ordered in a direct interval scale. Such computations as means, standards deviations, Pearson correlations, the t test, and the F test are all justified.

THE RATIO SCALE

On some occasions, when observational techniques are sufficiently refined, the serial order is such that a ratio scale describes it more accurately than a direct interval scale. The hypothetical example of the phonetician studying pitch percepts in Chapter 12 illustrates such an order. He discovered that a direct interval scale was not appropriate for the measure of pitch percepts, but that a ratio scale was suitable. The essential observational technique in determining a ratio scale is the discovery of equality of ratios. When the phonetician discovered that a ratio of two to one in cycles per second of the stimulating sound wave was perceived as an octave change in pitch he had made the basic observations required for a ratio scale. Ratio scales require a zero point for reference. The measure of loudness in terms of decibels requires a base point such as the hearing threshold for the ratio scale. Interval scales may also have a base point referring to an important feature of the data that is fixed. The centigrade measure of temperature, for example, is tied to the freezing point of water. Many other direct interval measures are flexible in their applications and the base point of reference is relative to the use to be made of the measurement. One might begin measuring a table at the end of the yardstick or in the middle of the yardstick. Suitable statistical treatments for ratio scales include those that can be used with direct interval scales, plus such statistical measures as the geometric mean and the coefficient of variation.

STATISTICAL ASSUMPTIONS AND PROCEDURES

DESCRIPTIVE AND INDUCTIVE USE OF STATISTICS

Statistics are useful to bring order and meaning to large masses of data. Statistical mathematics provides a way to take a host of specific statements of fact and reduce them to understandable generalizations, reconcile disagreements, discover variations, and keep the relevant information while dropping the irrelevant. Quite often the researcher wishes to describe certain characteristics of a group of people or a number of speech events. He might proceed in such a task by generalizing on the basis of complete enumeration in the sense discussed in Chapter 4. He could then use statistics to describe the characteristics of such a population by outlining the central tendency of various important features and by indicating the nature and extent of the variation. Let us say he has the computers in the registrar's office of a large university tabulate certain features of every student. For example, he might program the computer to count such things as the age, class, grade point, sex and religious preference of each student. He then could treat this mass of information statistically and simplify its presentation. He could select the relevant features for his investigation and the data would be much more useful because of the statistical interpretation. He could present summaries of information such as the distribution of students in the various classes, the average grade point, the way the grades vary around this average, average grade point for each of the classes, and the range of the distribution of grade points around these averages. The use of statistics to order a mass of complex data compiled by the complete enumeration of a class (or, population, to use the statistical term) is called *descriptive* statistics.

The researcher in speech may use statistics descriptively, but for the most part he uses statistics to generalize beyond the data he has observed. *Inferential* or *inductive* statistics deal with the rules for making such generalizations. In some studies, the investigator makes statistical inferences as a short cut to approximate the information resulting from a description by complete enumeration of the population. Public opinion polls and audience analysis surveys in the mass media use statistics in this way. The pollster observes a *sample* from the total population he wishes to describe, describes the sample in statistical terms, and then infers, with the aid of statistical models, what the results of a complete enumeration of the population would be. He estimates parameters in the total population on the basis of the parameters in his sample drawn from that population.

GENERALIZING FROM A SAMPLE TO THE POPULATION

The procedure for making a statistical estimate of some feature of a population of events on the basis of a sample drawn from that population is less complicated than other inferential uses of statistics. Indeed, for the most part, the more elaborate inductions build upon this procedure. For this reason, we shall examine the use of statistics to generalize from a sample to the entire population first. We begin by assuming that a number of random samples have been repeatedly drawn from the specified population. For example, if we wish to discover the proportion of potential viewers watching television at 9 P.M. on a given Sunday evening we would proceed as follows. First, we must make the assumption that if an unlimited number of random samples are drawn from the population of potential viewers of television at 9 P.M. on Sunday evening the average of all these sample results would be the same as if we had enumerated the entire population and discovered the proportion of viewers in this way. The assumption is that although each sample yields an answer that varies from the right answer, the average of the results of repeated samples approaches closer and closer to the right answer. Next, we must construct a probability distribution of the results of such an unlimited sampling of potential television viewers. On the basis of this distribution we can determine the odds that any given sample will fall on a part of the probability curve describing the results of unlimited sampling.

As sometimes happens with deductive reasoning, an indirect approach to an explanation of this argument is clearer than proceeding directly. Assume that the actual proportion of viewers in the total population on the given night was one-half or .5. The Law of Large Numbers discussed in Chapter 5 in relation to the assumption of pure chance and the flipping of coins indicates that the more samples we take, the closer the results approach the value of .5 heads. We make the same assumption in this case. Indeed, when we determine the standard deviation of the theoretical distribution, we may use a formula that includes the N of the samples in the denominator, which means that the larger the N, the smaller the variation of scores around the actual proportion. We assume, therefore, that the larger the sample size, the closer the results of each sample will be to the actual proportion of the parent population.

We often make this assumption in our conduct of everyday affairs. When we evaluate a poll or survey, for example, we frequently ask how large a sample of respondents was used as a base to generalize to the larger population. Consider the implications of this assumption to our problem. We know the actual proportion of viewers is .5 and we wish to predict the results of taking samples of different sizes from this population. We begin with a sample of twenty-five people. How likely are we to get the right answer? If we bet that the results will be .5 we are quite likely to lose. We are better advised to follow the example of the professional gambler and give ourselves a range of points to improve the odds. Our problem thus becomes: how wide a range of results must we set up to assure that our bet will be a sure thing?

We can answer this question, by the aid of statistics, with considerable accuracy. First, we compute (the technical details of this computation need not concern us here) the theoretical distribution of a large number of samples of 25 from this population. We examine this distribution of outcomes to find where the great majority of them will fall. We decide that we want to bet on the basis that we will be right 95 times out of a 100 or 95 percent of the time. We can now examine the theoretical distribution and find the range of points that will give us this degree of certainty. The theoretical distribution yields a range from 30 percent to 70 percent. Therefore, we can predict that 95 times out of a hundred a random sample of 25 from this parent population will yield an outcome that will fall between 30 percent and 70 percent reporting that their television set is turned on.

Keeping the odds the same, namely 95 out of a 100, and increasing the number of people interviewed will enable us to give a smaller number of points. For example, if one hundred people are sampled, the bet can be made that the proportion reporting their set turned on will fall between 40 percent and 60 percent. If the number of people in the sample is increased to 1,000, the same wager can be made that the proportion of people reporting their sets turned on will fall between 47 percent and 53 percent.

Of course, we are usually interested in estimating the proportion of television sets turned on in the parent population on the basis of the number turned on in a sample population. In short, we wish to argue not about the possible results of sampling a population that we know about, but rather we would like to know something about the parent population on the basis of what we know about a sample from that population. The argument proceeds in an analogous way. With a given size sample (N) we compute the points that we would have to give in order to bet on a relatively sure thing in regard to the actual state of affairs in the parent population. We can argue that on the basis of the sample results we are quite confident that between 30 percent and 70 percent of the television sets in the country were turned on at the time in question. The wider the brackets, the more confident we can be of the estimate. Of course, we pay for this increased confidence, because the wider the brackets, the less use we can make of the information. If I want to know which of two programs or candidates is the most popular, the narrower the brackets, the more I know. If I know that between 20 percent and 80 percent of the television sets were tuned to program A, and that between 25 percent and 75 percent of the sets were tuned to program B, I do not know very much about which program is most popular. Thus, we must always balance how sure we wish to be of our bet and how narrow we want the brackets to be to help us in our study. If we decide on the confidence level we want and the size of the sample that we have available, we can compute the size of the interval. In common-sense arguments of this sort the notion of "confidence" is similar but more ambiguous. The statistical argument results in an estimate that expresses the degree of confidence and the number of points in precise numerical terms. The measure of confidence is called the *confidence coefficient* and in many empirical studies in speech it falls somewhere between 90 percent and 100 percent of confidence. Another way to describe confidence is by a *confidence level*. A confidence coefficient of 95 percent would be expressed as the 5 percent level of confidence. A confidence coefficient of 99 percent would be expressed as the 1 percent level of confidence.

If we select the confidence coefficient of 95 percent, for example, two figures are computed from the sample statistics, one larger than the proportion discovered in the sample and one smaller; these describe the limits of the bracket that are required to assure that 95 percent of the time a sample such as the one discovered would be drawn from a population with a proportion that fell between these two limits. These two statistics are called the *confidence limits* and the interval between them is called a *confidence interval*. Thus, if a sample of $N =$ 1,000 is randomly drawn from the population and the proportion of television sets turned on is .5, the researcher could select the confidence coefficient of .95 and assert that the confidence limits are 47 percent and 53 percent. The odds are 95 to 5 that the number of sets actually turned on was between 47 percent and 53 percent.

ACCEPTING OR REJECTING A HYPOTHESIS

Often the researcher wishes to make inferences that are more analogous to the generalizations that result in laws of nature rather than the procedure outlined above for estimating the results of complete enumeration on the basis of a sample statistic drawn randomly from the population.

In this instance, the researcher has a reason to believe that a certain hypothesis or hunch is implied by a theory or by clinical practice or by experience. He wishes to collect empirical data that will yield evidence about the acceptability of the hypothesis. He frames his hypothesis in operational terms so that his data can be collected as objectively as possible. He proceeds to evaluate the hypothesis *indirectly*. The first step in this indirect chain of reasoning is to state the *null* hypothesis (the hypothesis of no difference) which can be referred to as H_0. Next he chooses a suitable statistical test of the null hypothesis. He must decide how certain he wishes to be in testing the null hypothesis and how large a sample he can afford in light of the odds and the practical problems confronting him in gathering the data. He estimates or computes the sampling distribution of the statistical test in regard to H_0. Next he picks the set of results that will require the rejection of the null hypothesis. He is now ready to do the study and evaluate the data. He computes the value of the statistical test and compares it with the set of results that require his rejecting the null hypothesis. If his statistical test yields a value that is one of the values of his rejection sets, he decides to reject the null hypothesis. If it is not, he decides that he cannot reject the null hypothesis. If the null hypothesis is rejected, the research can be viewed as an argument for the acceptance of the research hypothesis at the specified level of confidence.

A simple hypothetical example will exemplify how such a statistical inference is developed. Assume that we have reason to believe that a certain tranquilizer will aid in stuttering therapy. Our first step is to develop operational definitions for the key concepts in statement of the hypothesis. This becomes the *alternative hypothesis* or H_1. Our next step is to state the null hypothesis. In this instance our null hypothesis is that the results obtained from the experiment are due to chance. Put another way, that there was no difference between the stutterers who received tranquilizers during therapy and those who did not. Our next step is to select a statistical test for the null hypothesis. Assume that we decide to use matched pairs of stutterers and select the experimental member of each pair randomly. The test we select is a *sign test*. We pick this statistical test because it can be used with evaluations. The sign test requires only the assumption that we can compare the two members of each pair at the conclusion of the treatment and judge that one has improved more than the other. The member of the pair that is judged to show greatest improvement, either the experimental or control subject, is given a plus *sign*.

We must next select the significance level that we want for our study and the number of subjects that we can use. We pick the 5 percent level of significance and decide to use five matched pairs of subjects in our study. We then determine the sampling distribution in regard to H_0. With five pairs and two possible outcomes for each pair there are thirty-two possible results for this experiment. Table 5 indicates the hypothetical distribution of outcomes for our study. The most likely results are to have two or three experimental subjects receive pluses. The probability of all five experimental subjects doing better than the controls or of all five controls exceeding the experimental subjects is quite small. The odds against either of the last two outcomes are 32 to 1. Our alternative hypothesis was that the tranquilizers have a *beneficial* effect on the experimental subjects. We, therefore, look at the end of the sampling distribution in which the experimental subjects exceed the controls for the results that will cause us to reject the null hypothesis. The critical region is concentrated on this side and a *one-tailed* (also one-sided) test is appropriate. Had we used as an alternative hypothesis the statement that the drug was either helpful or harmful then the critical region would have to include the other side of the distribution where the controls exceeded the experimental subjects. In this case we would have to use a two-tailed (also two-sided) test. Since we placed a risk level of 95 percent on our study and selected a five-matched pairs design, there are only a few results that can be used as evidence to justify rejecting the null hypothesis. The chances of getting the five experimental subjects ranked higher than the five control subjects are $\frac{1}{32}$ or .03. This is smaller than the $\frac{1}{20}$ or .05 level of significance selected earlier. The outcome of all five experimental subjects exceeding the control sub-

Table 5

PROBABILITY DISTRIBUTION OF THE NUMBER OF SUBJECTS THAT SHOW
MORE IMPROVEMENT THAN CONTROLS IN A HYPOTHETICAL STUDY OF
THE EFFECT OF TRANQUILIZERS ON STUTTERING, USING FIVE
MATCHED PAIRS

Number of Subjects Showing More Improvement Than Controls	Pair 1 2 3 4 5	Frequency	Probability According to Chance
5	+ + + + +	1	$\frac{1}{32}$
4	+ + + + − + + + − + + + − + + + − + + + − + + + +	5	$\frac{5}{32}$
3	+ + + − − 9 others with 3+	10	$\frac{10}{32}$
2	+ + − − − 9 others with 2+	10	$\frac{10}{32}$
1	+ − − − − 4 others with 1+	5	$\frac{5}{32}$
0	− − − − −	1	$\frac{1}{32}$

jects is clearly in the region of rejection. What of the instance where four out of five experimental subjects are pluses? We must consider the outcome of four experimental subjects ranked positive and one control subject exceeding the experimental in conjunction with the case in which the experimental subjects exceeded the controls in all five pairs, because when we determine the odds on a more likely outcome we need to include the more unlikely results. The chance of getting four experimental pluses is thus $\frac{1}{32} + \frac{5}{32} = \frac{6}{32}$ or .188. This is much larger than the .05 level of significance, so if four experimental subjects exceed four controls, we could not reject the null hypothesis. We, thus, select the results of all five experimental subjects improving more than the five controls as the *critical* set for our experiment. When dealing with large populations distributed according to the normal curve, the area under the normal curve occupied by the critical set is referred to as the *critical region*.

You should always select the results that you will use as your critical set for rejecting H_0 before you do your experiment. You do this on the basis of your level of significance and your alternative hypothesis. You should not juggle the risk level and the alternative hypothesis after doing the study. Once the critical set has been selected, you should complete your study under these ground rules. To be sure, you might discover a hypothesis for another study by modifying the alternative hypothesis in light of the results of a given study, but this new alternative hypothesis must be tested by another experiment in which the level of significance, alternative hypothesis, and critical set or region have been established before the data are interpreted.

We now conduct our experiment. We select, match, and randomly assign stutterers as either an experimental or control member of the pair. We administer tranquilizers to the experimental members and at the conclusion of the experiment we have judges make comparison rankings. The judges pick all five experimental subjects as less severe stutterers when matched with their controls. These results we interpret as five pluses for the experimental subjects. The outcome is part of the critical set (in the critical region) and we reject the null hypothesis. Our study indicates that the alternate hypothesis (that tranquilizers are helpful in stuttering therapy) can be retained.[5] We cannot infer that the experimental hypothesis is conclusively demonstrated as true. What we can safely assert on the basis of this statistical argument is that the alternative hypothesis is not inconsistent with the observed sample of data. If our results had been that four experimental subjects had less severe stuttering and one control had shown more improvement, the outcome would not be part of our critical set and we could not reject the null hypothesis. If we cannot reject H_0 we should not conclude that the alternative hypothesis is conclusively demonstrated as false. What we can conclude in this case is that the sample observed can be explained by the operation of chance in taking a random sample from a population. We should not conclude that there was a tendency for the experimental group to exceed the control group but that the difference was not statistically significant. The purpose of our elaborate probability argument is simply to discover if the results are likely or unlikely and if they are likely on the basis of pure chance then we cannot infer trends or tendencies in the results.

---

[5] Our example is purely hypothetical and should not be interpreted as, in fact, supporting the use of tranquilizers in stuttering therapy. Indeed, research results do not support the hypothesis that tranquilizers are beneficial in the treatment of stuttering. See, for example, Louise R. Kent, and Dean E. Williams, "Use of Meprobamate as an Adjunct to Stuttering Therapy," *JSHD*, XXIV (February 1959), 64–69; Louise R. Kent, "The Use of Tranquilizers in the Treatment of Stuttering," *JSHD*, XXVIII (August 1963), 288–294.

If we feel that despite the results of our statistical analysis there was a meaningful difference between experimental and control groups we can present our evidence for this interpretation but we must argue on other than statistical grounds.

STATISTICAL INFERENCE AND ERROR

Although the odds are against them, long shots do win races, powerful bridge hands are dealt, and quintuplets are born. We might have gotten the results of the experiment with tranquilizers and stutterers by chance even though the odds were 32 to 1 against them. We should use statistics to draw the soundest conclusions that we can from our data but since statistics are based on the assumption of chance, they are inherently unpredictable. Our problem is simply stated but not always easy to solve. We should not reject the null hypothesis when our data are, in fact, the results of chance and we should not fail to reject the null hypothesis when the results reflect effects predicted by the alternative hypothesis. Rejecting the null hypothesis when it should not be rejected is an *error of the first kind.* Failing to reject the null hypothesis when it should be rejected is called an *error of the second kind.*

The risk of making an error of the first kind varies inversely with the risk of making an error of the second kind. If we reduce our risk of making a mistake in rejecting the null hypothesis when we should not do so, we must make our requirements for a critical set more stringent. For example, we required five positive results for the experimental members of our tranquilizer experiment. When we did this we increased the risk of failing to reject the null hypothesis when we should, in fact, have done so. The tranquilizer may have a beneficial effect even though only four of the five experimental subjects were judged to be more improved than the controls. Perhaps other variables clouded the results or perhaps the comparison rankings of our judges were not reliable. If we relax our significance level to keep from making an error of the second kind by allowing the five outcomes of four plus experimental members to be part of our critical set, we increase the probability of making an error of the first kind.

The student using statistical inference to interpret his data must, therefore, balance the risks of making an error of the first kind against the risks of making an error of the second kind for his *particular* study. The level at which he sets the risk of rejecting the null hypothesis should be determined by the use and importance of his findings. What are the penalties for rejecting the null hypothesis when it should not be rejected for his particular study? Would support of the alternative hypothesis lead to the expenditure of a great deal of wasted time and effort on the part of speech therapists? Would it result in the wide usage of drugs in the treatment of stuttering to the possible detriment of the health of the stutterers because of side effects of the drugs? Is this an area where much money and effort is being expended and the researchers are looking for most any lead to help them make a beginning? Is this an area in which little is known and almost any sort of alternative hypothesis with some support from systematic investigation would be better than the current notions in the field?

Sometimes the student dodges the dilemma by accepting the tradition of using either the 1 percent or 5 percent level of significance. He has ample precedence for doing so but he may, on occasion, vary the level of significance to the .001 or .10 level. In any case, when he reports his findings the researcher should indicate the level of significance for all his results so that the reader of his study can decide for himself if the findings are significant. The researcher may set the level at .05 but the reader may be willing to accept a .10 level, or he may require a .03 level.

The risk of making an error of the first kind also varies with the size of the sample. The notion of the *power* of a test is a statistical concept that refers to the ability of a test to reject the null hypothesis when it should be rejected. Power, in this sense, is dependent on two considerations. Generally, the power of a statistical test increases with an increase in the size of the sample. The smaller confidence intervals with larger samples discussed previously reflects this increased accuracy of large numbers. In addition, statistical tests themselves vary as to power. For example, when we selected a one-tailed test for our study of five matched pairs of stutterers, we picked a more powerful test than if we had selected a two-tailed test. With the two-tailed test, the critical set would have contained both the outcome of five pluses for the experimental members and five pluses for the control members of the pairs. With the two-tailed test the result of the experiment in which all five experimentals exceeded the controls would be interpreted as having $\frac{2}{32}$ of a chance instead of $\frac{1}{32}$. The level of significance then becomes .0625 instead of .0313. In general, the two-tailed tests are less powerful than the equivalent one-tailed tests. All things being equal you should select the most powerful statistical test for your study.

PARAMETRIC AND NONPARAMETRIC STATISTICS

All things, however, are seldom equal and often a less powerful test should be selected. As we have seen above, the quantification procedure may result in nominal, ordinal, direct interval, or ratio scales. Some statistical tests are developed from assumptions that require the use of arithmetic in the manipulation of the numbers and therefore require *measurements* that result in a direct-interval or ratio scales for their use. In addition, all statistical tests make some assumption about the data, the sampling procedure, and the distribution of the scores. The common statistical tests can be grouped into two classes to point up the importance of plugging the statistical model into the data by fulfilling the assumptions of the deductive system. The first group makes the most restrictive assumptions about the nature of the scores and their distribution and, when these assumptions are fulfilled, tests of this kind are the most powerful. This group of statistical tests are sometimes called *parametric* statistics. The second group of statistical tests makes fewer assumptions about the nature of the data and may be used in studies that use quantification procedures that yield ordinal scales and, for some of the tests, nominal scales. The second group is called distribution-free or *nonparametric* statistics.

The crucial differences between the two types of statistical tests involve their assumptions about the use of arithmetic in the computations, and their assumptions about the nature of distribution of the measures. We have often stressed the importance of selecting the statistical test appropriate to the numbers collected in a given study. The student should, also, examine his data in light of the additional assumptions of the various tests. Parametric statistical tests, such as common t and F tests and the Pearson product-moment correlation coefficient, assume certain things about the data. To use these tests you should assume the data is a sample from a normally distributed population. That is, if the scores from the entire population were plotted according to the assumptions of analytical geometry, they would approximate the bell-shaped *normal* curve. The central tendency of such a population can be described by the *arithmetic mean*. The scatter of the scores around the mean (their variation) is described by the *standard deviation*. In addition the student should assume the observations are independent in the sense that the selection of any one event for observation must not affect the chance of any other event being observed. The score assigned to any property must not bias the score assigned to any other property. Some parametric tests also assume that the populations have the same variance or a known ratio of variances around the measures of central tendency.

A common statistical treatment is to test a hypothesis about the value of the mean of a population. If the data fulfills the assumptions required for parametric statistics, the distribution will be normal. If the null hypothesis is that the mean of population is 4, and the alternative hypothesis is that the mean is larger than 4, then a decision must be made about how much larger the mean of the sample must be to limit the risk of not recognizing the difference between means. Figure 3 indicates a normal distribution of a mean 4. The region of rejection is a part of this distribution selected so that the results falling along this part of the curve are so unlikely they will cause us to reject the null hypothesis. If we set the significance level at 5 percent, a point A is chosen so that only 5 percent of the curve of the population is to the right of A. The risk of making a type one error is held to 5 percent. The two-tailed test with the alternative hypoth-

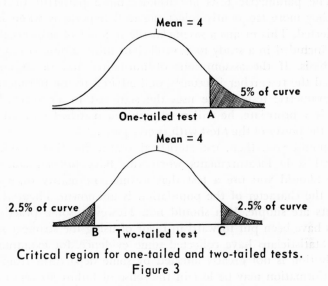

Critical region for one-tailed and two-tailed tests.
Figure 3

esis that the mean is either larger or smaller than 4 is set up at the 5 percent level of confidence by selecting two numbers B and C so they are equidistant from the mean and so that .025 of the curve lies to the right of B and to the left of C. If the mean of the sample falls either to the right of B or to the left of C, the null hypothesis will be rejected. Tests such as this require scores that have a normal distribution and reflect a direct interval or ratio scale.

In much research in speech the measurement requirements and assumptions of normality cannot be made and other statistical tests should be used. Nonparametric tests require neither the assumption of a normal distribution nor the assumption that the measures are additive. Most of these tests assume that the observations are independent in the sense that the selection of an event or the assignment of a number to properties does not bias the selection of any other event or the assignment of any other numbers to properties. In addition, they usually assume that the variable under study is distributed continuously. Many nonparametric tests can be used with data in an ordinal scale and some can be used with nominal scale data. An example of a nonparametric test is the *sign* test used in the example of the five matched pairs of stutterers and the tranquilizer. Common nonparametric tests include the χ^2 tests and Spearman rank order coefficient.

SELECTING A SUITABLE TEST

The parametric tests are usually more powerful in the sense that they more frequently reject the null hypothesis when it should be rejected. This means a saving in the number of subjects that need to be included in a study to get sufficient information to test the null hypothesis. If the assumptions of normality and measurement are fulfilled the researcher is usually well advised to use the more powerful parametric tests. If he uses the sign test in a study where the t test is appropriate, he will need eighteen matched pairs of subjects to get the power of the t test with twelve pairs.

Should you, then, use statistical treatments that assume equal-interval scale measurements when you have ordinal scale evaluations? Should you use a test that assumes normality of population when the character of the population is unknown? Theoretically the answers are simple. You should not. However, some practical arguments have been put forward in favor of using the stronger statistical tests. Statisticians have collected some evidence, for example, that t-distribution is not greatly affected by some departures from normality. Information may be lost in the sense of failure to reject the null hypothesis when it should be rejected when a nonparametric test is used. Nonetheless, you should be aware of the dangers in the use of parametric statistics if you are not sure of the scale you are using or the normality of your data. Using the parametric test may add misinformation and your conclusions may be unwarranted. When in doubt, you should seek the best professional advice that you can get about the kinds of statistical treatments that are suitable for your study, and be careful not to use an inappropriate statistic out of ignorance.

SUMMARY

The empirical researcher in speech often studies speech events that cannot be measured. In such a case he may quantify evaluations. The essential difference between measurements and evaluations is that measurements deal with statements of fact about properties that fulfill the assumptions of arithmetic, and evaluations deal with statements of taste and opinion which cannot fulfill these assumptions. If inaccurate techniques are used to assign numbers to measurable properties, the numbers will not fulfill the assumptions of arithmetic. In this case the researcher is using an estimation procedure.

Another way in which empirical researchers in speech quantify their observations is by testing procedures. A test establishes a set of responses which are presumed to be correlated with the responses under study. The process of establishing validity, which is troublesome in measurement of speech events, is more difficult for estimations, evaluations, and tests. Systematic procedures have been worked out for the establishing of the validity of tests. Content validity requires the subject to furnish a sample of the behavior being tested for evaluation. Predictive validity involves correlating the test responses with subsequent performance of the behavior being tested. Concurrent validity requires the test to discriminate between groups that have demonstrated different amounts of the response being tested. Construct validity utilizes every available means of determining the relevance of the test for the behavior under study. The theoretical constructs that served as the basis for the test's development will be used to justify the validity of the test. Statistical tests are useful in the examination of predictive and concurrent validity. A yardstick, which is often some index of the behavior under study, is selected to evaluate the test. This yardstick is called the criterion and the correlation computed statistically between test scores and criterion scores is an index to the validity of the test.

Validity is the primary problem in quantification but reliability is also important. Validity is influenced by reliabilty of quantification and an unreliable quantification will necessarily have a low validity. The statistical test for reliability between counters or observers is the coefficient of correlation. Evaluation tends to be less reliable than measurements and estimations. Judges can make more reliable evaluations if the events to be judged cover a wide range of excellence. Techniques for checking the reliability of tests include testing and retesting the same subjects with the same test form, with alternate forms of the same test, and dividing the test into halves and computing the agreement between the two halves.

The numbers that are assigned to properties of events under study can be thought of as a *scale*. Numbers assigned by measurements fall along scales that can be manipulated according to the rules of arithmetic. These scales are called ratio and direct-interval scales. Numbers assigned by estimation are often arranged according to an ordinal scale. Quantification by evaluation procedures may, when the evaluations are highly reliable, fall along an ordinal scale.

Evaluations quite often must be thought of as arranging the data in a nominal scale.

The nominal scale is the simplest type and numbers assigned to events in this fashion are used in place of names or labels. The number "5" could be used in place of the label *superior debater* on an evaluation blank. The basic observational process for a nominal scale is the determination of equality. The nominal scale does not fulfill the assumptions of arithmetic and few statistical treatments are fulfilled by data arranged along this scale.

The ordinal scale is more elaborate and contains more information. It assumes an order of events along some relevant dimension although the distance between events is not described by the numbers of the scale. It does not fulfill the assumptions of arithmetic completely, but it does exhibit the basic relations required for a serial order. This scale fulfills the assumption of a larger number of statistical treatments, particularly those referred to as nonparametric statistics.

The direct-interval and the ratio scales both result from measurements. They assume a difference along some dimension and require a unit of measurement to describe numerically the amount of the distance. The basic observational technique for a direct interval scale is the determination of equality of intervals. For the ratio scale, the observational technique is the discovery of equality of ratios. The majority of parametric statistical tests can be applied to direct-interval scale and ratio-scale measurements if the data fulfill the other assumptions of a given statistical treatment.

Statistics are used in interpreting data gathered from total population. In such cases, *descriptive* statistics are employed. The researcher in speech more often uses statistics to generalize beyond the observed data. In doing so he uses inferential or inductive statistics. One of the main uses of inferential statistics for research in speech is to generalize from the data in a sample to a description of the population. Another way in which inferential statistics are used in research in speech is to accept or reject a hypothesis. In testing a hypothesis in this fashion the researcher proceeds indirectly by first setting up the null hypothesis of no difference. He then selects a significance level, and the number of subjects, and then computes the theoretical sampling distribution according to the null hypothesis. With this as a basis, he determines the critical set of results that would cause him to reject the null hypothesis and accept the alternative hypothesis. He then runs the experiment and determines if the outcome falls into the critical region he has established. If it does, he rejects the null hypothesis at the specified level of significance.

In developing this statistical argument the researcher is faced with the dilemma of balancing the possibility of rejecting the null hypothesis when it should not be rejected with the possibility of not rejecting it when it should be rejected. If he makes a mistake in rejecting the null hypothesis, he has made an error of the first kind. If he fails to reject it when he should do so, he has made an error of the second kind. The power of a test refers to the ability of a statistical test to reject the null hypothesis when it should be rejected. Power is dependent on two considerations, the size of the sample and the number and nature of the assumption implied by the statistical test. Generally, the larger the sample size, the greater the power of the test. The number and nature of the assumptions implied by the statistical test vary but there are important similarities in the tests called *parametric* statistics. The assumptions of parametric statistical tests are restrictive and for the most part result in greater power. In addition to requiring a direct-interval scale or ratio-scale measurement, the parametric tests usually assume normality of distribution of the population. The observations must be independent and some parametric tests also assume that the populations have the same variance or a known ratio of variances around the measures of central tendency.

In much research in speech the measurement requirements and assumptions of normality implied in parametric tests cannot be made and other statistical treatments should be used. Nonparametric statistical tests do not require the assumption of a normal distribution of the population and many of them can be used with nominal-scale and ordinal-scale data. If the assumptions of the parametric test are fulfilled by the data, it will generally be more powerful than the equivalent nonparametric test. All things being equal, the researcher should select the test with the most power for his study.

Suggested Readings

Becker, Samuel L. "Research on Emotional and Logical Proofs," *SSJ*, XXVIII (1963), 198–207.

Berlo, David K. "Problems in Communication Research," *CSSJ*, VII (Fall 1955), 3–7.

Clevenger, Theodore, Jr. "A Synthesis of Experimental Research in Stage Fright," *QJS*, XLV (April 1959), 134–145.

Festinger, Leon and Daniel Katz, eds. *Research Methods in the Behavioral Sciences*. New York: Holt, Rinehart and Winston, Inc., 1953.

Hays, William L. *Statistics for Psychologists*. New York: Holt, Rinehart and Winston, Inc., 1963.

Lindquist, E. F. *Design and Analysis of Experiments in Psychology and Education*. Boston: Houghton Mifflin Company, 1953.

Siegel, Sidney. "Nonparametric Statistics," *The American Statistician*, XI (June 1957), 13–20.

————. *Nonparametric Statistics for the Behavorial Sciences*. New York: McGraw-Hill Book Co., Inc., 1956.

Stevens, S. S. "Mathematics, Measurement, and Psychophysics," S. S. Stevens ed., *Handbook of Experimental Psychology*. New York: John Wiley & Sons, Inc., 1951.

Walker, Helen M., and Joseph Lev. *Statistical Inference*. New York: Holt, Rinehart and Winston, Inc., 1953.

Wilson, E. Bright, Jr. *An Introduction to Scientific Research*. New York: McGraw-Hill Book Co., Inc., 1952.

U. S. House of Representatives. Committee on Interstate and Foreign Commerce. *Evaluation of Statistical Methods Used in Obtaining Broadcast Ratings*. Report No. 193, 87th Cong., 1st Sess., 1961.

PROJECTS

1) Write a paper discussing the difference between a listener using a rating scale to evaluate a speech and using the same rating scale to estimate the attitude of another listener to the same speech.

2) Select a thesis submitted for an advanced degree in speech at your school. The thesis should be one that reports quantitative research. Write an evaluation of the study which includes:

   a) a classification of the quantification procedure as a measurement, estimation, evaluation or test
   b) a determination of the type of scale resulting from the quantification procedure (nominal, ordinal, direct interval, or ratio scale)
   c) a discussion of the advisability of using parametric or nonparametric statistics with such a scale
   d) a discussion of the validity and reliability of the quantification procedure
   e) an evaluation of the suitability of the statistical interpretation made of the information in the scale.

3) Select three research articles from publications in speech—one that uses statistics descriptively, one that uses statistics to infer a feature of the parent population on the basis of a sample drawn from that population, and one that uses statistics to test a hypothesis. Write a short paper describing the statistical interpretations made in each article.

4) Select a topic from your area of interest that could be investigated quantitately. Give an operational definition to the alternative hypothesis and discuss the quantification that would result from such operational definitions.

   a) classify the quantification procedures as measurements, estimations, evaluations, or tests

b) discuss if the resulting scale would be a nominal, ordinal, direct interval, or ratio scale

c) discuss the advisability of using parametric or nonparametric statistics with such scales

d) discuss the problems of reliability and validity that you would foresee in doing such a study.

Questions for Discussion

1) What is the relationship between operational definitions and quantification procedures?

2) Compare and contrast the assumptions of parametric and nonparametric statistics. Why can the sign test be used with paired comparison evaluations?

3) Why might a researcher prefer to take a sample from a population rather than study the entire population?

4) What are the advantages and disadvantages of describing certain features of a population statistically?

5) Which study would furnish stronger evidence for the alternative hypothesis in the example used in this chapter in reference to the use of tranquilizers and stuttering therapy: the study with five matched pairs that was significant at the 5 percent level of confidence or a study with fifty matched pairs that was significant at the 10 percent level of confidence? Why?

6) Can a measurement, as defined in Chapter 12, ever have low reliability?

7) Can an evaluation, as defined in Chapter 12, ever fulfill the assumptions of arithmetic so that addition of the resulting numbers would provide a conclusion that could be checked empirically?

8) Is it possible for a measurement to have a high reliability and still have low validity?

INDUCTION AND EXPERIMENTAL DESIGN

████████████████████████

INDUCTION

ANALOGY

Man is continually fighting to order his confusions and his perceptions. Aware that he cannot step in the same river water twice, he must nevertheless try, for if he does not he will be engulfed by chaos. He knows that there really are no identical twins, that every individual is different, yet he must strive to find identities if he is to deal with many individuals. The basic intellectual process involved in sorting out experience is the process of analogy. Analogy is basic to the work of the scientist; searching for a law of nature in the laboratory, he tries to find a similarity in his experiments, a common bond, a pattern that he can catch in a generalization. If he is searching for a grand design or an embracing theory with only a blackboard and chalk to aid him he still needs the fruitful analogy to develop a theory. Analogy is basic to the work of the artist who searches to express and communicate the inexpressible by comparing events and forming new patterns. Analogy is basic to the teacher trying to increase his skill and comparing student A to student X and deciding to use the same teaching technique on student A that was successful with student X.

The finding of similarity charms man. He feels exhilarated in the laboratory when he has an insight into the principle that governs a process. He experiences an emotional feeling of appreciation when he grasps the analogy in Newton's theory. He has a feeling of satisfaction when he sees that student A is analogous to student X and that he has been successful in his work with student A. He hears the sonorous roll of analogies from an actor reading Shakespeare and is amused or exalted.

The basic process of analogy is the perception of sameness, similarity, equivalence. The perception that one sample of fluid is like another sample of fluid, so that they can both be treated in the same fashion and both be called by the same name, is the process of analogy. The perception that "All the world is a stage," or that the "quality of mercy" is like the "gentle rain from heaven" is also the process of analogy. When the sameness or similarity is idiosyncratic or the result of a unique imaginative perception it can be thought of as a figure of speech. When the sameness is consistent and public it often results in the formation of a concept. By the perception of analogies man constructs concepts and generalizations that simplify and order his experience so his environment becomes manageable. The empirical researcher who attempts to understand and order the results of his systematic observations utilizes this same process. The development of concepts and generalizations by perceiving analogies is the process of induction.

RULES FOR INDUCTION

When empirical research was getting under way in Western civilization a number of philosophers attempted to systematize the process of induction. They wanted to work out a set of rules for discovery. Foremost among these early thinkers was Francis Bacon, whose book, *Novum Organum,* was one of the first systematic attempts to work out a method for inductive logic. Bacon's method essentially was one of encyclopedic observation of specifics and the classification of facts with respect to a common property. He suggested, for example, one table for all observed facts with the property of heat, another table for all observed facts without the property of heat, and a final table for observed facts that had varying degrees of heat. Bacon hoped that such exhaustive listing of specifics would automatically result in the development of inductive generalizations.[1]

Despite all the attempts of the early philosophers to develop rules for induction the process has remained essentially a creative one. The psychology of discovery is still little known and studies in this area are just getting under way. Concept formation, which is a feature of the process of analogy, has been studied, however. Bruner, Goodnow, and Austin have, for example, discovered four "strategies" used by subject in forming concepts in different experimental situations.[2] As such research results are collated and studied, some suggestions about increasing the probabilities of making worthwhile inductions may be developed. Until such time, the general advice given in the discussion of the creative process in Chapter 7 is the best guide-line for the empirical researcher interpreting his data.

---

[1] See Hans Reichenbach, *The Rise of Scientific Philosophy* (Berkeley, 1951), pp. 78–94.

[2] Jerome S. Bruner, Jacqueline J. Goodnow, and George A. Austin, *A Study of Thinking* (New York, 1956).

FINDING HYPOTHESES

Empirical research projects are often designed to test a hunch or hypothesis. The hypothesis itself is a preliminary sort of induction to be further tested inductively. On occasion a study is designed to test a hypothesis developed for an earlier study. If the hypothesis is important and held tentatively such a study might well be justified. When empirical research techniques are first applied to a discipline, the investigators often borrow a hypothesis that has been discovered by scholarship and practice. For example, researchers may borrow an induction discovered by speakers, actors, or directors and test it systematically. The hypothesis that abdominal breathing is superior to upper-chest breathing in terms of pleasant voice quality might be investigated or the notion that the anticlimactic order of argument is more persuasive than the climactic order. Indeed, many empirical studies in speech have begun in this fashion.[3]

As research programs develop and research results accumulate, investigators often pursue the implications and unanswered questions raised by previous research. An excellent way for a student to develop a hypothesis is to become familiar with some phase of the research literature in his fields and to note the gaps in knowledge or the interesting suggestions for future research that grow out of the previous work.

Having come upon a hypothesis by the process of induction, the empirical researcher must still design an experiment to test his hypothesis. The testing is also a part of the process of induction, for it involves observation and the development of concepts and generalizations. For this latter phase of induction the empirical researcher has a number of systematic guidelines which have developed over the years and which enable him to test generalizations and judge the efficiency of his inductions.

Guidelines for testing hypotheses fall into two general areas: (1) guidelines for the selection of events to observe, and (2) guidelines to aid in dealing with the things that matter in the events under observation. The first set of guidelines deal with sampling procedure

[3] See, for example, H. H. Bloomer, "A Roentgenographic Study of the Mechanics of Respiration," *SM*, III (1936), 118–124; E. Mary Huyck and Kenneth D. A. Allen, "Diaphragmatic Action of Good and Poor Speaking Voices," *SM*, IV (1937), 101–109; Gordon L. Thomas and David C. Ralph, "A Study of the Effect of Audience Proximity on Persuasion," *SM*, XXVI (November 1959), 300–307; Howard Gilkinson, Stanley F. Paulson, and Donald E. Sikkink, "Effects of Order and Authority in an Argumentative Speech, *QJS*, XL (April 1954), 183–192; Harold Sponberg, "The Relative Effectiveness of Climax and Anti-climax Order in an Argumentative Speech," *SM*, XIII (1946), 35–44; Robert S. Cathcart, "Four Methods of Presenting Evidence," *SM*, XXII (August 1955), 227–233.

and the second set with the control or manipulation of relevant variables.

SAMPLING PROCEDURE

Once the empirical researcher has established a quantification procedure suitable for his research problem, he faces the further problem of selecting the events that he will quantify. He is often interested in measuring certain features of a population of events. Let us say he wishes to measure certain aspects of television-viewing events in homes in the United States between 8 P.M. and 10 P.M. on a given Sunday evening in November. The events in this population number in the millions and the researcher could spend the rest of his life on the task if he tried to observe each one. The United States Census Bureau does try to count certain features of the population by observing each individual in the country every ten years. Taking the census requires a huge staff and many observers and years of work. The investigator must select, in some fashion, from all the television-viewing events a *sample* that he will observe and measure or evaluate. The main qualification for this selection is that the sample must be such that he can generalize his findings to the entire population of television-viewing events.

DEFINING THE POPULATION

Before making his selection of events to study the researcher must clearly set up the limits of the population of events that he wants to study. If he is studying all the television-viewing events on a given Sunday evening, he must not limit his selection to a subclass of those events such as the viewing events in homes that have telephones, or, a sublcass of viewing events in homes costing $20,-000.00 or more, or a subclass in homes in towns of 25,000 population or more. The statistical concept of population refers to all the outcomes that would result from an infinite number of replications of the sampling procedure. The student should keep this statistical concept of population clearly in mind as he defines the limits of his study.

He can generalize the findings of the study to the entire population most confidently if the selection procedure is such that every event in the population under study has an equal chance of being selected for study. Every television-viewing event on the night in question should have an equal opportunity to become part of the sample. If it does not have such a chance, a bias is introduced that will have to be taken into account when the investigator generalizes the results of his study to the entire population of events. In Chapter 13 we discussed the statistical assumption that the observations are independent, which is an assumption common to both parametric and nonparametric statistics. The implementation of the statistical assumptions of independent observations is a sampling procedure that guarantees that each event in the population has an equal chance of being selected in the sample.

RANDOM SAMPLE

The technique that enables the strongest generalization from a sample of events to the entire population of events is the *random* sampling technique. A random sample, in this context, should not be confused with the common sense use of the term to refer to an unsystematic picking of events. Random, in the technical sense, means that every individual event in the population has an equal likelihood of being picked according to the rules of probability mathematics. We could get a random selection from numbering the events in the entire population and drawing the numbers for the sample from a hat. We could also get a random sample by using flips of an unbiased coin for selection of the sample. One of the most practical ways of selecting a sample is to use tables of random numbers.

When using a random sampling procedure for his study, the researcher must consider whether the sample will be taken with or without *replacement*. Without replacement the individuals selected are withdrawn from the population and have no opportunity to be drawn again. A lottery with replacement would require that a winning number would be put back in the drum and might win again.

When the number of individual events in the population is large and the sample small, the two methods are quite similar; but if the population is small, replacement may make a difference and the investigator should weigh the advisability of taking the sample, with or without replacement, preferably with expert advice to help in making his decision.

When taking a random sample from a population you can compute statistically the likelihood that the results obtained from observing the sample can be generalized to the total population. If the researcher studying the television-viewing events in the United States had a random sample of 5,000 observations, he could compute, using inferential statistics as discussed in Chapter 13, the number of television sets in use in the country on the basis of the number in use in the sample.

In practice you may find that a random sample is difficult to obtain and so compromises are sometimes necessary. The concept of a random sample is an important theoretical one, however, because it serves as the statistical model for many generalizations drawn from other samples and is the basis for modifications of statistical theory to deal with more complicated sample designs. Many statistical formulas assume a random sample and the student must be sure that this sampling procedure fulfills these assumptions before he uses such formulas.

STRATIFIED SAMPLE

Sometimes the study lends itself to a *stratified* sampling technique rather than a random sampling one. If, for example, a student wished to survey the extent and nature of musical-drama productions in colleges and universities of the United States in which the production was the joint responsibility of music, speech, and theatre departments, he might decide that a stratified sample would be more practical than a random sample. For a random sample he would need a list of the colleges and universities that formed the population of his study. He could then number the institutions on the list and select the sample by the use of a table of random numbers. To make a stratified sample from the same list, the researcher would need additional information about each institution to help him divide the population into parts or strata. He then would develop some hypotheses about relationships between certain parts of the population and the musical-drama productions put on at these institutions. Thus, if he had a hypothesis that the size of institution is related to the extent and nature of such productions, he could divide his list into *strata* according to size. He could have three strata, (1) institutions with an enrollment of 500 or less, (2) those with enrollments of 500 to 10,000, and (3) institutions with enrollments of 10,000 and more. He could then select a random sample from each stratum. Or he might feel that geography has a bearing on his study and make a second stratification according to geographical divisions of the United States such as Northwest, Southeast, and so forth. Or he might have a hypothesis that the type of institution is a factor in musical-drama production and divide his strata in terms of state supported universities, private liberal arts colleges, and so forth.

PROPORTIONAL STRATIFIED SAMPLE

On occasion, the investigator may decide to select his sample in such a manner that the proportion of individuals in each stratum reflects the proportion of each stratum in the total population. When we talk of a representative sample in everyday language, we often have a proportional stratified sample in mind. Some years ago a motion picture satirizing public opinion polling and marketing-research techniques was based on the premise that a pollster had discovered a town which, by chance, was a proportional stratified sample of the entire country. The proportion of wealthy people, professional people, housewives, laborers, factory workers, and members of various minorities in the town mirrored the proportion of these various groups in the entire country. Not only that, but within their proportional stratum the citizens of the town represented a random sample, so that all the mythical pollster had to do to predict public opinion and buying behavior was to study this town. (Unfortunately he had to keep his discovery secret for fear that once the citizens discovered how typical they were they would become atypical.)

To make a proportional stratified sample for a survey of musical-drama production, for example, the student might divide the list of colleges and universities in the United States into three strata according to their size and if one-tenth of the institutions on the list had enrollments of 10,000 or more then one-tenth of the total sample would be drawn from institutions of this size.

The proportional stratified sample might seem like the ideal procedure but it certainly is not necessary for an adequate sample. In many cases the gains from using such procedure are small. Often the hypotheses used as the basis of the stratification is obvious and important variables may be missed. Sometimes, the student overestimates the precision of stratified sampling procedures and assumes that if he designs a study using a stratified sample he can ignore the necessity of making a random selection within each stratum. He should not make such an assumption. Each stratum is a population in its own right and probability sampling procedures should be used within each stratum. Nevertheless, when practical, a proportional stratified sample generally results in a gain in precision even if these gains be modest ones. The results are seldom worse than if the proportional stratification is not used and they may be better. Often the development of a proportional stratified sample is feasible and requires a small amount of additional time and effort, as in the case of the study of musical and drama productions, and should be used. Finally, the proportional stratified sample is self-weighted and makes for simpler calculations.

The graduate student using a questionnaire, whether he is using a simple random sample or stratified sample of the population he is studying, faces the practical problem of deciding if the percentage of questionnaires that are returned represent a random sample of the population. Perhaps some bias is introduced by the process of sending out and filling in and returning the questionnaires. Returning the questionnaire may be a function of the respondent's interest in joint speech-music productions of drama, or it may be a function of an unusually frustrating experience with such productions, or it may be a function of a gratifying experience. The recipients of the questionnaire that threw it away may have been extremely busy or they may have thought the subject unimportant or they may have a bias against all questionnaires. The student would be misled if the questionnaires were returned, for the most part, by people who had taken part in joint musical-drama productions. Such biases are crucial to the generalizations that can be made about the entire population on the basis of the sample.

If the researcher, after careful study of the replies, feels that he cannot assume that the returned questionnaires represent a random sample of the entire population of questionnaires, he should send another copy of his questionnaire with a letter explaining that this is another attempt to get the information and tactfully asking for help and suggesting the importance of the study. He can expect to get about half of these questionnaires back and by statistical computations, he can judge if the follow-up questionnaires represent a sample drawn from the sample population as the original returns. If the second sample resembles the first, he has a firmer basis for concluding that he has succeeded in approximating a random sample. If he judges that his sample closely approximates a random sample, he can generalize his findings to the entire population of his study with more confidence. He should make this generalization carefully, with the full realization and careful explanation of the confidence limits involved in such inductions. The generalization must also be made with a full realization of the limitations of the questionnaire. If the researcher has doubts about the validity of some of the data, this reservation must be included in the generalizations he makes from the data.

SYSTEMATIC SAMPLE

Because random sampling is not always practical, researchers sometimes use *systematic*-sampling procedures. You should not confuse systematic sampling with random sampling, for they are not the same in a statistical sense. A typical way for taking a systematic sample from a list, for example, is to take every Nth item from the list. The survey team investigating television-viewing events in a metropolitan area might take every 99th name in the telephone book and call them to ask about their television viewing. (Of course this would restrict their population to viewers who had telephones listed in the directory.) If the original list was made up in random fashion such procedure would result in a random sample but most lists are not made up in this way. The telephone listings, for example, are alphabetical and members of the same family are clustered on the list and important variables may be associated with family membership. The student, contemplating a systematic sample, should watch for two important variations from randomness—trends and cyclical fluctuations. For example, if a student wished to survey the discussion courses in colleges and universities in the United States he would need to define the population to be sampled. Let us say that he obtains a list of the members of The Discussion and Group Methods Interest Group of the Speech Association of America that was compiled by adding new members to the end of the list. His list would have the members with most seniority at the top and newer members at the bottom. If he began with the first name on the list and selected every tenth name (1, 11, 21, 31, . . .) he would have a sample of members with more seniority in the interest group than if he selected the ninth name on the list and then took every tenth name (9, 19, 29, 39, . . .).

A student who wishes to take a random sample of Japanese television programming to perform a content analysis would not get a random sample by selecting every seventh day. Japanese television, like American, has a cyclical pattern of programming week by week. If he took every Monday night he would get a much different sample than if he took every Saturday night. Sometimes, indeed, if the survey team takes a systematic sample of a population of events and if this survey goes on over a period of time and is known to the group being surveyed or the persons responsible for the events, the survey itself may change the behavior of the people surveyed in significant fashion. For example, when television-rating services take their sample of television audiences systematically during the first week of each month the producers tend to load their best scripts and most expensive guest stars into this period.

COMBINED SYSTEMATIC AND RANDOM SELECTION

The random-sampling technique may be combined with the systematic-sampling procedure to increase the randomness of the sample. You could do this by selecting a number of systematic samples but starting each systematic cluster randomly. Let us say that ten systematic samples are to be taken from the telephone book, each sample starting with a number taken from a table of random numbers. We might take every 19th name starting with the 5th, 73rd, 71st, 3rd,

11th, 66th, 37th, 44th, 29th, and 42nd name in the telephone directory. (The starting numbers are taken from a table of random numbers.) We will have increased the likelihood of a random selection by using this combined procedure. However, even this addition of randomness to systematic procedures may not overcome trends and cyclical fluctuations in the original data.

PRACTICAL PROBLEMS AND IMPLICATIONS

Many times, of course, the method of selection is restricted by practical considerations and the sampling procedure of necessity falls short of random selection. If the student wishes to study some aspect of stuttering, he may have available only the ninety-eight stutterers who are undergoing therapy at his speech clinic. A student investigating the effect of prestige appeals on audience attitudes may have available for experimental audiences only the members of the fundamentals of speech classes at his school. The old saw that empirical researchers in speech are well on their way to developing an experimental rhetoric for college sophomores points up the lack of randomness in the selection of subjects for many research designs. Another way to look at this problem is to say that the populations that are sampled by such research are restricted.

Quite often the student finds that for his study there is no easy solution to this problem. One of his most difficult tasks will be to design his research project in such a way that he can make inductive inferences about his observations. The larger the population covered by his inferences the more useful his results are likely to be. If he is aware of this problem at the beginning of his planning, he should find it easier to adjust his sampling procedure to enable his inferences to cover large populations and he should find it easier to interpret the results of his study.

SEQUENTIAL SAMPLING

A sampling technique that is not frequently used in speech research is the sequential method. Sequential sampling is most suitable for investigations requiring expensive equipment. In this method the investigator does not select the number of subjects he will use during the course of the designing of the experiment. He plans, instead, to keep repeating the experiment until his results are conclusive. He does select a suitable statistical treatment and he sets up the critical set or region of rejection for his null hypothesis. For example, if a researcher were studying the effect of a certain experimental treatment on the movement of the vocal folds and his observational techniques involved the use of high speed motion pictures of the vocal folds, he might, of necessity, have to study one subject after another in sequence. Sequential sampling has been more widely used in the natural sciences than in speech. The procedure has some virtues in that the tests may be terminated with a smaller number of experiments than expected. E. Bright Wilson, Jr. warns, however, that using this procedure is "no job for an amateur statistician" since "conditional probabilities are involved." However, standard plans of procedure have been worked out for some situations.[4]

VARIABLES

INDEPENDENT, DEPENDENT, AND CONTROLLED VARIABLES

After the graduate student has made his decision about the events, subjects, or responses to be observed, he must make some additional basic decisions about the things that matter in the phenomenon under study. These important features are called *variables* and *controls*. When we specified the necessary conditions for water to boil in Chapter 4, then we also specified the *relevant variables*. In the case of water boiling the relevant variables included temperature, air pressure, and the purity of the water. Assume that we set up an experiment to study the invariable relationships in this case. We design the experiment in such a way that the *purity* of the water is kept constant. We systematically change the air pressure while bringing the water to a boil. We measure the temperature of the boiling water under various air pressures. In this case the purity of the water was a *controlled variable* since it is kept constant. The *independent variable* is air pressure, since we change it to see what the result will be. The *dependent variable* is the boiling point of the water. Our experimental design is neat and simple. Very seldom does the experimental researcher in speech have a chance to study the homogeneous events that exhibit such easily measured properties. Still, the experimentalist in the speech laboratory often operates from the same set of basic assumptions as the experimental researcher in the natural sciences. He often tries to specify the crucial similarities (the relevant variables) that control the events he studies.

VARIABLES IN REAL VERSUS EXPERIMENTAL SITUATIONS

The number of known variables that can be controlled will influence the researcher's decision about using a "real" or "experi-

---

[4] E. Bright Wilson, Jr., *An Introduction to Scientific Research* (New York, 1952), pp. 225–226.

mental" setting for his study. On occasion students will criticize experimental work in speech because it is "unnatural." The laboratory situation is so different from the actual situation, they charge, that the results of laboratory experiments in speech tell us little about "real life" situations. Such criticisms have merit. The variables under study are more likely to operate at full strength in the real or field situation than in the experimental setting. If the discussion takes place at an actual meeting of a management group, the variables will be more powerful and, perhaps, easier to observe than if the group is composed of fundamentals of speech students discussing "Should eighteen-year-olds be allowed to vote?" If the subject is giving a speech for an audience that has assembled specifically to hear him and he has something definite that he wants to say to his audience, the variables involved will be more powerful than if the audience is composed of students assembled to hear a tape-recorded speech as part of an experiment.

The number of things that count in the "real" situation, however, may make the sorting out of variables almost impossible. Perhaps the management group has been meeting for a number of years. The group may include members with the same church affiliations, and other social ties. The old feuds, friendships, and cliques may form such a complicated and overlaid network of variables that the researcher finds it extremely difficult to study enough of the important variables to find out anything. The same problem faces the student trying to study the "real" theatrical phenomenon or the "real" speech situation. The age, sex, educational background, color-perception skills, and previous theatrical experience of the audience will influence their reaction. The barometric pressure, humidity, air conditioning or lack of it in the theatre will introduce variability. The hardness or softness of the chairs and the ability of a given audience member to see the stage will influence his response. The artistry of the designer, the skill of the carpenters and painters, the quality of the light, the voice quality of the leading man, the shape of the ingénue's nose may all be variables operating in a real theatrical performance.

Setting up the study in a laboratory situation where many of these variables can be controlled and where the ones under investigation can be manipulated may be the best solution for some studies. The student may find the laboratory study more satisfactory even though it results in weaker effects and even though the variables are not always satisfactorily controlled or manipulated in the laboratory. Of course, some phenomenon cannot be created in the laboratory and must therefore be studied when and where they appear. Astronomy would be hard put to operate as a laboratory study. If the researcher wants to study mass persuasion or the voting behavior of the American people he must wait until a project in mass persuasion takes place or until he has an election to study. Of course analogues of mass persuasion can be developed. For example, a computer could be programmed to simulate the electorate. The difficulty with field studies is that participants are often reluctant to have a researcher observe them and they may resist his attempts to manipulate variables.

As he begins to design his experiment, therefore, the graduate student must make an attempt to classify the kind of events that he is studying. He should then decide on the basis of previous research, hints from theory, or hunches which variables are likely to be the relevant ones. Of these relevant variables he will find some can be controlled and some cannot. Of those that cannot, some may be available for measurement at the time of the experiment, so that their values, while beyond his manipulation, may be ascertained. Some of the variables will undoubtedly remain unknown. Thus, most experimental studies in speech fail to isolate and control or manipulate the relevant variables in the neat straightforward way that the relevant variables in heating and boiling water can be isolated, controlled, and manipulated.

VARIABLES INTRODUCED BY THE STUDY

One set of variables will be introduced by the experiment itself. The student should isolate and manage these variables as carefully as he isolates and manages the variables inherent in the events under study. If the child with an articulation problem is brought to a clinic room and a clinician administers an articulation test, what effect has the different environment on the speech sample? If a person says "ahhh" with his mouth wide open and a dental mirror back in his throat so high-speed motion pictures can be made of his vocal folds, how typical is the vocal-fold motion under these circumstances? If members of an audience are asked to push a button when they like or dislike something about a play or speech how different is their reaction from what it would have been had they not been asked to do so?

These problems, important as they are, are not the major ones for the graduate student doing an experimental study. The major task he faces in designing his experiment is to manipulate the variables he wishes to study and to control the variables he wishes to control.

MANIPULATING VARIABLES

THE DIFFICULTY OF ISOLATING AND MANIPULATING VARIABLES

The greatest challenge to the ingenuity of the student is posed by the problem of manipulating the variables he wishes to study. Sometimes, to be sure, the problem is straightforward, or a pattern that has frequently been used in previous research can be applied to a given problem. The variable may be the method of instruction used in some speech course. The other variables are controlled by using the same instructor and a random selection of students for each experimental group. One section is taught by the lecture–discussion method, another by television, another by television plus discussion sections. The variable may be pitch level and subjects can be instructed to vary their pitch level without much difficulty. Even with such straightforward variables and with simple directions the researcher can be surprised. One researcher was conducting a study of the voice characteristics of subjects with multiple sclerosis. He was measuring vital capacity and giving a standardized direction to the effect, "Exhale and then inhale as much as you can, then inhale a little bit more and blow out as much as you can into this tube." For the most part his directions were followed in the way he expected them to be until one of the subjects stuck the tube in his nose! After this the experimenter had to modify his instructions.

Often the problem of manipulating the variables is more difficult. Should the researcher be undertaking a project that requires him to vary the logical proof in an argument from "sound" to "fallacious" or the persuasive power of a speech from "highly" to "slightly" or the structure of a speech from "less important" to "more important" arguments, he is faced with a problem requiring imagination and ingenuity.[5]

On occasion the investigator may be able to manipulate a variable but the results of the manipulation may be so weak that his observational techniques cannot detect the change. For example, if he wanted to test the effect of variations in emotional language on audiences, or the effect of variations in ethical proof, or the levels

---

[5] See, for example, R. C. Ruechelle, "An Experimental Study of Audience Recognition of Emotional and Intellectual Appeals in Persuasion," *SM*, XXV (March 1958), 49–58; Jack Matthews, "The Effect of Loaded Language on Audience Comprehension," *SM*, XIV (1947), 176–186; for a discussion of the problems involved in manipulating variables associated with emotional and logical proofs see Samuel L. Becker, "Research in Emotional and Logical Proofs," *SSJ*, XXVIII (Spring 1963), 198–207.

of clarity in speeches, he would have to find a means to create powerful enough changes in the variable so the effect can be noticed.[6]

MANIPULATING VARIABLES WITH PREEXPERIMENTAL INSTRUCTIONS

The variables can sometimes be manipulated in the period when the subjects are being given their instructions. For example, in many of the studies of ethical proof (source credibility, prestige) the researcher attempts to manipulate the variable by asserting before the speech is heard that a given speech is from different sources. He might say to one group of subjects that the speech is given by a college professor and to another that this same speech is by a college student.[7] The subjects in a group discussion investigation could be told that they are to be graded and one member of the group will be ranked first, or they might be told that their group will be competing with other groups and that every member will receive the same grade depending on how well they compete with the other groups. Such instructions might be an attempt to manipulate the competitive-cooperative variable within each group.[8]

In this period before the experiment begins and the subjects are being briefed the variable may sometimes be manipulated by distributing directions or information differently to different subjects, or by adding false information. The studies of ethical proof in which the same speech is attributed to different speakers is an example of this technique. In a study by George Shapiro and the author an attempt was made to manipulate the perceived confidence of student speakers by having classes of fundamentals of speech students pick the three most confident and the three least confident speakers in their class. Experimental and control groups were selected from these classes and each experimental subject was told in an interview that he had been selected by his classmates as "one of the most confident speakers in the class." The ostensible purpose for the interview was to find out how the experimental subject had achieved this poise, but the real purpose was to manipulate the image of each one as a speaker by suggesting that his classmates saw him as a poised

---

[6] For a discussion of the problems involved in manipulating variables associated with ethical proof see Kenneth Andersen and Theodore Clevenger, Jr., "A Summary of Experimental Research in Ethos," *SM*, XXX (June 1963), 59–78; for an example of a study manipulating rhetorical clarity see Roger E. Nebergall, "An Experimental Investigation of Rhetorical Clarity," *SM*, XXV (November 1958), 243–254.

[7] See Andersen and Clevenger.

[8] See, for example, M. Deutsch, "An Experimental Study of the Effects of Cooperation and Competition Upon Group Processes," *Human Relations,* II (1949), 199–232.

speaker.[9] In a classical study employing this technique, Asch gave different instructions to his experimental and control subjects to study group pressures for conformity. He told the subjects that they were to participate in an experiment to test perception and the experimental subjects were told to report their observations as accurately as they could. The other participants in the study were coached to report the opposite of what they saw. In each group of nine he placed eight coached participants and one naïve experimental subject. They were then presented with visual stimuli and asked to report what they perceived. One stimuli, for example, was the matching of the length of a line with other lines. The stimulus was not ambiguous, the line was a clear match with one of the lines, but each coached participant gave the wrong answer and the naïve subject then had to report his perception and go counter to the decision of the group or agree with the group and go counter to his perceptions. In another phase of the experiment each naïve subject had a supporter; in another phase each naïve subject had a supporter at the start who later switched to follow the group, and in the fourth phase, each naïve subject began alone but one of the members of the group switched to his position during the experiment. Thus, the group pressure on the experimental subject was manipulated by making it unanimous, giving the subject one supporter, having him lose a supporter, and having him gain support.[10]

By managing in this way the information supplied to the subjects a researcher can sometimes manipulate a variable. Deception of this sort does raise an ethical question, however. Each researcher must make a decision about these matters according to his own lights. Some degree of deception is often used because it is helpful in manipulating variables that might otherwise be difficult to vary. The general defense of the practice is that the subjects who are deceived must be given a full and complete explanation of the study and the results after it is completed.[11]

MANIPULATING VARIABLES BY CHANGING THE ENVIRONMENT

Variables can be manipulated by restricting the environment. The effect of communication channels on group processes, for ex-

[9] Ernest G. Bormann and George L. Shapiro, "Perceived Confidence as a Function of Self-Image," CSSJ, XIII (Autumn 1962), 253–256.

[10] Solomon E. Asch, "Effects of Group Pressure Upon the Modification and Distortion of Judgments," in Group Dynamics: Research and Theory, eds. Dorwin Cartwright and Alvin Zander (Evanston, Ill., 1953), pp. 151–162.

[11] See, for example, Leon Festinger, "Laboratory Experiments," in Research Methods in the Behavioral Sciences, ed., Leon Festinger and Daniel Katz (New York, 1953), p. 170.

ample, could be studied by placing the groups in such an environment that only certain channels of communication are open to the members. If member *A* is able to talk to member *B* through a telephone connection but with no other member of the group, and if member *B* can talk with member *C* but with no one else, and so on, the communication channel would be manipulated by the restrictions of the environment.[12] The principle that an audience that fills the room or auditorium is more easily welded into a psychological unit than an audience scattered through a room or auditorium with many empty seats would have as one of its relevant variables the size of the room in relation to the audience. This variable could be manipulated in an experimental study by changing the environment.

MANIPULATING VARIABLES BY CHANGING STIMULI

Sometimes variables can be manipulated by modifying some stimuli that impinge upon the subjects of the experiment. Thus, intelligibility can be tested by cutting out part of the sound wave. The variable being manipulated is the amount of sound wave available in the stimulus. Portions of the sound wave can be cut out or interrupted or parts of the wave can be filtered out electronically to manipulate this variable.

MANIPULATING VARIABLES BY CHANGING REINFORCEMENT

Variables can be manipulated by modifying the consequences of the subject's response or behavior. This technique is widely used in experimental work in animal psychology. The experiment may be set up so certain responses or behaviors in rats may result in food or electric shock, and if the behavior is conditioned (modified) it becomes a dependent variable, the manipulation of food or of electric shock becomes the independent variable. Reinforcement can be changed in studies of human behavior also. For example, a number of psychological studies in verbal behavior manipulate variables by selecting certain responses on the part of the subjects to "reinforce." Reinforcement in this sense is often some indication of social approval. Thus, for example, if an investigator wished to study the development of influential roles in group discussion he might set up small groups with one naïve subject and the other members instructed to agree with every attempt the naïve subject makes to influence the group. He could then place the naïve subject in a second group in

---

[12] For a discussion of some ways to manipulate communication patterns see Alex Bavelas, "Communication Patterns in Task Oriented Groups," in Cartwright and Zander, pp. 493–506.

which the other members were instructed to ignore every influence attempt the naïve subject makes. Thus, by changing reinforcement of behavior, the reward or punishment that is a consequence of the response, variables can be manipulated.

CONTROLS

CONTROLLING RELEVANT VARIABLES

Although designing an experiment in such a way that important variables are manipulated challenges the ingenuity of the student, a more difficult problem may be that of controlling important variables that are not under study. Probably the second most significant way in which men and women differ is in the amount, quality, and nature of their speech. Sex is, therefore, an important variable in some speech events. The voice scientist must usually take measures to control the sex differences of his subjects when studying pitch, loudness, and voice quality. Studies of stage fright, attitude change, persuasibility, and meaning usually need to take sex differences into account.

Sex is but an example of the many variables that typically need to be controlled. The content of a speech is often a relevant variable and if other things are being studied, this should be controlled. The same holds true for such variables as the speaker's appearance, gestures, and voice quality. The setting of the study may be an important variable and in some research sound-proof rooms are used to insulate the experimental situation from factors that might influence the results. The complete speech event involves not only an actor or reader but an audience and a host of audience variables which may be relevant. The intelligence, personality, knowledge, and motivation of members of the audience may be significant variables. The time of day, the particular mood or states of alertness and fatigue at the time of the experiment may be important and attempts sometimes are made to control these variables.

CONTROL GROUPS

Because the most frequently employed research designs do not make an attempt to isolate and control all relevant variables, the student should have some basis for correcting his results from the effects of the uncontrolled variables. The most widely used technique for this purpose is to set aside a group of subjects as a comparison group. This comparison group is then given the same treatment as the experimental group, except that the experimental subjects are exposed to a manipulation of the variable or variables under study.

The assumption is that although the known and unknown relevant variables were not measured or controlled during the course of the experiment they would operate on the experimental group and the comparison group in the same fashion. If this is the case, then any significant differences between the two groups can be attributed to the experimentally manipulated variables. The subjects set aside for comparison purposes are called *controls* or the *control group*. Actually, the technical meaning of controls in this sense is somewhat misleading because the control group does not function as a way of controlling the variables but rather as basis for comparing the effects of uncontrolled variables with the effects of the same group of variables in which some have been manipulated.

BIAS IN SELECTING CONTROLS

Great care must be exercised in the selection of controls, for biases can easily be introduced into the study. If an experiment were designed to test the effect of tranquilizers on stutterers, a bias might be introduced because of an unconscious desire on the part of the student, who believed in the beneficial results of the drug, to put the stutterers he most wanted to help into the experimental group. A classic example of this sort of bias is furnished by the Larnarkshire milk trials. Over ten thousand school children were subjects of the study, and over ten thousand were controls. The test was designed to examine the effect of milk on the height and weight of these school children. The experimental group was given a daily ration of milk. The selection of experimental and control subjects was, to some extent, randomized but the teachers were allowed some choice if they felt the selection unbalanced. The result was that the teachers introduced a systematic bias into the selection by picking shorter and thinner children for the experimental group because they felt they needed the milk more. The control group was distinctly heavier and taller before the trials began and the results of the expensive test were difficult to interpret.[13]

PSYCHOLOGICAL BIAS AND CONTROLS

In addition to bias introduced by improper selection of experimental subjects and controls, psychological biases are easily introduced into speech research. The subtlety with which psychological bias can be introduced into an experimental research project and add new variables or skew the manipulation of intended variables has been convincingly demonstrated in medical research. For exam-

---

[13] Reported in Wilson, p. 43.

ple, the use of the *placebo* has revealed the problems of getting accurate data about the effects of drugs and medicines. Placebo is a neutral pill or medicine given in the same form as the drug or medicine under study. The placebo consists of sugar and flour or other ingredients that are not considered relevant variables. Using the placebo, medical researchers discovered there often was a marked improvement in both experiment and control groups even when the controls were given placebos. Indeed, until the development of wonder drugs, very few medicines were effective for specific ailments and for thousands of years much of the effectiveness of medication was a result of the "placebo effect." [14] In addition, subjects often made greater improvement when they knew that they were getting the medication under study than when they were blind to the fact. To guard against this psychological bias an experiment such as the one to test the effect of tranquilizers on stuttering should be set up in such a way that the subjects and the controls would both be administered pills and they would not know if they were getting the drug or not.

A bit more surprising was the discovery that if the doctor administering the drug knows the subjects from the controls the results may be biased. He may well see what he wants to see when examining the patients. Even in such straightforward tasks as checking numerical lists of data, the experimenter may unconsciously make errors that increase the likelihood of the experiment turning out in the way he desires. To return to the experiment with tranquilizers, a good technique to guard against either subject or experimenter bias is to keep both the subjects and the experimenters ignorant as to which individuals are actually receiving the tranquilizers. This *double-blind* approach helps guard against the contamination of the variables. With the increase in team research, the possibility of using the double-blind approach is facilitated. However, should the doctoral candidate be designing and administering the experiment personally he can still arrange for the experimental group and the control group to be selected by another person and the decision about who is to get the tranquilizers can be kept from him until he finishes his evaluation of the effects of the pills on all subjects both experimental and control.

Empirical researchers in speech have not always been as careful as they should be about these psychological biases which can enter into the comparison of experimental and control groups. The impressive evidence from medical research indicates that such effects

---

[14] For a more detailed discussion of the placebo effect see Arthur K. Shapiro, "A Contribution to a History of the Placebo Effect," *Behavioral Science*, V (April 1960), 109–136.

are widespread and important and the empirical researcher in speech should design his experiments in such fashion that these biases are accounted for or guarded against.

MATCHED PAIR DESIGN

A good procedure to follow to avoid sources of bias in the selection of subjects and controls is to match each experimental subject with a control as closely as possible on as many relevant variables as feasible. If critical thinking is a possible variable, they should be matched on the basis of a critical thinking test. If sex is a possible variable, they should be matched as to sex. In like fashion, depending on the study, they should be matched for intelligence, personality scores, attitudes, or verbal proficiency. The ideal of matching is exemplified by pairs of identical twins. The difficulty with such close and careful matching of all factors is that it restricts the number of subjects and increases the cost of the study because a large number of potential subjects and controls must be available for a small number of carefully matched pairs.

After the subjects have been matched on as many important features as possible, the actual selection of a member of the pair for the experimental group should be made on the basis of a random selection. The best procedure is to toss a coin. Certainly the decision should not be left to the researcher or a colleague, nor should an accidental order be used, for there is little assurance that it is indeed accidental and no statistical assumptions are fulfilled by an accidental order. Using a random selection, however, enables the researcher to interpret his results on a statistically sound basis. In addition the random selection guards against human biases of the researcher entering into the selection of controls and experimental subjects.

EXPERIMENTAL AND CONTROL GROUPS

Because of the practical difficulties of using the matching of subjects and controls, the empirical researcher in speech often uses a rather large number of subjects and selects his experimental and control groups randomly from this larger population. In this instance, he expects that by randomizing his selection and using larger numbers of subjects, whatever mismatching is done will be randomized in such fashion that it will be cancelled out in the final results.

REPLICATION OF EXPERIMENTS

Generally, research in speech requires that experiments be repeated several times to check the results. How many times an experiment should be replicated is dependent upon such practical considerations as finances, time, and administrative difficulties, as well as the conclusiveness of results. Generally, the smaller the size of the differences under examination, the larger the inaccuracy of observation, and the more heterogeneous the events under study, the more often the experiment will need to be replicated.

COMPLETE VERSUS FRACTIONAL REPLICATION

When empirical research was getting under way in speech the notion of replication of experiments was essentially the precise duplication of all elements. Currently there is a trend toward setting up experimental situations in which the replications are *not* carried out in exactly the same way. For example, should the investigator be interested in comparing the effectiveness of two different tranquilizers in the treatment of stutterers, the testing of one stutterer with the two tranquilizers would not be a sufficient sample, so the tests would have to be replicated with other stutterers. One approach would be to repeat the study exactly keeping all things constant except the two subjects and the two different kinds of tranquilizers. If the first test was run on a person with a severe case of stuttering who was not undergoing speech therapy, the second replication would be conducted on a severe stutterer who was not undergoing therapy.

Varying the experimental conditions, however, is often more efficient and realistic than the straight replicative design. If the experimental conditions are varied the effects of the two tranquilizers can still be determined and, in addition, more information can be gathered. Thus, in the study in question, the tranquilizers, if helpful, might be used not only in severe cases but also on less severe cases and in conjunction with therapy and without therapy. Table 6 indicates such a replication with hypothetical values for the improvement of stutterers under the various conditions. We will also assume that these numbers represent measurements.

Let us now examine how we can interpret this data so that we

Table 6

HYPOTHETICAL IMPROVEMENT SCORES FOR A REPLICATION
OF THE TRANQUILIZER EXPERIMENT WITH A MILD AND
SEVERE STUTTERER

Stutterer	Tranquilizer	
	A	B
Severe	13	14
Mild	9	12

gain more information than we would from a simple replicative experiment. First, we can add all four measures of improvement together and divide the result by four to estimate the average improvement for all treatments at 12 $(13 + 9 + 14 + 12 = 48 \div 4 = 12)$. The basic purpose of the study, of course, was to study the difference between the two tranquilizers. We can compute an average value for the superiority of tranquilizer B over tranquilizer A by adding the comparative advantage of 1 in the severe case and 3 in the mild case, and dividing by 2. The answer is that the average value for the superiority of tranquilizer B over tranquilizer A is 2. Since the drug will be used by both mild and severe stutterers, 2 is a more realistic figure than the 3 that would have been obtained from employing only mild stutterers.

As a byproduct of this design we can estimate the relative efficiency of tranquilizers in dealing with severe and mild cases of stuttering. The difference in the gains made by the severe stutterer over the mild stutterer with tranquilizer A is 4 $(13 - 9 = 4)$. The The difference for tranquilizer B is 2 $(14 - 12 = 2)$. Taking the average effect of severity of stuttering on improvement $(4 + 2 = 6 \div 2 = 3)$ results in an estimate of 3 as the average increase of efficacy of tranquilizers for the treatment of severe cases over the treatment of mild cases. We can make additional computations to determine if tranquilizer B has a more marked advantage in treating mild cases than in treating severe stuttering. To do so we take the gain of tranquilizer B over tranquilizer A from the mild case $(12 - 9 = 3)$ and subtract the gain of tranquilizer B over tranquilizer A in the severe case $(14 - 13 = 1)$; in this instance, $3 - 1 = 2$ is a measure of the relative efficacy of tranquilizer B over tranquilizer A in treating mild cases. Another way of computing the relative effect of B over A for mild cases is to calculate the greater increase for tranquilizer A from the mild to severe case. This increase is the difference between the increase for the first tranquilizer from mild to severe $(13 - 9 = 4)$ minus the increase for the second tranquilizer from mild to severe $(14 - 12 = 2)$ or $(4 - 2 = 2)$. These last two computations result in identical conclusions because they are simply two ways of looking at the same thing, namely the *interaction* between the two variables of different tranquilizers and variations of severity of stuttering.

The experiment could be doubled to four replications by introducing the variable of speech therapy as indicated in Table 7. There would then be four interactions, tranquilizer and severity of stuttering, severity of stuttering and therapy, therapy and tranquilizer, and the higher interaction of all three variables. In addition, tranquilizer A is compared with tranquilizer B in terms of severity of stuttering and use with or without therapy, the difference between using tran-

Table 7

Four Replications of a Tranquilizer Experiment

	Tranquilizer			
	A		B	
	Therapy		Therapy	
	With	Without	With	Without
Severe	ACE	ACF	BCE	BCF
Mild	ADE	ADF	BDE	BDF

A is tranquilizer A
B is tranquilizer B
C is severe stutterer
D is mild stutterer
E is with speech therapy
F is without speech therapy

quilizers with severe and mild cases of stuttering can be determined. When conducting experiments in which several factors are relevant (and almost all speech research is overly blessed with apparently relevant factors) the factorial design of experiments yields a larger amount of information from the same number of observations.

LATIN SQUARE REPLICATION

A modification of the factorial design that allows the researcher to take observations of all combinations of the values of the different variables is the Latin Square and Graeco-Latin Square design. For example, if a graduate student wished to study the reliability of untrained observers using five different articulation tests, he could use a Latin Square design by selecting five untrained observers and five children to be tested. If he did not use the Latin Square design there is a possibility that if one observer uses the five tests on the same child there will be a bias because of learning about the child's articulation and becoming acquainted with the child. If the observer uses the same test on five different children there is the bias resulting from the tester learning to use the test. The Latin Square solves these problems by having each tester use each test once and test each child once. Table 8 indicates a Latin Square layout for this situation, each row represents a child to be tested, each column is a different articulation testing technique and the letters A, B, C, D, and E represent the untrained testers.[15]

---

[15] Helen M. Walker and Joseph Lev, *Statistical Inference* (New York, 1953), p. 373. See also Leon S. Feldt, "The Latin Square Design in Speech and Hearing Research," *JSHR*, II (September 1959), 216–228.

Table 8

LATIN SQUARE FOR ARTICULATION TESTING

	Tests				
Subjects	I	II	III	IV	V
1	A	B	C	D	E
2	B	C	D	E	A
3	C	D	E	A	B
4	D	E	A	B	C
5	E	A	B	C	D

A, B, C, D, E represent the five testers.

If the student feels that the order in which the children are tested makes a difference, he might decide that each child will be tested first by one tester, second by another tester, third by another, fourth by another, and last by the final tester. A way to accomplish this is to use the Graeco-Latin Square design to add another dimension to the square. In this case, he would use the Greek letters, α, β, γ, δ, ϵ to represent the order in which the children are tested. The Greek is simply a touch of elegance and the same effect can be obtained by using numerals or a, b, c, d, e. Table 9 indicates the layout for the Graeco-Latin Square for this problem.[16]

Table 9

GRAECO-LATIN SQUARE FOR ARTICULATION TESTING

	Tests				
Subjects	I	II	III	IV	V
1	Aα	Bγ	Cϵ	Dβ	Eδ
2	Bβ	Cδ	Dα	Eγ	Aϵ
3	Cγ	Dϵ	Eβ	Aδ	Bα
4	Dδ	Eα	Aγ	Bϵ	Cβ
5	Eϵ	Aβ	Bδ	Cα	Dγ

A, B, C, D, E represent the five testers.
α, β, γ, δ, ϵ represent the order of testing.

One of the statistical treatments for dealing with these designs is the analysis of variance. In general terms, the analysis of variance tests whether a given factor has changed the character of the results by asking if the results of the observations of each factor can be thought of as samples from the same general population. On the

---

[16] Walker and Lev, p. 374.

basis of the variance within each subpopulation and the variance of
the means of each subpopulation a decision can be made statistically.

The procedure for developing an analysis of variance is complicated and a researcher planning a study of this sort should become
familiar with the statistical basis for interpreting data in this way
before he finishes planning the pattern of replication for his study.

SUMMARY

Induction is the process of finding data patterns, similarities,
and trends that can be described by concepts or generalizations. Despite all the attempts of philosophers to develop a set of rules for
the process of induction, the important first phase remains a creative one. The planning and design of an empirical research project
is usually worked out to test a hunch or hypothesis. The discovery
of such hunches is only a part of the process of induction. Having
found such a hypothesis, the researcher must still design an experiment
to test his hypothesis. The testing procedure is also part of the process
of induction. Most of the methodology that has developed in empirical
research in speech relates to the latter phase of induction.

The methodology for testing hypotheses can be examined in two
general areas: (1) methods for selecting events and responses to observe, and (2) methods for isolating, manipulating, or accounting
for relevant variables in the phenomenon under study. In selecting
events or responses to study, the main requirement is to allow for
some generalization of the findings to a larger and more significant
population. The first step in such a procedure is to define clearly
the population of the study. The statistical concept of population
refers to all the events that would be selected by an infinite number
of replications of the researcher's selection procedure. The findings
of the study can be generalized to the entire population most reliably
if the sampling is such that every event has an equal chance of being
selected for study. (If this is not the case, a bias is introduced that
must be accounted for when the researcher interprets his data.)
The sampling procedure then fulfills the assumption that the observations are independent. Such a selection procedure results in a
random sample. In practice random samples are sometimes difficult
to obtain and compromises may become necessary, but the concept
remains the theoretical basis for most statistics and for evaluating
results that are not random.

More complicated sampling techniques include stratified sampling and proportional stratified sampling. Another way that is not
random is the systematic sampling procedure. If a list of events to

be studied is used for the sample and every Nth item is selected, the result would be a systematic sample rather than a random one. Systematic samples are often easier to make but unless the original list is a random sample the results will not be random. Two important variations from randomness in the original list may be trends and cyclical fluctuations of relevant variables. The systematic and random sampling techniques can be combined by starting each systematic sample with a random number. Sequential sampling results from performing one experiment at a time until conclusive results are achieved.

After the researcher has selected the events to be studied he must determine the features of the events to which he will attend. These are called *variables* and *controls*. A given event may consist of many variables but, perhaps, only a handful of them will be pertinent to the investigation. When the necessary and sufficient conditions for a phenomenon are specified, then the relevant variables have been found. In studying the relationships that hold among the relevant variables some of them may be kept constant and thus controlled. Others may be manipulated and the effect of this change may be computed for other relevant variables. The manipulated variables are called *independent* and the variables changed as a result of this manipulation are called *dependent*.

The major justification for studying complex events in a laboratory situation is that the discovery, control, and manipulation of relevant variables is facilitated. This advantage must be weighed against studying speech events in real-life situations where the variables are likely to operate at full strength.

One set of variables will be introduced by the experiment. The student should isolate and manage these as carefully as he manipulates and controls the other variables in his study. Variables may be manipulated by instructions prior to the actual experimentation, by insulating or changing the environment during the experiment, or by modifying the stimuli upon the subjects during the experiment, or by modifying the consequences of the subject's response.

Equally important in the over-all design of the study is the control of relevant variables not under investigation. If these are known and measurable they can be accounted for by measuring them before and after the experiment to discover their contribution to the results. Quite often this is impossible. In those cases in which the researcher cannot isolate, control, or measure all relevant variables, he may use a comparison group to help him correct his data for the effects of unknown and uncontrolled variables. The comparison group is called a control group. In selecting members for the experimental and control groups and in observing the effects of the experiment, the student must guard against psychological bias. Membership in the two groups should be based on random sampling procedures. Neither the observer nor the subject should know whether the subject is a member of the experimental or control group.

The important stock approaches to designing experimental studies in speech include the matched-pair design, matched-group design, and the fractional-replication design. The matched-pair design requires a careful matching of pairs of subjects on as many relevant variables as possible. A more commonly used technique is to select a larger group of experimental and control subjects. The fractional-replication design yields more information by systematically manipulating a greater number of variables. The Latin Square and Graeco-Latin Square replications are examples of this approach. Controls of some sort are usually required because of the placebo effect or the effect on the subjects of being singled out to be in an experiment.

The design of an experimental study in speech is a systematic approach to the second phase of the inductive process where a hypothesis resulting from the first phase of the process is subjected to empirical testing. The major problems in this second phase involve the selection of events or responses to observe and the manipulating of relevant variables.

SUGGESTED READINGS

Clausen, John A., and Robert N. Ford. "Controlling Bias in Mail Questionnaires," *Journal of American Statistical Association,* XLII (December 1947), 491–512.

Festinger, Leon, and Daniel Katz, eds. *Research Methods in the Behavioral Sciences.* New York: Holt, Rinehart and Winston, Inc., 1953.

Hays, William L. *Statistics for Psychologists.* New York: Holt, Rinehart and Winston, Inc., 1963.

Hyman, Herbert H. *Survey Design and Analysis.* New York: The Free Press of Glencoe, Inc., 1960.

Lillywhite, Herold, and Waldo Phelps. "The Survey Method in Speech Education," *SSJ,* XVII (May 1952), 241–248.

Lindquist, E. F. *Design and Analysis of Experiments in Psychology and Education.* Boston: Houghton Mifflin Company, 1953.

Oppenheimer, Robert. "Analogy in Science," *American Psychologist,* XI (March 1956), 127–136.

Parten, Mildred. *Surveys, Polls, and Samples: Practical Procedures.* New York: Harper & Row, Publishers, 1950.

Reichenbach, Hans. *The Rise of Scientific Philosophy*. Berkeley: University of California Press, 1951.

Sellitz, Claire, *et al. Research Methods in Social Relations*. New York: Holt, Rinehart and Winston, Inc., 1959.

Sidman, Murray. *Tactics of Scientific Research: Evaluating Experimental Data in Psychology*. New York: Basic Books, 1960.

Townsend, Howard W. "The Survey as a Method of Research," *SSJ*, XIV (November 1948), 115–118.

U. S. House of Representatives. Committee on Interstate and Foreign Commerce. *Evaluation of Statistical Methods Used in Obtaining Broadcast Ratings*. Report No. 193, 87th Cong., 1st Sess., 1961.

Walker, Helen M., and Joseph Lev. *Statistical Inference*. New York: Holt, Rinehart and Winston, Inc., 1953.

Wilson, E. Bright, Jr. *An Introduction to Scientific Research*. New York: McGraw-Hill Book Co., Inc., 1952.

Young, Pauline V. *Scientific Surveys and Research*. Englewood Cliffs, N. J.: Prentice-Hall, Inc., 1956.

Projects

1) List twenty hypotheses suitable for investigation by the empirical method.

2) Select a published report of a survey and evaluate the sampling procedure and the generalizations to the parent population made by the investigator. The following list contains examples of such reports.

Casmir, Fred L. "A Telephone Survey of Religious Program Preferences Among Listeners and Viewers in Los Angeles," *CSSJ*, X (Spring 1959), 31–38.

Cripe, Nicholas M. "A Survey of Debate Programs in Two Hundred and Forty-six American Colleges and Universities," *ST*, VIII (March 1959), 157–160.

Davison, Louise D. "Speech Correction in the Public Schools of Georgia," *QJS*, XXXV (February 1949), 62–64.

Dietrich, John. "Dramatic Activity in American Colleges: 1946–1947," *QJS*, XXXIV (April 1948), 183–190.

3) Select one of the hypotheses you developed for project one above.

a) State the hypothesis in operational terms.
b) On the basis of your present knowledge list the possible relevant variables.
c) Which of these variables could be controlled?
d) Which of these variables could be quantified prior to the experiment?
e) Which of these variables could be manipulated? How?
f) Which variables would you select to be independent variables? Which variables would you select to be dependent variables?

4) Take one of the hypotheses you developed for project one above.

a) State the hypothesis in operational terms.
b) Define the population to be sampled.
c) Discuss the sampling procedure you might employ in picking subjects for your study.
d) What kinds of generalizations might you make on the basis of this sampling procedure?

5) Select a thesis reporting a study employing the experimental method that was submitted for an advanced degree at your school and write a short paper evaluating the following:

a) The worth of the hypothesis tested.
b) The skill with which the variables were controlled.
c) The skill with which the variables were manipulated.
d) The type of sampling procedure used to select the subjects or the responses for the study.
e) The author's interpretation of his data.

6) Find an article in a speech journal reporting research that used a factorial replication design. Write a short paper discussing the use of this particular design in the study.

QUESTIONS FOR DISCUSSION

1) In what way can both the discovery of a hypothesis and the testing of that hypothesis be thought of as phases of the process of induction?

2) Discuss the statement, "The development of concepts and generalizations by perceiving analogies is the process of induction."

3) Why did the attempts to systematize the process of induction fail?

4) On what basis can we say that some factors in a speech event are relevant variables and others are not?

5) How important is the notion of a random sample for empirical research in speech?

6) How are relevant variables controlled in experiments that employ some form of factorial replication in their design?

7) How might the psychological bias of an investigator contaminate the results of an empirical research project in speech?

CHAPTER FIFTEEN

COLLECTING DATA

The design of an empirical study in speech furnishes the framework for the collection of data. During the planning of the research project the investigator selects the events to be studied, picks the statistical treatments, and decides whether to quantify the results or not. If he decides to quantify, the general characteristics of the quantification procedures will have been specified by the statistical assumptions made in the design of the study. His remaining problems are largely the practical ones of selecting specific observational procedures, drafting questionnaires, planning interviews, selecting tests, developing scaling procedures, or discovering measurement techniques. The large number of tests, scales, rating blanks, inventories, and category systems that have been developed by researchers in speech and the behavioral sciences indicate the importance of this step in an empirical research project. In theory, the actual collection of data should pose few problems, but empirical research, like politics, must be the art of the possible, and the practical problems posed by the collection of data are often the most basic and troublesome ones he faces. The work on this problem has been so voluminous that in this chapter we shall only survey the major techniques and indicate some of the more important tests, scales, and measurements. The selection, evaluation, and application of a standard quantification procedure or the development of a new one to fit the needs of the project requires extensive study of the literature relating to the problems posed by such procedures and some practice in using the technique. The purpose of this chapter is to indicate the range of techniques available and point the way for the student to find a bibliography for studying a specific procedure.

The student may collect data for an empirical research project in speech in a wide variety of ways. However, any specific technique will be based primarily upon indirect or direct observations. In the first case the phenomenon under study will be observed by someone else and the empirical researcher must rely on the account of this witness to verify his descriptions. Thus, the descriptions of the event will be expressed, for the investigator, in indirectly verifiable statements of fact. In the second case, the researcher observes the phenomenon under study and his descriptions are, for him, expressed in directly verifiable statements of fact. In either case, the student using the empirical method may quantify his descriptions or not. Quantification is not a function of direct or indirect observation in collecting data but rather a function of the purpose, hypothesis, and design of the study.

INDIRECT OBSERVATION AND THE COLLECTION OF DATA

The researcher cannot always arrange his study in such a way that he can personally see the things he wants to study. On occasion, he can observe some of the events but must depend on the observation of others for the rest of his data. On other occasions, he must rely entirely on the reports of those who observe or take part in the events.

STATISTICAL RECORDS

The student working on a thesis in speech may use the reports of various data-collecting agencies. For example, a student wishing to examine the relationship between intellectual attainment and speech problems might use statistical data collected by a group of secondary schools. Statistics are available in the Minneapolis, St. Paul, and suburban schools, for example, regarding the referral of students to speech correctionists in the school system. The correctionists keep records of the nature and severity of these speech problems. Statistics are also available in the same school systems in regard to grade records and intelligence-test scores of the students who have been referred to speech correctionists. Using this information the student could examine the incidence and nature of speech problems in a group of students with high grades and high intelligence-test scores in the public schools of Hennepin and Ramsey counties. A host of governmental agencies, federal, state, and local, collect data that may be of use to the graduate student in speech. Private organizations and businesses do likewise.

DOCUMENTS

On occasion, the empirical researcher will search out documents in somewhat the same way as the historian does. In addition, the empirical researcher may have the documents prepared for his study under more controlled conditions. He may, for example, gather data by asking the members of a number of controlled discussion groups to keep a diary recording their impressions and experiences in the group or by asking a selected sample of a given television audience to keep a diary recording their television viewing during the month.

When dealing with such documents the student can borrow the appropriate techniques from history and criticism for the evaluation and testing of evidence, that is, follow the same procedures outlined in Chapter 9. Like the historian, the empirical researcher has a viewpoint. His viewpoint is essentially that of empiricism as developed in the discussion of the philosophy of science in Chapter 4.

INTERVIEWS AND QUESTIONNAIRES

Sometimes the graduate student cannot find or develop documents for the events under study. Two important ways in which data can sometimes be gathered under these conditions are the use of the interview and the questionnaire.

These two techniques are quite similar and the same basic principles apply to both methods. The essential differences relate to the way in which the witnesses are questioned. Questionnaires are usually distributed by mail and the respondent answers them at his leisure. The interview technique requires the witness to be questioned directly. If a skillful interviewer probes for details and persuades the witness to give truthful answers, the interview can assure more complete and accurate results. The subject sometimes finds it easier to give incomplete answers on a questionnaire than in a well-conducted interview. Furthermore, the questionnaire can easily be put aside and forgotten. An interviewer might well get a response from a subject who would ignore or forget a questionnaire.

On the debit side, the interview technique is more time-consuming and generally more expensive. As a result, the student using the interview as a research tool might have to restrict the sample size of his study and this may overbalance the other virtues. In deciding which of these two methods to use, therefore, you should evaluate the nature and complexity of the information you seek and the time and money you have available for the study. If the information is factual and you wish to survey a large number of subjects on a small budget, the questionnaire is a good technique to select. If the data are more complex and likely to arouse emotional reactions and if you prefer a thorough understanding of a small number of subjects to a more superficial response from a larger number of people, you should consider using the interview.

The student using the interview or the questionnaire is faced with many of the same problems that the historian or critic faces in dealing with testimony. You may solve these problems in analogous fashion. For example, the student conducting an empirical study wants, as does the historian, the primary source for the information. Like the historian he searches for eyewitness testimony to the events under study. If he is studying the production of musical dramas in colleges and universities, he must send his questionnaire to the faculty members who know something about these productions. If he is studying television-viewing events, then he must interview the people who watch television. If he is studying speech activities in a given state's high schools, the superintendents of these high schools might not be the best source of information because often they have little firsthand information about these matters.

In addition to surveying those who are in a position to provide him with the data he is seeking, the student must try to elicit accurate information. He must examine his questioning procedures carefully to make sure that he does not introduce a bias either in the way the questions are worded, ordered, or asked. He must try to ask the questions that will result in the information he wants. To do so he must be aware of possible distortions in his information and he must guard against this distortion working its way into his data. If he cannot keep his data from being contaminated, he must guard against the distortion influencing his interpretation of the data.

PREPARING THE QUESTIONNAIRE AND THE INTERVIEW

The first step in preparing either a questionnaire or an interview is to decide what information to seek. At first glance this may seem simple but, on occasion, the student finds this first step difficult. Suppose, for example, the student decides to study discussion courses in colleges and universities in the United States.[1] He might wonder about how many courses there are, who teaches them, what textbooks are used and how many students are enrolled. But this information, while necessary, may not tell him things he wants to know such as what is taught in the course and how it is taught. He now finds himself asking about some of the less tangible aspects. How important is the discussion course in the speech curriculum? Are there trends indicating a changing emphasis in the teaching of discussion across the country? Has the course been growing or declining in popularity? When the student reaches this point, he must make some decisions about the scope of his survey. Perhaps, he decides to investigate the number of courses, the background of the instructors, the textbooks used, student enrollments over the past

---

[1] For an example of survey-of-discussion courses see John Keltner and Carroll C. Arnold, "Discussion in American Colleges and Universities," *QJS*, XLII (October 1956), 250–256.

five years, and the content of the courses. He can use direct questions to get such factual information as the textbooks for the course and the size of the enrollments. He will not be able to get information about course content so easily. However, questions about the goals of the course, the testing and evaluation of student work, the balance between participating in discussions and studying about discussion processes, and the textbook, may furnish him with information that he can use in inferring the course content.

The student is now ready to make some decisions about the factual information the questions elicit and about interpretations, evaluations, opinions, or attitudes he wishes to discover or test. He has a choice of framing questions directly or in such a way that the information he wants may be inferred from the responses. If the information is noncontroversial, a direct question is often indicated. However, if the information deals with controversial issues, attitudes, or biases, a direct question may result in misleading answers. For example, interviewers for a marketing survey asked housewives if they would buy a new margarine if it were introduced in super markets in the area. The results were overwhelmingly negative. The results were so negative, in fact, that they seemed invalid. Louis Cheskin of the Color Research Institute was consulted. He investigated the study and decided that the answers to this question gave very little information about the actual buying habits of the housewives because the question was put to them directly. They interpreted the question as asking, does your husband provide so poorly that you would have to buy a substitute product for your family in order to save a few pennies? To find out if they really would buy the product an indirect questioning procedure was necessary.[2]

A student investigating the censorship of dramatic productions given at small denominational colleges would have to be very careful about this problem. Direct questions to college administrative officers such as, "Do you censor the dramatic productions presented at your school?" might well result in wrong information.

When the student has thought through the information that he wants to get with his questionnaire, he should outline the topics he wants covered and arrange them in a list. The topics should be ordered in such fashion that they seem to follow logically, with no abrupt transitions or breaks in thought or mood to interrupt continuity of the questions. The arrangement should be psychologically

---

[2] Louis Cheskin, "Subliminal Research: Implications for Persuasion," *Today's Speech*, VII (April 1959), 19–21.

sound as well. Questions that are likely to cause resistance should be placed after less controversial ones. Those asking for noncontroversial facts can often precede questions that probe for attitudes and opinions. If the content of a given topic is likely to influence the response on another topic, the two should be separated by other subjects. The student should examine each topic to see if it is led up to naturally.

DRAFTING THE QUESTIONS

With the topics arranged in order, the next step is to write questions for each. At this point, a basic decision must be made about the kinds of questions to be used. The choices are analogous to selecting an objective form of test as opposed to an essay form. Both the interview and questionnaire procedure may use either check responses or free responses to questions. In the development of a check-response questionnaire, one in which the subject is asked to check a response such as "yes" and "no," the items are carefully worked out and pretested. The free-response question is open-ended and results in answers that are not standardized and are more difficult to tabulate. Essay answers need to be weighed, evaluated, and interpreted. The check-response technique results in an interview or questionnaire that is simpler to administer, and a great deal easier to tabulate. However, the time saved in the latter stages is frequently required in preparing questions that will draw out the information desired.

The free-response question will often reveal unexpected data and is more useful for depth studies. The problems of administration and interpretation, however, often restrict the size of the sample that can be interviewed by this technique. On the other hand, a limited sample of subjects skillfully interviewed can yield much valuable information. Free-response questions elicit answers that need imaginative interpretation; indeed, such work is very close to the artistry of the historian or critic.

Sometimes, of course, the student will combine check-response with free-response items on the same questionnaire.

Factual information is the easiest to gather and can be collected with either type of question. For example, the student surveying the background of instructors in discussion courses might use a question of this type:

Name of instructor _____ academic rank _____
highest degree held _____ institution granting this degree
_____ major areas of interest _____.

An open-ended question could be used as follows:

List names of instructors teaching courses in discussion, the institutions they attended, and degrees received with major area of concentration.

_____

_____

_____

_____

Check-answer questions are easiest of all for the respondent, for example:

Academic Rank
        Graduate Assistant   _____
        Instructor   _____
        Assistant Professor   _____
        Associate Professor   _____
        Professor   _____
Highest Degree Held
        BA   _____
        BS   _____
        MA   _____
        MS   _____
        MFA   _____
        Ph.D.   _____

The problem of studying attitudes, opinions, and matters of taste by questionnaires or interviews is more difficult. Open-ended questions about opinions and attitudes are often difficult to interpret. The student has few guidelines to help him evaluate the answers. Check-response questions can be used for studying these matters but the construction of a suitable questionnaire is an extremely complex and difficult task. A student undertaking such a job should be familiar with the field of attitude scaling and utilize these findings in developing his questionnaire. Two-valued check-response questions are sometimes used to get data about attitudes. For example, a value judgment could be studied by a series of check-response questions of this type:

Yes   No
_____ _____ The discussion course should be the core of the public address curriculum.
or,
Disagree Agree
_____   _____ I would rather teach a course in public discussion than a course in persuasion.

The bivalued type of question works best when the student wants to offer a limited choice of alternatives and in a situation where the response is likely to be definite and certain. If the respondent objects to the black and white nature of a bivalued question, he may reject the question and not answer it on the grounds that neither answer reflects his position. Or he may be forced to make a response that does not reflect his attitude accurately. The student can mitigate these problems by adding a response category such as "doubtful," "undecided," or "no difference." Adding a neutral category has the drawback, however, of giving the respondent a way to dodge touchy or difficult questions.

The scaling kind of question, to be discussed later in the chapter, can also be used in questionnaires; for example,

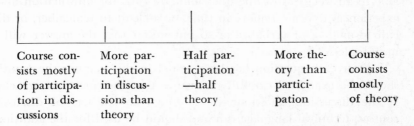

| Course consists mostly of participation in discussions | More participation in discussions than theory | Half participation —half theory | More theory than participation | Course consists mostly of theory |

A cafeteria type of check-response question can be used in much the same way:

> Put a *1* in front of the most important criterion for evaluating a participant in public discussion, a *2* in front of the second most important criterion, and so on until you have ranked every criterion,
>
> ———— speaking skills
> ———— human relations skills
> ———— analysis of topic
> ———— use of evidence

Checklists of this sort can easily become long and must be carefully prepared to make sure that there is no overlapping of alternatives and that the items are balanced and impartial. Because items on a checklist tend to be overlooked or under-used by the respondent simply because of their position on the list, the items should be rotated in random fashion when the final forms of the questionnaire are prepared.

EVALUATING THE QUESTIONS

The student should now begin to write questions that cover the topics on his list. After he has prepared a first draft of the questionnaire, he should examine each question in terms of how it relates to the other questions, his purpose in making the survey, and the sample of respondents he has selected. He could ask, among other things, "Is this question necessary?" "Does it cover the topic adequately or are several questions needed?" Several are indicated if the question is general, or if more detail is needed, or if it covers two or more points. If the question asks for opinions, attitudes, or tastes, the researcher should examine it to see if it gives the respondents the information they need to answer it. Other questions the student may well raise are: "Are the respondents unlikely to answer honestly even if they have the necessary information because their answers may go counter to the accepted norms and mores, or because they may embarrass or degrade them?" "Are the respondents unable to answer because the questionnaire calls for information about experiences that are remote in time, or difficult to remember, or difficult to analyze or verbalize or so unfamiliar that the answer will be meaningless?"

After each question has been tested in this manner the wording should be examined carefully to assure that the questions are clear. If the discussion questionnaire is to go to teachers of discussion courses, technical language can and should be used for the additional precision that will result. If it is to go to high school principals, technical language probably should not be used.

The student should ask: "Can the question mean anything other than what is intended? Are certain assumptions implied that may be misunderstood or challenged? Do the questions grow out of a frame of reference that the respondents may not share? Is the wording likely to be objectionable to any of the respondents? Would a personalized or less personalized wording improve the accuracy of the response?"

PRETESTING THE QUESTIONS

When the questions have been revised, the student should conduct a "dry run" of his study. This will enable him to discover questions that result in useless information, responses that are difficult to tabulate or interpret, and information that is needed but not provided. He can do this by filling in a number of questionnaires himself and then trying to analyze the results. Also, drawing up dummy tables of possible results often reveals weaknesses in the questions.

When the questionnaire seems to be in good order, the student should do a pilot study by using it in an interview situation with a limited sample of subjects. He can use a few open-ended questions in this pilot study to elicit unexpected information and spontaneous responses that will help in drafting additional check-response questions for the final draft of the questionnaire. The student will get immediate reactions to ambiguity in the questions or to emotion-arousing wording in the interviews. After he revises his questionnaire following the dry run and the pilot study, he should be ready to mail it to the sample of subjects he has selected to survey.

INTERVIEW SCHEDULES

As we have noted earlier, mailing out questionnaires is relatively inexpensive but sometimes not as satisfactory as the personal interview. If the interviewer is inexperienced and not expert in the field under study, a detailed schedule of questions can be furnished him. An interview schedule is often developed in the same manner as a mail questionnaire. The interview schedule, in such a case, would be a checklist and the entire study would be carried out in the same way as the pilot study for the mail questionnaire discussed above.

The interviewer asks the questions and records the proper check marks during face-to-face or telephone conversations with the respondents. Although it poses some special problems the data gathered by an interview with a checklist is likely to be more accurate than the same information gathered by a mail survey.

One of these special problems is that of interviewing every individual in the sample. If a given member is not at home or misses an appointment, the interviewer may be tempted to substitute some other respondent. Systematic biases can be introduced into surveys because interviewers fail to interview every member in the sample. In surveying women's fashions, for example, the women who are not at home during the day may have significantly different tastes than those who are at home.[3] Interviewers who worked only during the day would eliminate the working women from the sample and thus introduce a systematic bias. Sindlinger and Company found a similar bias in television surveys. In doing their studies they used follow-up techniques to make sure that a maximum number of the original sample was interviewed. The Sindlinger surveys indicated that people who were difficult to interview because they were seldom home at night watching television had significantly different viewing habits than the stay-at-homes. The people who were often away from home

---

[3] For a discussion of the problems of interviewing women about opinion leaders in fashions see Elihu Katz and Paul F. Lazarsfeld, *Personal Influence* (Glencoe, Ill., 1955).

at night tended to select public affairs and cultural programs more often than did the other group.[4]

TRAINING INTERVIEWERS

The student using interviewers should select them with care and train them, if necessary. They need to become skillful in finding all the respondents in the sample and in persuading the unwilling ones to agree to be interviewed. The great majority can be found and persuaded with tact and perseverance.

CONDUCTING THE INTERVIEW

The interviewer's manner should be direct, courteous, and objective. If it is not he can bias the answers. His vocal inflection can indicate disapproval or suggest a negative or positive response. For example, one interviewer appeared at my door conducting a marketing survey for a whiskey company. He proceeded through the checklist, asking his questions in a straightforward manner, until he came to a question close to the end of the list. With a sheepish look on his face he stopped and muttered something about it not being a good question and he was not asking it. My curiosity was aroused and I prodded him until he read the question. The question was not as skillfully worded as it might have been but the interviewer's manner and bias successfully destroyed whatever effectiveness it might have had.

When the interview is being conducted each question should be asked as worded and in the order presented by the schedule. The same manner and procedure should be used and impromptu explanations avoided. A question should be repeated slowly and with proper emphasis if the respondent says that he does not understand it. The interviewer should supply additional information only if it has been authorized. If the interviewee still does not understand the question, the no-response category can be used.

The interviewer should be alert for incomplete or vague answers. He should have a standardized set of follow-up questions to use in these instances. Such questions as "Do you think of any other reasons?" "Are there other things that come to mind?" "Could you give me an example?" or "Could you go into that a little more?" are often useful.

The interview technique with the use of a carefully specified checklist is appropriate for surveys that require a large number of interviews and ask for specific information or attitudes. The use of

---

[4] *Broadcasting*, LXII (January 1, 1962), 25.

such a checklist enables the student to use a number of interviewers with some assurance that he will get the information he needs for his study. The checklist also simplifies the training of interviewers.

THE OPEN-ENDED INTERVIEW

The open-ended interview, which may vary from directive to nondirective, is particularly useful for depth studies of complicated psychological processes or sociological phenomenon. For example, Robert Merton and his associates studied the psychological response to a radio appeal by Kate Smith to buy war bonds. They used a structured-interviewing technique called the "focused interview" to study the psychological mechanisms that caused people to buy war bonds as a result of listening to the Kate Smith program.[5] Open-ended interviews were also used to study the panic caused by the radio dramatization of the *War of the Worlds*.[6] A number of studies of voting behavior have used the interview technique and in some of these studies the same people have been re-interviewed periodically during a political campaign.[7] The political "style" of the American people was studied by David Riesman and his associates by means of the open-ended interview technique. The results of their work was published in the book, *The Lonely Crowd*.[8] The Riesman study is as much a work of art as it is a work of science. The selection of subjects to be interviewed was unsystematic and certainly not random. In this regard, the study is open to criticism, but it is a good example of the advantages of the open-ended interview method when skillfully and artistically employed. The study was based on approximately 180 interviews with high school students, graduate students, residents of Harlem in New York City, residents of a Vermont community and any additional individuals who could be persuaded to participate. Only in the study of the Vermont community was a systematic attempt made to get a representative sample of interviewees in terms of a strata. Greater care was taken with interpretation of the data than with interviewing. Again, careless interviewing is not to be encouraged, and the study is open to criticism on this count as well, but the great care that was taken with the interpretation of the interview protocols (records) is one of the strengths of the study and worthy of emulation. Each protocol was read over again and

---

[5] Robert K. Merton, with Marjorie Fiske and Alberta Curtis, *Mass Persuasion: The Social Psychology of a War Bond Drive* (New York, 1946).

[6] Hadley Cantril, Hazel Gaudet, and Herta Herzog, *The Invasion from Mars* (Princeton, 1940).

[7] Paul F. Lazarsfeld, Bernard Berelson, and H. Daudet, *The People's Choice: How the Voter Makes up His Mind in a Presidential Campaign* (New York, 1944).

[8] New Haven, 1950.

again by the investigators to find its main implications. Answers were grouped together for further study. The investigators did not allow their curiosity to be inhibited by their method. They used all the interviews having "laid it down as a rule that there was no such thing as a 'bad' interview, but that inadequacies of communication could be as revealing as full and conspicuous rapport." [9] In interpreting the interviews Riesman and his associates used all the knowledge of human nature that they had available if they judged it to be relevant. As Riesman put it, "there is no rule against bringing to the work all we know about people and the way they talk . . . protocols are to be read in the glare of our whole knowledge of man and not in some artificially filtered light." [10] The artistic approach to interpretation of open-ended interview protocols has much to recommend it since such data are difficult to quantify in a meaningful way.

QUANTIFICATION OF INTERVIEW AND QUESTIONNAIRE DATA

Check-response interview schedules and questionnaires yield data that are easily quantified. The investigator can usually count such things as, for example, the number of discussion courses or the number of associate professors teaching them. He can assign numbers to check marks on a scale and count the number of yes answers to questions calling for a yes or no response. He must remember, however, that such quantification often yields nominal scale data or, at the strongest, ordinal scale data.

The student will find the quantification of free responses on questionnaires or interviews more difficult. One technique he might use for this purpose is to make a content analysis of the responses. In Chapter 12 we gave a simple example of content analysis using a carload of vegetables that could be categorized as potatoes, onions, carrots, and so forth. A similar category system would need to be worked out to make a content analysis of responses to open-ended questions. In addition to developing a meaningful set of categories, the student using content analysis would have to determine what would be counted as a unit. He might select each word, each complete thought, or each new theme, for example. He would then go through the protocols sorting each unit into the appropriate category and counting the number of units in each. Content analysis has been used to study many kinds of communication, both oral and written, and will be considered in greater detail later in the chapter.

---

[9] David Riesman, *Faces in the Crowd* (New Haven, 1952), pp. 28–29.
[10] Riesman, *Faces in the Crowd*, p. 30.

DIRECT OBSERVATION AND THE COLLECTION OF DATA

DIRECT OBSERVATION WITHOUT QUANTIFICATION

Speakers, broadcasters, clinicians, and dramatists are usually empiricists even though they do not always use statistics in their work. The empirical method is essentially observation followed by induction and further observation to test the induction. The speaker, playwright, actor, or director usually takes the audience into consideration in his work. If, on the basis of past experience, the director gets a hunch about a technique of staging he tries it and observes the audience's reaction. His approach may be unsystematic but it is empirical and much of the knowledge we have about the practice of drama and speechmaking is the result of such procedure. The empirical researcher may employ the same method of direct observation in a more systematic fashion.

The student using direct observation without quantification first selects the phenomenon he wishes to study and then observes as carefully as he can. He may use whatever observational techniques and whatever research procedures seem appropriate to his problems as the study proceeds. He collects all the available evidence from every source that can help him explain the event he is studying. If he examines an individual, or a social unit he is making a *case* study. If he examines a variable or a series of variables or a phenomenon in a "real" life situation, he is making a *field* study. Field studies are much like surveys except that surveys are usually based upon careful sampling procedures so the results will be generalizable to a larger population, and surveys are seldom conducted in as much depth as a field study. In any event, if the student is making a case study or a field study he will often use direct observation. He will observe the events under study, make a record of his observations, and draw his conclusions on the basis of this record supplemented by whatever other evidence he finds.

Clinical data is gathered in this fashion. Field studies of communication in industry and educational institutions often proceed in this way. Considerable research in discussion and group methods has been conducted along these lines and some research in theatre has utilized this technique.

The student might, for example, be studying the emergence of leadership roles in leaderless group discussions. He could observe the groups directly and tape their meetings. These tapes could then be played back and, if useful, typescripts could be made from the tapes. Other indexes and data could be collected by interviews, or questionnaires and on the basis of all this evidence the researcher could draw some conclusions about the way the emergence of leadership roles is perceived by the members in discussion groups that begin without a leader.[11]

An empirical study of directing technique could be done in the same fashion if the investigator attended rehearsals conducted by a number of directors, observing carefully and recording what he observed. He could then draw some conclusions about the techniques that made for effective or ineffective direction of plays. Marian Gallaway used this approach to study the effect of rehearsals on the rewriting of playscripts. She observed most of the rehearsals of four New York plays and kept a careful record of changes made in the scripts during rehearsals.[12]

In observing directly, the speech researcher must decide on the explanation he will give for his presence, the extent to which he will become involved in the events under study, and the method that he will use to record his data.

EXPLAINING THE PRESENCE OF THE OBSERVER

One of the first problems the student must consider is the change that may be introduced in the events under study simply because an observer has been added to the situation. Research into this problem indicates that on occasion the presence of observers does modify behavior.[13] For example, Deutsch found that members of small groups seemed to be aware of the presence of observers at the beginning of three weeks of frequent meetings but had almost forgotten them at the end of that time.[14] Bales studied some groups with observers sitting where they could be seen and some groups with observers hidden behind a one-way mirror. Sometimes the subjects were told they were being observed from behind the mirror and sometimes they were not. Bales found no significant difference in the behavior of these groups that could be attributed to the influence of observers.[15]

The student should try to find out if the presence of an observer modifies the behavior under study in significant ways. If it does, he should try to adjust his findings to account for this modification. Cer-

---

[11] This was the procedure used by John Geier in his study, "A Descriptive Analysis of an Interaction Pattern Resulting in Leadership Emergence in Leaderless Group Discussion," Ph.D. dissertation, University of Minnesota, 1963.

[12] Marian Gallaway, "An Exploratory Study of the Effect of the Medium on the Manuscripts of Plays," *SSJ*, XXIV (Winter 1958), 75–83.

[13] N. Polansky, *et al.*, "Problems of Interpersonal Relations in Research on Groups," *Human Relations*, II (1949), 281–291.

[14] M. Deutsch, "An Experimental Study of the Effects of Cooperation and Competition upon Group Process," *Human Relations*, II (1949), 199–231.

[15] Robert F. Bales, *Interaction Process Analysis* (Cambridge, 1950).

tainly the way in which observers are introduced will make a difference in the behavior of the subjects. William Foote Whyte, on the
basis of his experience as a participant observer in such diverse set-
tings as the industrial plant and the street-corner gang, suggests that
in making field observations the researcher's explanation to the people under observation should be brief, simple, and general enough to
cover all behavior of the observer.[16]

To introduce observers without explanation is certainly unwise,
but to describe in exact detail the things the observer is watching for
may also be unwise. Subjects may be more inhibited if they are given
detailed information. If the instructor in a public-speaking course
tells a student that during this speech the instructor will be watching
for vocalized pauses, he may modify the speaker's behavior significantly. Some investigators suggest to the subjects that the observer is a
neutral person. Other investigators make clear, in a general way, what
the observers are up to but try to create as unobtrusive and nonthreatening an observational situation as they can. Roger W. Heyns
and Alvin F. Zander, for example, suggest one way in which observers
might make themselves nonthreatening to discussion groups. First,
observers should let the group know beforehand that they will be
present at the meeting and that they will be there to study the group.
Second, observers should come to the meeting early enough to talk to
the chairman and get his cooperation, and to explain to the group the
general purpose of the research and to stress that they are watching
not for specific content or to evaluate personalities but to study the way
in which the group goes about its business. They should suggest that
it would be best if the group members ignored the observers. Insofar
as possible the group should go about its business as though the observers were not there. The observers should then say a word or two
about what they will be doing. If they plan to take notes or use a tape
recorder, this should be described. Finally, their manner should be
such that members of the group feel that they are there to record objectively the events that take place and that they are not there to spy or
make evaluations.[17]

PARTICIPANT AND NONPARTICIPANT OBSERVATION

The student's decision about the degree of involvement necessary
for successful observation has a bearing on the way in which observers
are introduced. An observer might need to be involved in the events

---

[16] "Observational Field-work Methods," in *Research Methods in Social Relations,* eds., Marie Jahoda, M. Deutsch, and S. W. Cook (New York, 1951), 493–513.
[17] Roger W. Heyns and Alvin F. Zander, "Observation of Group Behavior," in
Research Methods in the Behavioral Sciences, eds. Leon Festinger and Daniel Katz
(New York, 1953), p. 382.

under study. If the student is studying techniques of direction, he might ask: would it be advisable for the observer to be part of the production crew, or a member of the cast? Or would it be better for him to be sitting unobtrusively in the back of the rehearsal hall, or at the director's elbow? If studying speech therapy, he might ask: would it be more useful for the observer to be watching the therapy session from behind a one-way mirror or would it be better if the observer were the therapist? If studying groups, he might ask: would it be better if he watched the discussion group from the back of the room or if he were a member of the group?

For some studies a nonparticipating observer might be advisable; for others a participating observer would be better. The student studying the points of greatest confusion in group meetings might decide to be a nonparticipating observer. As a nonparticipant he might better describe these points and account for them by examining the things that happened in the meeting preceding and following these moments of confusion. On the other hand, if he wishes to observe some of the pushes and pulls of personality, and the emotional tone and climate of a group, he might wish to be a participant.

RECORDING DATA

One of the more troublesome problems for an observer is presented by the need to record and organize data. Speech events are suitable for recording on a tape recorder or on a video-tape recorder or on motion picture film. Such recordings are of great value when they can be made, and when supplemented by the recollections of the observer, are the most helpful sorts of records.

If this is not possible, the nonparticipating observer may make notes as he watches. A tape recorder, a camera, or a pencil and note pad may all prove distracting to the subjects. Often the advantages of an audio or audio-visual recording outweigh the disadvantages but quite often if he must use notes anyway the nonparticipating observer and certainly the participating observer may prefer to rely on his memory and record his impressions later. He will need considerable training to write up his observations after the event. Some observers follow the practice of dictating their impressions into a tape recorder or dictaphone; others write them out in long hand and type them up. The beginning observer should experiment with ways that suit him best. The writing up of observations should be done as soon as possible after the events observed. It is better to err in the direction of being too comprehensive than in the direction of being too sketchy. First records are likely to be on the sketchy side. Further experience with the observing of events will help the student to stretch his powers of observation and recollection.

From the beginning the researcher should organize his data into a plausible pattern. He should also discriminate between statements of fact and statements of opinion and evaluation while making his notes. In general, he should concentrate on the statements of fact that result from his observations and leave the detailed interpretations for later. If the student organizes his material as he proceeds he will discover the gaps that he might otherwise overlook and he will be able to avoid the interesting but irrelevant byways that plague all researchers.

Direct observational techniques are suitable for empirical investigations of speech events that have been little studied by empirical means. They are quite useful for the study of complex phenomenon and for the study of speech events as they occur in the field.

DIRECT OBSERVATION AND QUANTIFICATION TECHNIQUES

Usually the next step in the investigation of such phenomena is the development of procedures to aid the observer increase the accuracy of his observations. One useful device is the development of rating scales or category systems to use in evaluating and describing the behavior under study. Take the case of the teacher of speech who wishes to evaluate the speaking abilities of his students. He might begin by observing the student speaker and making notes on his speeches. Or he might make tape recordings of his student's work for later playback and study. After some experience with this sort of observation, he may develop a rating scale to aid him in evaluating the performances. He might give a numerical rating from 1 to 5 to a speech, 5 indicating superior, 4 excellent, and so forth; in addition he might develop a set of categories such as choice of topic, development of ideas, organization, language, and delivery and give a numerical rating to each of these categories for a given speech.

Rating scales and category systems of this sort tend to ask for an absolute rating against some standard of considerable generality. That is, the teacher might ask himself what he means by superior in this context. He might answer that a superior speech meets certain absolute standards of excellence or he might decide that a comparative rating with other student speeches would be a more meaningful evaluation for his purposes. In the latter case he might use a ranking system or comparison system. Let us say that the teacher is having a class meeting in which five students give speeches. He could keep a record of each speech and continually rank the students after each performance. He would rank the first speaker as one until the second speaker completed his speech, then he would pick the better of the two and rank him first and the other second. The third speaker would be ranked against the other two and the process repeated until the five speeches were given and each speech placed in rank order. The teacher might assign numbers in another fashion by making the first speech the "standard" against which to judge the others. He might, for example, assign the first speaker a score of 75 arbitrarily no matter how excellent the speech might be. He would then compare each subsequent speech with the standard speech and assign an appropriate score. Thus, the second speaker might be judged as 5 points better than the standard speech and be given a rating of 80, the third speaker might be judged 3 points less than the standard and be given a rating of 72. Whenever speech teachers make such attempts at systematizing their observations by the use of quantification procedures they are doing the same sort of thing as the empirical researcher who wishes to improve the accuracy of his observations and therefore develop such techniques as observational aids.[18]

The development of research in discussion and small groups demonstrates this feature of empirical research. Researchers in this area soon moved from direct observation of groups to the use of various observational aids. Rating scales were frequently used. Sometimes these scales called for periodic ratings during a meeting and sometimes for a rating of certain aspects of the entire meeting. For example, the Conference Research Project of the University of Michigan included an observer's rating of certain aspects of the meetings studied on scales such as the following: [19]

1. Understandability: To what extent were the participants getting the meaning of one another's statements?

0	1	2	3	4	5	6	7	8	9	10

They were "talking past" one another; there was much misunderstanding.

Communicated directly with one another.

18 See, for example, Wayne Thompson, "An Experimental Study of the Accuracy of Typical Speech Rating Techniques," *SM*, XI (1944), 67–79; Keith Brooks, "The Construction and Testing of a Forced Choice Scale for Measuring Speaking Achievement," *SM*, XXIV (March 1957), 65–73; Wilmer E. Stevens, "A Rating Scale for Public Speakers," *QJS*, XIV (April 1928), 223–232; Franklin Knower, "A Suggestive Study of Public-Speaking Rating Scale Values," *QJS*, XV (February 1929), 30–41; Walter H. Wilke, "Subjective Measurements: A Note on Method," *QJS*, XXI (February 1935), 53–59; Keith Brooks, "Some Basic Considerations in Rating Scale Development: A Descriptive Bibliography," *CSSJ*, IX (Fall 1957), 27–31; Harvey Cromwell, "Decisions in Extemporaneous Speaking Contests," *SSJ*, XVIII (December 1952), 116–121.
19 Heyns and Zander, p. 386.

Category systems were developed to enable observers to make a content analysis of the flow of discussion. The observers used a form containing the categories and a suitable space for counting the units. One of the important category systems in the area was developed by Robert Bales and his associates. It contained twelve categories. Observers using the Bale's categories code each interaction into one of the categories. The results are expressed quantitatively and furnish a description of the number of interactions in each category along a time dimension.[20] In all these instances, the purpose of the rating scale, category system, or evaluation procedure is to refine the data collected by direct observation and secure additional information that might be overlooked by less systematic direct observation techniques.

EVALUATING SPEECHES

Evaluations of speech events may be made under controlled laboratory conditions or in the field. In some instances the purposes of the study are best served by making the evaluation at the time the event occurs, in which case the student must be alert for the following problems.

The evaluations made at the time the event occurs have been extensively studied particularly as they relate to evaluation of speeches. One important feature of such evaluations is that the judgment will tend to be affected by the order and nature of the surrounding stimuli. The *ordinal position effect* refers to the tendency of the order of stimuli to affect their selection and evaluation. Becker studied the ordinal position effect on the judgment of speakers in the Northern Oratorical League's Annual Contest and found that the first speaker in the contest seldom won first in the competition.[21] The evaluation may also be influenced by the evaluations made of the prior event. If a speaker follows a very good speaker or a very poor speaker this may effect the judge's evaluation.

If the student can record the event for evaluation under more rigorously controlled conditions, some of these problems can be avoided. For some studies, a tape recording of the speech may be adequate for evaluation. For other studies, television tape recordings

---

[20] Bales, *Interaction Process Analysis.* For other category systems used in small group research see L. F. Carter *et al.,* "A Note on a New Technique of Interaction Recording," *Journal of Abnormal and Social Psychology,* XLVI (January 1951), 258–260; L. F. Carter *et al.,* "The Relation of Categorizations and Ratings in the Observation of Group Behavior," *Human Relations,* IV (1951), 239–254; M. B. Freedman *et al.,* "The Interpersonal Dimension of Personality," *Journal of Personality,* XX (December 1951), 143–161; E. Brandenburg and P. A. Neal, "Graphic Techniques for Evaluating Discussion and Conference Procedures," *QJS,* XXXIX (April 1953), 201–208.

[21] "The Ordinal Position Effect," *QJS,* XXXIX (April 1953), 217–219.

or motion pictures would be more suitable. Such records can be re-arranged in random order so that the same speech events can be eval-uated in a way to guard against ordinal position effects or the effects of preceding and following speech events.[22]

Should the student decide to use carefully controlled stimuli for evaluation he must determine the length of the stimuli adequate for the purposes of his study. Should the speech be five minutes or thirty minutes long? Should the speech sample be five seconds or thirty seconds long? If the speech is to be recorded, randomized, and played for judges to evaluate, the length of the sample becomes an important practical problem. How long must a speech sample be to change atti-tudes to the point where the change can be detected? How long must a speech sample be to yield retention scores that are valid and relia-ble? How long must a speech sample be before a judgment as to sever-ity of stuttering or presence of harshness is possible? Researchers in experimental phonetics, speech pathology and audiology have done some work in reference to the length of speech samples used to eval-uate voice quality, articulation, and stuttering.[23] But for most other areas of speech we have little research evidence bearing on these and related problems.

QUANTIFICATION OF EVALUATIONS

Several different procedures are available to the student who wishes to quantify evaluations. The judges can be asked to label each stimulus event with a term such as *superior, excellent, good,* and *fair,* or the judges can be asked to assign letters or numbers to these values. Teachers often use a similar grading procedure in the classroom. Quantifying evaluations in this way results in a nominal scale. The investigator can refine this technique by asking the judges to select a point on a scale that reflects his evaluation of the stimulus on a continuum of excellence. The number of divisions on such rating scales usually range from three to eleven. A five-point scale might look like this:

The number of divisions should depend upon the discriminating ability of the judges. The investigator need not furnish the judges

---

[22] Richard Martin used 15-second kinescope recordings of stuttering presented to his evaluators in random order in his study, "Direct Magnitude-Estimation Scal-ing of Stuttering Severity Utilizing Auditory and Auditory-Visual Stimuli," Ph.D. dissertation, University of Minnesota, 1963.

[23] Dorothy Sherman, "Clinical and Experimental Use of the Iowa Scale of Se-verity of Stuttering," *JSHD,* XVII (September 1952), 316–320.

with an eleven-point scale if they are likely to use only three points in their evaluations. A teacher in grading students may use a fourteen-point scale of the order A, A−, B+, B, B−, . . . , F−, but for the most part he may use only a three-point scale of the order A, B, C. The student developing a rating scale to evaluate speech events might begin with a five- or seven-point scale and change to more units if necessary, after using the scale in preliminary investigations. He should select a suitable scale on the basis of his experience in using a variety of scales to evaluate the events he wishes to study.

Judges often find rating scales helpful in making evaluations. The rating scale may help unify the criteria of evaluation by encouraging all the judges to consider the same features of the speech event. Rating scales also furnish the judges a common basis for assigning numbers to their evaluations. The investigator may find the evaluations resulting from a rating scale easier to compute and interpret because he does not need to transform the information from various raters into equivalent numbers. The student using a rating scale must be aware that numbers gathered in this way should not be treated as direct-interval or ratio scales when they will be, for the most part, nominal or ordinal scales.

Another technique for the quantification of evaluations is to compare in some fashion one sample of the thing to be judged with all the other samples. A relatively straightforward way to do this is for the investigator to ask each judge to rank the events under study. If five speakers are to be evaluated, the judge could be asked to rank the speakers from first to fifth in order of excellence. A more complicated comparison method is to have each judge presented with the events in pairs in such a way that every event is paired with every other event. The paired-comparison technique, as this is called, was used in a study of voice quality and effectiveness by Lewis and Tiffin. Six voices were used in this study and each voice was compared with every other voice.[24] Thompson studied the "accuracy" of rating scales, ranking procedures, grade assignment, and paired comparison evaluations of student speakers and found the paired comparison evaluations to be the best technique according to his criterion of accuracy which was the mean evaluation of all the judges.[25]

Another method of systematizing evaluations is called the direct magnitude-estimation scaling procedure. Stevens and his associates have used this technique to scale psychological percepts such as loud-

---

[24] Don Lewis and Joseph Tiffin, "Psychophysical Study of Individual Differences in Speaking Ability," *Archives of Speech,* I (January 1934), 26–43.

[25] Wayne Thompson, "An Experimental Study of the Accuracy of Typical Speech Rating Techniques," *SM,* XI (1944), 67–79.

ness and brightness.[26] Prather applied the technique to the evaluation of articulation defects and Martin studied its use in evaluating stuttering severity.[27] Martin had his raters evaluate samples of stuttering recorded on audio tape and kinescope. The rater assigned a number to his evaluation of the first sample of stuttering and this became his standard. He compared each succeeding sample of stuttering to the standard sample. The rater was allowed to assign any sample of stuttering a number that was proportional to the 100 points assigned the standard. The second sample of stuttering could be assigned a number indicating it was one-half as severe as the standard or twice as severe. Brooks has developed a forced choice scale for evaluating speech effectiveness that forces the judge to select a phrase that is descriptive of the speaker's skill.[28]

The nature of evaluations is such that reliable judgments are difficult to achieve. Even the most sophisticated aids such as rating scales, paired comparison techniques, or direct magnitude-estimation procedures, are unlikely to result in highly reliable scores. The use of a number of judges does tend to increase the reliability of evaluations. Statistical procedures are available that can help predict the number of judges needed to reach a given level of reliability.[29]

Evaluations have been useful in studies of the effectiveness of teaching methods, various therapy techniques in the speech clinic, and in selecting subjects for the voice scientist. For example, a series of studies dealing with the habitual and natural pitch levels of superior speakers required the evaluation of a number of voice samples and a final selection of superior voice samples.[30]

EVALUATIONS AND ESTIMATIONS

When a judge is asked to select a winner in a speech contest or decide which of two voices has the more "superior" voice quality, he is obviously making an evaluation. Rating scales can also be used to

[26] S. S. Stevens, "The Direct Estimation of Sensory Magnitudes—Loudness," *American Journal of Psychology*, LXIX (March 1956), 1–25; S. S. Stevens and E. H. Galanter, "Ratio Scales and Category Scales for a Dozen Perceptual Continua," *Journal of Experimental Psychology*, LIV (December 1957), 377–411.

[27] E. Prather, "Scaling Defectiveness of Articulation by Direct Magnitude-Estimation," *JSHR*, III (December 1960), 380–392; Richard Martin, "Direct Magnitude-Estimation Scaling of Stuttering Severity Utilizing Auditory and Auditory-Visual Stimuli," Ph.D. dissertation, University of Minnesota, 1963.

[28] Keith Brooks, "The Construction and Testing of a Forced Choice Scale for Measuring Speaking Achievement," *SM*, XXIV (March 1957), 65–73.

[29] See, for example, Franklin H. Knower, "A Study of Rank Order Methods of Evaluating Performances in Speech Contests," *Journal of Applied Psychology*, XIV (October 1940), 633–644; Theodore Clevenger, Jr., "Retest Reliability of Judgments of General Effectiveness in Public Speaking," *WS*, XXVI (Fall 1962), 216–222.

[30] See, for example, Wilbert Pronovost, "An Experimental Study of Methods for Determining Natural and Habitual Pitch," *SM*, IX (1942), 111–123.

estimate the amount of a measurable property present in a stimulus or to quantify a mixture of estimation and evaluation. Gilkinson and Smith draw the distinction between observations for "appraisal" and for "description." They suggest research may require a "sharper departmentization of data involving appraisal, and data involving description." [31]

An observer may be asked to rate a speaker in terms of the severity of the speaker's stage fright, or the severity of the tremor in the speaker's voice, or the shaking of his knees, or of his hands. Giving an operational definition to "tremor" or misarticulation of the [s] sound would make the following assertions statements of fact: "Speaker *A*'s voice had a tremor in it," "Subject *A* misarticulated the [s] sound in the word *sea*." When the rater is asked to decide the truth or falsity of a statement of fact there is, theoretically, more likelihood that the ratings will be reliable. Even such ratings are not always reliable as attempts to identify the presence or absence of voice quality problems such as harshness in speech samples indicate.

On occasion, raters will be asked to both describe and appraise, both estimate and evaluate, the event or stimulus. If the judge must not only decide if stuttering is present but also how severe or bad the stuttering is, he may both estimate and evaluate.

Careful methodological work has been done in the development of quantification procedures for the evaluation of the severity of stuttering and articulation problems. The problems posed by estimation and evaluation procedures have been dealt with extensively by researchers in speech and hearing disorders and by voice scientists, and their techniques should be examined by any researcher in speech who plans to use evaluation or estimation procedures as part of his observational technique.[32]

TESTING PROCEDURES AND QUANTIFICATION

A second tool that is widely used to help refine observational techniques is the test. The field of psychological testing has furnished

[31] Howard Gilkinson and Donald K. Smith, "Measurement in Speech," in *An Introduction to Graduate Study in Speech and Theatre*, ed. Clyde Dow (East Lansing, 1961) , p. 297.

[32] See, for example, D. Lewis and Dorothy Sherman, "Measuring the Severity of Stuttering," *JSHD*, XVI (December 1951), 320–326; D. Sherman, "Reliability and Utility of Individual Ratings of Severity of Audible Characteristics of Stuttering," *JSHD*, XX (March 1955), 11–16; D. Sherman and R. McDermott, "Individual Ratings of Severity of Moments of Stuttering," *JSHR*, I (March 1958), 61–67; D. Sherman and C. E. Moodie, "Four Psychological Scaling Methods Applied to Articulation Defectiveness," *JSHD*, XXII (December 1957), 698–706; Mildred C. Templin, "Spontaneous Versus Imitated Verbalization in Testing Articulation in Preschool Children," *JSHD*, XII (September 1947), 293–300; Mildred C. Templin and F. L. Darley, *The Templin-Darley Tests of Articulation* (Iowa City, 1960).

many an empirical researcher in speech with the tools to be used in studies to evaluate the relationship between speaking ability and various psychological traits, interests, and abilities. Tests have also been used to explore the characteristics of actors, the effect of speech training on achievement and personality, and the result of debate experience on mental tests.[33] Graduate theses in speech have reported studies using personality inventories, intelligence tests, critical thinking tests, and personal interest inventories. In addition, investigators in speech have developed tests designed specifically for studying speech events. Representative of such testing procedures are the Speech Attitude Scale, the Personal Report on Confidence as a Speaker test, the Personal-Social Adjustment Inventory, and the Brown-Carlson Test of Listening Comprehension.[34]

A student who wishes to make an investigation that requires tests should investigate a publication such as the *Mental Measurements Yearbook* which lists and evaluates a number of commercially available tests.[35] Such evaluations typically include considerations of a given test's reliability and validity. If the researcher fails to find suitable tests he may have to develop his own. The development of a useful test is a contribution to the research in the field and the construction and validation of such a test is a worthwhile research project.

The student faced with the problem of developing a test should study the ways in which analogous tests have been worked out for clues as to the best way to proceed. In addition, he should seek expert advice about specific procedures and suitable statistical treatments for the testing of reliability and validity of his test.

ATTITUDE SCALES

Another observational aid used by researchers in speech has been the attitude scale. While it resembles the rating scale in some respects

---

[33] See, for example, John R. Shepherd and Thomas M. Scheidel, "A Study of the Personality Configuration of Effective Oral Readers," *SM*, XXIII (August 1956), 298–304; Ernest H. Henrikson, "Some Relations between Personality, Speech Characteristics and Teaching Effectiveness of College Teachers," *SM*, XVI (September 1949), 221–226; William Smiley Howell, "The Effects of High School Debating on Critical Thinking," *SM*, X (1943), 96–103; Francis E. Drake, "A Study of the Personality Traits of Students Interested in Acting," *SM*, XVII (June 1950), 123–133; Donald E. Sikkink, "An Experimental Study Comparing Improvers and Non-Improvers in the Beginning Speech Course," *WS*, XIX (May 1955), 201–205. Stanley F. Paulson, "Changes in Confidence During a Period of Speech Training," *SM*, XVIII (November 1951), 260–265.

[34] For a further discussion of these tests see the following articles. For the Speech Attitude Scale, Franklin H. Knower, "A Study of Speech Attitudes and Adjustments," *SM*, V (1938), 130–203. For the Personal Report on Confidence as a Speaker, Howard Gilkinson, "Social Fears as Reported by Students in College Speech Classes," *SM*, IX (1942), 141–160. For the Brown-Carlson Test of Listening Comprehension, James I. Brown, "The Construction of a Diagnostic Test of Listening Comprehension," *Journal of Experimental Education*, XVIII (December 1949), 139–146.

[35] Oscar Krisen Buros, ed., *The Mental Measurements Yearbook*, 5th ed. (Highland Park, N. J., 1959).

it is a quantification procedure designed to assign numbers to the *internal states* of the subjects. The rating scale aids in assigning numbers to an evaluation of the stimulus; the attitude scale aids in assigning numbers to a feature of the response. Like a pitch percept or a loudness percept, the attitude is present or absent in the subject. Statements about the presence or absence of the attitude are thus statements of fact. Relational statements about the quality of the attitude are similar to relational statements about loudness percepts such as "this percept is louder than that percept." Whether the relations ordering attitude percepts are such that attitudes can be measured is a question of fact and when observational techniques have been suitably refined this question can be decided once and for all. In the meantime, theoretically, the measurement of attitudes remains a possibility. Since ratings are evaluations and attitudes may be measurable the two quantification procedures should be separated. In practice the two procedures are much the same. The same scale may be presented to the judge as is presented to the subject and the same speech stimulus played to both; however, the inferences that the experimenter makes about the marks the judge puts on the scale compared to the marks the subject puts on the scale are quite different. From the judge's mark of a 4 on a five-point scale of excellence, the investigator infers that the stimulus speech was a good speech, better than the other speeches that the judge marks as less than 4. From the subject's mark of a 4 on a five-point attitude scale, the researcher infers the presence of an attitude state of a certain intensity within the subject. Of course, the researcher could infer something about the judge's internal psychological states from his mark on the rating scale. (Debaters frequently do so after losing a debate.) In this case the mark of 4 on the evaluation scale would lead to an inference that the judge had an evaluation percept of 4 as part of his internal psychological states at the moment he made the mark. The investigator can run his inferential chain in this direction; however, he may not be studying the internal states of the judge. He, often, is studying the stimulus event and he uses the internal states of the judge as a yardstick to quantify some feature of the speech stimulus.

Like the phonetician measuring pitch percepts, the empirical researcher investigating attitudes must rely upon an introspective report of the subject as to the presence or absence of an attitude percept and its intensity. The similarities between the two problems, however, are largely academic because the phonetician can manipulate pitch percepts quite easily and precisely. The practical problems involved in manipulating attitudes and getting accurate reports about them are much more difficult. The student investigating attitude changes would have a much simpler time of it if he had the equivalent of a pure tone generator. With a pure attitude generator that would create a stimulus capable of minute changes and precise tuning, he could ask his subjects to report when they first perceived the attitude, at what point they were aware of a just noticeable difference in attitude, and in this way develop a scale to measure attitudes.

Lacking such a device, the student often must use an attitude scale of some sort. A common technique is to use an equal-appearing interval scale with appropriate labels describing the attitude under study. Table 10 indicates a sample of such a scale with the hypo-

Table 10

PRETEST AND POST-TEST SCORES FOR THREE SUBJECTS ON AN ATTITUDE SCALE

			Subject A			
			X		X	
			Pretest		Post-test	
-3	-2	-1	0	1	2	3

			Subject B			
			X		X	
			Pretest		Post-test	
-3	-2	-1	0	1	2	3

			Subject C			
			X	X		
			Pretest	Post-test		
-3	-2	-1	0	1	2	3

thetical results from pretests and post-tests for three subjects. All subjects checked the neutral position on the pretest. After the experimental treatment both subject *A* and subject *B* checked 2 in the positive direction on the scale and subject *C* checked 1 in the positive direction. The investigator must now interpret these scores. If he goes beyond the assertion that all three subjects report an attitude shift in a positive direction, he must proceed with caution. He could misinterpret the results in the following fashion. Since both *A* and *B* moved from a neutral position to a position of plus 2 he could infer that both of them changed their attitude by the same amount. Subject *C*, on the other hand, while he had the same attitude as the other two subjects on the pretest has moved only half as far in a positive direction on the post-test. The investigator might, therefore, interpret the results as indicating that subjects *A* and *B* have the same attitude after the experiment and their attitude is twice as favorable as C's attitude. This set of conclusions is only tenable if the assumption is made that the various divisions of the scale are applied by the subjects to the same attitudes in such a way that they are additive; that is, the scale enables the subjects to determine equality of intervals as required in a direct interval scale *measurement*. If the researcher can demonstrate that the attitude scale results in a direct interval-scale measurement, he is justified in using parametric statistical results in interpreting his data. In the present example, he would often be better advised to use a nonparametric test in his study.

In an attempt to meet this problem, more elaborate scaling procedures have been worked out to approximate the assumptions required for a direct-interval scale. The psychologist L. L. Thurstone developed one of the more famous scales.[36] His scale is constructed in such a way that there is evidence of equality of intervals. In the construction of Thurstone's equal-appearing interval scales the first step is the preparation of many statements about a given subject. Each of these statements is selected to carry different loads of positive or negative connotations toward the subject being studied. A group of judges then sort the statements into eleven piles, ranging from the least to the most favorable. The judges are instructed to assume that each pile is equidistant from the next. The middle pile (6th) is assumed to be composed of statements that reflect a neutral attitude toward the proposition. Of course a given statement may be placed in different positions by different judges. Thus, statement A may be sorted into the 6th, 7th, 8th, 9th, and 10th piles. To determine whether statement A will be included on the scale and at what point, all the statements are analyzed in detail. For each statement the mean or median position is computed. If the median is used, and statement A is placed in the eighth position most frequently, then this would be determined as well as the range of each item. The range is determined by the number of piles into which the statement is sorted. Statement A, for example, had a range from the 6th pile to the 10th. Similar information is gathered for all other statements and those with low range and with median-scale positions of approximately equal distance are picked for the scale. Subjects taking the test select the statements with which they agree and the test is scored by assigning the scale value of the median item checked. The Thurstone Scale may yield a better index than an intuitive selection of statements but the judges must still pick state-

---

[36] L. L. Thurstone, "Attitudes Can Be Measured," *American Journal of Sociology*, XXXIII (January 1928), 529–554; L. L. Thurstone and E. J. Chave, *The Measurement of Attitude* (Chicago, 1929).

ments that they perceive as being equal distances apart and the problem remains.

R. A. Likert has developed a method for scoring an attitude scale
that is an extension of mental testing procedures.[37] The items for
the scale are picked by taking statements of opinion that are so extreme that few people will reject them as not being extreme enough.
A scale is applied to each item with intervals from 1 to 5. The test is
then given to a sample of subjects and the items are analyzed for
their consistency with one another and with the entire test. In the
first procedure correlations are made of scale values of test scores
among individual items. In the second procedure correlations are run
between scores for individual test items and the total test score. In the
first procedure, the final form of the attitude scale is composed of items
with the highest-average correlation. In the second procedure, the
final form is composed of items which correlate most highly with the
total scores on the entire test.

Louis Guttman has developed a third method for quantifying
attitudes.[38] The method differs from the Thurstone and Lickert methods in that it is designed to create an ordinal scale suitable for ranking attitudes. The Guttman technique is as elaborate as the other two
and need not be outlined here. The researcher who plans to quantify
attitudes will need to examine the whole field of attitude scaling and
testing carefully before selecting a quantification procedure. I have
sketched the outlines of the Thurstone and Lickert techniques to indicate the nature and problems of attitude scaling.

THE SEMANTIC DIFFERENTIAL

Closely related to attitude scaling is a technique developed by
Osgood and his associates to quantify meaning.[39] Osgood's scaling device, called the semantic differential, is similar to an attitude scale in
that the same quantification procedures are used and the inferences of
the researcher move from the data of the check marks on the scales to
the internal states of the subjects. Insofar as meanings, or to use Osgood's terminology "representational mediation processes," are present
or absent within the subject, the semantic differential is similar to an
attitude scale. The semantic differential consists of a list of scales,
each scale labeled with a different set of polar adjectives. Some typical

---

[37] Helen Peak, "Problems of Objective Observation," in Festinger and Katz, pp.
252–253.

[38] S. Stouffer *et al., Measurement and Prediction* (Princeton, 1950).

[39] Charles E. Osgood, George J. Suci, and Percy H. Tannenbaum, *The Measurement of Meaning* (Urbana, 1957). For an interesting critical review of this book
see Uriel Weinreich "Travels Through Semantic Space," *Word,* XIV (August–
December 1958), 346–367.

sets of adjectives include: weak and strong, sweet and sour, hot and cold, active and passive, and strong and weak.

The main difference between an attitude scale and the semantic differential is that attitude scales are usually prepared for a specific investigation of a specific attitude. The semantic differential is often used to scale meanings across investigations and topics. The semantic differential is a generalized scale of meaning. The meaning of a concept, an individual, or a picture may be scaled by the same set of items on a semantic differential. The generality was achieved by the use of *factor* analysis.[40] The final set of polar adjectives used in the scales was developed in this way. A great number of antonyms were selected and scaled and given to groups of subjects. The results were then examined by means of factor analysis. This is a complicated statistical procedure designed to simplify the explanation of a series of statistical correlations. In the case of the semantic differential, intercorrelations between test items present a complicated set of data. If patterns can be discovered in such a table of intercorrelations that can be accounted for by assuming a smaller number of underlying *factors,* the data can be explained in more parsimonious fashion. Osgood and his associates submitted large lists of polar adjectives to this procedure and *factored* out three basic dimensions to explain the intercorrelations between items. They called these factors potency, evaluation, and activity. They then selected the items that were most heavily loaded with a given dimension for their final testing instrument.

The semantic differential has much to recommend it as a practical research tool. Although the validity and reliability arguments are elaborate and esoteric, as the brief comments about factors analysis above indicate, the actual test is short, easy to take, and easy to score. These virtues, plus the need of experimentalists in communication to quantify meaning, have resulted in widespread use of the semantic differential as a research tool in speech.[41] Indeed, Raymond G. Smith has done extensive work in adapting the original Osgood scale to the problems of researchers in public address and theatre. He has followed the same statistical procedures but has introduced new polar

---

[40] For an explanation of factor analysis applied to a cup of coffee see Raymond B. Cattell and William Sullivan, "The Scientific Nature of Factors: A Demonstration by Cups of Coffee," *Behavioral Science,* VII (April 1962), 184–193.

[41] See, for example, Carl H. Weaver, "Semantic Distance Between Students and Teachers and Its Effect Upon Learning," *SM,* XXVI (November 1959), 273–281; D. K. Berlo and H. Kumata, "The Investigator: The Impact of a Satirical Radio Drama," *Journalism Quarterly,* XXXIII (Summer 1956), 287–298; David K. Berlo and Halbert E. Gulley, "Effect of Intercellular and Intracellular Speech Structure on Attitude Change and Learning," *SM,* XXIII (August 1956), 288–297. Sidney Kraus and Raymond G. Smith, "Issues and Images," in *The Great Debates,* ed. Sidney Kraus (Bloomington, 1962), pp. 289–312.

adjectives at certain points as being more appropriate to speech.[42]

If meaning could be quantified, many of the interesting questions facing the researcher in speech could be examined more systematically. A speaker's skill in arousing meanings could be studied. The playwright's meaning of a character in his play could be quantified, the character's meaning for the director, the actor, and the audience could also be quantified and comparisons of these scores would give some index of success by the author and the production in communicating the meaning of the character.[43] If meaning can be scored, then a speaker's skill in arousing meaning in an audience could also be measured. Nebergall used the semantic differential to study "rhetorical clarity." Part of his procedure was to have subjects look at a modern painting and quantify their meaning by use of the semantic differential. He then had them tell other subjects about the picture and he used the semantic differential to compare the meaning of the speakers and listeners to see which subjects spoke more clearly.[44]

The semantic differential grew out of a theory of meaning and is called a *measurement of meaning* but it should not be accepted as such without careful examination. The semantic differential does not fulfill the criteria for a measurement as the term has been used in this book. When we interpret the scale values of the semantic differential we must not assume that they are additive. The student in speech who wishes to quantify meaning may well decide to use the semantic differential but he should become thoroughly conversant with the construct-validity arguments developed in the *Measurement of Meaning* and recognize the limitations of this scale in the design of his study and the statistical treatment of data.

CONTENT ANALYSIS

As we have said, an important way to quantify observations is to find some aspect of the event under study that can be counted. Many speech events do have features that recur and that can be treated as individuals and counted. The cycles in a sound wave, the number of words in a speech, the number of nouns and adjectives in a play, can be counted. The similes and metaphors and the allusions to Diety in a

---

42 Raymond G. Smith, "Development of a Semantic Differential for Use with Speech Related Concepts," *SM*, XXVI (November 1959), 263–272; "The Semantic Differential for Speech Correction Concepts," *SM*, XXIX (March 1962), 32–37; "A Semantic Differential for Theatre Concepts," *SM*, XXVIII (March 1961), 1–8; "Validation of a Semantic Differential," *SM*, XXX (March 1963), 50–55.

43 For a study using the semantic differential in theatre see Percy M. Tannenbaum, Bradley S. Greenberg, and Margareta Leitner, "Changes in Semantic Compatibility During the Production of a Play," *SM*, XXX (November 1963), 340–345.

44 "An Experimental Investigation of Rhetorical Clarity," *SM*, XXV (November 1958), 243–254.

speech can be counted. The number of misarticulations of the [s] sound in a sample of two hundred words by a preschool child can be counted. The number of blocks a stutterer makes in a five-minute speech can also be counted.

The difficulty with much of what is countable in speech events is that such counting does not furnish the researcher with a measure or index of the property he wishes to study. If he is studying rhetorical clarity, counting the number of words may not help him very much. If he counts the number of nouns and adjectives in a message he has little indication of how clear the message is. On the other hand, if he could compute a workable clarity index by counting personal references, sentence length, number of prefixes and suffixes, the counting would be worth doing.[45]

Content analysis is a procedure used by investigators in speech to find or create units in speech events that can be counted in such a way that the resulting numbers are useful measures or indexes to important features of the communicative event. A rhetorical criticism of a speech is often a qualitative analysis of the content of a speech text. A content analysis of the same text would be quantitative. Such an analysis involves two operations: first, the careful definition of the unit to be counted, and, second, a set of categories used to tabulate the counts.

Suppose a researcher wishes to make a content analysis of a speech. He might decide to use as a unit the individual words. Counting words is very much like counting potatoes and would result in reliable results. To be sure he would face some problems because of typographical errors, contractions, and hyphenated words. In most of these instances, however, he could solve these problems with arbitrary decisions, such as counting hyphenated words as one word. He might decide to use as a unit each sentence. At this point the arbitrary nature of punctuation would enter in and complicate his problem but the counting would remain relatively straightforward. He might decide to count "thought units," in which case he would have to define his category carefully. If he uses thought units, paragraphs, column inches, or seconds as his unit, he has created the property of number in his data. In a sense, each unit is treated as though it were an equal-interval and the resulting numbers can be treated with arithmetic.

The first step, difficult as it sometimes is, does not pose the problem to the student that developing a meaningful set of categories often does. The category system should be practical in that the units can be placed into categories by coders with a high degree of relia-

---

45 For an attempt at developing such an index see Rudolf Flesch, *The Art of Plain Talk* (New York, 1946).

bility. The number of ambiguous units must be small. Above all the categories should give some insight into speech events as a result of the counting. If the category system allows the student to draw inferences about the speaker, his purpose or his skill, or some inferences about the audience, its prejudices, mood or attitude, or some inferences about the message, then the category system is successful.

Much research has been done on analyzing messages with this technique by researchers in journalism investigating the content of newspapers and magazines. The content of radio and television programming has been analyzed in this manner. Speeches and small group discussions have been studied in this fashion.[46]

INSTRUMENTATION

Empirical investigators in speech have developed machines to aid in the collection of data, to aid in measuring and manipulating variables, and to simulate speech events. Three machines that have been used to facilitate the collection of data are the Wisconsin Sequential Audience Analyzer, the Meier Recorder, and Esterline-Angus Recorder.[47] These gather and tabulate audience responses. They are no more accurate than the paper and pencil tests or scales that are used for the same purpose. They do, however, sample and summate the results. In addition to performing such functions, instruments are used to aid the researcher in measuring the variables he wishes to study. The instruments that create observable effects from sound waves that enable the measure of the sound pressure, the fundamental frequency, and the distribution of energy in the sound wave, are examples of this use of machines.[48] Instrumentation is also useful in manipulating or controlling variables in the sound wave so the investigator can better observe the effect of the variable under study or to interrupt or mangle the sound wave to enable the researcher to study the variable important in the intelligibility of speech. Finally, instruments have been used to simulate speech events. The development of vocal analogues and speech synthesizers illustrates this use of instrumen-

---

[46] See Bernard Berelson, *Content Analysis in Communication Research* (Glencoe, Illinois, 1952); David W. Shepard, "An Experiment in Content Analysis: The Radio Address of Henry J. Taylor: 1945–1950," Ph.D. dissertation, University of Minnesota, 1953; Donald L. Wolfarth, "The Inaugural Addresses of the Presidents of the United States: A Content Analysis," Ph.D. dissertation, University of Minnesota, 1959.

[47] Herman H. Brockhaus and John V. Irwin, "The Wisconsin Sequential Sampling Audience Analyzer," *SM*, XXV (March 1958), 11–13. E. C. Mabie, "The Responses of Theatre Audiences, Experimental Studies," *SM*, XIX (November 1952), 235–243.

[48] See, for example, M. D. Steer and T. D. Hanley, "Instruments of Diagnosis, Therapy, and Research," in *Handbook of Speech Pathology*, ed. Lee Edward Travis (New York, 1957), pp. 174–245.

tation.[49] Computers can be programmed to simulate psychological responses such as discriminating between shapes and the responses of large audiences such as the electorate of the United States. Programming a computer to simulate a given audience or a speech mechanism shows promise of being an important tool for research in speech.[50]

Concrete advice on the construction of instruments can only be given within the context of a specific research project. The development of such instruments is a highly technical and complicated project. Advice on such matters is beyond the scope of this book; however, certain general considerations need to be outlined to guide the student who is contemplating starting on a research project requiring instrumentation and to guide the reader of a research report which employed instrumentation in gathering its data.

The student contemplating the use of instrumentation should familiarize himself with previous work and the machines of a similar nature that have been built. Frequently many of the dead ends have been explored and there is no need to run them down again. Then, too, originality is a rare commodity and the researcher should use the originality of previous investigators whenever possible. Many of the instruments used in speech laboratories are electronic; thus, the student contemplating such a project should be conversant with electronics and enjoy constructing and modifying electrical gear. Indeed, a student who is not a handyman and who does not enjoy building things, is handicapped when it comes to developing suitable instruments for his study. He may, of course, get help from a technician, if he has a clear idea of what the apparatus needs to do and if he can work closely with the man building the machine. Often, however, the research is so closely tied to the instrumentation that a modification of the apparatus may result in a significant change in the direction of the research or in an important discovery. Such happy results are more likely if the student has a thorough understanding of his apparatus and how it can be modified.

Research hardware is impressive and the student may become so engrossed in his apparatus that he fails to keep his main goal in mind. Laboratory instruments, like most gadgets, are useful only if they can aid the student with his study. Hours may be spent in building and machining elaborate equipment and making fine calibrations of that equipment for a study that does not require an elaborate and sensitive measuring device. There is little point in shooting sparrows with

---

[49] For example, Wendahl and his associates have been studying harsh voice quality by use of laryngeal analog synthesis. See R. W. Wendahl, "Laryngeal Analog Synthesis of Harsh Voice Quality," *Folia Phoniatrica*, XV (1963), 241–250.

[50] The journal, *Behavioral Science*, contains a section on "Computers in Behavioral Science," in each issue which discusses computer programs of this nature.

a cannon. The hours spent on such instrument building might better be devoted to the design of the study and the careful gathering of data. The student who brings thousands of dollars of high-fidelity tape recording equipment to a research project when a lightweight and inexpensive recorder would provide all the information he needs for his study is falling into this error. On the other hand, a student using such an inexpensive recorder for his study should become aware of the response characteristics of the machine and its limitations.

If the study requires precise measurements, the student must be aware of the limitations inherent in various measuring instruments. He may decide to use a direct measuring device or a comparison technique for taking his measurements. An example of a direct measuring device is a spring scale in which the object to be weighed is placed on the pan of the scale and the weight is read directly from a dial indicator. The Fundamental Frequency Indicator is such a measuring device.[51] The comparison technique is exemplified by the balance scale in which the weight to be measured is opposed by other known weights until a balance is achieved and the weight to be measured is determined by computing the known weights of the balancing objects. A further example is the technique of measuring fundamental frequency by comparing the photographic representation of the electrical analogue of sound pressure of a sound wave with the electrical analogue of the sound pressure of a known frequency generated by a pure tone oscillator. In general, the direct measuring devices are easier to use and quicker but not as accurate as the comparison technique.

If the experiment requires comparative rather than absolute measurements, then there is a definite advantage in using comparison procedures rather than taking two direct measures and comparing them. Then, too, pointer-type instruments such as are often used in direct measurements limit the precision with which a measurement can be read. Many times the calibration of such dials is dependent upon mechanical springs which respond with some variability to the same stimulus. The comparison measures can be made with precision by using fine steps on the controls. If the measurements are taken by hand, however, the measurement by comparison techniques will usually take longer. If the added precision is unnecessary, then the ease of measurement makes the direct method preferable.

Absolute measurements depend upon the ability of the instrument to approximate the standards used in the measurements. The standards used for weighing, for example, are the standard kilogram weights kept at the National Bureau of Standards in Washington,

---

[51] See Harvey Hollein, "Fundamental Frequency Indicator," abstract of Convention Paper, *Asha,* V (October 1963), 784.

D.C. A scale used in an empirical investigation should be calibrated to a standard weight before the weighing begins.

If a machine is designed to measure the frequency of sound waves it must be calibrated in similar fashion against some standard sound wave. The standard wave may be generated by a pure tone generator or by a tuning fork, but even this standard must be periodically checked against a more basic standard. A student should be able to document the basic standards of his laboratory back to an authoritative standard such as the National Bureau of Standards. The student in his laboratory is in something of the same position as the householder attempting to measure time with a dozen clocks and watches. Should the householder build a clock he would have to check its accuracy against some standard. Radio time may be a good standard time for the householder; but if the measurements are more critical, the householder would have to trace the source of the radio station's time standard. Even the most elaborate and expensive electronic equipment prepared and checked by reputable commercial firms must be checked for accuracy against suitable standards before research is based on their use.

Many measurements in speech vary with time and some vary quite rapidly as, for example, the measurement of energy distributions and frequency of the sound wave produced during speech. Most instruments have inertia inherent in their construction. Certainly all mechanical measuring devices such as those requiring a needle to make a tracing on a moving graph or to point to a reading on a dial have this characteristic of inertia. Therefore, instruments often exhibit a time lag in their response to changes in the quantity being measured. The spring scale does not respond immediately to each increment of weight but there is a time lag as the inertia of the pointer and the other moving parts of the scale is overcome. Once the apparatus is in motion inertia causes it to stay in motion so that it overshoots the appropriate point on the dial. The scale's pointer oscillates around the accurate measurement before settling upon it. If a pen were fixed to the pointer of a scale and graph paper were pulled along at an even rate under the pen the tracing would resemble the graph produced by periodic sound waves. Therefore, the oscillations of the scale's pointer can be thought of as frequency responses and can be treated in theoretical terms. When a student is planning to measure quantities that vary rapidly through time he must ask about the *frequency response* characteristics of his instrumentation. He wants, in short, to know how much wobble is introduced in the measurement because of the inertia in the system and if this will make it impossible to measure accurately enough for his study.

To test the frequency response characteristics of instruments that measure the sound wave, for example, pure sinusoidal signals of varying frequencies can be measured and the deviation from this sinusoidal form in measurements will indicate the response characteristics of the instruments. The ideal for such a study is an apparatus that responds with equal accuracy to all frequencies and gives a measure proportional to the quantity being measured. This ideal is called a *linear response*. Most instruments do not have a linear response through all frequencies from zero to infinity because of the effect of the natural resonance of the system. Typically when a measure approaches the natural resonance frequency there is an amplification of the frequency response and as the measure recedes there is a corresponding damping effect. In electrical instrumentation it is sometimes possible to introduce compensating circuits that balance out the response characteristics of the original apparatus and increase the linear response characteristics of the instrumentation.

In making measurements that require accuracy through time of rapidly fluctuating quantities the response of the entire apparatus is of crucial importance. Although checks of the component parts individually may indicate good response characteristics the entire system should be coupled together and tested in the final check.

SUMMARY

Data for an empirical research project in speech may be collected in a wide variety of ways. But basically all of these methods may be divided into two classes depending upon whether the observations are made indirectly or directly. When gathering data indirectly the student must depend upon the observations of other people for his information. He may use documents and statistical records in much the same way that a historian or a critic would use them. The main techniques for indirect observation, however, are the interview and the questionnaire. The interview may be structured by a checklist and the interview itself conducted to hold as many variables as possible constant or be open-ended and relatively unstructured. The questionnaire can also be either a checklist or open-ended. Objective questions are useful for gathering factual material. The open-ended interview and questionnaire is useful for the discovery of attitudes and values. Interviews tend to be more thorough and expensive than questionnaires, which generally yield a larger sample with the same expenditure of time, money, and effort.

The student who observes the events under study directly may make qualitative or quantitative descriptions of these events or he

may use a combination of both. The researcher using the direct observational technique selects the phenomenon he wishes to study and
then observes it as carefully as he can. The major problems to be faced
in such a study deal with explaining the presence of the observer to
the people involved in the event, deciding whether to be a participant
or nonparticipant observer, and recording the data.

The direct observational techniques are often useful in opening
up a new area of research. Studies of this type can furnish hypotheses
for study by experimental methods. Such studies can furnish leads in
regard to relevant and irrelevant variables and may indicate the kinds
of quantifications appropriate to further research. The next step in a
continuing program of research might well be the quantification of
direct observations of the speech phenomenon under study. Evaluations have been quantified in several ways. Labeling the event with a
number rather than an evaluative word like *good* or *excellent,* ranking the events in order of excellence, making paired comparison, and
rating the events on a scale, are representative techniques used in
gathering evaluative data.

We must draw a clear theoretical distinction between an estimation of a measurable property and the evaluation of an event. In practice the problems of making estimations often causes this distinction
to be blurred. Many of the same procedures such as paired comparisons, ratings, and rankings used in evaluations are also used for estimation. On occasion the observer is asked to quantify a mixture of properties, some that can be described with statements of fact, such as those
that might deal with the stutterer closing his eyes when he blocked on
the letter [b] and others dealing with evaluations that are dependent
upon value statements or taste prescriptions of the order that all other
things being equal, the stutterer who closes his eyes when he stutters
distracts or disturbs the listener more than one who does not. An
important aid to quantification of observations in some studies is the
use of a test that evokes a response that can be assigned a number and
correlated with another set of responses. Attitude scales have been
widely used in speech research and resemble the rating scale in some
respects. The main difference is that the attitude scale is used to study
the subject making the response. The rating scale is used to study the
speech event to which the judge responds. Insofar as the subjects do or
do not have internal psychological states accurately described by the
notion of attitude the researcher is dealing with statements of fact.
Experimental psychologists have gone a long way toward measuring
such internal psychological states as pitch and loudness and this suggests that theoretically, at any rate, attitudes may be measurable. The
aids to quantifying attitudes have been the use of the equal-appearing

interval scale, the Thurstone, Lickert, and Guttman scales. Closely related to attitude scaling is the work of Osgood and his associates in developing a scale to quantify meaning called the semantic differential.

Content analysis is a way of quantifying observations of speech events by carefully defining a unit of the phenomenon and then setting up significant categories into which the units are sorted. If the discovery that there are twice as many units sorted into category *1* than there are in category *2* allows for significant inferences about the events under study this technique is successful. If the assumption that each unit represents an equal amount of the relevant variables under study can be made, then the content analysis procedure will result in a measurement.

Instruments have been used to gather and tabulate data, to aid in measuring variables, in manipulating and controlling variables, and to simulate speech events. Much of the measurement in speech required instruments to aid the researcher in his observations.

The large number of tests, scales, rating blanks, category systems, and instruments used by researchers in speech indicate the practical importance of such aids to observation in the collection of data for empirical studies. The work on these practical problems is so voluminous, detailed, and technical that this chapter contains only a survey of the major techniques to indicate some of the more important ways in which data have been collected.

Suggested Readings

Anastasi, Anne. *Psychological Testing*. New York, The Macmillan Company, 1954.

Berelson, Bernard. *Content Analysis in Communication Research*. New York: Free Press of Glencoe, Inc., 1952.

Berlo, David K. "Problems in Communication Research," *CSSJ*, VII (Fall 1955), 3–8.

Bingham, Walter Van Dyke, and Bruce Victor Moore. *How to Interview*. New York: Harper & Row, Publishers, 1959.

Festinger, Leon and Daniel Katz, eds. *Research Methods in the Behavioral Sciences*. New York: Holt, Rinehart, and Winston, Inc., 1953.

Gilkinson, Howard and Donald K. Smith. "Measurement in Speech," *An Introduction to Graduate Study in Speech and Theatre*. ed. Clyde W. Dow. East Lansing: Michigan State University Press, 1961.

Guilford, J. P. *Psychometric Methods*. New York: McGraw-Hill Book Co., Inc., 2nd ed., 1954.

Lindzey, Gardner, ed. *Handbook of Social Psychology*. Cambridge, Massachusetts: Addison Wesley Publishing Co., Inc., 1954, Vol. I.

Maloney, Martin. "Mass Communication Research in Radio, Television and Film," *An Introduction to Graduate Study in Speech and Theatre.* ed. Clyde W. Dow. East Lansing: Michigan State University Press, 1961.

Sellitz, Claire, et al. *Research Methods in Social Relations.* New York: Holt, Rinehart and Winston, Inc., 1959.

Travis, Lee Edward, ed. *Handbook of Speech Pathology.* New York: Appleton-Century-Crofts, 1957.

Young, Pauline V. *Scientific Surveys and Research.* Englewood Cliffs, N. J.: Prentice-Hall, Inc., 1956.

Projects

1) Select a thesis using either interviews or questionnaires that has been submitted for an advanced degree at your school. Write a short paper evaluating:

   a) the questions that were asked
   b) the interpretation of the answers.

2) Select a subject from your area of interest that you could study by use of direct observational techniques. Write a short statement that would serve as a suitable explanation for your presence as an observer.

3) Select a research article reporting a content analysis study of communication. Write a short paper evaluating the category system in terms of the usefulness of the results.

4) Select a research article reporting a study that used standardized tests to quantify important variables. Write a short paper evaluating the validity and reliability of the tests. You may need to consult sources other than the test manuals to get a complete picture of the usefulness of the tests.

5) Select a variable of a speech or theatre event that you are interested in and write a short paper discussing ways in which this variable might be quantified.

6) Select one of the following and make an analysis of the standardized tests that are available in this area. Write a short paper indicating which standardized test is, in your opinion, the best one.

   a) articulation
   b) listening
   c) critical thinking
   d) personality
   e) intelligence
   f) hearing

Questions for Discussion

1) Discuss the advantages and disadvantages of various scales designed to quantify attitudes or meaning.

2) What is the difference between an equal-appearing interval scale and a direct-interval scale?

3) If you were teaching a first course in your area of interest what kinds of test questions would you use—open ended (essay) or check response (objective)? Why?

4) What kinds of information about speech and theatre would be useful enough to students and teachers so that a master's thesis that used the questionnaire or interview method to gather the information would be justified?

5) What would be the advantages and disadvantages in trying to quantify observations of play production technique by studying rehearsals?

6) What would be the advantages and disadvantages in trying to quantify audience reaction during the performance of a play or during the delivery of a speech?

7) Discuss the advantages and disadvantages of a rating scale or blank as an aid in evaluating voice quality, speeches, oral reading, or acting?

8) List and discuss five hypothetical situations in which raters might be asked to both describe and appraise on the same rating scale.

9) Compare and contrast the semantic differential with the Thurstone-type attitude scale.

10) Evaluate the statement, "While a content analysis of a play or speech is similar, in some respects, to a qualitative critical study, the crucial difference is that the content analysis is more *objective* and therefore more scientific."

11) Evaluate the statement, "Machines that quantify the audience's reaction to a play or speech by having each member of the audience press a button or push a lever are useless because the situation is so unnatural the audience is atypical."

CHAPTER SIXTEEN

PLANNING, CONDUCTING, AND REPORTING EMPIRICAL RESEARCH

DOING EMPIRICAL RESEARCH

FINDING A QUESTION FOR STUDY

The empirical researcher's habits are as personal and idiosyncratic as the historian's, the critic's, or the playwright's. The man in the voice-science laboratory or the speech clinic or the communications-research center is often no less creative and haphazard in his work than the critic or historian. His work is by no means always as straightforward as his research reports would suggest. To be sure, important work can be done in the investigation of hypotheses already formulated by other researchers. Reading extensively in the literature of a research area can yield a hypothesis for investigation and a suitable quantification procedure and research design. Such work is necessary and important, although there is some danger that a research project developed in this fashion will be mechanical and sterile insofar as generating understanding or hypotheses for future research is concerned.

The discovery of significant new questions for research is often the result of a more active, less focused, and more random searching procedure. The investigator in such instances may be struck by a contradiction or he may be particularly curious about some phenomenon. He begins by observing the events that he wishes to study. At first these observations may be casual and unsystematic but the more he works with the phenomenon, the more certain features of the events intrigue him. Now he begins to systematize his observations. He tries to develop observational techniques that will yield sounder data. He begins to manipulate certain variables. In short, he is in the middle of an active, searching, period of preparation. During the course of the preparatory work he observes carefully, alert to the paradoxical or strange, ready to have the experiment tell him something. He is not disturbed by the unexpected or the unplanned, rather he is aware of the possibility of discovery at such moments. When he gets such a hint from his work the good investigator grasps the implications and follows them up. This moment of finding a significant lead is one of the most important and exciting features of empirical research. A lead may come only after an extended period of frustration. It may come by accident or, seemingly, through luck, but it usually comes only after the researcher has prepared the way by first trying this and then that and actively manipulating his research.

Hitting upon something exciting after such a period of preparation is of course analogous to the moment of insight discussed in Chapter 7. A hunch of this sort will serve as the central question for more sharply focused and systematic research activity.

After the discovery of a significant question for investigation, the researcher continues with essentially the same procedure as before. Again he tries to break out of old mental sets when they prove fruitless, again he tries various approaches, observing carefully and daydreaming about his problems as he shaves or drives to work. Again he keeps in close touch with his experiments, alert to any communication from them.

The second moment of insight is the one that may yield a possible answer to his question. Now, he, indeed, has a hypothesis that he can submit to experimental test. Not only that but he has a wealth of practical know-how to help him plan the experimental design. He knows the pitfalls to watch for in quantifying variables. He knows a great deal about the subjects or the responses he is studying. He can now proceed to draw up an experimental design that will enable him to extract the maximum amount of information and develop a statistical treatment to aid in interpreting the data.

FINDING A TOPIC: CASE STUDY ONE

Seldom do empirical researchers in the behavioral sciences reveal the way they have made important discoveries. However, Skinner (7) has written in detail about how he came to the discoveries that he reported in his book *The Behavior of Organisms*.[1] Skinner's work exemplifies the active, change-direction, haphazard, and indirect nature of empirical research and the way in which topics for investigation can be developed.

Skinner began with a general notion that he would look for "lawful processes in the behavior of the intact organism." He used rats for his subjects. To aid in the investigation he built a gadget that released the rat from a dark tunnel into the light. Skinner then undertook to observe the exploratory action of the rat when modified by food, and frightening clicks on other occasions. He was hopeful that he could

---

[1] The use of footnotes and citations to references in this chapter will follow the recommended procedure for articles in the *JSHD* and *JSHR*.

discover reaction patterns that were lawful. After carefully timing the reactions of rats coming out of the dark tunnel into the light under these conditions Skinner came to the conclusion that the major result of his efforts to this point was the discovery that some of his rats had babies. (In short, he found no lawful processes.) The way the baby rats behaved next attracted his attention. They acted like certain mutilated cats in previous animal experiments. Skinner changed the direction of his study. He decided to study "the postural reflexes of young rats." The first reflex that intrigued him was the result of pulling a baby rat's tail. Skinner found that if he held a young rat in the palm of one hand and gently pulled its tail, the rat would lean forward and then lunge forward sharply so as to pull loose and leap into space. But again his investigations came to a dead end. His next approach was a modification of his earlier effort. He built an eight-foot runway of light wood and mounted it on glass plates so that when the rat moved the runway also moved. The movements of this runway were recorded on a kymograph. The long runway became the floor of a tunnel which was equipped with a soundless release box. He ran a number of trials measuring the reaction of adult rats to the clicks.

As his investigations proceeded Skinner tired of carrying the rat from the front of his eight-foot runway to the back to begin another trial, so he built a back alley that allowed the rat to run back to the starting place by himself.

Again the research seemed to have reached a dead end. Skinner could find no regularity or pattern to his measurements. In addition, he was annoyed because the rats would often delay their return trip. The delay was bothersome but Skinner did not ignore it or try to eliminate it. Alert to this slight hint from his research, he began to time these delays. They seemed to show orderly changes. Skinner had his first major insight. In his words, "I forgot all about the movements and began to run rats for the sake of delay measurements alone."

He now had a new question to investigate and for this question his present apparatus was unnecessarily cumbersome. After several modifications of equipment Skinner found that he could save himself further work by feeding the rats by having them reach into a covered tray. This covered tray worked so well that Skinner was again motivated to change his investigation. Pushing a tray cover was not a normal part of a rat's eating behavior. The rats had learned to reach into the covered tray in order to get the food. Perhaps they could learn a more complicated routine. He added a lever mechanism that the rat had to push to get his food.

The rats did learn to press the lever to receive the food and Skinner's investigation was going along nicely when one day the food magazine jammed and the rat did not receive his reward for pushing the lever. When Skinner discovered the jammed mechanism he promptly repaired it, but the record made by the rat as he at first diminished the rate of his presses on the lever and then stopped pressing it altogether, caused Skinner to have his second major insight. He began to jam his mechanism on purpose. He called the record of diminishing behavior an "extinction curve" and said, "I can easily recall the excitement of that first extinction curve. I had made contact with Pavlov at last!" Now Skinner had a hypothesis that he could test in systematic fashion. He built four sound-proof ventilated boxes and was on his way to "intensive study of conditioned reflexes in skeletal behavior."

The results of these experiments were embodied in his book *The Behavior of Organisms* and were part of the impressive contributions of Skinnerian psychology.

Skinner sums up his experience as a researcher in the following principles.

1. When you run onto something interesting, drop everything else and study it.

2. Some ways of doing research are easier than others.

3. Some people are lucky.

4. Apparatuses sometimes break down.

Given the present state of empirical research into the higher mental processes, these principles of Skinner's embody, perhaps, better guide-lines for the researcher in speech than a learned monograph summarizing the results of empirical research into the psychology of discovery.

Skinner began with a general notion of what he wanted to study —"lawful process in the behavior of intact organisms." He got several rats and began building gadgets to enable him to observe their behavior. He tried first this and that. He was active. He did something with the behavior that he wanted to study. He did not speculate about a good research question or a good hypothesis to test with eighty-four rats systematically submitted to four experimental conditions by a Latin-square research design. As he proceeded with his experiments he saw something one day that interested him and that seemed significant, and so he changed his focus, dropped everything else, and began to study it. He had experienced his first insight into an area of investigation. He had discovered a significant question for study.

Again, he continued his active approach, and, as he proceeded with his experimentation he demonstrated at various times the beguiling operation of serendipity—the art of finding one thing while looking for something else. When his machine jammed, he capitalized on the accident, and when he got an extinction curve, he grasped the implications. He saw that he had made contact with Pavlov. He had a hypothesis to put to empirical test. Now he was ready for the question of how many rats, how many trials per rat, and what statistical treatment of the data would be most suitable to test the hypothesis. He could safely build his four Skinner boxes and go to work.

FINDING A TOPIC: CASE STUDY TWO

The way Berg (2) found the topic for his doctoral dissertation illustrates the creative and active characteristics of the preliminary searching in an empirical study. Berg began, in a general way, to study small group behavior. In a group methods seminar he was given a small task-oriented group to study. The group was part of a discussion course and the same individuals worked together on various projects for a period of several months as part of their course work. Berg observed the group as it met and kept a tape recording of its work sessions. At first, he was intrigued by the emergence of roles in the leaderless group. He watched for signs of role collision, ambiguity, and stabilization. To help him systematize his observations, he began to keep a quantified record of the interactions in the group using the category system developed by Bales. After several weeks of such observation his studies seemed to come to a dead end.

At this point, during a seminar meeting, he was discussing the group and remarked that the work sessions seemed chaotic and disorganized. Group members frequently said that they were lost or did not seem to be getting anywhere. The members seemed to Berg to "free associate" a good deal and to drift from one topic to another until they were often far afield. As he expressed it, the group seemed to have a short "attention span." The members of the seminar were struck by the analogy of a group's attention span with an individual's attention span. Berg decided to drop his study of role emergence and concentrate on examining attention span. He began by using the tape recordings of the group meetings and clocking with a stop watch the length of time the group spent considering a topic. The results were surprising. The group's average attention span was about one minute in length. As Berg continued timing the attention span, he perceived what seemed to be systematic variations in the length of time devoted to topics. The variations seemed to be a function of the member who introduced the topic and the kind of topic it was. He decided to categorize the topics to check his hunch. He classified the topics into substantive, procedural, and irrelevant categories. He worked out a numbering system to indicate which member introduced each new topic. By placing the member's number in the appropriate category whenever he introduced a new topic, Berg was able to keep track of both the length of time devoted to topics introduced by each member and in each category. The term was very nearly over and Berg decided to code all the records of the group's meetings with his category system. The results of the pilot investigation were promising. The group's attention span was not only short but it was remarkably stable over all meetings. Other interesting patterns were suggested by the data, such as: various members seemed to specialize in introducing certain kinds of topics; early in its life the group seemed to devote equal amounts of time to topics introduced by leader contenders but after one member had emerged as leader, the group seemed to devote more time to topics introduced by the leader and less time to the topics introduced by the unsuccessful leader contenders.

The observational technique promised to yield useful information, so Berg turned to the question of its reliability. He trained other observers to use his category system and checked the reliability of the results. In the process he worked out some refinements and developed a clearer and more reliable set of categories. When his category system proved reliable he had a method of investigation as well as a focus for his work. He decided to make "A Descriptive Analysis of the Distribution and Duration of Themes Discussed by the Task-Oriented, Small Group." He was ready to make records of many different groups in different contexts and begin his systematic investigation.

Of course another way to find a topic is to search the literature for clues. A worthwhile study can also result from a replication of a previous study to further examine a hypothesis partially supported by the research. Once a fruitful line of investigation has been opened up, considerable further research may be indicated. In such cases, the student should still be alert to find better methods of observation and quantification. He would do well to remember Skinner's principle that some methods of doing research are easier than others and he should watch for the unexpected or accidental that can lead to new discoveries.

Empirical researchers in speech have investigated a wide range of topics. To give some indication of this range and the nature of topics investigated by this method here is a list of representative titles of master's theses reported in *Speech Monographs*.

A Comparative Study of Several Procedures for Scaling Articulation

Judgments of Stuttering Frequency from Audio, Visual, and Audio-Visual Cues.

Speech Defects among Gifted Children

Psychosocial Factors in Functional Articulation Disorders Revealed through Parent Interviews

A Comparison of the Bekesy-Type Test with Reger's Monaural Test or Fowler's Binaural Test for Recruitment

Lipreading Performance as a Function of Light Levels

An Experimental Study of the Habitual and Natural Pitch Levels of Untrained Speakers

A Comparative Study of Techniques of Data Reduction from Cinefluorograms of Normal Velopharyngeal Functions Exposed at Different Film Speeds

Some Acoustic Correlates of Hoarseness

The Relationship between Some Aspects of Communicative Speaking and Communicative Listening in Freshmen Men and Women

The Relation between Sentence Order and the Comprehension of Written English

Mediated Attitudes as Indices of Noncongruity Factors in Attitude Change

An Experimental Study of the Effects of Trustworthiness and Expertness on Source Credibility

The Construction and Testing of a Forced Choice Scale for Debate Judging

An Experimental Study of the Relationship between a Conscious and an Unconscious Measure of Audience Response to a Motion Picture Film

An Investigation of the Effects of Personality, Sex, and Age upon the Selection of Television Programs

An Attitude Survey of University of Wisconsin Freshmen Regarding Mass Communication Media

A Record of an Experimental Production of *Hansel and Gretel*, Including a Survey of Audience Reaction

An Analystic Survey and an Eclectic Synthesis of Current Practices in Arena Theatre Lighting

Personality Factors of Dramatic Creativity

CONDUCTING THE STUDY

PREPLANNING

The student should search the literature of his field for the previous work done in the area of his study as he develops an interest in a general area. For example, Berg was searching the research literature on small groups as he developed the notion to investigate something relating to the group's attention span. He was also searching for the work done on individual attention span. The student should have this search largely completed by the time he makes his detailed and specific plans for his research project. Usually these plans are written out and often are submitted to the graduate school for formal approval. The blueprint for the study is called a "prospectus." Chapters 8 and 9 deal with the scholar's method for researching the records of the past. The same rigorous techniques are to be applied by the student in his search for previous empirical investigations in his area of study.

The student should try to find studies that are pertinent to his research in two different ways. First, he should find out what has been done in the study of the same general topic. Thus, if he is studying stuttering severity by the use of direct estimation scaling procedures, he will search for studies that have dealt with quantification of stuttering severity, regardless of the technique of quantification that was employed. Secondly, he will also be interested in studies employing the same procedures to study different materials. Thus, he will want to know about the use of direct estimation scaling procedures in studies of articulation problems.

The student will find the results of his search of the previous literature useful in drawing up the research proposal or prospectus that he submits to the graduate faculty for review and approval. He will also find the previous research helpful in the selection of quantification procedures and statistical treatments.

Even if the student finds suggestions about statistical interpretations in his search of the literature he should get the most competent statistical advice that he can as he plans his extensive research project. New developments in statistics are coming with great rapidity and are adding considerable refinement and precision to the design and interpretation of empirical studies in speech. The student should get statistical advice *early* during the planning stages of his study. Many institutions have statistical centers that furnish graduate students and faculty members with advice on these matters. Even where such centers are not available students can usually find professional help with these problems.

If the student obtains a statistician to help with both the design of his study and with the computations, he should become thoroughly conversant with the statistical treatments used. He needs to get a clear understanding of how the problem is being set up and solved. He should not abdicate his responsibility by having a statistician "take care of the statistics." In a sense, if he publishes the results of his study, he testifies as to his expertise in the use of the statistics reported in the article. In addition, the inductive and deductive phases of a study are so closely related that the student must be able to talk intelligently to his statistical advisers about his study.

The final prospectus should be prepared with considerable care and according to the recommended form of the graduate school. This prospectus will be prepared after the research is clearly focused and the preplanning well advanced. Earlier drafts of the prospectus should aid the student as he works through his study and consults with his advisers about the selection of the subjects, quantification procedures, statistical interpretations, and the administration of the study.

The student may well begin as Berg did with an idea developed in a seminar that leads to a preliminary investigation of a general problem. After he has come upon a question such as "How long is a small group's attention span?" he might draft a preliminary prospectus. As he continues his work, perhaps with a pilot study, he should come to a greater understanding of his problem and be able to develop another draft of a prospectus or a planning paper that he can use for his own good as a map. This prospectus can be evaluated by his peers and his adviser and his study can be revised in light of these evaluations. At this point, he is ready to write the final prospectus which blueprints his study and which is submitted for the approval of his department and the graduate school.

This final prospectus should include a statement of the purpose of the study, a justification of its worth, and a description of the method and design to be used in the project. If the study is designed to search for information and not to test a hypothesis, the purpose of the project can be stated in the form of a question, such as "What is the status of the discussion courses in speech departments in colleges and universities of the United States?" If the study is designed to test a hypothesis, the purpose of the study can be stated in terms of the hypothesis, such as, "The use of meprobamate will be a beneficial adjunct to stuttering therapy." Of course a survey study or a search for factual material can be explained as a test of a hypothesis. The student might suggest that his questionnaire in regard to discussion courses is designed to test the hypothesis that these courses are low status in relation to such courses as rhetoric, argumentation, public speaking, and history and criticism of public address courses. He need not do so, however. After all if he is on a fishing expedition to find out what is the case, the question will serve to explain the purpose of the study as well as a hypothesis. Indeed, a question is a bit less confusing than to state the purpose of the study is the test of a hypothesis. If the student uses a hypothesis in his plan for a study that is essentially an attempt to describe what is the case, he may try to force his study into the experimental pattern. In short, not all empirical studies need to test a hypothesis. However, if the study is designed to test a hypothesis, then a clear statement of that hypothesis in operational terms is a very important feature of the prospectus.

After clearly stating the purpose of his study, either as a question or in terms of an alternate hypothesis, the prospectus next contains a section discussing the worth of the study. The search of the literature for previous research bearing on the subject matter or the proposed method is useful in the section justifying the research proposal. If the area has not been studied, this justification section must answer the question "Why is this problem worth studying?" A corollary question is, "If this problem is worth studying, why has it been overlooked so long?" Should the area have been intensively studied, the student must answer the question, "In what way do you hope to add anything new to all the work that has been done?" A second major question to be dealt with in this section is "Why is this research method worthwhile?" If the method has not been used in previous research, he must answer the corollary question "Why do you think this untested method will work?" If the method has been often used he must answer the question "How do you hope to add anything significant when you are using the same research techniques that have often been used in the past?"

If the subject has not been studied previously the student should develop an argument to demonstrate its importance by criteria external to the previous research and then he can suggest that since this important area has not been investigated there is all the more reason to do so. Should the subject have been intensively studied previously, the student must demonstrate that his work will add a new dimension to previous results and he can then suggest that the intensive study of the area is evidence that it is an important one and to make a contribution to such an important area would certainly be worthwhile.

If the student is using a new method of investigation, he must demonstrate its feasibility and he can then argue that his study will have as an important byproduct the development of a new research technique in the area. If the method has been used very often he may be able to demonstrate that its popularity is soundly grounded and that it is the most appropriate and best method available.

The next section of the prospectus is the most important and describes the events to be observed, and the observational techniques to be used, the research design, and the statistical interpretations that will be made. The student develops the actual blueprint of his study at this point in his prospectus. He deals with such matters as the number of subjects, their characteristics, the use of controls, the tests, measures, evaluations, or estimations to be used, the replication of the study, the use of parametric or nonparametric statistics, and the confidence level to be used in testing the null hypothesis. In short the prospectus is a plan that outlines the main decisions made in preplanning the design of a study. A sample prospectus for an empirical study is to be found in the appendix.

Quite often the postdoctoral investigator faces a similar problem in drawing up a request for a grant to support his work. He may wish to apply to a governmental agency, a foundation, or a university for such a grant. He will need to draft a request outlining his study. These research proposals are usually less formally structured than a graduate student's prospectus but they often deal with the same topics. The proposals for support for a research project or program are often more extended but they generally include an explanation of the purpose of the project, an indication of its importance, including some reference to previous work, a discussion of why this particular research program should be undertaken at this particular institution by this particular set of researchers, a precise and detailed description of the research work envisioned in the proposal, and, the most important departure from the graduate student's prospectus, a detailed budget of the use to be made of the money requested. A checklist of items to keep in mind when drafting a request for a grant is to be found in the appendix.

MOBILIZING RESOURCES FOR THE STUDY

Decisions about such matters as the subjects to be used in the study need to be made by balancing theoretical factors against practical considerations. The student must plan a study that he can do with the resources at his disposal. (The student should make it clear in his prospectus that he can mobilize the resources necessary to complete the study.) Can he get enough college students for his study? Would it be better to get a range of subjects from various sectors of the community? Is this practical? Are there organized groups in the community that would furnish subjects for the study? Can the subjects be motivated? (Students in classes can usually be motivated to attend the experimental sessions and do the tasks set for them.) Will the subjects drawn from the community do the same? Is it possible to find suitable space for the administration of tests? Such space should be available at places and times that assure that potential subjects will be able to attend the experimental sessions. If the study must be done in a soundproof room in the speech clinic or voice-science laboratory, can arrangements be made to bring the subjects to these places? Will the researcher have to arrange transportation? Are the rooms or laboratories busy during most of the day and available only in the evenings and on week ends for the study? What effect will this have on the availability of subjects? If students from classes are used, how much time will the instructors allow during class periods for necessary explanation and actual testing? What effect will the use of classes have on the sample selected?

A special question is "How large should the sample be?" Here again the theoretical must be balanced with the practical. In some cases, an increase in sample size results in considerable gains in information. In other cases, a rather large increase of sample size will not increase the amount of information to any great degree and the added cost of the larger sample may be unwarranted.

MAKING OBSERVATIONS

A second important set of decisions that need to be made in the preplanning stages, involves when to make observations. Sometimes tests or evaluations or measures need to be taken before the experiment proper begins. Usually such preexperimental observations are used to furnish a basis for comparison with similar postexperimental observations or as a basis for matching pairs of subjects or control and experimental groups in an attempt to control relevant variables. Decisions need to be made about where and how such preexperimental observations or tests will be conducted. Can the entire group be assembled and given the test? Would it be better to try to schedule smaller groups at different times? Will giving the tests or making the evaluations or taking the measurements at different times introduce an unwanted variable? How long will it take to evaluate the data before the experiment proper can be run?

Often observations are made during the experiment. These may be observer's ratings, measures, or evaluations as the experimental activity is in progress. In some experiments the subject may make a record that serves as part of the data of the experiment. Sometimes the experimental activity is interrupted for questionnaires or interviews about the activity. The scheduling of experiments and the rooms available for such work pose an important administrative problem. If observers are going to watch the experiment, they must be scheduled and given a suitable environment in which to make their observations. They will probably need at least some briefing, and perhaps some training, before the experiment. If apparatus is used in the study it must be carefully calibrated and checked out before use. If changes in the apparatus seem necessary, never try more than one change at a time. Generally, if the hardware is working properly during the course of observation it is wise to leave well enough alone. A carefully prepared checklist of things to do during the course of an experiment is extremely helpful both in studies using instrumentation and those using more direct observation techniques.

A most important feature of observations made during the course of a study is the keeping of records. Laboratory notebooks should be of good quality and permanently bound, if the experimenter is recording day-to-day observations. Loose-leaf notebooks will not stand the rough day-to-day usage they get in an extended research project. If the study requires many routine evaluations or measurements, special blanks can be prepared to record them. Data should be entered directly into the record at the time of observation in permanent ink. Notebooks and records of observations made during the course of the experiment should contain the name of the observer and the date of the observation. Every record should be clearly identified. Duplicate copies of these work sheets should be made. The loss of such records before the study is completed could mean the loss of months of work. A filing system for the records of observations made during the study is indispensable.

Observations may also be made after the experiment, as in the case of a reapplication of certain evaluations, tests, and measures to check the results of the experimental treatment. Here again such practical matters as scheduling the time and place of the observations is quite important. Must the preexperimental situation be replicated closely? Should all of the postexperimental observations be taken at the same time? What follow-up procedures should be developed for the subjects who fail to show up for postexperimental testing or evaluations? Can the researcher plan in such a way that a percentage of each group, control and experimental, can drop out along the way without damaging his results? Or must he try to assure that the groups remain intact and plan for follow-up procedures to allow those who become ill, or forget, or have other responsibilities at the scheduled time for postexperimental observations, to be included in the experiment.

ADMINISTERING THE STUDY

The most brilliantly conceived and carefully planned study can go astray during its administration. The student must be prepared to adapt to these administrative problems. No matter what techniques are used to inform subjects of the time and place that they are to report for the study some may not appear. This problem can be minimized by clear verbal briefings, reminder cards or letters, and telephone reminders shortly before the study begins. If a minimum number of subjects is required, then the student would be wise to schedule more subjects than he needs. For example, if the study involves the effect of changing size on group discussions and the student needs groups of five for a certain part of his study, he would do well to schedule six potential subjects to be sure that five will be on hand. He can always explain the situation and dismiss one subject if all six appear.

The subjects need to be oriented to the study. They will usually be curious and, sometimes, a bit on their guard. The explanation should account for every feature of the study, and whatever the subjects are required to do should appear plausible within the framework of this explanation. The explanation should be standardized throughout the study, for one way to manipulate a variable is to change the set of the subjects during their orientation. If the student unwittingly changes the mental set of his subjects while giving them preliminary directions, he may change a relevant variable that he would prefer to keep constant. Typical questions should be handled with standard replies if possible and unexpected questions must be answered carefully with an eye to the effect on the study.

Checklists of administrative duties that need to be handled during the study are helpful. Space requirements should be checked out, scheduled, and then rechecked before the experiment. Even so, some rooms may become unavailable during the course of the study and alternate rooms should be kept in reserve if possible. Always the student should allow himself some flexibility of operation for the unexpected occurrence or some of his data may be lost.

If instrumentation is required for the study, additional trouble can be expected from periodic malfunctions. Even such a simple device as a tape recorder can prove troublesome and must constantly be checked to make sure it is working properly. Careful administration of the study can overcome to some extent the problems of psychological bias discussed in Chapter 14. If necessary, the observers may be kept naïve about which subjects are experimental and which are controls. The tabulation of results may also be done by research assistants who do not know these things. If the student administers the study and does most of the observations himself he must deal with this problem as carefully as possible.

THE INTERPRETATION OF RESULTS

TABULATING RESULTS

The first step in interpretation of the results of an empirical study is to work out a clear and efficient method of tabulation. Data from laboratory notebooks or test forms or evaluation scales can then be transferred to these tabulation sheets for final processing. In some instances large cardboard sheets can be used to tabulate the results of a study. In other cases regular dittoed tabulation forms on 8½ by 11 sheets are more efficient. The mathematical interpretations that are to be made from the results will determine, to some extent, the most helpful sort of tabulation method for the student. If he is using a certain statistical formula, he should tabulate the results so that they transfer easily into the formula. If the results are to be presented in forms of percentages, graphs, or tables, the methods of tabulation should be designed to facilitate such presentations.

The student might well try several different ways of recording his results, for looking at his data in one way and then another sometimes gives him insights into the material that are helpful in drawing interpretations for future studies as well as making interpretations for the study itself. Of course, the statistical model including the level of significance, alternative hypothesis, and critical set, will have been decided upon before the study was run and the student cannot abandon these decisions as he interprets his results. The student must interpret the results of his study in the manner in which he planned it. He cannot move to another way of analyzing the data because the first way did not result in significant results. In some studies, however, the investigator is searching for information or patterns in events and when doing a descriptive study of this sort, inspecting the results and looking at the data from several different angles can reveal patterns that are helpful.

STATISTICAL INTERPRETATION

Statistical computations need to be carefully done and all work sheets should be clearly written and kept for future checking. Tabular representations in the text of the study will be easier to develop if the work sheets used during statistical computations are legible and clearly organized. In a theoretical sense, the use of a computer poses somewhat the same problems as the use of a statistician to help interpret the results of a study. However, computers are becoming so important to empirical research in speech that they deserve separate consideration.

THE USE OF COMPUTERS IN EMPIRICAL RESEARCH

Computers are used in two major ways in empirical research. Computers are most useful for data processing and they hold considerable promise in terms of simulating complicated phenomena. The first is perhaps the most common use of computers and second is the most intriguing one. If a researcher compiles information about television audiences he can store such information on cards or on tape and the computer can be programmed to process the data and compute statistical descriptions of the results. The major use of computers in speech research has been to process data in this fashion. Computers are most useful for processing data that are repetitive and detailed and for the solution of equations or mathematical computations of great complexity. For example, if a research program required a repetitive and detailed processing of information resulting from the content analysis of many small group discussions over a number of years the computer would be a great aid in computation. The content analysis information could be kept on IBM cards and a program analyzing the data prepared for data processing. This program too could be stored on cards. As data are accumulated from the analysis of many different groups over a period of years, the same program could be used to analyze each batch of new data. The basic program could be modified over the years by branching in new subroutines to check out new hypotheses developed during the course of the research. A computer program is essentially a line of deductive reasoning mapped out for the computer to follow in the processing of data. This line of reasoning is analogous to a network of roads. Just as the driver of a car may choose to take several different roads as he travels along so may the programmer of a computer guide the reasoning of the machine into different subroutines. Adding these new paths does not destroy the old network but simply modifies it and offers more alternatives. Therefore, all of the data accumulated from past coding of the content of groups could be used in these new subroutines to test new hypotheses.

The computer is also helpful for the solution of extremely complicated mathematic computations. For example, the computer greatly facilitates making a factor analysis of a set of data. The use of a computer program to make a factor analysis of various foils of the semantic differential would be an example of this use of computers. In terms of the solution of complicated mathematical formula computers are becoming more and more helpful because many *program subroutines have already been worked out to solve these problems.* In other words, the work of programming the computer has been done and all that is required in addition is to adapt the subroutine to the specific problem posed by the study. Even if a subroutine is not available for the computations, a number of translation programs, such as the IBM Fortran system, can be used to write a new program tailored to the student's problem. We shall not attempt to give an exhaustive explanation of the programming of computers, however, a general explanation of the use of a translation program will enable the reader to decide if his research is such that he should investigate the possibility of using a computer.

Every step of a deductive problem must be planned and the computer must be told in step-by-step fashion how it is to go about the computation, for computers may be thinking machines but they are extremely simple minded. The complicated set of directions that spells out this procedure is called a program in absolute or machine code. Programming a computer in this fashion requires a great deal of time, effort, and planning. Since many of the programs developed in absolute code contained repetitive patterns, shorthand codes have been developed to facilitate programming. Fortran is such a shorthand system. Theoretically Fortran is a translation system that takes the directions written in the shorthand code and converts them to the longer absolute or machine code. In practical terms, the Fortran system is simply a special and generalized program for the computer that causes it to act as the translator. This is the way it works. The Fortran program can be placed on a deck of punch cards and run through the computer. This run programs the computer so it can act as a translator. Next, the program that will be used to work out the computations is written in the Fortran shorthand language and punched on cards. When the computer processes these cards it punches out the same information on a larger deck of cards in absolute or machine code. This is the place the programmer would have to start if he did not have Fortran available. Next, the cards containing the translated program in machine code are fed through the computer and this pass programs the computer so it is ready to process data. Since Fortran is an easy language to learn and allows a programmer to write solutions to mathematical problems quickly and easily it is feasible for a student to learn to program a computer using Fortran language.

A second way in which computers have been used is to program them to simulate some phenomenon to be studied. For example, Wendahl and his associates at the University of Minnesota have studied harsh voice quality by means of a laryngeal analog synthesis accomplished by a computerlike machine. Computers have been programmed to simulate nerve-fiber action. They have also been programmed to simulate audiences. For example, in the case of the televised reports of national elections, they have been programmed to simulate the national electorate. This use of computers opens up exciting possibilities for researchers in speech because they enable quick computations of complicated probability estimates of the reactions of very large audiences. Perhaps, if we are ever to achieve a science of mass persuasion the shape of such a science will be much more analogous to meteorology than it will be to physics. If this is the case the use of computers will be crucial to such developments. One of the interesting features of probability statements is that they achieve greater precision with estimates involving large numbers. The simulation of audience reactions of large mass audiences by means of computers is particularly suggestive. Just as the scientist can predict the rate of decay of radioactive substances quite accurately, although he cannot predict when a given particle will break away, so the empirical researcher in speech may, with the help of a computer, be able to predict with considerable accuracy the reaction of the American people to a given speech or issue, such as the effect of a candidate's religion on his chances for the presidency, even though the reaction of individuals would be impossible to predict.

Most large schools now have data-processing centers with computers available to aid in graduate research. On occasion the centers will develop programs for the student, but other centers require that the student develop his own program for the problem he is working on. If the problem is a relatively straightforward one, the development of a program is simple enough, but requires a close liaison between the student and the expert at the computer center. Indeed, even if the program is worked out by someone else the researcher should seriously consider becoming a programmer in his own right. The process may give him new hunches and new hints for his research, as well as help him to see how a slight change in the program will enable him to gain considerable additional information from his data without having to expend much more time and effort. If the student finds it impractical to become his own programmer, he should read the manuals for the computer that will process his data and become familiar enough with the way it works so that he can talk intelligently with his programmer.

WRITING THE RESEARCH REPORT

The historian and critic are engaged in literary pursuits and need to be excellent writers. The empirical researcher, however, can manage with less talent if he writes carefully, clearly, and accurately. Indeed, writing up the results of an empirical investigation is but a small part of the student's work. Months of labor can be written up in a dissertation of less than one hundred typewritten pages.

If the research report is to be submitted as a thesis or dissertation in partial fulfillment of a graduate degree, the student should write the report according to the recommended style for his department and his graduate school. Examination of dissertations written in an acceptable style also will be helpful.

Quite often there is a conventional way of organizing the research report for an advanced degree. The order of chapters and the kinds of material required are frequently similar from study to study. In general, a discussion of the problem that was investigated, a survey of previous research, and a summary of the research method and the design of the study, is usually included early in the study. If there is anything unusual or unique in the observational techniques employed, a new test, a new machine, or a new measurement or evaluation, this should be explained carefully and in enough detail so that other researchers could duplicate the techniques if they wanted to do so. The statistical procedures or other interpretative devices should likewise be explained so that the readers of the report can make a critical evaluation of their appropriateness and effectiveness. The way the study was conducted should also be described. If plans were modified during the course of the study, if the sample was modified, or if certain observations were discarded, these things should be reported. Finally, the results of the study with the supporting evidence should be presented.

In short the research report should contain a write up of the problem, the methodology used to investigate the problem and the results, plus the justification for drawing these conclusions. The report should be complete enough so that a critical reader will have enough evidence to judge the soundness of the research methodology and the statistical interpretations drawn from them.

The student preparing a thesis reporting an empirical research project faces the same blank sheet of paper that the student writing a historical or critical study does. He has the same problems of outlining, writing, and revising. The advice on writing a scholarly paper given in Chapter 10 is pertinent to the writing of an empirical research paper as well.

Articles prepared for such journals as *SM, QJS, ST, Journal of Broadcasting,* and *ETJ,* as well as theses in the areas of theatre, radio, television, film, oral interpretation, and public address, usually employ the footnoting style discussed in Chapter 10, whether the study was an experimental, quantitative, historical, or critical one.

A style different from that discussed in Chapter 10 is used for noting references in articles presented to the *JSHD* (3) and *JSHR* (4) and to journals in psychology, acoustics, and phonetics as well as in theses in speech pathology, audiology, voice science, and communications. References for such studies are often prepared on separate pages following the last page of the text. The proper form for such references is given in Chapter 8. The references are listed alphabetically by author's surnames, much like a bibliography, and numbered consecutively. Notes to sources on the reference list are indicated by inserting the appropriate number in parenthesis within the text. For example:

> Bloodstein (5) reported that from 33 to 65 percent (depending upon the age level) of 418 young stutterers seen by him between 1950 and 1956 exhibited some form of associated or secondary symptoms.

When a direct quotation is taken from a reference the page number is often added in the parenthesis. For example:

> Templin and Darley (16, p. 5) take cognizance of these disparate findings and suggest that "It is possible that the discrepancy between the Findings of Templin and those of Snow and Milisen may be attributed, at least in part, to differences between the samples studied."

Content footnotes can also be used in the scientific paper. A good procedure is to number content footnotes separately from references inserted in parenthesis within the text. Begin with the numeral "1" and number consecutively throughout the paper. To distinguish these from the references to literature, the numbers should be superscripted as in other types of research papers. For example:

> Prior to the widespread use of disc, wire, and tape recorders [1] in the late 1940's and early 1950's. . . .

Content footnotes may contain references in parenthesis as part of their explanatory material. For example:

> [1] The "communicative responsibility" research of Eisenson and Wells (13) in 1942 was the first study relative to stuttering reported in the *JSHD* in which the criterion measure was obtained from mechanically recorded samples of the speech of stutterers.[2]

---

[2] The material in the footnote examples was drawn from studies by Martin (5) and Siegel, Winitz and Conkey (6).

Scientific papers usually contain more numerals, symbols, formulas, tables, figures, and illustrations than do historical or critical theses. Since the reporting of results of quantitative research requires a widespread use of numbers and percentages, the student writing such a thesis will use figures, symbols, and abbreviations to an extent not considered good form for nonscientific writing. Most numbers will not be spelled out, except at the beginning of a sentence. The writer should spell out expressions referring to units of quantification when they are not preceded by numbers. For example, write out "cycles per second" unless preceded by a number such as 440 cps. The term *percentage* should be used rather than "percent" or "%" when no figure is given in the text.

Only simple mathematical expressions should be run into the text. Complicated, lengthy, or important formulas should be centered on separate lines with a space above and below.

Tables should be typed on separate pages as uniformly as possible. They should be numbered consecutively and all references to the table should use the table number. Tables should carry titles even if the titles are obvious. Footnotes referring to items on the table should be placed below the table. Ideally, a table should follow the first mention of it in the text of the study. Wide tables may be placed broadside. If too wide for this, they may be arranged on two facing pages. Long tables may be continued from page to page.

Illustrations usually consist of graphs, charts, and diagrams of machines and instruments. Graphs and charts are often drawn on cross-ruled paper and then traced on plain bond paper with India ink or reproduced by some photographic process. The latter technique, if permitted by the graduate school, has much to recommend it. Legends, keys, captions, and other symbols may be made either with a typewriter or by hand in India ink.

Frequently empirical research studies require elaborate tables and illustrations to supplement the written test. The preparation of a dissertation may be complicated by the need to duplicate such materials. Reproduction techniques can be used to make excellent and inexpensive copies of such material. If the graduate school or publisher will accept such reproductions in lieu of carbon copies the use of such processes will simplify the actual preparation of the research report.

The written description of the tabular material should not repeat information that is clear from an inspection of the table. However, the description should aid the reader in interpreting the table and should point out significant features of the results presented by the table that are not readily apparent.

The student should guard against stylistic problems that often appear in empirical research reports. The first of these is the danger of timidity. The student may be tempted to draw conclusions with reluctance and to hedge on the statement of his findings, so that the reader is hard put to decide what the student has discovered. Such timidity is understandable. The candidate must defend his thesis, frequently in oral examination. Nevertheless, the student must be careful not to qualify his results with so many modifiers that the effect is one of inconclusiveness. The student should do his study justice and claim for it the results that he honestly believes have been demonstrated by the evidence, and he should explain these results clearly.

A second danger in writing the research report is the danger of obscurantism. The student may be tempted to restate common sense in pretentious terms. After all, in most of the natural sciences the key concepts are often esoteric and expressed in technical jargon. To the nonspecialist a study entitled "Reaction of Aldehydes with Monosubstituted Malonic Acids" seems like a meaningless mumbo-jumbo.[3] Still, such language is apparently essential to the natural sciences. If science uses esoteric terms then it is easy to assume that empirical researchers in speech must also employ such terms. Assume that a student is studying small group discussion and he finds some members of the group are better liked than other members. He also finds in some of his groups that several of the members have been frustrated in some way by the group's progress. The frustrated members tend to form cliques that join together to discuss the common grievances of their members. He concludes that people tend to form animosities and attachments as they work in groups. At this rather gross level of observation he can give some impression of the nature of these attachments and animosities but he certainly cannot give operational definitions to them. He could, in short, give an adequate and accurate description of them in common sense terms. But he could, on the other hand, fall into the trap of obscurantism and begin to coin terms to describe these things. He might begin with a tentative step away from direct language by thinking in terms of attraction and repulsion. Next, he could talk of attraction and repulsion nets; from here he might move to a discussion of attraction and repulsion matrixes. Next, he might explain the attraction and repulsion matrixes. Perhaps, he knows some chemistry and hits upon the analogy of group attraction with the chemical concept of valence. He now discusses attraction and repulsion valences. Valence, of course, brings with it the notion of molecules, atoms, electrical charges, elements, and compounds. He might well end up with a

---

[3] This example is from Barzun (1). The chapter on "The Language of Learning and of Pedantry," in this book is an excellent treatment of the topic.

study entitled "The Valences of Personality and Group Elements as They Apply to the Formation of Molecular Patterns of Attraction and Repulsion in Small Group Quanta Matrixes."

Technical terms have their place. Reporting research on the vocalis muscle in the *Journal of Speech and Hearing Research* would require using the technical terminology of anatomy. Here such terms as *arytenoid cartilage* and *conus elasticus* would be appropriate. Such terms serve a legitimate function of naming with precision features of the research materials and they should by all means be used. Complicated matters cannot be treated in simple fashion and research reports should not be oversimplifications or popularizations, however unnecessary new terms for the purpose of the research report may serve to obscure the results of the research.

Closely related to the danger of obscurantism is the danger of impressiveness. Impressiveness is the obverse of timidity and the graduate student is less likely to fall into this error than the young postdoctoral researcher. Our hypothetical researcher looking into patterns of attraction in small group discussion is well on his way to writing up his report in this fashion. He might, for example, start with observations of fifty groups and proceed to the construction of an elaborate explanatory system or "theory" on this slender base.

The research report should be written with all the technical terms required for clarity and precision. It need not be easy reading, for complex ideas are seldom easy to write up or to read about, but it should not be unduly obscure because of unnecessary jargon introduced because it sounds more like the language of science. The student should claim for his research all that he can in honesty maintain the research demonstrates. He should present his findings with no more or no less reservation than the evidence justifies in his considered judgment. On the other hand, he should not write up his research, which may be but a small part of a large program of investigation that is just getting under way, as though from his work with two-hundred college students he has made a major contribution to communications theory.

SUMMARY

The empirical researcher is often no less creative and haphazard in his work than the critic or historian. He is often struck by a contradiction or an unexpected event may arouse his curiosity. He begins by observing the events that he wishes to study. Usually he has some general notion of what he wants to do and he actively works with the phenomenon he is studying. While manipulating variables and developing better observational techniques, he goes through a period of active preparation. During this phase he should work carefully and be alert for intriguing and unexpected developments. When he gets such hints from his work, he should be conscious of their implications and run down these new leads. Hitting upon something exciting after a period of such preparation is a moment of insight like the illumination of a creative writer. This hunch can serve as a question to focus the work. Such questions are often half of a good research project. With the question to guide his investigation, the researcher should continue his work. The next moment of illumination should yield a tentative answer to his question. This tentative answer can serve as the hypothesis for a carefully designed experiment. During the course of this preliminary investigation, and as he prepares the design for his experiment or investigation, the researcher must search the literature for previous work done in the area of his study. He will get leads for his preliminary work and a survey of previous research is helpful in justifying the study. Studies that have investigated the same events and studies that have used the same research techniques to study different materials will be helpful to him.

The prospectus is a blueprint of the study that is submitted for review and approval to the graduate school or fund-granting agency. The preparation of a prospectus for a research project requires detailed preplanning. This involves balancing the theoretical requirements of empirical research against the resources available to the researcher. Decisions involving the number and selection of subjects, the discovery and scheduling of rooms or laboratory space, and the selection and use of observational techniques must be made at this point.

The administration of a study requires the ability to adapt to the unexpected so that bias is not introduced and data not lost. Care must be taken so that psychological biases are not introduced into the gathering of data, and a clear and efficient method of tabulating the results will guard against loss of data and aid in the interpretation of results. Statistical computations should be carefully checked and all work sheets preserved. If the student uses a data-processing center or a research center to help him process his data, he should begin consultation with his statistical advisor early in the planning stages of his study. Should his study be such that computer processing would be helpful the same general procedure can be followed. If extensive use is to be made of computers, the researcher would be wise to learn to program the computer himself.

Writing up the research report is often a small part of conducting an empirical study. Months of work can be written up in a short dissertation. Nevertheless, a clear and accurate report is an important culmination to an empirical project. The research report should be written with all the technical terms required for clarity and precision. It need not be easy reading for complex ideas are seldom easy to write up or read about, but it should not be unduly obscure because of unnecessary jargon. The report should claim all that the researcher can honestly maintain his study has discovered and no more.

REFERENCES

1) Barzun, Jacques. *The House of the Intellect.* New York: Harper & Row, Publishers, 1959.

2) Berg, David M. A descriptive analysis of the distribution and duration of themes discussed by the task-oriented, small group. Unpublished doctor's dissertation, University of Minnesota, 1963.

3) Information for contributors to the journal of speech and hearing disorders. *J. Speech Hearing Dis.,* 26, 1961, 99–103.

4) Information for contributors to the journal of speech and hearing research. *J. Speech Hearing Res.,* 3, 1960, 86–98.

5) Martin, Richard R. Direct magnitude-estimation scaling of stuttering severity utilizing auditory and auditory–visual stimuli. Unpublished doctor's dissertation, University of Minnesota, 1963.

6) Siegel, Gerald M., Winitz, Harris, and Conkey, Harlan. The influence of testing instrument on articulatory responses of children. *J. Speech Hearing Dis.,* 28, 1963, 67–76.

7) Skinner, B. F. A case history in scientific method. *Amer. Psychologist,* 10, 1955, 245–259.

SUGGESTED READINGS

Auer, J. Jeffery. *An Introduction to Research in Speech.* New York: Harper & Row, Publishers, 1959.

Baker, Sheridan. "Scholarly Style, or the Lack Thereof," *AAUP Bulletin,* XLII (1956), 464–470.

Barzun, Jacques, and Henry F. Graff. *The Modern Researcher.* New York: Harcourt, Brace and World, Inc., 1957.

Dickens, Milton. "Laws of Experimental Research," *WS,* XXIV (Fall 1960), 197–200.

McCartney, Eugene S. *Recurrent Maladies in Scholarly Writing.* Ann Arbor: University of Michigan Press, 1953.

Sidman, Murray. *Tactics of Scientific Research: Evaluating Experimental Data in Psychology.* New York: Basic Books, 1960.

Turabian, Kate L. *A Manual for Writers of Term Papers, Theses, and Dissertations.* Chicago: The University of Chicago Press, 1955.

Wilson, E. Bright, Jr. *An Introduction to Scientific Research.* New York: McGraw-Hill Book Co., Inc., 1952.

Projects

1) Select an article reporting an experimental study in speech or theatre arts and write a short paper criticizing the organization, the presentation of tabular material, the discussion of the reliability and validity of the quantification technique, and the clarity of the writing.

2) Select a thesis presented for an advanced degree at your school that reports quantitative research and examine the style of reference, bibliography, footnoting and format and compare the form of the thesis with the form suggested in the *MLA Style Sheet* and in the suggestions for contributors to the *JSHR.*

3) Examine several theses (or research articles) and collect examples of what you judge to be timidity, obscurantism, and impressiveness in the style of writing used in these reports.

4) Select a question or hypothesis suitable for investigation by empirical techniques. Write a prospectus in which you describe the plan for conducting such a study. Check the proper form for such a prospectus with your department and graduate school and write your prospectus so it is in the proper form.

5) Make a survey of the research facilities available to the graduate student doing an empirical study at your school. Check such services as aid with the planning of the statistical features of design and interpretation available through a statistical center, aid with programming and use of computers for the processing of data, aid in developing observational techniques and in design of research through consultation with researchers in other disciplines, financial aid from research funds within your school, duplication services available to help in the preparation of the thesis copy.

Questions for Discussion

1) What should be the role of technical terms in the writing of research reports?

2) Compare and contrast Skinner's preliminary searching in his study of the learning behavior of rats and the work of a playwright planning a play.

3) What are some of the strengths and some of the weaknesses of topics selected for empirical study in your area of interest?

4) How would you characterize a style of language appropriate to the writing of an empirical research report?

CHAPTER SEVENTEEN

RESEARCH IN PERSPECTIVE

Since Chapter 1, the main emphasis of this book has been upon theory and method in speech research. The treatment has ranged from the general and philosophical analysis of the structure of speech theories to the specific treatment of how to take notes or frame a question for an interview, but the focus has been on research isolated from the cultural context. We shall sum up as we began, with an examination of the functions of research and, balancing the ideals with the realities, place research in perspective.

In the first chapter the functions of research in a college or university were described as being to contribute new knowledge, to vitalize teaching, to serve the community, and to train graduate students. These functions outlined the ideal role of research. You have now been a graduate student for several months at least and these ideals may sound like platitudes to you. You may begin to wonder if they have any relevance for the academic life. In Chapter 1 reference was made to the sociologists and journalists who have commented upon the facts about research as they found them. The time has now come to consider some of these realities. How does research, in fact, function in the academic community and in society at large?

RESEARCH AS A CRITERION OF EXCELLENCE

The continued evaluation of men, colleges, and universities is unavoidable. We decide where we wish to teach and where we wish to have our children taught. The government and the foundations decide what institutions should be given money and what professors should be given research grants. The deans and department heads hire, promote, and give merit raises. Research and its most tangible evidence, publication, has come to assume, in large measure, the function of determining status and prestige within the academic communities of this country. Faculties tend to be judged as good or poor in terms of the quality and quantity of their research. The academic community judges the individual faculty on similar evidence. We need only recall the pressure on the early members of the National Association of Academic Teachers of Public Speaking to gain respectability by doing research to realize that this is not a recent development. In 1942, however, Logan Wilson made a study of *The Academic Man* and discovered that research was becoming more important as a criterion of excellence in assigning prestige and status in college and university circles.[1] Caplow and McGee in their study of *The Academic Market Place* reaffirmed Wilson's findings and cited evidence to indicate that this trend to use research as a status symbol had increased since the Second World War.[2]

FACTORS MAKING RESEARCH A CRITERION OF EXCELLENCE

One of the clichés of our time is that rapid improvements in the speed and efficiency of communication and transportation facilities have caused our world to grow much smaller in recent decades. The increased mobility of faculty members and the expansion of communications within academic disciplines nationally and internationally has caused a similar feeling among professors. They can assert that the scholarly world has grown smaller not because it has less population but because the lines of communication drawing it together are much stronger than the geographical distances that divide it. As a result many professors strive for a national reputation within their field rather than a local campus reputation. A professor of speech, for example, may want to be well thought of by other speech professors across the country and he may be less interested in his professional reputation on his own campus. This within-discipline and national (even international) frame of reference for status rankings is in marked contrast to the older tradition in which professors were more interested in their reputation within the college or university community. Of course, most professors are interested in both their national and local reputations, but Caplow and McGee concluded that the emphasis is changing and that the national reputation is becoming the more important consideration, particularly for young men beginning their professional careers.

Since World War II, the turnover of faculty members has increased. The determined effort of many institutions to upgrade their faculties and the natural increase in the number of jobs because of larger enrollments has contributed to this mobility. The young Ph.D. looking for a permanent position is joined by the established pro-

---

[1] (New York, 1942.)
[2] (New York, 1958.)

fessor on the move. Every year a number of scholars with national reputations change institutions. When such a man moves he sets off a chain reaction that may effect a number of schools. His former department must look for a replacement. In order not to lose much status as a department they look for the next best man in the country to replace the man they lost. If they can hire this man his school must now look for a replacement. The faculty member who views his current position as a temporary one often is more interested in his national reputation than in his status on campus.

Concomitant with this development was the increase in the number of and efficiency of the channels of communication within academic disciplines. The national professional associations play an important part in establishing and maintaining this communications network. They sponsor journals in which research results are published. They hold national meetings where members deliver oral research reports. These functions, as will as formal business sessions and informal meetings of all sorts, enable the members of a given association to get to know and recognize other members of their discipline from other campuses. Such lines of communication are necessary before national reputations can be efficiently established. Certainly the general increase in communication channels in the country at large has expanded the dissemination of information that contributes to the process of evaluation, but the national associations play a large part in making it possible for their members to agree in approximate, sometimes tacit, and unofficial fashion on the status and prestige rankings within the discipline.

The national meetings and publications of such organizations as the Speech Association of America, the Educational Theatre Association, the Speech and Hearing Association, and the National Society for the Study of Communication enable one to make an approximate answer to such questions as: Who are the foremost scholars in ancient rhetorical theory? Who are the best theatre historians? Who are the best authorities on stuttering? Who are the best communications research specialists?

The evidence that can be disseminated through nationwide channels, either orally at a national meeting, or in journals, encourages the use of research rather than teaching ability as evidence in determining the national reputations of college and university teachers. Certainly teaching and related skills are an important part of a faculty member's qualifications. Unfortunately, teaching ability can, for the most part, only be talked about at a national convention. It cannot be demonstrated. The results of research can, on the other hand, be presented at such conventions and can be published for evaluation and criticism. Publication is often good evidence of a professor's research skill. Testimony about a professor's teaching is often a less reliable kind of evidence for that ability. His peers within the discipline are likely to read and evaluate his research carefully; and, thus, his standing within the profession (petty politics aside) is apt to depend upon the quality of this work. His peers are not so likely to make an investigation of his teaching ability, and his standing within the profession seldom depends upon the quality of his teaching.

Teaching ability is, however, an important criterion of excellence in determining a professor's local reputation. The faculty, administration, and, particularly, the students, evaluate teaching ability within the local campus community. Even in this context, however, there is a tendency for faculty members and administrators (if not students) to use research publications as a measure of a professor's worth. Since the school's standing is linked to the national reputation of its faculty, the administration must weigh this dimension in their evaluation of individual professors. More important is the sheer size and complexity of higher education today. Deans and department heads lose contact with classroom teachers and find it difficult to evaluate teaching ability. In addition, teachers are reluctant to allow administrators to observe and evaluate their classroom performance. The faculty and administration can easily check up on the publications of a professor. Publication thus fills a real need for a quick and available source of evidence for evaluating the talents of a faculty.

THE GENERAL PUBLIC'S RESPECT FOR RESEARCH

In addition to the importance of research in establishing academic reputations, it is also important in giving professors status outside the academic community. In the words of an article printed in the literary supplement of the *London Times,* "every American citizen has learnt to regard research as sacred and indispensible." [3] Indeed, Jacques Barzun, a knowledgeable and popular commentator on the academic scene, was moved to write an article on the excesses of this veneration—"The Cults of 'Research' and 'Creativity.' " [4]

The research worker is honored by the general public because of the practical results that have come from applied research in such fields as medicine, engineering, and agriculture. Such advertising themes as "Better things for better living through research" reflect

---

[3] (November 6, 1959), xxxii.
[4] *Harper's Magazine* CCXXII (October 1960), 69–74.

the popular image. Research enables us to control our environment, to stop the spread of polio, to take tranquilizers and wonder drugs, to conquer space.

More and more research projects are supported because of this veneration of research. This escalation of research funds is affecting the nature, organization, and function of it in the modern American college and university. Both industry and government, with popular approval, are supporting it. Research centers, some based on campuses and some not, fostered by money from the federal government or from such private sources as foundations and business corporations have mushroomed in this century. The research work of the campus-based centers may or may not be tied in with the instructional efforts of the college or university. A grant confers upon the recipient an increase in prestige, and since he can usually take his grant with him when he moves, he becomes attractive to other schools. These institutions may bid for his services and he is thus rewarded in many ways by his grants. Some of these rewards are less tangible than the increased income that results from his value to the schools that bid for his services but they are nevertheless important. The researcher will probably not be able to supplement his salary with money from his grant, but he usually can get a reduction in his teaching load. The research subsidy frequently enables the professor to give financial aid to graduate students who work on the research with him.

The large-scale support of research programs has increased the number of cooperative projects employing a team of investigators. These programs often span a number of years and undertake a comprehensive attack on some particular set of research problems.

PRESSURES TOWARD EXCESS AND ABUSE

The large rewards of research exert considerable pressure on professors to publish research reports or to get a research grant. These pressures compromise the ideals of research in several ways. The volume of publications is on the increase. New scholarly journals spring up year by year, and the pressure of manuscripts on each of them increases. From London, the *Times* literary supplement appraised the state of American scholarship in 1959 and found "an abundance of trivialities designed chiefly for committees on promotion." [5] Such a sweeping judgment is probably unfair; but certainly the material and psychological rewards of publication are so great

---

[5] (November 6, 1959), xxxii.

that they tempt many professors to publish research for the sake of publication regardless of worth. Teachers, who have little interest in research, are sometimes bent in the direction of publication by these pressures. Research undertaken for publication rather than discovery is liable to result in "trivialities designed chiefly for committees on promotion" and thus cheapen the whole enterprise of research.

The current pressures also compromise the function of research in improving teaching. As the prestige of research increases, the prestige of teaching declines and the motivation of the faculty for expending talent and effort in the classroom is lessened. The language of the campus clubs reflects this decline of motivation for teaching. The responsibilities of teaching are referred to as a "load" while research is referred to as "my work" and a "reduction in the teaching load" so the faculty member has more time for "research" and "his own work" is often considered a desirable thing. This attitude can result in half-hearted or poorly prepared teaching. In addition to the value system and the attitudes fostered by these pressures for research, teaching sometimes suffers simply because the research specialist has little time for teaching. He is often busy setting up and administering research programs. He is often in demand as a consultant for government and industry. He is frequently called away from the campus and this very absence makes him a less effective teacher.[6] The controversy over whether research aids or hinders teaching is a symptom of the problems caused by the veneration and rewarding of research.[7]

These same forces can make research a less valuable educational experience for the graduate student. Research centers often use the team approach to research problems. The exciting part of the research, such as the discovery of a suitable question to investigate and the development of the tools and the research design to gather data, may be done by the senior professor. If the graduate students do the routine work of collecting and processing the data they may not benefit as they should from their work. The research administrator may select a topic or an area of research that is likely to be supported. At its worst this practice involves identifying a grant and then searching for a project that will win the award. Thus, the genuine curi-

---

[6] For an exposé developing this argument see Spencer Klaw, "The Affluent Professors," *The Reporter*, XXII (June 23, 1960), 24.

[7] For a typical exposition of the opposing viewpoints in this controversy, see John Q. Academesis, "Too Many College Teachers Don't Teach," *The New York Times Magazine* (February 21, 1960), 14, and Charles A. Fenton, "The Sweet Sad Song of the Devoted College Teacher," *AAUP Bulletin*, XLVI (December 1960), 361–364.

osity important for worthwhile investigation may be supplanted by an analysis of the granting agencies. Sometimes, too, this research is aimed at serving narrowly practical ends. The making of a better sausage casing is research, too.

Serving the community through research is not always free of problems, either. The professor undertaking a project to serve the community may find that he is serving some special-interest group. Thus, a speech professor who specializes in industrial communications may discover that the managers of a company will be glad to underwrite research if the project promises them greater success in manipulating their employees. Accepting such a project can erode several important ingredients of worthwhile research including an honesty of purpose and a loyalty to the discipline and to the facts.

Sometimes the various functions of research are at cross purposes. When a graduate research program begins to emphasize the role of research in graduate training, it may become unimportant whether a graduate student's research makes a contribution to knowledge or not. The main concern then becomes that he learn something of research technique. De-emphasizing the importance of the results tends to create a climate in which the graduate students view the research requirement as simply another hurdle in the path to a degree. A student encountering this emphasis may be tempted to find a research project that will get him over this hurdle as gracefully and easily as possible.

A POINT OF VIEW

We must understand the niggardly and status-seeking elements in research. We need to be aware of the pitfalls and the abuses. The analysis, however, must always be balanced with the positive aspects of current research. The graduate student may no sooner become committed to research and determined to make it an important part of his life work, than he decides that most research is trivial. He comes to the conclusion that there is not really a first-rate research man in his discipline. In point of fact, much good research is being done with a commitment to increasing knowledge. There will always be trivial scholarship and trivial scientific investigation, just as there will always be trashy creative projects and useless consumer goods produced; but there are also some good plays and some good products and the good things make the whole enterprise worthwhile.

Research will continue to function as a gauge of academic prestige, probably increasingly so. There is no indication that the trends now under way will be arrested. Publication will continue to be important. Imperfect as it may be, it is probably the best available indicator of scholarly excellence. Research should not become an idol of the academic community. It should not be above criticism and above reproach. Certainly there are many research practices that need to be criticized. Many of these excesses stem from researchers' striving for promotion and status rather than searching for knowledge.

The ideals of research outlined in the first chapter thus still have considerable relevance for the practice of research. Research should be sought for its own sake. Curiosity should be the motive power, and under the prodding of his curiosity the researcher should take time from the important matters of teaching to go where his interest leads him. If he does, the material bounties that flow from research are more likely to seek him. If he seeks them through research, he may fail to find them. Research should serve one major function in higher education. It should make a contribution to the knowledge, wisdom, and standards of criticism and appreciation of the various arts and sciences. The cynical who say that it is ridiculous to expect every graduate dissertation to make a "contribution" put the thing all wrong. Whereas it is ridiculous to expect every graduate dissertation to make a contribution, it is not ridiculous for every graduate student to attempt to make a contribution. *Many have done so.* They might not have if they approached the project as a hurdle on the way to their degree to be avoided or topped as easily as possible.

In the final analysis, of course, pure saints and sinners do not exist in the research libraries and laboratories. Rather, these workshops are inhabited by mortals motivated by complex and, sometimes, inconsistent aspirations. A man with a sincere commitment to discovery, scrupulously careful of the facts in his research work, may be extremely jealous of his reputation and testy about sharing credit. He may not turn his back upon the affluent life his research earns him and he may bask in the prestige it generates. A man may begin his research career because he is aggressive and ambitious and has discovered that research, as Winans remarked many years ago "is the standard way into the sheepfold," and he may yet become a skillful researcher and make important contributions to his field.

Both of these men would have one thing in common, however. They would have talent. There is no substitute for talent when it comes to doing research in speech. Talent plus method or craft can enable even a scoundrel to do good work while the best intentions and the best attitudes will not enable saintly men of little talent and no method to produce good work. Whatever his motivations, the good research worker, once in his workshop, will have high personal standards of performance and a sure hand with the tools of his research method. These very methods contain an internal ethic. In the laboratory or the library, you must make certain truth decisions about statements of fact on the basis of observations. Asserting such statements of fact to be true when you know they are false—in short, fabrication and lying—is intolerable. Thus, a thorough grounding in research method is one component of successful work. A knowledge of theory is another. Given these two qualities, a pure heart should prove no hindrance.

SUGGESTED READINGS

Barzun, Jacques. "The Cults of 'Research' and 'Creativity,'" *Harper's* (October 1960), 69–74.

Berelson, Bernard. *Graduate Education in the United States.* New York: McGraw-Hill Book Co., Inc., 1960.

Caplow, Theodore, and McGee, Reece J. *The Academic Marketplace.* New York: Basic Books, Inc., 1958.

Graduate Education in Speech Pathology and Audiology. Washington, D. C.: American Speech and Hearing Association, 1963.

Klaw, Spencer. "The Affluent Professors," *The Reporter* (June 23, 1960), 24.

Mills, C. Wright. *The Sociological Imagination.* New York: The Grove Press, 1961.

Pronovost, Wilbert L., *et al.* "Research: Current Status and Needs," *JSHD,* Monograph Supplement 8 (June 1961), 114–123.

Smith, Raymond G. "The Dignity of a Profession," *CSSJ,* XIV (May 1963), 83–87.

Wilson, Logan. *The Academic Man.* New York: Oxford University Press, 1942.

PROJECTS

1) Make a survey of some topic of interest to you and try to discover the graduate-research projects that have made a contribution to our understanding of the topic.

2) Compile a list of authorities in an area of speech. Determine the basis for their reputations.

QUESTIONS FOR DISCUSSION

1) What do you think of the statement that scholarly journals publish "an abundance of trivialities designed chiefly for committees on promotion?"

2) The most common role for a social scientist doing applied research,

according to C. Wright Mills, is "to become an adviser to the king." This role, he goes on to say, "is a difficult role to fulfill in such a way as to maintain moral and intellectual integrity, and hence, freedom to work on the tasks of social science." *The Sociological Imagination* (New York: Grove Press, Inc., 1961), p. 180. What is your reaction to Mills' position?

3) To what extent is it advisable for a graduate student to select a topic that he thinks will please his graduate adviser?

4) What should be the criteria for excellence in evaluating educational theatre directors? Debate coaches? Speech clinicians? University professors? College professors?

APPENDIX

A. SAMPLE PROSPECTUSES WITH TABLES OF CONTENT ATTACHED

B. CHECKLIST TO AID IN APPLYING FOR RESEARCH GRANTS

C. A SHORT GLOSSARY OF BASIC STATISTICAL TERMS

D. PREPARING MANUSCRIPTS FOR JOURNAL PUBLICATION

A. SAMPLE PROSPECTUSES WITH TABLES OF CONTENT ATTACHED

PROSPECTUS ONE

The Rhetoric of Isolation: A Burkeian Analysis of the America First Committee by Donald Walter Parson, University of Minnesota.

On December 8, 1941, the major isolationist pressure group prior to World War II disbanded. It disbanded believing that war would have been avoided had its principles been followed; it disbanded believing that the United States had been tricked into war by a combination of foreign and domestic interests. That pressure group was the America First Committee.

America First was organized in September of 1940 to keep America out of war. During its short life, it attracted over one-half million members, set up a speaker's bureau of over sixty speakers who delivered over a hundred addresses under the auspices of the National Committee. Such speakers from various professions and political affiliations included: Charles Lindbergh, Burton K. Wheeler, Robert Hutchins, Gerald P. Nye, Chester Bowles, Hamilton Fish, Philip LaFollette, and Karl Mundt.

America First drew upon a tradition of isolationism dating back to George Washington, a tradition which dominated the American liberal tradition. It reflected, according to historian Adler, "the isolationist impulse," which has been "woven into the warp and woof of the American epic." [1]

Several studies have been made of the America First Committee. The most comprehensive has been done by Wayne S. Cole at Wisconsin for his doctoral degree.[2] Since then he has published the history of the Committee.[3] Cole's study pays little attention to the speeches, partly because in his own words he "knows almost nothing about rhetoric." [4] James R. Johnson at Cornell studied the America First speeches for his doctoral dissertation; he reconstructed the speeches into an isolationist "debate case," in which America First upheld the negative on the question of entering the war.[5]

The materials for investigation of America First are scattered and incomplete. The largest single collection is housed in the Hoover Institution

---

[1] Selig Adler, *The Isolationist Impulse* (New York, 1961), p. 15.
[2] Wayne S. Cole, "America First," Ph.D. dissertation, University of Wisconsin, 1949.
[3] Wayne S. Cole, *America First* (Madison, 1953).
[4] Letter from Wayne S. Cole, August 3, 1963.
[5] James R. Johnson, "The Rhetoric of the America First Committee," Ph.D. dissertation, Cornell University, 1964.

Archives, at Stanford University, California. Various newspaper accounts and taped recordings of speeches have been used to supplement the primary materials. The Hoover collection contains several handwritten, typed, or dictated speech manuscripts, along with many mimeographed copies of speeches delivered. The collection contains the personal correspondence of General Robert Wood, National Director, to various speakers as well as the correspondence of other heads of the organization, Robert Bliss, Page Hufty, and Robert Stuart.

The tools of investigation are borrowed from the critic, Kenneth Burke.[6] The Burkeian approach has been used more extensively in literary criticism, but there have been studies in rhetoric using his ideas. Marie Hochmuth Nichols cites the thesis of Jack Armold on the Compromise of 1850 as a good example of the use of this method.[7] This study is not "Burkeian" in the sense that it attempts to build on a chronological or topical exposition and application of Burke; in fact Burke's writings prevent the critic from systematizing his ideas into preconceived forms. What Burke provides is a series of insights by which the critic may discover the rhetorical patterns peculiar to a movement.

This study of the America First Committee will develop the argument that the rhetoric of isolation largely failed to accomplish its purpose. It will attempt to assess the Committee's strategic potential, how that potential was employed, and its results. Burke suggests that speakers seek identification with an audience.[8] This study discusses the America First attempt to gain identification with "the people" which it claimed to represent. To Burke, speakers develop strategies for dealing with specific problems; the strategies chosen reveal both an attitude toward the problem and suggest a course of action. This study seeks to uncover the strategies of America First. America First employed public opinion polls to demonstrate its identity with "the people"; when the polls began to indicate popular support for those measures isolationists opposed, they attempted to discredit the polls, to substitute their own polls, and finally to claim that their failures were the result of a "conspiracy." This study analyzes the isolationist attack on three "conspirators": the Jews, the British Government, and the Roosevelt Administration. This study will attempt to explain why the choice of the Jew as "devil figure" was inconsistent and inappropriate to the audience with which America First sought to identify; why the isolationist claim of a "British invasion of America" was never sustained; and why America First was never able to successfully alienate Roosevelt, the "War Lord" from "the people." This investigation suggests that America First failed to take advantage of the potential available to it; that the isolationists failed to turn consistent defeats into victories.

---

6 The major works used for this study are, *Attitudes Toward History* (Boston, 1959), *The Philosophy of Literary Form* (New York, 1957), *A Grammar of Motives and a Rhetoric of Motives* (Cleveland, 1962), and *The Rhetoric of Religion* (Boston, 1961).

7 Jack Armold, "The Compromise of 1850: A Burkeian Analysis," Ph.D. dissertation, University of Illinois, 1959.

8 See Kenneth Burke, *A Grammar of Motives and a Rhetoric of Motives* (Cleveland, 1962), pp. 543–555.

Appended is a short description of projected chapters.

TABLE OF CONTENTS

PROSPECTUS TWO

Direct Magnitude-Estimation Scaling of Stuttering Severity Utilizing Auditory and Auditory-Visual Stimuli by Richard R. Martin, University of Minnesota.

PROBLEM

Both the researcher and clinician interested in the behavioral process of stuttering frequently find it necessary to assess the magnitude of the stuttering response. Physical scales have been utilized extensively to assess various behaviors thought to be related to, or integrals of, the stuttering process. All too often, however, these isolated physical measurements only partly account for observers' psychological perceptions relative to the existence of and variations within the stuttering behavior syndrome. As a result, some researchers have employed the instruments of psychophysics in an effort to scale observers' psychological perceptions of stuttering. The proposed study outlined in this paper concerns a heretofore untried technique for scaling observers' psychological perceptions of stuttering severity.

In the vast majority of studies in which rated severity of stuttering was employed as a criterion measure, the experimenters have utilized some form of the equal-interval scaling technique. This situation undoubtedly is due, in part, to the extensive work of Sherman and her colleagues (2, 5, 6, 7) with respect to the Iowa Scale of Severity of Stuttering—an equal-interval scale. The research with this nine-point equal-appearing interval scale has demonstrated quite conclusively that such a scaling method can be used to place, reliably, samples of stuttered speech in rank order of severity. There are, however, differences between observers or between rating sessions with respect to the absolute scale value of any sample.

The question arises, therefore, as to whether a ratio scaling method can be used to simply and reliably measure severity of stuttering. Although no work has been reported in which attempts were made to use a ratio scale for determining stuttering severity, Sherman and Moodie (8) have reported a study in which the method of constant sums (a ratio scale) was employed to scale defectiveness of articulation.

Stevens and his colleagues (11, 12, 13) at the Harvard Psychoacoustics Laboratories have been working with the method of direct magnitude-estimation in scaling such psychological attributes as loudness, pitch, finger span, and brightness. These experimenters have found the method usable and the results reliable.

Recently Prather (4) utilized the direct magnitude-estimation method to scale defectiveness of articulation. The experimenter interpreted her findings as indicative that the use of a direct magnitude-estimation method for scaling articulation defectiveness was justified. The method was practical and the scale values were reliable.

A second unresolved question in stuttering evaluation involves the almost universal procedure of presenting only auditory (tape recorded) stimuli to the observer and ignoring the visual or combined audio-visual cues. Tuthill (14) prepared sound motion pictures of stutterers and normal speaking individuals talking extemporaneously. The experimenter concluded that essentially the same frequency of stuttering was judged to occur when the sound track was presented alone as when the complete motion picture was played. These results are important, but bear primarily on the question of stuttering frequency and only indirectly on stuttering severity.

Luper (3), on the other hand, found that the severity ratings of visible samples (silent motion pictures) of stuttered speech were slightly but significantly higher than were ratings of audible samples.

The studies of Tuthill and Luper indicate that frequency of stuttering is much less subject to variations in the stimulus material employed than is severity of stuttering. The study proposed herein will be so designed as to yield information relative to the mean scale values and reliabilities of audio stimuli as opposed to combined audio-visual stimuli when the direct magnitude-estimation procedure of scaling stuttering severity is employed.

PROCEDURE

Subjects (Ss). Ss will be 30 adult stutterers, 16 years of age or older. The sex ratio will be approximately 4:1 in favor of males. The only restriction as to selection will be an attempt by the experimenter (E) to include Ss who represent a wide variety of stuttering severity and stuttering type.

Raters (Rs). Rs will be selected on the following bases. "Sophisticated" Rs will be defined as graduate students in Speech Pathology. "Unsophisticated" Rs will be persons not meeting the sophisticated classification.

Speech Samples. All speech samples will be obtained in the recording studio of KUOM. Each S will be requested to read orally a standard prose passage. Beginning at a fixed point in the reading passage, S will be filmed with a standard television camera for approximately one and a half minutes. The sound picture will be recorded on a single track kinescope tape. Simultaneously, a high quality magnetic tape recording will be obtained for each reading.

Rating Tapes. One permanent negative and one print of the sound film kinescope will be prepared in the KUOM laboratories. Samples of the oral reading of each S will be selected from the kinescope print. The first 15 seconds of tape of each S will be omitted. The next 15 seconds of tape will be cut from the print and used as a short sample. The next 10 seconds of the tape will be omitted, and the following 30 seconds cut from the print and used as a long sample. The thirty 15-second samples will be randomized and spliced with 15 seconds of blank tape between each sample. This will be *Tape 1.* The thirty 30-second samples will be randomized and spliced with 15 seconds of blank tape between each sample. This will be *Tape 2.* When Tape 1 and 2 are played back with only the audio portions being projected they will be referred to as *Tape 3* and *Tape 4,* respectively. When Tapes 1, 2, 3, and 4 are rerandomized for a second rating during the rate-rerate reliability procedure, they will be referred to as *Tape 1A, Tape 2A, Tape 3A* and *Tape 4A,* respectively.

The magnetic recording tape obtained during the filming session will be cut into 15 and 30-second samples identical to those included in Tapes 1 and 2. The thirty 15-second samples will be randomized and spliced into *Tape 5,* and the thirty 30-second samples will be similarly constructed into *Tape 6.*

Rating Procedure. For the 10 tapes (1, 1A, 2, 2A, 3, 3A, 4, 4A, 5 and 6) the procedure for accomplishing the direct magnitude-estimation scaling of stuttering severity will be as follows: E will present the samples of a given tape to R one at a time and instruct R to assign whatever numbers represent the relative position of each sample on a severity of stuttering continuum. The number assigned to the first sample will become R's *standard.* On any succeeding sample R is free to assign whatever number he chooses, except that he will be required to use a number which indicates the position, proportionally (i.e., one-half, one-third, twice, ten times, etc.), of that sample on the severity of stuttering continuum relative to the numerical designation of the standard. For example, if R assigns the number "20" to the first reading sample, and if he judges the second sample to be twice as severe in terms of stuttering severity, he will be forced to assign the number "40" to that second sample.

A group of 14 sophisticated Rs and a group of 14 unsophisticated Rs will accomplish direct magnitude-estimation ratings of stuttering severity for Tapes 1, 2, 3, 4, 5 and 6 in two rating sessions. Assignment of tapes to each rating session will be counterbalanced. Not less than two nor more than three weeks later, the same Rs will rate Tapes 1A, 2A, 3A and 4A in a single session. Both groups of Rs will be present during all rating sessions.

Thus, there will be eight rating conditions for the kinescope tapes. *Condition I* will involve sophisticated Rs, short samples, combined stimuli (14 sophisticated Rs rating Tape 1). *Condition II* will involve sophisticated Rs, short samples, auditory stimuli (14 sophisticated Rs rating Tape 3). *Condition III* will be sophisticated Rs, long samples, combined stimuli (14 sophisticated Rs rating Tape 2). *Condition IV* will be sophisticated Rs, long samples, auditory stimuli (14 sophisticated Rs rating Tape 4). *Condition V* will include unsophisticated Rs, short samples, combined stimuli (14 unsophisticated Rs rating Tape 1). *Condition VI* will be unsophisticated Rs, short samples, auditory stimuli (14 unsophisticated Rs rating Tape 3). *Condition VII* will include unsophisticated Rs, long samples, combined stimuli (14 unsophisticated Rs rating Tape 2). *Condition VIII* will include unsophisticated Rs, long samples, auditory stimuli (14 unsophisticated Rs rating Tape 4).

In addition, there will be four rating conditions for the magnetic sound tapes. *Condition IX* will include sophisticated Rs, short samples, magnetic sound stimuli (14 sophisticated Rs rating Tape 5). *Condition X* will include sophisticated Rs, long samples, magnetic sound stimuli (14 sophisticated Rs rating Tape 6). *Condition XI* will be unsophisticated Rs, short samples, magnetic sound stimuli (14 unsophisticated Rs rating Tape 5). *Condition XII* will be unsophisticated Rs, long samples, magnetic sound stimuli (14 unsophisticated Rs rating Tape 6).

ANALYSIS OF DATA

Since each R will be free to assign any number to the first sample on any tape, and will then assign to all following samples any number proportional to the assigned standard, there will not be agreement between Rs relative to the magnitude of scale values assigned. Corrected scale values will be computed by bringing assigned scale values into coincidence for all Rs by using a constant correction factor. Every standard will be converted to a numerical rating of 10, and the remaining samples for any given tape for each R adjusted according to the ratio between assigned standard for the first sample and the converted numerical rating of 10. For example, assume that R1 assigned a value of "50" to the first sample, the standard, on Tape 1. Assume that the assigned values for samples two, three and four on Tape

1 were "75," "25," and "100," respectively. The assigned standard value of "50" would be converted to "10." This would represent a reduction of four-fifths, so every other assigned value would be reduced by the same amount, i.e., by four-fifths. Thus, the corrected values for samples two, three and four would be "15," "2.5," and "20," respectively. This correction procedure will be accomplished for all ratings by all Rs under all conditions.

Frequency distributions of the corrected scale values will be computed separately for each of Conditions I through VIII. Each frequency distribution will contain 420 scale values (14 Rs X 30 Ss). These frequency distributions will be utilized to determine which rating condition results in the closest approximation to a normal distribution of severity of stuttering scale values.

Rate-rerate reliability will be determined for each R under each condition by computing a reliability coefficient. The mean reliability coefficient for Condition I will be determined by averaging the reliability coefficients of Rs 1 through 14 on Tapes 1 and 1A. For Condition II, the mean reliability coefficient will be the average of Rs 1 through 14 on Tapes 3 and 3A. The mean reliability coefficient for Condition III will be the average of the reliability coefficients for Rs 1 through 14 on Tapes 2 and 2A. The Condition IV mean reliability coefficient will be the average of Rs 1 through 14 on Tapes 4 and 4A. Condition V, VI, VII and VIII mean reliability coefficients will be computed in the same manner, except that the reliability coefficients of Rs 15 through 28, the unsophisticated Rs, will be averaged in each condition.

The mean reliability coefficients for the eight conditions will be submitted to a 2 x 2 x 2 (Rater Type x Sample Length x Stimulus Type) analysis of variance. Significances, or lack of them, for the various main effects and first- or second-order interactions will give some indication as to the conditions under which direct-magnitude estimation of stuttering severity can be reliably accomplished.

Inter-rater reliability will be determined in much the same manner as for intrarater reliability discussed above. Scale values will be corrected in the same way. In each of the eight conditions (for Tapes 1, 2, 3, and 4) the Rs in each condition will be randomly paired, yielding seven pairs. A reliability coefficient will be computed between the scale values assigned by the paired Rs for each of the 30 Ss in each of the eight conditions. The mean split-half coefficient will be determined for each condition, and subjected to the same type of analysis of variance as described for the rate-rerate reliability data.

The data analysis of distribution and reliability of scale values will yield information relative to the following questions: Under which condition is the distribution scale ratings most normal? Do the mean scale ratings differ between the various conditions? Are there differences in the rate and rerate mean scale ratings for each condition, i.e., what is the "practice" effect? What are the rate-rerate reliability coefficients of each condition? Are there significant differences between the eight conditions in terms of rate-rerate reliability coefficients? What are the split-half reliability coefficients of each condition? Are there significant differences between the conditions in terms of split-half reliability coefficients?

The severity ratings assigned by Rs to the magnetic sound tape samples (Tapes 5 and 6) under Conditions IX, X, XI and XII will be converted by the standard correction procedure discussed above. Mean corrected scale values for each S in a given condition will be computed by averaging the value assigned by all Rs. Correlation coefficients will be computed between the mean corrected scale values of Ss in Conditions IX and II, X and IV, XI and VI, VII and VIII. Inspection of these correlation coefficients will yield information relative to the effects of different qualities of sound recordings on rater judgment of stuttering severity. From an acoustic standpoint, the fidelity of a high quality magnetic tape recording is somewhat superior to that of a sound portion of a single track kinescope tape. If the above correlation coefficients are relatively substantial and positive, this would be evidence, albeit not conclusive, that the differences in the two sound recordings are not sufficient to affect differentially the severity of stuttering ratings assigned to the respective auditory stimuli.

TABLE OF CONTENTS

REFERENCES

1. Anderson, N. H. Scales and statistics: parametric and nonparametric. *Psychol. Bull.*, 58, 1961, 305–316.
2. Lewis, D. and Sherman, D. Measuring the severity of stuttering. *J. Speech Hearing Dis.*, 16, 1951, 320–326.
3. Luper, H. L. Consistency in stuttering in relation to the goal gradient hypothesis. *J. Speech Hearing Dis.*, 21, 1956, 336–342.
4. Prather, E. (Moodie). Scaling defectiveness of articulation by direct magnitude-estimation. *J. Speech Hearing Res.*, 3, 1960, 380–392.
5. Sherman, D. Clinical and experimental use of the Iowa Scale of Severity of Stuttering. *J. Speech Hearing Dis.*, 17, 1952, 316–320.
6. Sherman, D. Reliability and utility of individual ratings of severity of audible characteristics of stuttering. *J. Speech Hearing Dis.*, 20, 1955, 11–16.
7. Sherman, D. and McDermott, R. Individual ratings of severity of moments of stuttering. *J. Speech Hearing Res.*, 1, 1958, 61–67.
8. Sherman, D. and Moodie (Prather), C. E. Four psychological scaling methods applied to articulation defectiveness. *J. Speech Hearing Dis.*, 22, 1957, 698–706.
9. Sherman, D., Trotter, W. and Goodwin, F. A scale of the audible characteristics of individual moments of stuttering. Unpublished study, State University of Iowa, 1954.
10. Siegel, S. *Nonparametric Statistics* (New York: McGraw-Hill Co.), 1956.
11. Stevens, S. S. The direct estimation of sensory magnitudes—loudness. *Amer. J. Psychol.*, 69, 1956, 1–25.
12. Stevens, S. S. and Galanter, E. H. Ratio scales and category scales for a dozen perceptual continua. *J. Exp. Psychol.*, 54, 1957, 377–411.
13. Stevens, S. S. and Stone, G. Finger span: ratio scale, category scale, and JND scale. *J. Exp. Psychol.*, 57, 1959, 91–95.
14. Tuthill, C. E. A quantitative study of extensional meaning with special reference to stuttering. *Speech Monogr.*, 13, 1946, 3–20.
15. Woodworth, R. S. and Schlosberg, H. *Experimental Psychology*. Rev. ed. (New York: Holt, Rinehart & Winston, Inc.), 1954.

B. CHECKLIST TO AID IN APPLYING
FOR RESEARCH GRANTS

1. Have you prepared a succinct, accurate description of the project?
2. Have you included a discussion of the reasons for doing such a research project at your institution with the research workers included in your proposal?
3. Have you considered the possibility of associating representatives from other disciplines with you in a multidisciplinary approach to your problem? (Many foundations are interested in encouraging interdisciplinary approaches to research.)
4. Have you phased your project carefully? Is it to run for one year? Two years? Five years? Have you considered the interval required for staffing the project, developing necessary plans or research materials? Have you allocated the required budget *year by year* in your application?
5. Have you taken into account all the resources needed for the success of your research project? Faculty requirements? Visiting scholars? Fellows and research assistants? Civil service personnel (particularly secretarial help)? Equipment and supplies? Physical accommodations? Library acquisitions (you can often make a contribution to the holdings of your library as a by-product of your research grant)? Travel? Translations? Publication subsidy?
6. Have you provided a short summary budget of the entire project? Have you provided a detailed breakdown of the budget year by year according to personnel, research equipment, secretarial services, office supplies, library, travel, publication, and administrative costs?

C. A SHORT GLOSSARY
OF BASIC STATISTICAL TERMS

Arithmetic Mean is the common-sense notion of arithmetic average. The mean is computed by adding up all the scores of a distribution and dividing the sum by the total number of scores in the distribution.

Correlation Coefficient is a commonly used measure of relationship between paired factors or the tendency of two or more variables or attributes to go hand-in-hand. The correlation coefficient ranges in value from −1.00 for perfect negative correlation through .00 for no correlation to +1.00 for complete positive correlation.

Frequency Distribution is a tabulation of scores distributed from high to low or low to high which indicates the number of individual observations resulting in equivalent scores or falling in a score interval. (May be used with measurements, evaluations, and estimations as well as test scores.)

Median is the midpoint of a frequency distribution, the point that divides the scores into two equal parts so that 50 percent of the scores fall below this point and 50 percent fall above this point.

Mode is the most frequent score in a distribution of scores.

Normal Distribution is sometimes called the normal curve because it is a frequency distribution that has a distinctive bell-shaped appearance when presented in graphic form. The scores of a normal distribution are distributed symmetrically about the mean with as many cases at various distances above the mean as below it. In addition, the scores are concentrated near the mean with fewer scores at each end of the distribution.

Standard Deviation is a measure of the variation or dispersion of a set of scores. It expresses the nature and extent of the deviation from the mean by the scores of a frequency distribution. If the distribution is a normal one the standard deviation describes the variability of the scores. In this case approximately two-thirds of the scores would fall within the limits described by one standard deviation above and below the mean. About 95 percent of the scores would lie within two standard deviations above and below the mean.

D. PREPARING MANUSCRIPTS
FOR JOURNAL PUBLICATION

A research project is really not complete until it has been written and published. The sooner you make the contribution of your work available to other investigators the more useful it will be. When your study has been completed you should begin to look for a suitable publication outlet for it. The best way to do this is to read a number of journals and see if they publish articles along the lines of your work. The professional journals all have guidelines that they follow in selecting articles for publication. In addition, each editor and each editorial staff mark the publication with their interests and preferences during their tenure in office.

Also, when preparing the manuscript for publication, you should keep in mind the audience that reads the journal for which you are writing. You should write the article so it can be understood by all members of that audience. You should also put yourself in the role of the consulting editor who will read the article when you submit it. The editors will be asking the following sorts of questions about your article. Is the article appropriate for this journal? Does it make an important enough contribution to justify the space it will require in *this* journal? Are the methods and procedures satisfactory for this type of article? Is the preparation of material up to publication standards? Is the article clearly suitable for publication? Clearly unsuitable? Can the article be revised so it will be acceptable?

You should realize that there is a difference between a clear rejection and having your manuscript returned with suggestions for revision. You should not view a return of your manuscript with suggestions for revision with a view to possible publication as the equivalent of a rejection. Quite often the revised article will be accepted.

Journal articles usually vary between two to twenty typewritten pages (500 to 5,000 words). Some journals will accept longer articles but the average journal article will fall somewhere between 3,000 and 4,000 words. Short research reports in the form of letters or research notes are now published by a number of journals in speech and related fields and the results of your research may achieve publication in this fashion.

You should select the title for your article with considerable care. It should be brief, descriptive, and clear. The title is one of the most important determinants of the audience that your article will receive once it is published. It is important in the indexing of your article and subsequent scholars are likely to find or to overlook your material depending upon the accuracy with which your title is indexed.

Some journals require abstracts of your paper to follow the title. The abstract should be written with great care. It should be an expansion of the title and it should describe the matter of the paper. A potential reader will often decide whether to continue and read the article or not on the basis of the abstract. In addition some abstracts are collected and published in abstract journals. The reader of such a journal may decide whether to look up your paper or not on the basis of the abstract itself.

After the title and abstract (if required) you should proceed to the text of the article itself. If you are reporting empirical research you can organize your text around an introduction (background of the study), statement of purpose, method, data, interpretation, and conclusions. If you have used standard statistical methods you need not describe them beyond naming them and furnishing a reference where they are described in detail.

If you are reporting a critical or historical study your organization may be more topical or chronological. In any event the text should unfold your thesis in a clear and complete fashion.

If the work is the result of your thesis or dissertation you should indicate this on your manuscript and name the director of the study. You should also identify yourself on the first page of the manuscript.

The article should be typed on twenty-pound white bond paper of the $8\frac{1}{2}$ by 11 inch size. You should place your name in the upper left-hand corner of each page. The first page of the text should have the number of words typed in the upper right-hand corner. The number of words can be computed by counting all words on three or five pages and discovering the average for this sample and then multiplying by the total number of pages in the article.

The first page should begin with the title of your article centered at the top of the page and typed in capital letters. The names of the author or authors are centered two spaces below the title and typed in capital and lower-case letters. When useful, you should provide heads and subheads to increase the clarity of presentation. Footnotes and tables should be typed on separate pages and added to the end of the text itself.

Leave a margin of about two inches on the left-hand side, top and bottom and about an inch and a half on the right-hand side. Type an original and two carbon copies of your paper. You may use either elite or pica type. Use a clean ribbon and keep the typewriter keys cleaned. You owe the editors the courtesy of a neat and clean manuscript. In preparing it for mailing pack the manuscript flat unless it is only several pages in length. Mail the original and first carbon copy to the suitable editor. Usually the editor will have several associate editors read your paper and the additional copy will speed up editorial response. Even so, you may not hear for a matter of weeks and sometimes months because of the burden of manuscripts some editorial boards have to process.

INDEX OF SUBJECTS

INDEX OF NAMES